Jewish Art

Journal of the Center for Jewish Art
The Hebrew University
Jerusalem

Jewish Art, formerly the *Journal of Jewish Art*, was started in 1974 by Maurice Spertus and Professor Bezalel Narkiss. The first five volumes were published by the Spertus College of Judaica Press, Chicago, Illinois. Volumes 1–11 were edited by Professor Bezalel Narkiss.

Layout	Pini

Copy Editor	Doron Narkiss

Jewish Art is published annually by the Center for Jewish Art of the Hebrew University, Jerusalm.

Subscriptions

Center for Jewish Art
P.O. Box 4262
Jerusalem 91042

ISSN 0792-0660
ISBN 965-391-004-3

Jewish Art is set in 10 point Baskerville on a body of 13, and printed on 115 gramme chrome paper.

Produced by Pini at HaMakor Press, Jerusalem

Cover: Painted sukkah from Fischach, southern Germany, after 1836/7. Jerusalem, Israel Museum, 196/1. Courtesy of the Israel Museum. Photo Yoram Lehrmann.

EDITOR'S NOTE

This double volume of Jewish Art celebrates the fifteenth anniversary of the Center for Jewish Art of the Hebrew University. It also appears just before the Fourth International Seminar on Jewish Art which will be held in Jerusalem from 29 May to 3 June 1994.

The Seminar, organized by the Center for Jewish Art, boasts a large group of speakers, three times as many speakers as at the first seminar, held nine years ago. For the first time it has become necessary to conduct concurrent sessions in order to accommodate all lectures. The broad range of subjects on each of the six topics reflects the universalism of Jewish art. Spanning ancient to contemporary times, as well as a wide range of cultures, the lectures encompass general art history, ethnography and history, addressing social, economic and political issues.

This universalism is also expressed in our annual, Jewish Art. *The iconography of the Temple in Jerusalem and its components throughout the ages is dealt with in this issue, from a Bar Kokhba coin, to a tenth century Karaite Bible, to the art of Percival Goodman.*

A number of articles shed light on patrons and makers of manuscripts and on the iconography of these manuscripts, as well as the iconography of wall paintings, seals and bridal gifts. One article examines the exquisite ritual objects created by a family of silversmiths from Bratislava, priceless treasures which were recently stolen from the Jewish Museum in Budapest; others take a closer look at the art of the Soyer brothers, of Jacques Lipchitz, and of Frida Kahlo, revealing surprising Jewish elements.

This issue follows special volume 18, on the Jewish art of Spain, which marked the beginning of a new series devoted to specific topics. Volume 21, also part of this new series, will be dedicated to the art of the Jews of the Commonwealth of Independent States. It is most gratifying to see how the number of contributions to Jewish Art *has increased and it is another indication that the study of Jewish art has matured from a fledgling into a recognized discipline.*

Aliza Cohen-Mushlin

TABLE OF CONTENTS   VOLUME NINETEEN-TWENTY / 1993–1994

6

Fig. 1. Painted sukkah from Fischach, southern Germany, after 1836/7. Jerusalem, Israel Museum, 196/1.

FISCHACH AND JERUSALEM: THE STORY OF
A PAINTED *SUKKAH**

Naomi Feuchtwanger-Sarig

To my grandfather, in memoriam

The village of Fischach is located approximately 20 kilometers southwest of Augsburg, in Bavarian Swabia — a region in the south of Germany. Fischach became known to historians of Jewish art thanks to the painted *sukkah*, which was originally the property of the local Deller family (Fig. 1).[1]

Jewish settlement in Fischach is probably connected with the expulsions of the Jews from Augsburg in 1560 and 1564.[2] Unwilling to give up commercial assets, they chose to continue to dwell as close as

This study was carried out in honor of the 25th anniversary of the passing away of Dr. Heinrich Feuchtwanger, my late grandfather, in 1988. The enigma of the *sukkah* from Fischach, which he so treasured, has now been solved through items from his own collection, thus rendering the bond between him as a scholar and collector of Judaica and this extraordinary work of German Jewish folk-art inseparable. May his memory be blessed with love for the Jewish heritage and the beauty of the arts.

All photographs of the Fischach *sukkah* were taken by Yoram Lehrmann, and are reproduced courtesy of the Israel Museum.

1   Jerusalem, The Israel Museum: 196/1. The *sukkah* was installed in the Renée Lang Wing, and was relocated, following the resetting of the Judaica exhibition halls, in the Max Mazin Wing. This unique relic of Ashkenazi folk-art has so far been subject to very little research. Short, popular essays were written on the *sukkah* in various journals and periodicals. See H. Feuchtwanger, "Herr D. aus F.," *Mitteilungsblatt der Hitachduth Olej Germania* 5 (1938), 6; H. Boas, "A Show of Succot," *Palestine Post*, 22 October 1948, p. 4; S. Ben Chorin, "Von Fischach nach Jerusalem. Ein Unikum jüdischer Folklore," *Jedioth Chadashoth*, 11 October 1954, p. 2. It was presented for the first time at the Bezalel National Museum in Jerusalem in 1948 within the framework of a special Sukkot display, which was organized under the auspices of Mishmar Ha'am. The *sukkah* was again a special feature for Sukkot in 1954. In 1963 it was shown for the first time in its original homeland, at the exhibition on the history of Rhine Jewry, *Monumenta Judaica*, which was mounted in the Municipal Museum of Cologne (*Monumenta Judaica. 2000 Jahre Geschichte und Kultur der Juden am Rhein*, E 596. See Catalogue, color plates VII and IX. The entry was written by the late Dr. Heinrich Feuchtwanger). In 1968 the *sukkah* was lent to the exhibition *Israel a travers les ages* at the Petit Palais in Paris, and was accorded a brief entry in the accompanying catalogue, No. 378, plate IV. See also I. Schachar, *The Jewish Year* (Iconography of Religions, XXIII, 3, Institute of Religious Iconography, State University of Groningen, Leiden, 1975), p. 10 and pl. XVI.

2   For a detailed history of the Jews in Fischach, see B.Z. Ophir, *Pinkas Hakehillot, Encyclopaedia of Jewish Communities from their Foundation till after the Holocaust*, vol. 2: *Germany — Bavaria* (Jerusalem: Yad Vashem, 1972), pp. 633–636 (Hebrew). See also E. Gebele, *Die Juden in Schwaben* (special volume, reprinted from *Schwabenland*), 2/3 (1938), 35; M. Piller, "Die Fischacher Judengemeinde und ihre Synagoge," *Kirche + Kunst* 6, Heft 2 (1985), pp. 50–52; and the anonymous essay "Eine jüdische Landgemeinde," *Gemeindeblatt der jüdischen Gemeinde zu Berlin*, 26. Jg., Nr. 5, 2 (February 1936), p. 12.

possible to the trade center at Augsburg, and took up residence in neighboring townships. They were granted dwelling privileges by the Barons of Burgau, whose attitude towards the Jews was rather favorable at the time.

Among the newly inhabited localities was Fischach. Documents recording Jews as burghers exist from 1573 onwards. Following the expulsion of the Jews from Scheppach, Günzburg and Burgau in 1617, the Fischach Jewish population expanded considerably, and the original nucleus of the small community developed into a well-established, institutionalized one. The year 1739 was an historical milestone in the annals of the Jewish community of Fischach: the new synagogue was consecrated, and a *Memorbuch* was begun.[3] In 1811/12 there were already 219 Jews in Fischach, constituting 47 percent of the overall population of the village. In 1860, they totalled 283 souls, in spite of the migration to the larger cities which has already begun several decades earlier.[4] A marked decline in the proportionate ratio of Jews to Christians is apparent in the statistics of the Jewish benevolent societies in Germany for 1928/29. Of about 900 inhabitants of Fischach, only 160 were Jews.[5]

The majority of the Jews of Fischach were stock-breeders and dealers, and only few were small merchants and peddlers.[6] It is most likely that such was also the occupation of Mr. Deller, who lived in the late eighteenth and first half of the nineteenth century — the original owner of the painted *sukkah*.

Little is known of his life, but some information can be gathered about his family. They are first recorded in Fischach in a legal document, which was drawn on the 4th of Tevet 580 (22 December 1819), and deals with the debt of the widow Breindel Deller to the local Jewish community. In 1822, Itzik and Shmuel Deller are recorded in another official community document.[7] The statistical yearbook of the Jewish communities for 1889 names a certain H. Deller as the chairman of the *Verein Chevrath Neorim* in Fischach.[8] He kept this position until 1897, while also being the chairman of the *Binjan Bes Almin-Verein*. A. Deller served as head of the *Armenverein*.[9] In the records of 1898, however, H. Deller appears to have been succeeded by G. Deller,[10] who kept his position until 1901, whereas the *Binjan Bes Almin Verein* was chaired by another member of the family , N. Deller.[11] In 1909, a certain A. Deller is mentioned as the person in charge of the *Synagogen Kasse*,[12] a position which he still held in 1911.[13] Later on, the almanac of the various institutions of the Jewish communities in Germany for 1932/33 mentions Hugo Deller as the second community chairman in Fischach.[14]

One may, therefore, surmise that, for decades, members of the Deller family enjoyed a certain esteem in the community, perhaps on account of their economic well-being.

The *sukkah* of the Deller family was discovered in 1935, following information which had become known to Dr. Heinrich Feuchtwanger.[15] After having located the former Deller residence, he set about scavenging the attic, and was rewarded by finding the painted wooden planks and roof beams which had once formed the *sukkah*.[16] After long negotiations,

[3] Published by M. Stern, *Memorbücher from the 16th–19th Centuries in the Holy Community of Binswangen,... Fischach,... Hurben... in Schwabia* (Jerusalem, 1941), p. 30 (Hebrew).

[4] *Führer durch die Wohlfahrtspflege in Deutschland. Zentralwohlfahrtsstelle der deutschen Juden* (Berlin, 1928/29), p. 127.

[5] Gebele, *Juden in Schwaben*; see also A. Kober, "Jewish Communities in Germany from the Age of Enlightenment to their Destruction by the Nazis," *Jewish Social Studies: A Quarterly Journal Devoted to Contemporary and Historical Aspects of Jewish Life* 9, no. 3 (July 1947), pp. 199–200.

[6] See P. Weiner-Odenheimer, *Die Berufe der Juden in Bayern. Berlin: Verein für die Statistik der Juden in München* (Berlin: Veröffentlichungen des Büros für die Statistik der Juden, 1918), vol. 10, pp. 90–106, especially pp. 97 and 100–103. Cf. also Gebele, *Schwaben*.

[7] Both documents are kept in Jerusalem, Central Archives for the History of the Jewish People: 5456/אג.

[8] *Israelitisches Jahrbuch des Deutsch-Israelischen Gemeindebundes* (1889), 45. The same person is mentioned in the *Statistisches Jahrbuch des Deutsch-Israelischen*

Gemeindebundes 13 (1898), 86.

[9] *Statistisches Jahrbuch* (n. 8), 11. Jg. (1896), p. 71; 12. Jg. (1897), p. 77.

[10] 10. Idem, 9. Jg. (1898), p. 77; 10. Jg. (1899), p. 90.

[11] *Israelitisches Jahrbuch* (n. 8), 8. Jg. (1893), p. 59; 9. Jg. (1893), p. 62; 10. Jg. (1894); 15. Jg. (1901), pp. 102–103; 16. Jg. (1903), p. 105; 19. Jg. (1908), p. 126.

[12] *Handbuch der Jüdischen Gemeindeverwaltung und Wohlfahrtspflege (Statistisches Jahrbuch)*, 19. Jg. (1909), p. 126.

[13] Idem, 20. Jg. (1911), 138.

[14] B. Schlesinger, ed., *Führer durch die jüdische Gemeindewervaltung und Wohlfahrtspflege in Deutschland, 1932–33* (Berlin, Zentralwohlfahrtsstelle der deutschen Juden, 1933), p. 305.

[15] The historical data concerning the discovery of the *sukkah* was supplied by my late grandmother, Mrs. Henni Feuchtwanger, to whom I am deeply indebted for encouraging me to pursue this study.

[16] Due to its deteriorated condition, the *sukkah* could no longer be in use since around 1910. See H. Feuchtwanger, *Mitteilungsblatt*, and *Monumenta* (n. 1).

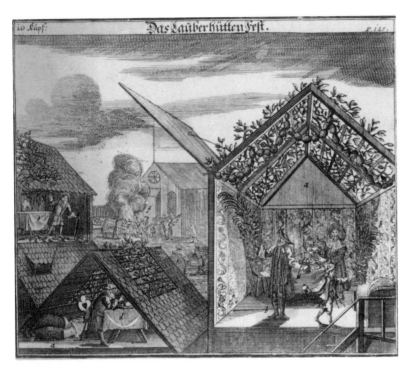

Fig. 2. "Das Lauber hütten Fest." Engraving by J.G. Puschner in Paul Christian Kirchner, Jüdisches Ceremoniel, Nuremberg 1726, no. 10, facing p. 126.

Fig. 3. Sukkah from Goßmansdorf, Franconia, date unknown. Detail. Courtesy Erich Weiß, Goßmansdorf.

the *sukkah* was subsequently presented to the Bezalel National Museum in Jerusalem by the widow of Mr. Deller's great-grandson, and was thus saved from inevitable destruction.

In fear of the Nazi regulations, which strictly forbade transfer of artworks outside of Germany, the *sukkah* had to be smuggled out. Aware of the grave danger involved in committing such a deed, and convinced beyond doubt of the necessity to salvage such a rare specimen of religious folk-art, the Fraenkel family of Munich, close relatives of Dr. Feuchtwanger's, agreed to transport the *sukkah* along with their belongings on their refugee voyage to Palestine in 1935. It was installed, painted side inwards, against the walls of a wooden container, and made a safe journey to Jerusalem.[17] In the same year, the last of the Deller family left Germany for Quito, Ecuador.[18]

The *sukkah* is a square structure,[19] with a door and a window in its façade, and a window on each

of its lateral walls. A metal chain with a hook at its end is attached to the top of the wall on the left, and similar ones are still affixed to the other walls as well. These devices probably served to keep the roof-covers open as long as there was no danger of rain. A similar wooden flap can be seen in the copper engraving, executed by Johann G. Puschner, which is reproduced in Paul Christian Kirchner's book *Jüdisches Ceremoniel*, published in Nuremberg in 1726 (Fig. 2).[20]

Two main types of *sukkot* were customarily in use by the Ashkenazi Jews from the eighteenth to the twentieth century. In many homes, the shingled roof was designated to serve as a *sukkah*. When in use, some of the shingles would be removed, and thatching placed in their stead. Remains of such a *sukkah* were recently discovered in a private home, now owned by Christians, in Goßmansdorf in Franconia, near Würzburg (Fig. 3).[21] The whitewashed

---

17 These details were verified by Mrs. Esther Pinczower, née Fraenkel, of Jerusalem and her brother, Mr. Michael Fraenkel of Haifa, based on their childhood memories.

18 Thanks are due to Mr. Meir Meyer of the Israel Museum in Jerusalem for providing important information concerning the *sukkah* and the history of the Deller family.

19 Its dimensions are: 2.90 x 2.90 m., height 2.10 m.

20 P.C. Kirchner, *Jüdisches Ceremoniel, oder Beschreibung derjenigen Gebräuche...* (Nuremberg: Peter Conrad, 1726). Engrav-

ing number 10, facing p. 124, is entitled "Das Lauber hütten Fest," and is signed at the bottom right corner: M.P. Sc. In other engravings, such as those facing pp. 78, 106 and 216, he signed his full last name. The copy which was consulted is the one in Wolfenbüttel, Herzog August Bibliothek, Gv 890.

21 I am most grateful to Mr. Hermann Suß of Fürstenfeldbruck, Mr. Joachim Braun of Ochsenfurt, and Mr. Erich Weiß of Goßmansdorf, who have all provided me with useful information and photographs of the *sukkah*.

Fig. 4. Sukkot meal of an Ashkenazi family in Amsterdam. Engraving in Bernard Picart, Ceremonies et coutumes ..., Amsterdam, 1783, I, facing p. 123.

REPAS des JUIFS pendant la FÊTE des TENTES.

Fig. 5. Moritz Oppenheim, "Das Laubhütten-Fest," 1869. After L. Stein, Bilder aus dem altjüdishen Familienleben, Frankfurt, 1882, pl. 16.

walls and the wooden panels of the construction bear remnants of decorations in red and blue. These consist of inscriptions pertaining to the festival of Sukkot and of simple, naive illustrations, which do not allow for explicit dating. A similar *sukkah* is evident in the above-mentioned engraving by Puschner, which appeared in Kirchner's study. The collapsible roof still prevailed in the late nineteenth and early twentieth century, as recorded, for example, in the memoirs of Clara Geissmar from her home-town of Eppingen, Bavaria: "In every house there had to be a room, through whose roof-beams the open sky could be seen. This room served as a *sukkah*. A kind of folding-door or a board was lowered upon the beams, in order to protect the room from rainfall..."[22]

The other type of *sukkah* was constructed annually outside Jewish synagogues or homes. In smaller com-

---

[22] Translated from C. Geissmar, *Erinnerungen* (Mannheim, 1913), quoted in M. Richarz, ed., *Jüdisches Leben in Deutschland, Selbstzeugnisse zur Sozialgeschichte 1780–1971* (New York, 1976), p. 456.

munities, a communal *sukkah* was often used by all the members of the congregation.[23] Family *sukkot* were, of course, most popular, wherever they were permitted by the local authorities.[24] The famous engraving by Bernard Picard provides an example of such a structure, being used by an Ashkenazi family in Amsterdam (Fig. 4).[25] The *sukkah* on the right seems to be an attic-type one, and is clearly being used by members of the local bourgeoisie. The *sukkah* shown in the background to the left, on the other hand, is filled by people who, according to their attire, belong to a lower class. Vertical lines, engraved at set intervals, suggest that this structure, too, was made of wooden planks.

Another collapsible wooden *sukkah* was depicted by Moritz Oppenheim in his painting *Das Laubhütten-Fest* (1869), reflecting a very similar construction to that of the Fischach *sukkah* (Fig. 5).[26] The Oppenheim *sukkah*, however, differs from the Fischach one in its interior decoration. It comprises only a hanging plaque, inscribed with the benediction recited upon entering the *sukkah*. Mr. Deller, on the other hand, owned a *sukkah* whose interior, except for the floor, is completely covered with artwork.[27]

The artist who painted the Deller *sukkah* incorporated motifs inspired by both secular and Jewish sources. The entrance wall and most of the lateral walls are covered with genre scenes. The entrance wall bears a gazelle-hunting scene, with two male figures and a dog (Fig. 6).[28] Fischach itself is depicted on the wall on the right, including the two *Judenhöfe* and the local synagogue.[29] Mrs. Deller, in village Biedermeier attire, is shown standing in front of her house (Fig. 7). The flowers in the basket, painted on the inner side of the door to the *sukkah*, are also typical of local folk-art scenes.

Such themes are totally devoid of Jewish meaning, and can indeed be found in a large variety of works of folk-art in the entire German-speaking realm from the sixteenth century onwards. Landscapes, hunting scenes and floral motifs form the common secular decorative repertoire for small boxes, cupboards and even home interiors.[30] Painted chambers must have been very costly, and were consequently owned only

23 E. Silbermann, *Erinnerungen 1871–1917* (Munich, 1916), relates his childhood in Kolmsdorf, Upper Franconia, in Richarz, *Jüdisches Leben*, p. 165, n. 21.

24 See the letter by Low Seeligmann, written in Munich on 19 September 1799, in S. Schwarz, *Die Juden in Bayern im Wandel der Zeiten* (Munich and Vienna, 1963), Appendix II, pp. 322–323, after the original in Munich, Staatsarchiv für Ober-Bayern, ex. GL 2783/1163.

25 B. Picard, *Cérémonies et coutumes religieuses de tous les peuples du monde Représentées par des Figures desinées de la main de Bernard Picard* (Amsterdam: J.F. Bernard, 1723), I, facing p. 123.

26 After L. Stein, *Bilder aus dem altjüdischen Familien Leben nach Orginal-Gemälden von Moritz Oppenheim Professor* (Frankfurt a.M.: Heinrich Keller, 1882), pl. 16. See also the English edition ed. J. Gutmann, with an introduction by Alfred Werner, *Pictures of the Traditional Jewish Family by Moritz Daniel Oppenheim* (New York: Library of Jewish Art, 1976); and the reproduction in *Moritz Oppenheim: The First Jewish Painter* (Jerusalem: The Israel Museum, 1983), no. IV.12 (cat. 238).

27 Another painted *sukkah* of the collapsible type has recently been discovered. It originates in Württembergisch-Franken (the Württembergian part of Franconia), in the village of Döttingen. Eleven of its panels were purchased by Mr. Egon Wetzel of Mainhardt, and are now in possession of the Hallisch-Fränkisches Museum in Schwäbisch-Hall. It was painted, or at least inscribed, by Abraham, the local *hazan*, as can be learnt from the inscription on one of its panels, providing also the date, the eve of the new moon of Elul 642 (=1882). The *sukkah* was first exhibited at the Germanisches Nationalmuseum in Nuremberg in 1988, in the exhibition *Siehe der Stein schreit aus der Mauer. Geschichte und Kultur der Juden in Bayern* cat. no. 3/111, pp. 109–110.

I am indebted to Dr. Cornelia Foerster of the Germanisches Nationalmuseum for providing me with her essay on the *sukkah*: "Ausstellung sichert Jüdisches Kulturgut. Zur Restaurierung einer Laubhütte," *Monatsanzeiger des Germanischen Nationalmuseums* 79 (October 1987), 630–631. Thanks are also due to Mrs. Evelyn Friedlander of London for sending me the article by N. Bar-Giora, "Ein Zeugnis aus dem siebzehnten Jahrhundert. Die bemalte Sukka aus Döttingen," *Israelitisches Wochenblatt* (Zurich), 42, 17 (October 1986), 15–16. The author, however, suggests 1682 as the date of the *sukkah*. Another *sukkah*, much more elaborate than that of Döttingen, was offered in an auction by Christie's in Amsterdam on 15 December 1988, Lot 196. See cat. pp. 60–61. It is of similar dimensions to those of the *sukkah* from Fischach and bears a resemblance to it in some of its iconographic features.

28 These figures have been identified as the local Baron and his hunter by Ben-Chorin (n. 1). They may, however, be portrayals of Mr. Deller and his son or servant. This interpretation seems more plausible in view of the inclusion of the image of Mrs. Deller on the opposite wall. However, there seems to be no absolute identification of these persons.

29 The synagogue, which also served as the community "school," is the last building on the Judengasse. It can be distinguished by its two entrances, to the main hall and to the women's gallery. Obviously, only a small number of Jewish houses in Fischach were depicted. In 1860, for example, the Jews occupied 38 houses and two Judenhöfe in the village. See Gebele (n. 2).

30 See, for instance, the cupboard from Tölz dating from around 1830, which was exhibited in *Volkskunst aus Deutschland, Österreich und der Schweiz*, 1968, cat. no. 71, pp. 63–64, and color plate on p. 65. The cupboard is decorated with sacred and floral motifs. Flowers in a basket are depicted also on the door of another cupboard produced in 1819 by M. Rossler, also

Fig. 6.   Gazelle-hunting scene, detail. Fischach sukkah, panels 6–7.

Fig. 7.   Deller residence and the village of Fischach. Fischach sukkah, panels 26–29.

Fig. 8.   Anonymous Franconian artist, "Ländliche Stube eines Rittersmannes," 1818. Gouache on paper. Munich, Bayerisches Nationalmuseum, NN 2510.

by those who enjoyed a higher economic or social status. For example, a painting by an unknown Franconian artist, dated 1818, depicts the combined living-room and bedroom of a cavalry officer, where the walls and the foot of the bed are richly adorned (Fig. 8).[31] It is conceivable that similar painted chambers were known to the panel artist, who was active in the region around Fischach, and was commissioned to perform the task of decorating a collapsible, temporary structure, to be used only seven days a year.

The idea of painting the interior of the *sukkah* may have originated from still another source, namely, the painted wooden synagogue of Kirchheim, of 1739/40.[32] It was most probably known to Mr. Deller, as the village of Kirchheim is close to Fischach.

Mr. Deller's identity as a Jew is clearly manifest in five painted panels, interspersed arbitrarily on the walls of the *sukkah*. They depict the Offering

---

from southern Germany: ibid. no. 68, p. 63 and pl. 17. For an architectural landscape, see the south German cabinet, dated 1833, no. 72, p. 64 and pl. 23. Further examples are brought by: B. Deneke, *Europäische Volkskunst* (Frankfurt a.M, Berlin, Vienna, 1980), Propyläen Kunstgeschichte, Supplement V, esp. nos. 86–89, 91–93, 99 and 101. For a survey of the medium and iconography of painted folk-art furniture see also idem, *Bauernmöbel. Ein Handbuch für Sammler und Liebhaber* (Munich, 1983), pp. 96–106, and the relevant examples.

[31] Munich, Bayerisches Nationalmuseum: NN 2510, reproduced in H. Glaser, ed., *Wittelsbach und Bayern. Krone und Verfassung. König Max I. und die neue Stadt* (Völkerkundemuseum, Munich, 1980), III, 2, no. 706, entry by Helmut Sperber on pp. 706–707, and photo on p. 375. Cf. also Deneke, *Europäische Volkskunst*,

no. 72 (n. 30). At times, people chose to decorate the exterior of their homes. See, for example, O. Schwindrazheim, *Deutsche Bauernkunst* (Vienna, 1904), p. 104 and pl. 54

[32] On the synagogue and its paintings, see mainly F. Mader, *Die Kunstdenkmähler von Unterfranken und Aschaffenburg. Die Kunstdenkmähler des Königreiches Bayern, III, 3: Bezirksamt Aschaffenburg* (Munich, 1911), pp. 80–83 and figs. 54–57; M. Untermayer, "Die Synagoge von Kirchheim," *Central-Verein Zeitung* 15, no. 16, 1, *Beiblatt*, pp. 1–2; M. Untermayer-Raymer, "German Synagogue Art: Notes and Drawings," *Menorah Journal* 25, no. 1 (January-March 1937), 66–68; D. Davidovicz, *Wandmalereien in alten Synagogen: Das Wirken des Maler Elieser Sussman in Deutschland* (Hameln-Hannover, 1969), pp. 19–21 and pls. 21–23.

9

10

11

12

*Fig. 9.   Offering the Paschal Lamb at the Temple.
Fischach sukkah, panel 23.*

*Fig. 10.   Giving of the Law on Mt. Sinai. Fischach
sukkah, panel 22.*

*Fig. 11.   The Binding of Isaac. Fischach sukkah, panel
20.*

*Fig. 12.   The High Priest performing the sacrifice on the
Day of Atonement. Fischach sukkah, panel 16.*

Fig. 13.   Haqafot on Sukkot. Fischach sukkah, panel 15.

of the Paschal Lamb at the Temple (panel no. 23,
Fig. 9), the Giving of the Law on Mt. Sinai (panel
no. 22, Fig. 10), the Binding of Isaac (panel no. 20,
Fig. 11), the High Priest Performing the Sacrifice on
the Day of Atonement (panel no. 16, Fig. 12), and
the *Haqafot* with the Torah Scrolls on Sukkot (panel
no. 15, Fig. 13). Dr. Feuchtwanger identified these
scenes as representations of the major festivals of the

Jewish year — the High Holidays and the Pilgrimage
feasts,[33] though without pointing to their immediate
visual model.

In 5587 (1826), Seckel Arnstein and Sons printed in
Sulzbach a five-volume *mahzor* for Passover, Shavu'ot,
the New Year, the Day of Atonement, and Sukkot.[34]
Each volume of the *mahzor* opens with a copper
engraving, appended to the first title-page,[35] executed

[33] Feuchtwanger, *Monumenta* (n. 1).

[34] The Arnstein-Frankel printing firm succeeded that of Johann
Holst, following a privilege granted to Aaron Frankel on 12
August 1699, which permitted him to print Hebrew books.
See J. Benzing, *Die Buchdrucker des 16. und 17. Jahrhunderts
im deutschen Sprachgebiet* (Wiesbaden, 1982, 2nd edn.), 459.
See also J. Prijs, "Hebräische Buchdruckereien im Gebiete des
heutigen Bayern," *Bayerische israelitische Gemeindezeitung* 1
(1925), 91–93; B. Friedberg, *History of Hebrew Typography... in
Central Europe...* (Antwerp, 1953), pp. 76–78 (Hebrew). On the
printer of the mahzor, Seckel b. Aaron Frankel-Arnstein, see M.
Weinberg, "Die hebräischen Druckereien in Sulzbach 1669–1851.
Ihre Geschichte, ihre Drucke, ihr Personal," *Jahrbuch der
jüdisch-literarischen Gesellschaft* pp. 101–114; 1 (1903), idem,
Die hebräischen Druckereien in Sulzbach (1669–1851) (Frankfurt

a.M., 1904 85–98. The printer's marks of the Frankel-Arnstein
family are discussed by G.H. Seidel, "Die Druckerzeichen von
Fürth und Sulzbach," *Nachrichtenblatt für den jüdischen Bürger
Fürths* (September 1982), pp. 29–32.

[35] Following the first title-page, another one was added. It includes
the specific contents of each respective volume, as well as data
concerning the place and year of publication and the name of
the publishers in German. These title-pages provide a clue for
the sequence of the printing of the five volumes. The mahzor for
Passover and the one for Sukkot bear a printing error which has
subsequently been corrected in the remaining volumes. In the
mahzor for Shavu'ot, on the other hand, the date of publication
is printed in a slightly smaller font. The full set of the Sulzbach
mahzor which was consulted is in Jerusalem, Jewish National
and University Library, S 36 A 1445.

Fig. 14. Mahzor. Sulzbach: Seckel Arnstein and Sons, 1826. Vol. II: Shavu'ot. Engraving and second title page. Engraver: Joseph Herz.

Fig. 15. Mahzor. Sulzbach: Seckel Arnstein and Sons, 1826. Vol. III: Shavu'ot. Engraving and second title page, with copper-plate engraving by Joseph Herz. Feuchtwanger collection, 491a,b. Jerusalem, Israel Museum, 184/95. Courtesy of the Israel Museum.

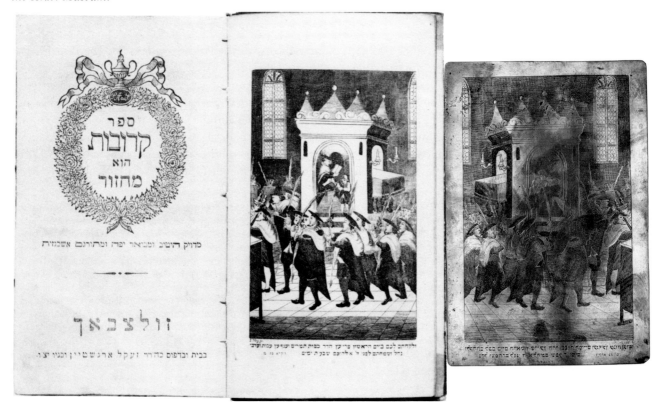

Fig. 16. Joseph Herz, Sacrifice of the Paschal Lamb. Engraving facing the second title page of Sulzbach Mahzor, vol. I: Passover.

Fig. 17. Joseph Herz, The Giving of the Law. Engraving facing the second title page of Sulzbach Mahzor, vol. II: Shavu'ot.

and signed by Joseph Herz (Fig. 14).[36] These illustrations are exclusive to this edition only. Two volumes of it are in the Feuchtwanger Collection at the Israel Museum, as are two of the original copper plates from which the engravings were printed (Fig. 15).[37]

The similarity between Joseph Herz's engravings and the Fischach panels is remarkable. In the latter, however, the inscriptions which accompany the illustrations, as well as the artist's name, were left out.

The folk-artist who painted the *sukkah* kept all the major elements of the scene as they are depicted in the *mahzor*, but felt free to alter the landscape and the architectural background to his own taste. Thus, in the Passover scene, for example, he omitted the Temple and suspended the lamp from above on an ornamental ribbon (Fig. 16). The Shavu'ot scene in the *sukkah* follows the *mahzor* more closely, though some landscape details have been discarded (Fig. 17).

---

[36] On Joseph Herz and his work see A. Wolf, "Etwas über jüdische Kunst und ältere jüdische Künstler," *Mitteilungen zur jüdischen Volkskunde* 15 (1905), 55; L. Lowenstein, "Zur Geschichte der Juden in Fürth (2. Teil)," *Jahrbuch der jüdisch-literarischen Gesellschaft* 8 (1911), 111–112; E. Toeplitz, "Joseph Herz (1776–1828), ein jüdischer Kupferstecher," *Aus alter und neuer Zeit. Illustrierte Beilage zum Israelitischen Familienblatt*, Beilage zu Nr. 24, 44 (13 June 1929), p. 347.

[37] The Feuchtwanger Collection, nos. 329 a, b (Sukkot) and 491 a, b (Shavu'ot) Jerusalem, The Israel Museum: 184/95 and 184/97, respectively. See I. Shachar, *Jewish Tradition in Art: The Feuchtwanger Collection of Judaica*, trans. R. Grafman (Jerusalem: The Israel Museum, 1981), cat. no. 78; no. 329, p. 125 and photograph on p. 126; and no. 491, p. 184, reproduced on p. 185.

ניתן שם אברהם את המזבח ויערך את העצים ויעקד את יצחק בנו וישם אתו על המזבח ממעל לעצים:

ויכפר את מקדש הקדש ואת אהל מועד ואת המזבח יכפר ועל הכהנים ועל כל עם הקהל יכפר:

Fig. 18. Joseph Herz, The Binding of Isaac. Engraving facing the second title page of Sulzbach Mahzor, vol. IV: New Year.
Fig. 19. Joseph Herz, The Sacrifice on the Day of Atonement. Engraving facing the second title page of Sulzbach Mahzor, vol. V: Day of Atonement.
Fig. 20. Joseph Herz, The Haqafot on Sukkot. Engraving facing the second title page of Sulzbach Mahzor, vol. III: Sukkot.

ולקחתם לכם ביום הראשון פרי עץ הדר כפות תמרים וענף עץ עבות וערבי נחל ושמחתם לפני ה' אלהיכם שבעת ימים:

The same holds true for the three remaining panels (Figs. 18, 19, 20).

Evidently, Mr. Deller owned a copy of the sumptuous 1826 edition of the Sulzbach *mahzor*, and the five small panels in his *sukkah* were copied directly from this model. Apparently, the villager from Fischach must have valued his mahzor very highly. With rightful pride, he commissioned the reproduction of all five copper engravings in his *sukkah*, regardless of their immediate relevance to the holiday. The identification of this iconographic source for the illustrations thus establishes a *terminus ante quem* for the dating of the *sukkah*, 1826.

Fig. 21. Painted sukkah from Fischach, southern Germany, after 1836/7. Jerusalem, Israel Museum, 196/1. Wall opposite the entrance. Courtesy of the Israel Museum.

The wall opposite the entrance to the *sukkah* is the most lavish of the panels. It bears a monumental depiction of the Holy Sites in Jerusalem, occupying the entire wall (Fig. 21). This panoramic vista, though schematic in concept, retains to some extent the city's actual semblance, with the Dome of the Rock to the left of the Wailing Wall, the Al-Aqsa Mosque to its right, and the row of cypresses in the platform above it.

Similar illustrations of Jerusalem as seen from the east were popular mementos produced in Jerusalem in the nineteenth century.[38] The first dated depiction of the Holy Sites in this manner is a lithograph which was drawn in Jerusalem in 1836/7 and printed elsewhere (Fig. 22). This data is provided by the inscription, which runs along its lower margin, and reads: "A token of love sent to my brethren who abide in the Diaspora, seeking (the welfare of) Zion and Jerusalem. Here, the Holy City of Jerusalem, may it be rebuilt and restored soon, in our days, Amen, (in) the year 597 of the minute count. Made by the youngster the lesser Yehosef Schwarz. And distributed among (the People of) Israel through my beloved brother Rabbi Hayyim Schwarz, may God guard and protect him, residing in the Holy Community of Hürben, may God protect it."[39]

---

[38] For examples of such works of art see Y. Fischer, ed., and H. Peled, *Arts and Crafts in Eretz Israel of the Nineteenth Century* (Jerusalem: The Israel Museum, 1979) (Hebrew), esp. 72–73 and 96–100.

[39] מנחת אהבה היא שלוחה לאחי יושבי הגולה דורשי ציון וירושלים. פה עיר הקדושה ירושלים תובבא שנת תקצז לפק. נעשה על ידי הצעיר הקטן יהוסף שווארץ. ואפיצה בישראל ע"י אחי חביבי מהורר חיים שווארץ נרו חונה בק"ק הירבען יע"א.

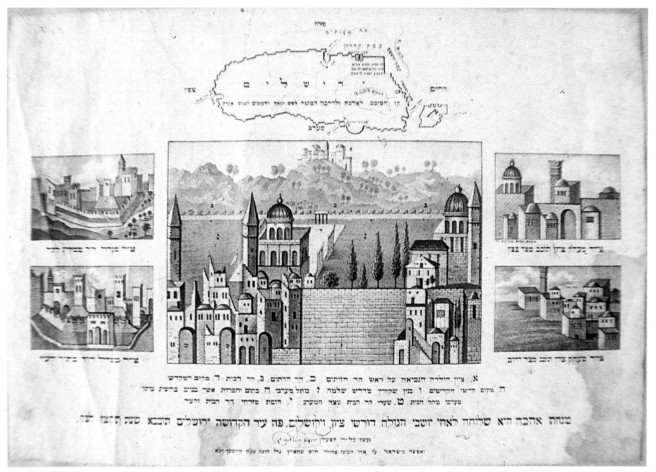

Fig. 22. Yehosef Schwarz, View of Jerusalem, 1836/7. Lithograph on paper. Israel Museum, Feuchtwanger Collection, 492, Israel Museum 177/102. Courtesy of the Israel Museum.

Yehosef Schwarz is a well-known figure in the history of Eretz Israel.[40] He was born in the Bavarian town of Floß in 1804, and immigrated to Jerusalem in 1833. As a scholar, his main interest was the study of Eretz Israel. In his publications he included lithographs of maps and landscapes of the sites under discussion.[41]

The art of lithography was, at the time, unknown in Eretz Israel, as Yehosef himself deplored in the introduction to his book, *Sefer Toledot Yosef*, which was published in 1845.[42] The place in which these lithographs were actually printed remains a matter of conjecture. It may be assumed that the original drawings were made in situ by the author, as he attests to have drawn maps and views of various sites

[40] The first biography of Yehosef Schwarz was written by A.M. Luncz, who edited and published Schwarz's *Tebuoth Ha-Arez* ("The Crops of the Country") in Jerusalem in 1900, and added a preface and a biographical note. On Yehosef Schwarz see pp. xi–xxiv. See also I. Schwarz, "Vorrede des Übersetzers," in: *Schwarz, Joseph. Das heilige Land, nach seiner ehemaligen und jetzigen Beschaffenheit...* (Frankfurt a.M., 1985), x–xiv; and A.J. Brawer, "Schwarz, Yehoseph," *Encyclopaedia Judaica* (Jerusalem, 1971), vol. 14, cols. 1022–1023. See also H. Peled, "Seven Artists in Eretz Israel," *Arts and Crafts*, pp. 110–111, n. 38.

[41] Lithographs relevant to our study appeared for the first time

in the English translation by I. Leeser of *Tevuot Ha-Aretz: Descriptive Geography and Brief Historical Sketch of Palestine by Rabbi Joseph Schwarz* (Philadelphia, 1850), and later in the German edition (n. 40).

[42] In the introduction to his work, written in Jerusalem in 1843, the author requests the readers' forgiveness for the imperfection of his book. The faults, he claims, are due to the fact that the appropriate aids for scientific research are wanting in Eretz Israel. He further states that it is impossible for him to "draw the drawings required for the understanding of my profound words (and this is the craft of lithography, which is not to be found in the country)." Translated after Luncz, (n. 40), ix.

in Jerusalem.[43] He then sent these drawings abroad to be reproduced in lithograph, most likely through the good offices of his brother, Hayyim, who served as the Rabbi in Hürben.[44]

The lithographs were distributed by the Rabbi of Hürben. One of the immediate markets must have been the nearby Jewish communities, including Fischach, which is located only about 25 kilometers to the northeast.[45] A copy of this memento from Jerusalem was apparently purchased by Mr. Deller, and was reproduced almost in its entirety in his *sukkah*, as a unified composition.[46] One must, therefore, ascribe the *sukkah* from Fischach to a date later than Yehosef Schwarz's drawing of 1836/7.

The depiction of Jerusalem occupies the most prominent place in the *sukkah*, and thus may have served as a reminder of Jerusalem, perhaps also alluding to the pilgrimage to the Temple, or as an elaborate, suggestive *Mizrah*-plaque.[47]

A hundred years after Yehosef Schwarz's illustration was drawn, another copy of this view of Jerusalem was acquired by Dr. Heinrich Feuchtwanger,[48] who rediscovered the *sukkah*.

Mr. Deller's *sukkah* from Fischach reveals something of the life style of a well-to-do Jewish merchant living in rural Germany in the middle of the nineteenth century. It provides evidence of his love of the book and to his taste for art. Above all, it is a manifestation of his longing for Jerusalem. In this sense, the *sukkah* has found its due home at the Israel Museum in Jerusalem.

43 For example, in his letter of 23 Iyar 5597 (28 May 1837) he promises his brother to send him an illustration of the Wailing Wall and the Holy Tombs of Jerusalem. The letter, originally written in Hebrew, was translated into German and published by his brother under the title "Aus einem Schreiben des Hrn. Joseph Schwarz aus Jerusalem, an seinen Bruder, Hrn. H. Schwarz, Rabbiner in Hürben," *Wissenschaftliche Zeitschrift für jüdische Theologie* 156–159 4 (1839), and 303–309. Reference here is made to pp. 157 and 305. Thanks are due to Dr. Falk Wiesemann of the Heinrich-Heine-Universität in Düsseldorf, who kindly brought this version of the correspondence in German to my attention. The letter was later retranslated into Hebrew and published by A. Yaari, *Igrot Eretz Israel* (Tel Aviv, 1943), 370–378 (Hebrew).

The relevant passages are on pp. 371 and 374.
44 Hayyim Schwarz's official seal, inscribed "Rabynat Hürben, Schwarz," is in the Feuchtwanger Collection in the Israel Museum, Jerusalem. See Shachar, *Feuchtwanger Collection* no. 620, p. 214. Israel Museum 105/171 (n. 37).
45 The village of Hürben was annexed to the city of Krumbach in 1902. See B.Z. Ophir, *Pinkas Hakehillot*, 637–639 (n. 2).
46 For some reason the artist omitted the upper left panel, depicting "David's Tower from Without."
47 Feuchtwanger, *Monumenta*, (n. 1), suggests that this may have been the eastern wall of the *sukkah*.
48 See Shachar, *Feuchtwanger Collection*, no. 429, p. 188 and photograph on p. 189 (n. 37). Israel Museum 177/102.

AMERICAN SEPHARDI SYNAGOGUE ARCHITECTURE

Laura Rachel Felleman Fattal

American Sephardim represent a minority of 350,000 within the larger American Jewish population of over 5.8 million people. Hitherto barely affiliated American Jews experiencing a renewed respect for orthodoxy have been attracted by the Sephardi maintenance of tradition in ritual and architecture. The exotic Sephardim lure the dominant Ashkenazi population with their prayer intonations reminiscent of Arabic and Spanish melodies, their distinctive holiday foods, and their often Near-Eastern complexions.

Sephardi communities in America have grown considerably in the last decade. Persian Jews, representing the latest group of Sephardi immigrants, have been moving to the United States since the Khomeini revolution of 1979. In addition there has been ongoing emigration from Israel, with its present majority of Sephardi Jews; the strong emotional, intellectual, and financial ties linking the American Jewish community and Israel have awakened a desire to know more about the Sephardi communities.

Synagogue architecture reflects the liturgical needs of a community and its integration into the larger society. At the same time, the synagogue represents an aesthetic view of spirituality. The synagogues to be discussed in this essay were chosen according to the following criteria: 1. The architect's intent to build a unique religious building; 2. Aesthetic and creative interpretations of style; 3. Geographic diversity; 4. The presence of a living congregation; and 5. Adherence to Sephardi rite, whether the Judeo-Arabic tradition or the more dominant Spanish-Portuguese siddur.

Salient examples of American Sephardi synagogues will be reviewed, with an emphasis on the post-World War II period. The history and architecture of ten

American Sephardi synagogues will be described and analyzed, and the relationship between the socio-cultural milieu and the architectural style of the main religious buildings of these communities, the synagogues, will be examined.

Few laws govern synagogue architecture.[1] Jews have prayed and come together as communities in dwellings as meager as tents and as opulent as the Hellenistic synagogue in Alexandria. Simplicity and religiosity have often been paired, thus precluding architectural innovation. There are few stylistic similarities between American synagogues in general and Sephardi synagogues in particular. In some instances American synagogues resemble the religious buildings of other faiths, as for example B'nai Amoona of St. Louis, Missouri, built by Mendelsohn in 1949; in others, synagogues are brazenly identifiable as in Goodman's B'nai Israel, of Millburn, New Jersey built in 1951.

Sephardi synagogues have existed in the United States since the colonial period. At that time Sephardi Jewry was made up of the later waves of those fleeing the religious persecutions of the Spanish Inquisition. The early American Sephardi Jews came originally from Curaçao in the West Indies and Amsterdam in the Netherlands, immigrating to New York City and Newport, Rhode Island.

Four noteworthy early American congregations continue to function today. The congregations of Shearith Israel in New York of 1730 and Mikveh Israel in Philadelphia of 1782 have redesigned their synagogues and moved several times; however, the Touro Synagogue in Newport, Rhode Island of 1763 is the original building of the early congregation, and the Hebrew Congregation of St. Thomas of 1833 is the extant synagogue of a congregation whose earlier synagogues were destroyed by fire in 1804, and again in 1831.

---

[1] Joseph Baumgarten, "Art in the Synagogue — Some Talmudic Views," *The Synagogue: Studies in Origin, Archaeology and Architecture*, ed. J. Gutmann (New York, 1975), pp. 79–89.

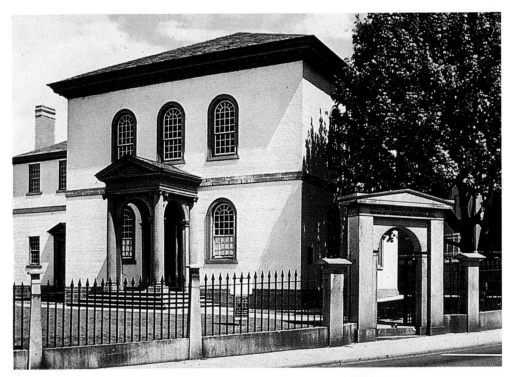

Fig. 1. Touro Synagogue, Rhode Island, ca. 1740, west façade.

Fig. 2. Touro Synagogue, ca. 1740, interior from central Bimah towards the Torah Ark in the east.

The Touro Synagogue, Newport Rhode Island

The Touro Synagogue of Congregation Jeshuat Israel is the oldest synagogue still functioning in the United States today, although the congregation rarely meets and the rite is no longer Sephardi.[2] The synagogue was named for its minister, Isaac de Touro, who came from Amsterdam to Newport in 1758. Even though the independent-minded merchants who made up the congregation had immigrated to the American colonies to improve their standard of living, they clung to the fashions of Europe. The British-born architect Peter Harrison, who had come to Newport in 1740, was hired to build the Touro synagogue. Harrison worked in the Georgian style, an austere but elegant form of Neoclassicism (Fig. 1). The building was to accommodate eighty congregants, seating men on the main floor and women in the balcony (Fig. 2). The balcony and ceiling of its white interior are supported by twelve grey solid wood columns, thought to be symbolic of the Twelve Tribes of Israel. Architecturally, they recall the twelve columns of the Portuguese Synagogue in Amsterdam of 1675 by Elias

[2] Marc Angel, "The Planting of Sephardic Culture in North America," *The Sephardim*, comp. J. Stampfer (Portland, Oregon, 1987), pp. 95–113, see especially p. 102.

Bouman, and London's Bevis Marks Synagogue of 1701. Wischnitzer has noted that although the columns of these three synagogues are similar in number, their structural function is quite different.[3]

Harrison's design and construction of the Touro synagogue has been much praised.[4] He was well versed in the English academic pattern books that were the source for the designs of most Neoclassical architects. He avoided ornate architectural details, offering a broad suggestion of sculptural relief in the broken entablature around the ark, the dentilled entablature along the lateral walls, the set-in windows, the large balustraded reader's platform, the ark, and the balcony.

Numerous chandeliers lighting the interior of the synagogue are customary for the Sephardi communities. Several brass-armed Walloon chandeliers are strategically placed to illuminate the Touro synagogue. The Walloon design, originating in the Low Countries, was thereafter used in the Sephardi synagogue of Beth Elohim in South Carolina built in 1794 (destroyed by fire in 1838), and in Mikveh Israel in Philadelphia of 1976. With their arabesque tendrils, Walloon chandeliers are now often used in synagogues because of their coveted association with early American synagogues, conveying the idea of the continued existence of Jewish communities in the United States.

The exterior of the Touro synagogue is constructed of brick imported from England. At present, the brick is painted an off-white color. Dark brown columns (part of a portico added later), brown outlined hemispherically arched windows, and a beltcourse between floors all articulate the exterior of the building. Women enter the synagogue not from the front door, but from the adjoining wing on the north side of the building. This entrance leads to the gallery upstairs. There is a hipped roof, as is typical of Neoclassical architecture. The lack of attention paid to the exterior design of the Torah Ark is in marked contrast to the stark and severe design of modern buildings. The architectural presence of this Jewish community was one of elegance and understatement.

The street plan of Newport in 1763 is unknown.

The present location of the synagogue is at an acute angle to the narrow street, due to its decidedly eastern orientation; if this has persisted from colonial times it suggests an attitude of tolerance for religious expression. Such an acceptance of diversity was the ideal of Roger Williams, the founder of the colony of Rhode Island.

Shearith Israel, Manhattan, New York

Originally established in 1730, Shearith Israel is the oldest Jewish congregation in the United States.[5] It has had several locations, moving in 1834 from Mill Street in lower Manhattan to Crosby Street, in 1860 to 19th Street, and finally in 1897 to its prestigious site on Central Park West at 70th Street.

There is a continuity of classicism among all of Shearith Israel's buildings. There is also an unbroken genealogy between the congregants of the 1730 Mill Street synagogue and some members of the congregation of Central Park West. Such architectural embellishments as the wooden ten commandments above the ark, the wooden ark, the four brass candlesticks, the eternal light, and the hanukkah lamp of the small sanctuary set apart from the main one (Fig. 3) all once belonged to the 1730 Mill Street synagogue. The siddur of the synagogue, with its Spanish-Portuguese rite, has been a model for Sephardi congregations worldwide.

Designed by Arnold Brunner in 1897 (Fig. 4), the synagogue is a monumental limestone building divided vertically in three parts on the exterior by attached giant Corinthian columns. The wreaths in the attic are separated by Doric pilasters supporting a sculptural pediment. Large, hemispherically arched stained glass windows are placed between the columns on the main façade and the giant pilasters on the lateral façade. The entire exterior design recalls a Roman triumphal arch, and according to Berger, the 1897 classicism of Shearith Israel was a political statement.[6] Earlier, the Palestine Exploration Fund, amongst others, had excavated synagogues built during the late Antique and Byzantine period in the Galilee;[7] by continuing to build in the classical tra-

---

[3]   Rachel Wischnitzer, *The Architecture of the European Synagogue* (Philadelphia, 1964), p. 104. Rachel Wischnitzer, *Synagogue Architecture in the United States* (Philadelphia, 1955), p. 15.

[4]   Wischnitzer, *United States*, p. 14.

[5]   Ibid, p. 11.

[6]   Maurice Berger, "Arnold Brunner's Spanish and Portuguese Syn-

agogue: Issues of Reform and Reaffirmation in Late Nineteenth Century America," *Art Magazine* 54.6 (1980), 164–167.

[7]   As for example Kapernaum, Kefar Bar'am, and Chorazin. For early photographs, some by the Palestine Exploration Fund, see H. Kohl and C. Watzinger, *Antike Synagogue in Galilaea* (Leipzig, 1916; Israel, 1973), pp. 4–58, 89–100.

3

4

5

Fig. 3.   Shearith Israel, New York, 1897, small sanctuary, interior.

Fig. 4.   Shearith Israel, New York, 1897, west façade.

Fig. 5.   Shearith Israel, New York, 1897, main sanctuary, interior.

dition, it was hoped that a bridge could be formed between ancient Israel and contemporary Jewry.

The interior of the main sanctuary (Fig. 5) repeats the elements of classicism found on the exterior and in the small sanctuary. The synagogue was built to accommodate seven hundred people seated on wooden pews, men on the main floor, and women in the balcony. The ark faces directly east, and lines up precisely with the grid pattern of midtown Manhattan. The sanctuary is dimly lit by outside light filtered through Tiffany stained glass windows, their colors suggestive of land formations and the movement of water, but devoid of narrative. Several small chandeliers hang above the lateral pews. The large wooden reader's platform is situated far back in the sanctuary, giving a bipolar emphasis to the room.

Painted salmon and veined with grey lines to simulate marble, the columns on the main floor support the balcony. Flanking the ark are columns and blind arches in simulated marble. In the center of the interior eastern wall is a classical temple front constructed of marble. The Ten Commandments perch atop the pediment of the classically styled ark, which suggests a building that has been turned inside-out.

The Hebrew Congregation of St. Thomas, Virgin Islands

Though not a part of the United States until 1917, St. Thomas was inhabited by Jews from the 1670s. From the seventeenth century until the early part of the twentieth century it was governed by Denmark. Although wealthy Jewish merchants lived on St. Thomas in the seventeenth and eighteenth centuries, they were most likely to worship on the island of St. Croix. The first congregation was established on St. Thomas in 1796.[8] We know of its wealth from a solicitous letter from the Philadelphia congregation of Mikveh Israel, asking for funds from fellow Jews to assist in building a new synagogue. In 1814 Denmark became the first modern nation to pass laws for the protection and liberation of Jews, and the most prosperous time for the Jews of St. Thomas was the early and mid-nineteenth century. Evidence of the Jews' tranquil existence on St. Thomas can be seen in the mutual efforts of Jews and gentiles to assist each others' charitable causes.

Fig. 6.   St. Thomas, Virgin Islands, 1833, façade.

The linguistic and financial skills of the Jewish merchants buoyed the island's economy. In 1868 shipping was their main livelihood, and St. Thomas became a transshipment center, a free port and a port of repair for sailing ships. Later in the century however, steamships provided most of the transoceanic transport. Coal, a natural resource of the United States and the countries of Europe, was loaded and used for fuel in these seafaring steamships. The loading and transporting of coal became more economically accomplished elsewhere and the economic fortunes of the Jews of St. Thomas declined.

The synagogue of the congregation of St. Thomas is an excellent example of regional Neoclassicism. The elegant building was designed in 1833 by a French architect whose name we do not know. Fourteen grey marble steps lead to the large, double-columned portico (Fig. 6). The columns, with their uniquely simple capitals, are of brick. A pointed, arched doorway opens into the sandy-floored sanctuary. Romantic lore explaining this sandy floor suggests that its simplicity recalls the time when Jews prayed in unfinished basements during the Spanish Inquisition. The synagogue of Mikveh Israel in Curaçao of 1732 also has a floor of sand, suggesting that this is a regional characteristic.

The sand on the floor augments the diverse textures filling the single-room sanctuary (Fig. 7), which is supported by four white Ionic columns said to symbolize the four mothers of Israel: Sarah, Rebecca, Rachel, and Leah.[9] Its walls are constructed of indigenous, irregularly shaped grey stone. Pointed windows

[8]   Stanley T. Relkin and Monty R. Abrams, eds., *A Short History of the Hebrew Congregation of St. Thomas* (1983), pp. 5–13, 22–32.

[9]   Ibid., p. 13.

are set into the wall and outlined with classical brick patterning. The brick was brought to St. Thomas as ballast for sailing ships; the mortar was made up of molasses and sea sand. The dark wood of the lateral pews, the ark, the reader's platform, and the low *mehizah* — the division between the men's and women's seating — is mahogany from the Caribbean.[10] These native materials are in stark contrast to the imported Baccarat crystal that protects the lights of the chandeliers, and the brass of the lower part of the Walloon chandeliers and candlesticks. A deep blue Decalogue with gold lettering is placed over the ark between two extended volutes.

The pews all face the center of the sanctuary. The reader's platform is situated on the western wall, with two single chairs placed in front for the *parnassim*, the leaders of the community. Brass candlesticks adorn the corners of the platform, in a manner similar to that of the small sanctuary of Shearith Israel in New York of 1730 (Fig. 3). A mahogany preaching pulpit stands slightly in front of the reader's platform and between the chairs of the *parnassim*.

Initially, sixty-four families from St. Thomas itself, England, France, St. Eustatius, and Curaçao commissioned the construction of the synagogue in 1833; all of the furniture now in the synagogue dates from that

time. In 1837, there were 400 Jews on St. Thomas. In its spatial proportions and use of classical orders and motifs, their synagogue exhibited a worldly knowledge of European design. Its modest size served a practical population with sophisticated taste.

The congregations of Touro, Shearith Israel and St. Thomas all adhere to the religious requirements of synagogue architecture. In their ground plans the reader's platform is separated from the ark. Limitations of space in Italy as early as the fifteenth century had created such a bipolar arrangement, which then developed a tradition of its own with the reader's platform of Sephardi congregations being located at the western end of every synagogue to this day.[11] This bipolar emphasis of the ark situated on the eastern wall, and a platform at the extreme western end of the sanctuary, enhances the ceremony when the Torah is brought out of the ark and paraded through the congregation, thus increasing its involvement in the service.

Separation of men and women is deliberate and marked. In Touro, the women enter the synagogue by a separate door from the men, and they sit upstairs. In Shearith Israel, women and men pass through the same exterior entrance; but the women's doors to the sanctuary are at the far sides of the main door,

---

[10] Ibid. p. 22.

[11] Wischnitzer, *European Synagogues*, p. 67.

Fig. 7.   St. Thomas, Virgin Islands, 1833, interior.

and lead upstairs to a large balcony. In St. Thomas, the women sit behind the men, separated from them by a low wooden barrier and on a slightly raised platform. The light of the raised chandeliers of these three sanctuaries appears to benefit the men seated on the main floor more than the women seated behind them or in the balconies.

There are no figurative representations in the synagogues. Though ornate, the Tiffany stained glass of Shearith Israel, the Baccarat crystal of St. Thomas, and the architectural embellishments of Touro all remain non-figurative.

Stylistically, Touro, St. Thomas, and Shearith Israel are classical buildings whose architects used successful formulae for synagogue building such as Bevis Marks of 1699–1701 in London, and the Portuguese Synagogue of 1671–75 in Amsterdam.[12] Their prominence in their respective cities has been linked directly to the size and wealth of their congregations. The practical question of where to build a synagogue — on a hilltop, near a river, or near other religious buildings — was overridden in most cases by a concern for being close to the Jewish community, to facilitate walking to services.

After the mid-nineteenth century, Sephardim no longer represented the dominant Jewish group in the United States. Ashkenazi Jews, with their different customs and rituals, began to enter the United States from many parts of Europe. Reform Jews from Germany and England brought with them a different seating plan for the synagogue. The Reform synagogue placed the reader's platform and the ark together at the eastern end of the sanctuary, exchanging the congregation-centered prayer for passive observance. Reform synagogues presented an atmosphere of decorum not sought after by traditional congregations. Ashkenazi Jews experimented with architectural styles for their synagogues. They built houses of worship in the Neoclassic, Romantic, Romanesque, Islamic, and, in this century, the International style.

Sephardi congregations also continued to build and remodel synagogues throughout the latter half of the nineteenth century, and at an accelerated pace in the twentieth century. Many of these congregations have been housed in older religious buildings of other groups of Jews or even of other religions, and in large

houses. Most of these communities which started in inner city neighborhoods moved later to affluent areas. We shall focus on synagogues built for a singular purpose in post-World War II America. A hiatus of over 130 years in Sephardi synagogue architecture is bridged by the congregation of Mikveh Israel in Philadelphia.

Mikveh Israel, Philadelphia

Mikveh Israel is a modern urban synagogue built in 1976. Its exterior (Fig. 8) is of brick, reminiscent of colonial Sephardi building materials and particularly appropriate, since its new location and design were to add to the celebration of the bicentennial of the American Revolution. Funds from its initial budget were siphoned off in 1973 when the congregation aided Israel in its war effort, and the existing building is smaller than was originally intended.

Mikveh Israel began building its first synagogue in 1782 on Cherry Street, and subsequently enlarged the building in 1822, commissioning the renowned architect William Strickland.[13] The building is noteworthy, since it was the only nineteenth-century Sephardi synagogue to use a Mideastern motif in its architecture. This motif exemplified the Egyptian revival style that was fashionable in other building projects. Thirty-eight years later, in 1860, John MacArthur was selected to redesign Mikveh Israel at a new location on North 7th Street. Then, in 1909, a new Neo-Roman style synagogue, the congregation's largest, was designed by Pilcher and Tachau and built in a prominent location on Broad Street. Finally, in 1976, the Philadelphia architectural firm of H2L2, headed by Robert Breading, built the present synagogue. Smaller in size than the previous three synagogues, it seats 400 people.

Men and women enter the transitional lobby together, then enter the sanctuary separately through large wood doors. They sit on lateral oak pews (Fig. 9), the women behind the men, separated by a double wood panel on the back of the last row of the men's pews. The women's section is slightly elevated. Acoustic refinements in the walls and ceiling improve the auditory clarity of the service; this is necessary since the participation of amateur speakers is encouraged.

[12] Carol Krinsky, *Synagogues of Europe* (Cambridge, MA, 1985), p. 413.

[13] Wischnitzer, *United States*, pp. 28–33.

Fig. 8. Mikveh Israel, Philadelphia, 1976, exterior.
Fig. 9. Mikveh Israel, Philadelphia, 1976, interior.

Hidden skylights are recessed into the ceiling, providing indirect lighting; there are no lower windows. The bipolar focus of the sanctuary lies in the tremendous Victorian white marble reader's platform, taken from the MacArthur synagogue in 1860, and the tall wood ark housing antique Torah scrolls. Above the ark is a dark wood Decalogue. The glittering eternal light, of Turkish design and similar to lamps in Shearith Israel, dates from the MacArthur synagogue. The regal reader's platform is crowned by an enormous Walloon chandelier. The architect's purpose in choosing this chandelier was to recall both colonial synagogues and their Sephardi tradition.

Aesthetically, Mikveh Israel demonstrates a proclivity for natural materials and a clear division of forms. Large, recessed, angular shapes on the eastern exterior brick façade of the synagogue suggest the abstract outline of the candelabra. The rest of the building is a self-contained unit, the interior of which is sparse yet elegant. The tactile contrasts of the marble reader's platform, the brass chandelier, the wooden ark, pews, and *mehizah* and the metallic eternal light are indicative of Modernism, a style that values the purity of materials for their intrinsic beauty. A lack of ornamentation on the blank white lateral walls, the absence of a balcony, the flat ceiling, and the uncarved flat ark offer an uncomplicated, functional space.

Two other Sephardi synagogues of architectural note share Mikveh Israel's use of Modernism in their design. They are Congregation Beth Torah of 1969 in Brooklyn, New York, and Or VeShalom of 1970 in Atlanta, Georgia.

Beth Torah, Brooklyn, New York

Beth Torah, located on the major walking and automobile artery of Ocean Parkway, was constructed by Dick Foster in 1969 and has been awarded a citation of architectural distinction by the American Institute of Architect's Guild for Religious Architecture.[14] Its brick exterior serves to insulate it from its urban surroundings. Its three sets of double entry doors use the Star of David as part of a linear pattern of wrought iron set against red glass. The vestibule that divides the outside, secular world from the inside, sacred world is often aglow in the red filtered light of the glass doors.

The congregation is of Syrian origin, mainly from the city of Aleppo. The fortress-like façade of the synagogue parallels the close-knit organization of the community, whose families engage in business, trade, and the professions. The first congregation of Aleppoans established a synagogue in 1912 in lower Manhattan; services were held in lofts or rented halls. After World War I, economic conditions began to improve for the Syrian Sephardi immigrants, and autonomous synagogues as well as day schools were established in Brooklyn. Many social activities still revolve around the synagogue and religious holidays, and the tight cohesion of the group has kept most of its young people from marrying outside the community for almost two generations. Intermarriage in this Syrian group is still much less common than for any other Sephardi groups: today there are 25,000 Syrian Sephardim, and they are the most cohesive, the best organized, and the richest of all the Sephardim in the United States. Even after they leave Brooklyn, the center of the Syrian Sephardi community, individual members of this group maintain their communal ties and assist in helping those Jews still living in Syria.[15] In 1976 there were 4,350 Jews living in Syria, a sizable number of people enduring in a hostile environment.[16]

Beth Torah is located in a heavily Jewish area of Brooklyn where there are competing synagogues within walking distance. The community distances itself from the non-Jewish world. Many Jewish immigrants who came to the United States from Islamic countries lived in very circumscribed freedom in their countries of origin.[17] As a result, and stemming from

Fig. 10.   *Beth Torah, Brooklyn, New York, 1969, interior.*

this history of self-effacement, even in a country of religious tolerance and an immediate community of fellow Jews, the Syrian community has built its houses of worship in an unassuming manner. In the interior (Fig. 10) the traditional use of wood for the reader's platform recalls the Great Synagogue in Aleppo; the patterning of the wrought iron doors, however, follows the Islamic tradition. Their repetitious, abstract lines suggest the intertwining designs of mosaics and wooden furnishings that can be seen in Mid-Eastern synagogues (such as the Ben Ezra synagogue in Cairo, the doors of which date from the eleventh century) and mosques.

The floor plan of Beth Torah is rectangular (Fig. 11). At the eastern end of the sanctuary, an off-white marble wall surrounds the ark. In the way up the lateral brick walls, protruding bricks form a wave-like pattern that punctuates the tall enclosing space. The lateral pews are of light wood; the women's section is caged off at the western end of the sanctuary by a similarly colored high wood *mehizah*. To allow for better visibility of the service, both the men's and the women's pews slope upwards toward the brick walls. There is an austerity in the use of accoutrements and space at Beth Torah, calling attention to the tension

[14]   Herbert L. Smith, *Architectural Record Awards* (New York, 1970), pp. 98–99.

[15]   Joseph Papo, *Sephardim in Twentieth-Century America* (Berkeley, CA, 1987), p. 313.

[16]   Chaim Raphael, *The Road from Babylon* (New York, 1985), p. 271.

[17]   Norman Stillman, *The Jews of Arab Lands: A History and a Source Book* (Philadelphia, 1979), p. 107.

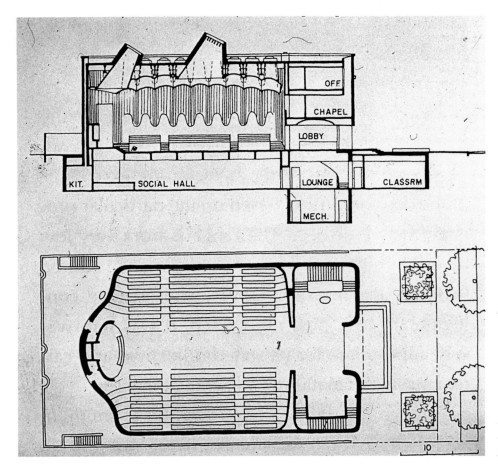

Fig. 11.   Beth Torah, Brooklyn, New York, 1969, plan.

between the two poles of the ark and the reader's platform.

The sumptuous quality of this modern sanctuary stems from the architect's use of diverse textures. The reader's platform in the center of the sanctuary and its overhanging chandelier, the minor preaching platforms near the ark, the ark's doors, and the large Star of David above, are all of burnished brass. The eyes wander from one shiny brass object to another, gathering together the total impact of the interior. The chandelier's radiating rings of brass circles, dotted by brass bulbs, pour down from the high ceiling to the central reader's platform. These rings increase in size as they approach the ground. The shape of the raining circles of the chandelier is repeated in the clear skylights, tangential to the wall, and in the two large circular lights in the ceiling.

Wischnitzer has concluded that American syn-

agogue architecture of the post-war era is fortunate in not being dependent on non-Jewish architects.[18] In contrast to past centuries, when non-Jewish builders, unfamiliar with the essential spirit of Judaism, searched for appropriate architectural styles, Jewish architects now could be self-expressive and free of any historical indoctrination.

Or VeShalom, Atlanta, Georgia

The synagogue of the congregation of Or Ve-Shalom in Atlanta, Georgia, was designed in 1970 by two Jewish architects, Benjamin Hirsch and Warren Epstein. Careful historical studies of synagogue design, the architects' own expectations of a Jewish spiritual ambience, and the needs of the congregants have worked together to create the new house of worship of the Sephardi community of Atlanta. The exterior of the building (Fig. 12), is jagged, its outline reminiscent of seventeenth-and eighteenth-century wooden Polish synagogues, having a pyramidal roof, jutting clerestory windows, and the high protrusion of the

[18] Rachel Wischnitzer, "The Problem of Synagogue Architecture — Creating a Style Expressive of America," *Commentary* III (March 1947), 241.

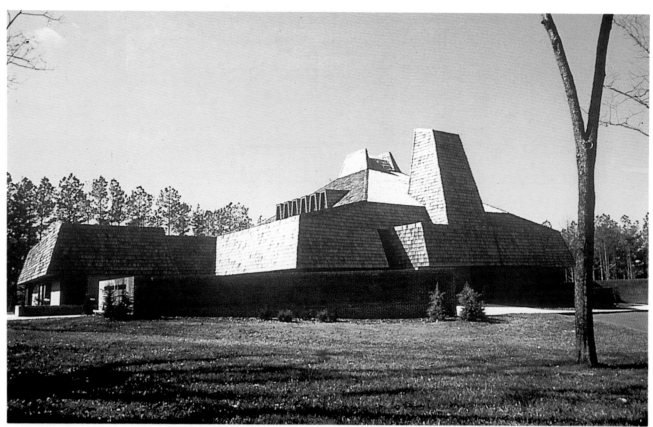

Fig. 12.   Or VeShalom, Atlanta, Georgia, 1970, exterior.

Fig. 13.   Or VeShalom, Atlanta, Georgia, 1970, interior.

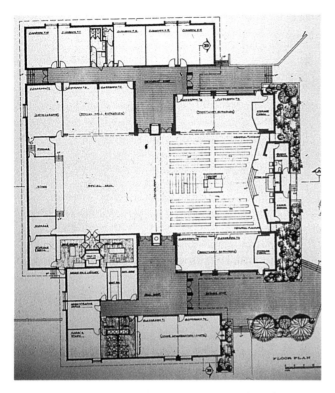

Fig. 14.   Or VeShalom, Atlanta, Georgia, 1970, plan.

ark. A shingled roof and brick lower walls combine the traditions of medieval Poland and colonial America. Or VeShalom is divided into three parts: the sanctuary, the classrooms of the Hebrew school, and the administrative offices. A suburban synagogue, it is surrounded by an expansive lawn.

The sanctuary blends art and architecture virtually indistinguishably (Fig. 13). Grainy coral stone is used for the supporting wall of the ark, to remind congregants of the Western Wall of the Second Temple in Jerusalem. A similar reference is apparent in the shape of the stained glass clerestory windows. Larger on the exterior than on the interior, the architects probably intended to embody the apocryphal idea that whereas in the Temple in Jerusalem the Shekhinah, or divine presence, is inside the sanctuary, in the Diaspora the Shekhina is outside and needs a large opening to enter the sanctuary. The pitched roof hugs the space, providing intimacy. A varied use of lighting illuminates much of the activity in the sanctuary: the fluorescent lights and the skylights near the ark, the ceiling-to-floor stained glass windows flanking the ark area, and the clerestory provide a religious aura.

Metal grillwork covers the front of the tall stained-glass ark. The wooden lateral pews accommodate both men and women who sit either separately or together. The reader's platform is of the same wood as the pews, and is placed at the far western end of the sanctuary.

The families of the congregants of Or VeShalom originated on the island of Rhodes. The first who came to Atlanta in 1906 found an already sizable German-Jewish Ashkenazi population. After 1910, increased Sephardi emigration from Turkey necessitated a Sephardi place of worship. The first Sephardi synagogue was built in Atlanta in 1920, for Jews from both mainland Turkey and the island of Rhodes. The community continued to grow to such an extent, that by 1953 it had expanded beyond its first quarters and sought a new sanctuary. The Sephardi community remodeled a Methodist church, and Turkish and Rhodeli members of the congregation worshipped there together.

The Atlanta congregation grew in numbers and in socio-economic position, and in 1970 the present Or VeShalom was constructed. In 1971, the building was honored by the Guild for Religious Architecture with a National Design Award for its architectural beauty and its functional attributes.

The architects of American synagogues in the post-World War II era have been concerned with providing a space for the social functions and the religious purposes of the congregation. The sanctuary space must be flexible to accommodate the well-attended High Holidays of Rosh Hashanah and Yom Kippur, and the Saturday morning minyans. Or VeShalom seats 265 people; if needed, however, the side walls of the sanctuary open to incorporate the adjoining social hall, expanding capacity by an additional 600 places. Life cycle celebrations, political meetings, adult education, a Hebrew school: all are events and programs that must be part of the synagogue complex. The flexible plan (Fig. 14) incorporates the ancient idea that the synagogue is a house of study, worship, and assembly.[19] Such a multipurpose synagogue mirrors, theoretically, the modern, twentieth-century stylistic notion of functionalism. Epstein and Hirsch have co-ordinated structurally the reception areas, classrooms, lecture halls and offices, with the sanctuary as the primary focus of the building.

19 Wischnitzer, *United States*, p. 135.

The Sephardi Temple, Cedarhurst, Long Island, New York

Turkish congregants from Monastir first founded a synagogue in lower Manhattan in 1907. Some members subsequently dispersed to the Bronx and New Lots, Brooklyn. Other Jews from Greece and Turkey also moved to the New Lots area of Brooklyn in the 1920s and 1930s. Their financial success and their desire to live outside the city brought them as a group to Cedarhurst, on the western edge of Long Island. In part, the cohesiveness of this congregation is in contrast to that of other Sephardi communities which moved from inner city locations to the suburbs.[20]

The use of Near Eastern building motifs can be seen in specific synagogues. The Sephardi Temple built in 1963 in Cedarhurst, Long Island, represents a conscious attempt on the part of the architect, Bertram Bassuk, to bring to mind buildings that pierce the skyline of Jerusalem. The large, parabolic dome and another dome which was not constructed were to remind the Turkish congregants of the Dome of the Rock and Al-Aqsa. The dominance of the dome recalls Lewis Mumford's proclamation that the dome is the most appropriate form for synagogue construc-

tion.[21] This general association of the dome with the Near East is more Islamic than Judaic in origin. Romantic notions of the Middle East conjured up visions of the centrally planned, domed mosques of Istanbul, Cairo, and Jerusalem. Alfred S. Alschuler's Temple Isaiah of 1924 in Chicago boasted a large dome and a vast central space, following the orientalizing conceptions of current architectural thinking on synagogues.[22]

The parabolic dome of the Sephardi Temple soars, appearing higher than its apex of 45 feet (Fig. 15). The spacious interior (Fig. 16) is filled with wooden pews that radiate around a large wooden movable reader's platform. There is no women's balcony or special architectural division separating the women from the men; pews are available to seat men and women together or separately, in keeping with the traditional nature of the congregation. Clear windows in the upper walls allow an uninterrupted view of the sky. A small section of the clear glass is decorated with a stained glass Decalogue. Muted gold-colored Hebrew inscriptions appear on a hinged, horizontal wooden beam near the ark. This writing resembles in design and message Hebrew inscriptions decorating medieval

[20] Papo, *Sephardim*, p. 319.
[21] Lewis Mumford, "Towards a Modern Synagogue Architecture," *Menorah Journal* XI (June 1925), 225–226.
[22] *Faith and Form: Synagogue Architecture in Illinois, An Exhibition Catalogue*, The Spertus Museum (Chicago, 1976), pp. 58–61.

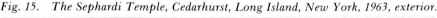

Fig. 15.   The Sephardi Temple, Cedarhurst, Long Island, New York, 1963, exterior.

Fig. 16.   The Sephardi Temple, Cedarhurst, Long Island, New York, 1963, interior.
Fig. 17.   The Sephardi Temple, Cedarhurst, Long Island, New York, 1963, small chapel.

Spanish synagogues (Nuestra Senora del Transito in Toledo of 1350–60 and the Cordova synagogue, renovated 1315).[23] The ark, which does not face directly east, is made of the same gold-colored fiberglass as the wall inscriptions. The flames of the fires of Moses's burning bush reach upward along the wood-backed ark, which is dotted with single-colored stained glass circles. Their translucence suggests a smoldering fire.

The small chapel of the Sephardi Temple (Fig. 17) is a miniature of that of the Spanish synagogue of Santa Maria La Blanca in Toledo. Its lateral walls are mirrors framed by white stuccoed horse-shoe shaped arches. They extend the space by their multiple repetition of these arches. As a design motif, repetition is seen in the wood slats of the dark wood pews, in

the rosette patterns of the Oriental carpets, and in the lamps placed between arches. The carved dark wood diamond-shaped doors of the ark are situated between floor-to-ceiling windows. The small wooden reader's platform is in close proximity to the ark, maintaining the cordiality of the room.

Bassuk explained the motivation for his architectural choices as springing from a poignant yearning for architectural symbols that would evoke images as-

23   Wischnitzer, *European Synagogues*, pp.18–40; see also the articles by Yom-Tov Assis, Bezalel Narkiss, Santiago Palomera Plaza et al., and Esther W. Goldman in *Jewish Art* 18 (1992), 7–69.

sociated with the congregation's ethnic background.[24] These yearnings, distilled from a mixture of Romanticism, archaeology, and myth, have been presented in specific architectural terms. Istanbul's Ahrida synagogue, founded in 1470, features a large central dome, elaborately carved wood embellishing the balustrade of the women's balcony, an oversized reader's platform, and numerous pews; the use of wood and the domed sanctuary of the Sephardi Temple are reminiscent of this Turkish precedent.[25]

The synagogue's enclosed patio, situated near the small sanctuary, also forms a platform for the Sukkah booth for the Feast of Tabernacles. The plan of the synagogue with its offices, attached Hebrew school classrooms, small and large sanctuaries, and spacious social halls was built for a growing suburban congregation. The back wall of the main sanctuary opens to allow for greater seating capacity during the High Holidays.

[24] Bertram Bassuk, "The Sephardic Temple of Cedarhurst," Faith and Form 2 (April 1969), 10–14.
[25] See E. Juhasz, ed., *Sephardi Jews in the Ottoman Empire* (Jerusalem, 1990), pp. 37–51, pl. 3, fig. 5.

Tifereth Israel, Los Angeles, California

Tifereth Israel in Los Angeles, 1969, is the sister congregation of the Sephardi Temple in Cedarhurst, Long Island. It merges the regional Mission-style architecture of the early Spanish settlers in southern California with the Jewish congregation's memories of Spain, Morocco, Turkey and Greece.[26] Of exterior white stucco with few windows (Fig. 18), shutting out the busy main thoroughfare of Wilshire Boulevard, it is joined by an enclosed landscaped courtyard, where indigenous trees provide shade from the sultry southern California climate. Arched openings are used for passageways to the courtyard, and occur singly in the main entrance. Its prestigious location attests to the prosperity of the Sephardi population in Los Angeles.

The first permanent group of Sephardi Jews in California arrived in 1905. In 1912, it was reported that 40 to 50 Sephardim resided in Los Angeles.[27] Most

[26] *Sephardim*, p. 30.
[27] Marcia Josephy, "Sephardic Synagogues of Los Angeles," College Art Association annual meeting (February 1986), New York, unpublished lecture.

Fig. 18. Tifereth Israel, Los Angeles, 1969, exterior.

of the early settlers were from Turkey and Rhodes, and participated in religious activities through small prayer groups. Because of continual divisions regarding diverse religious practices, no communal organizations could exist. In 1919, however, Tifereth Israel was founded with 37 members, and by 1920 between 250 and 300 Sephardim were living in Los Angeles.

Tifereth Israel was the term used to describe the allocations given to support Sephardi rabbis in Jerusalem. These funds were not considered charity but were rather regarded as fees or salary for settling and studying in Israel. The symbolic connection of the Los Angeles congregation with Israel was thus apparent in the naming of its synagogue. The congregation occupied temporary spaces until the construction in 1932 of a Spanish-style building on West Santa Barbara Street. In 1959, Temple Tifereth Israel and the Sephardi Community merged with the Sephardi Brotherhood Temple Israel to form the Sephardi Temple Tifereth Israel. A united effort to move to a more spacious facility began in 1965.

The design concept for the new building began in May, 1967 with the hiring of Nabas Shabazian. In 1969, Brent Goldman Associates were hired as the architects for the new building. The main lobby is L-shaped, with the main sanctuary and the library on one side, and the Candiotty chapel for daily services and the social hall on the other. The garden and the patio are accessible through the social hall. Classrooms for the Hebrew school are to be found on the third floor of the building.

In the planning stages, discussion centered on the design of the structure of the synagogue. The Amado family was active in planning and financing, and felt the need for a Sephardi statement as part of the architecture of the building. Their vision and their considerable financial gift spurred construction and the synagogue subsequently received an honor award from the Guild for Religious Architecture.

By 1978, although the sanctuary was incomplete, the building was in use. The synagogue's orientation, not to the east, but to the north, is in keeping with some religious thought: Posner notes that one must direct one's heart toward the Temple in Jerusalem, and not be dependent on the architectural setting of the synagogue.[28] A large wood ark in the sanctuary (Fig.

Fig. 19.   Tifereth Israel, Los Angeles, 1969, interior.

19), its front an ornate arcade, resembles the ark in the Portuguese Synagogue in Amsterdam. The upper part of the arcade is filled with repeated elongated lobe designs, in general reminiscent of Andalusian stucco designs and circular openings. The eternal light is Turkish in design. Its gold and silver latticework offers a striking contrast to the dark flat wood ark.

Two Persian rugs line the floor between the ark and the centrally located, carved wood reader's platform placed directly beneath a circular skylight entirely filled by a stained glass Star of David. The use, as here, of a skylight over the reader's platform, or the chandelier in Mikveh Israel and Beth Torah, acknowledges the importance of the tension between the ideal and the real. The living nature of Judaism is shown in the reality of the spoken Torah, while the ideal nature

28 Raphael Posner, "The Synagogue in Jewish Law," *Recent American Synagogue Architecture* (New York, 1963), pp. 14–15.

of the absolute is symbolized by the ark, the vault for the scrolls.[29]

The main sanctuary accomodates 600 families. Lateral wood pews running the length of the space seat men and women together. Lighting is by floodlights, not windows. The minimal use of windows was common in North Africa; however, windows have been thought to provide the advantage of letting one's prayers, petitions, and praise reach Jerusalem. The artist Joseph Young was commissioned to create the stained glass windows flanking the ark. Their brilliant color and abstract design present the universal message of a communal gathering place, rather than a specific Sephardi statement.

As in the main sanctuary, the Candiotty Chapel (Fig. 20) employs dark wood for the ark and the reader's platform though these are simpler in conception. The walls are white and unadorned except for a stained glass rose window above the ark. The ornate eternal light was taken from the previous sanctuary of 1932 on West Santa Barbara Street.

The solidity of the façade and the flat roof of Tifereth Israel recall some synagogues in Fez, Meknes, and Casablanca, all in Morocco.[30] However, the interiors of modern Sephardi synagogues built in the United States are in marked contrast to those of the Islamic world. The sanctuary space of the American Sephardi synagogue is unified and uninterrupted, while sanctuaries in the Islamic world often have numerous, repeated colonnades supporting the roof.

The Sephardi Temple and Tifereth Israel herald a change in synagogue design. In these synagogues, the architectural style of the building mirrors the ethnicity of the congregants. In addition the style of Tifereth Israel can be seen as concurring with the Mission architecture of the early Spanish settlers of California. In this instance, Moorish-style architecture represents an acculturated Sephardi presence in Los Angeles.

The use of Moorish design in synagogue architecture can be dated from the middle of the nineteenth century in Europe. It represents an aspect of the Romantic movement in art, a movement which sought the exotic in far-off places and distant times. European architects and artists saw the Islamic world of the Middle East and North Africa as distinct from themselves, and therefore appropriately Romantic. Jews, however, having originated in the Middle East, felt a kinship with this style.

The Orianenburgerstraße synagogue in Berlin 1859–66 is a domed, twin-towered synagogue with numerous arcades and window openings.[31] In Vienna, the Tempelgasse of 1853–58 was inspired in part by archaeological excavations in the Middle East.[32] Its turrets were reminiscent of the minarets and carved stone work that imitated Islamic floral designs. In the United States, Ashkenazi congregations borrowed from current European styles for their synagogues. Congregation B'nai Yeshurun at Plum and 8th Street in Cincinnati of 1866 is a minareted building with unending decoration, slender columns, and numerous domes.[33] Other mid-nineteenth-century Moorish-Ashkenazi synagogues are the Reform Congregation Keneseth Israel of 1864, the Rodeph Shalom of Philadelphia of 1871 as well as the Ahavat Chesed of 1872 and Emanu-El of 1968 in New York.[34] The oriental character of these synagogues is suggested by their frequent use of bulbous domes and lattice façades.

Ashkenazi congregations have valued the association with the Middle East in their architecture. Their sojourn in the United States has been a mere 150 years, after more than 1700 years in Europe. Nevertheless, these Jews found little irony in their use of the Romantic Moorish synagogue style; in fact, the Moorish architectural style filled a need by being fashionably Romantic in character, and Judaic by geographic association, and the monumental nature of such synagogues suggests the socio-economic security of European and American Jewry.

The expression of a renewed interest on the part of Ashkenazi Jews in Jewish history and its connection with the Middle East can also be seen in the creation

[29] Eugene Mihaly, "Jewish Prayer and Synagogue Architecture," *Judaism* 7.4 (1958), 315.

[30] J. Pinkerfeld, *Synagogues of North Africa — Tunisia, Algeria and Morocco* (in Hebrew) (Jerusalem, 1974), pp. 71, 107.

[31] *Synagogen in Berlin*, R. Bothe, ed., Berlin Museum, 26 Jan.–20 March 1983, exhibition in vol. I, pp. 87–97.

[32] H. Hammer-Schenk, *Synagogen in Deutschland, Geschichte einer Baugattung im 19. und 20. Jahrhundert (1780–1933)* (Ham-

burg, 1981, vol. I, pp. 302–307, vol. II, figs. 216–219.

[33] S. Winifred Smith, "Plum Street Temple Cincinnati," *Museum Echoes, Ohio State Archaeological Historical Society at Ohio State Museum, Columbus, Ohio* 21.19 (September 1948), 67–70.

[34] Grace Grossman, *Synagogue Architecture in America, An Exhibition Catalogue*, The Spertus Museum of Judaica (Chicago, 1975), pp. 3–5.

of the Alliance Israelite Universelle. This educational system, sponsored by Moses Montefiore and Adolphe Cremieux, brought Western languages and Enlightenment philosophy to the distant locales of the Sephardi Jews. The initial motivation for these schools was to alleviate the poverty and limited employment opportunities for the Jews of North Africa, Turkey, Iraq, Syria, and Lebanon. The contact between acculturated Ashkenazi Jews and non-Western Sephardi Jews reawakened a realization of the effects of antisemitism, since the protected status of non-Moslems in Islamic countries was one of insecurity, caution, and manipulation. These realities of the lives of the Sephardi Jews fueled nascent Zionist movements in Europe, and renewed the connection with the Middle East.

Sephardim in the United States have been a minority within a minority for the past century and a half. The congregations of Em HaBanim in Los Angeles 1985 and the Sephardi Center of North Miami Beach of 1985 have constructed hybrid synagogues. Modest nostalgia and efficiency converge in these buildings.

Congregation Em HaBanim, Los Angeles, California

The congregation Em HaBanim is predominantly Moroccan. Sephardim from Morocco have been slowly coming to the United States since the end of the last century. In 1948 there were 265,000 Jews in Morocco; in 1976 there were only 17,000.[35] After World War II, with the establishment of the State of Israel, emigration increased dramatically. Today, a close familial network exists among the Moroccan families still living in Morocco and those living in France, Israel, and the United States. In the naming of Em HaBanim, there was perhaps a conscious borrowing from similarly named synagogues in Fez, Morocco.

The new synagogue (Fig. 20) built in 1989 is of red brick on the exterior, with tall, narrow, arched windows across its façade. It is an unassuming edifice with a large off-center hemispherical portal. The interior (Fig. 21) is lit by a clear, six-sided low dome. Some light filters in through the symbol-laden stained glass windows of the façade (Fig. 22). The congregants sit

[35] Raphael, *The Road from Babylon*, p. 271.

Fig. 20.   Em HaBanim, Los Angeles, 1984, façade.

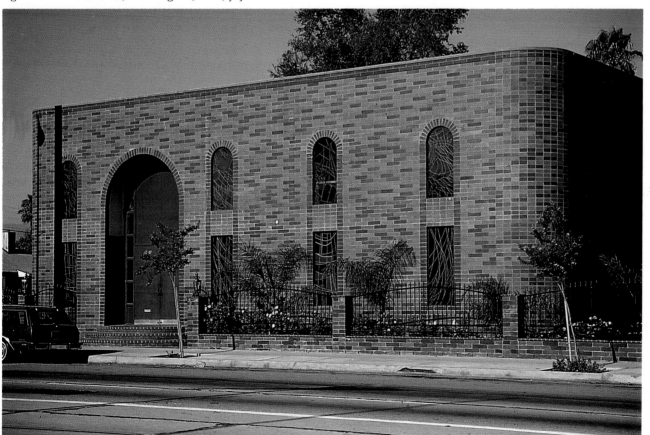

Fig. 21. Em HaBanim, Los Angeles, 1984, interior.
Fig. 22. Em HaBanim, Los Angeles, 1984, stained glass window.

on portable chairs. The ark and the reader's platform are large, dark wood pieces that stand in a bi-polar arrangement in the sanctuary.

Members of the Khalfon family of skilled wood craftsmen have carved the elaborate ark and reader's platform. The attention to wood craftsmanship has perhaps been influenced by the North African synagogue interiors of Meknes and Fez, familiar to some of the congregants.[36] The *mehizah* is a white screen. It stands as a movable unit on one side of the synagogue. The insistence on a *mehizah* as an architectural element of the synagogue attests to the strict observance of the congregation. Rituals and special holidays that were celebrated in Morocco, such as the last day of Passover, are also especially festive occasions in Los Angeles. Several glass-tasseled chandeliers (*Kandils*) illuminate the interior for evening services. Small chandeliers are traditional memorials to the deceased in Sephardi congregations.

[36]   Pinkerfeld, *Synagogues of North Africa*, p. 163.

The Sephardi Center of North Miami Beach

The congregants of the Sephardi Center of North Miami Beach are Cuban, Moroccan, Israeli, Greek, and Turkish in origin. Although their membership is ethnically diverse, they use the Spanish-Portuguese siddur. Many of the Cuban Jewish families emigrated from Turkey after World War I, and their entry in the 1920s into the United States was prevented by strict immigration quotas for southern European immigrants. They made their home in Cuba, often as prosperous business people, but after Castro's communist revolution in 1959, many came to the United States, particularly to Miami, Florida.

The Sephardi Center of North Miami Beach (Fig. 23) was built between 1976 and 1978 by the architectural firm of Gambach Associates, headed by a Sephardi Jew. It is of simple beige stucco, in a contemporary Middle-Eastern style as Safdie's buildings in the Jewish Quarter of Jerusalem. It has an affinity with Israeli building, which seeks a fusion of the substantiality of Arab stone dwellings and the sleekness of the International style. The ark's eastern placement is dramatically marked on the exterior by the arched outline of a bell tower or minaret-like protuberance. The paired narrow arched windows that encircle the building symbolically suggest the scrolls of the Torah.

The narrative of a stained glass window on one wall of the synagogue illustrates Jews praying at the Western Wall in Jerusalem. Its clear representation of figures, a break with traditional synagogue designs,

Fig. 24. Sephardi Center, North Miami Beach, 1976–8, stained glass window.

is not unusual. The interior is sparse, with portable seats; men and women sit separately. The reader's platform and ark are at opposite ends of the sanctuary. The wooden ark is highlighted by its placement in a skylit alcove, and the stained glass windows are narrative (Fig. 24).

Kol Israel Congregation, Brooklyn, New York

The dedication of new Sephardi synagogues is a frequent occurrence in the United States. In 1989 Kol Israel Congregation in Brooklyn, New York moved into a synagogue designed by Robert A.M. Stern Architects. It is situated in a residential community accommodating the congregants who walk to services. The brick building is inspired by thirteenth-and fourteenth-century Spanish synagogues with its articulated and patterned brickwork on its façade (Fig. 25). The broad decorative brick walkway around the synagogue augments the size of the building itself as well as creating a piazza-like gathering place for congregants to meet after the services. One enters the building and goes up to the balcony — reserved for women — and down the stairs to the main level of the synagogue. The main level is therefore subterranean, allowing the large windows on the lateral sides of the building to provide natural illumination in the sanctuary (Fig. 26). Because the synagogue is located in a residential community, there were height and set-back restrictions that the architect was required to obey. The inventive

Fig. 23. Sephardi Center, North Miami Beach, 1976–8, exterior.

solution of the below ground-level sanctuary created an enlarged space in height and width for the well-proportioned, wood accented interior. Special attention was given to handicapped accessibility, so that all congregants would be able to participate in communal events.

Kol Israel Congregation has its ark on the Eastern wall facing Jerusalem. The Torah Ark is separated from the central reader's platform: both the ark and the reader's platform material recall historical precedents. Both men on the main level and women in the balcony surround the reader's platform on three sides. The congregants for the most part are from the Levant, Syria, Israel, Lebanon, Iraq, and Egypt, with some from Central and South America. The ambience of the synagogue, in fact, recalls communities around the Mediterranean. The wrought iron accents, wooden seats, ark and reader's platform, decoratively painted wooden beams, the small windows on the frontal façade and the patterned brick of the exterior of the building, concurrently create a symbolic and tangible Sephardi presence. Kol Israel merges traditional aspects of Sephardi synagogue design (eastern orientation of the ark, separation of reader's platform and ark, separation of men and women surrounding the reader's platform), along with the accoutrements signalling a cultural difference.

Today, communal prayer is practiced in air-conditioned and centrally heated houses of worship. The ease in the mode of prayer is paralleled by the many choices in the architectural style of the modern synagogue. The plethora of stylistic possibilities for Sephardi synagogue architecture in the United States represents a cultural double-edged sword. Its diversity

Fig. 25. Kol Israel, Brooklyn, New York, 1987, exterior.

suggests a religious freedom that is often a product of assimilation,[37] while the choice of a particular style is a distinct statement of ethnic identity.

---

[37] Gary Tinterow, "Post World War II Synagogue Architecture," *Two Hundred Years of American Synagogue Architecture* (Waltham, MA, 1976), p. 34.

INTERIOR EAST ELEVATION

Fig. 26.   Kol Israel, Brooklyn, New York, 1987, interior.

44

Fig. 1. *The Torah ark installation at Temple Israel in Tulsa, Oklahoma (1955) with Seymour Lipton's sculptural group over the ark, his ner tamid, and menorah. (After Avram Kampf, Contemporary Synagogue Art.)*

THE TABERNACLE IN THE WILDERNESS: THE *MISHKAN* THEME IN PERCIVAL GOODMAN'S MODERN AMERICAN SYNAGOGUES

Evelyn L. Greenberg

Percival Goodman (1904–1989) left a unique architectural legacy. More than fifty synagogues throughout the United States were built to his plans in the decades following World War II. His innovations in synagogue construction introduced the entire vocabulary of modern architecture to this field. They have been so widely accepted that there is a tendency to forget how novel they were when he began his career. Gone would be the so-called traditional styles of the nineteenth and early twentieth century with their grandiose entrances, huge auditoriums, elaborate decorations and inadequate ancillary facilities. Instead, Goodman emphasized a more modest, human scale, built around the congregation and the religious service.[1] He was concerned with maximum utilization of space, new construction technologies and clean-cut lines highlighting the intrinsic beauty of natural materials — brick, wood and, on occasion, Israeli marble.

Seeing many of the synagogues *in situ*, one is struck by the elegance of his solutions to difficult problems of siting and the appropriateness of each building's setting in its landscape. The viewer notes the rationality of his unified plans for the multi-purpose, expandable structure which is typical of the American synagogue: sanctuary, educational facility and social center. Rabbis and laymen who worked with him speak repeatedly of his sensitivity to the needs of the individual congregation and his willingness to design a range of structures, from small ranch-type buildings to great temples for several thousand members.

Goodman was the first architect to integrate original works of art into his synagogue designs. He himself planned the Torah ark for he regarded it as the focal point of the interior. In addition, he commissioned work by first-rate artists, many of them in the early stages of their careers, like Adolph Gottlieb, Herbert Ferber, Helen Frankenthaler, Ibram Lassaw, Seymour Lipton, and Robert Pinart. They created Torah ark curtains, eternal lights, menorahs, stained glass windows, tapestries and mosaics whose color and form, together with the Torah arks which Goodman designed, provide *hiddur mitzva*, an aura of beauty and sanctity, to the prayer hall.[2]

As Avram Kampf has indicated, literally thousands of congregants learned to relate positively to abstract sculpture and non-objective art through these works.[3] They have had a long-lasting influence on the Jewish community's appreciation and continuing support for contemporary art.[4] Goodman had an intuitive sense of the direction in which the art world was moving. The *bima* assemblage in many of his synagogues, at Tulsa, Oklahoma and Bridgeport, Connecticut, for example, is an authentic installation that speaks to the most immediate art concerns of our time (Figs. 1 & 9).

[1] Goodman expressed his views on synagogue architecture in many articles, at conferences, and in connection with exhibitions. For such a discussion see *An American Synagogue for Today and Tomorrow*, ed. Peter Blake (New York: Union of American Hebrew Congregations, 1954), p. 87 ff.

[2] His contracts with the synagogues show that Goodman was responsible for selecting, supervising and approving the art work. The contracts are on file in the office at his home. See, for example, those with Temple Israel, Columbus, Ohio (1957) and Temple Israel of New Rochelle, New York (1959). The writer is most grateful to Mrs. Goodman for three extended interviews (30 October 1990, 7 November 1990, 5 March 1991) and for permission to study the files, photographs and slides in the office which Goodman set up in his home when he retired in 1979. Thanks also to Mrs. Goodman and the Slide Archives of the Union of American Hebrew Congregations for permission to reproduce Figs. 2, 3, 6, 7, 9–15.

[3] Avram Kampf, *Contemporary Synagogue Art: Developments in the United States 1945–1966* (Philadelphia: Jewish Publication Society, 1966), p. 52 ff. Kampf's work remains the only substantive treatment of contemporary synagogue art and architecture in all its aspects.

[3] Avram Kampf, *Contemporary Synagogue Art: Developments in the United States 1945–1966* (Philadelphia: Jewish Publication Society, 1966), p. 52 ff. Kampf's work remains the only substantive treatment of contemporary synagogue art and architecture in all its aspects.

[4] Mrs. Naomi Goodman (Interview 30 October 1990) relates that at first congregations were dubious about accepting the unfamiliar modern art. Goodman arranged with the artists, and the Kootz Gallery which represented many of them, to place the works on trial for six months to one year. The favorable publicity the art received led to willing acceptance by the synagogue membership. Nothing was ever returned. For an impression of the level of community interest in the new synagogue art see the *Jewish Times* of Baltimore, 25 April 1952.

Fig. 2   Chapel exterior, Fairmont Temple, Cleveland, Ohio. (Figs. 2, 3, 6, 7, 9–15, are reproduced courtesy of Mrs. Naomi Goodman and the slide archives of the Union of American Hebrew Congregations.)

Goodman's early life gave no indication that he would plan more synagogues than any other architect in our century, probably in Jewish history. He was born in America into an assimilated family of nineteenth-century German immigrants of Sephardic origin. After studying architecture in Paris he established a successful firm in New York and was also appointed professor of architecture at Columbia University, where he taught until his retirement. His main interest was in the design of public rather than private buildings and in the larger social issues that relate to architecture. Together with his philosopher brother, Paul, he published a widely-read book on city planning and environmental design, *Communitas*.

Deeply affected by the Holocaust, he began to study Judaism by reading Martin Buber. His interest in synagogue architecture was first expressed in articles in early issues of *Commentary* magazine in 1947 and 1949

in response to an essay by Rachel Wischnitzer.[5] These led to contacts with rabbis and synagogue leaders just as the post-war explosion of synagogue building was getting under way.

Through the influence of several of the rabbis with whom he worked, Goodman became increasingly familiar with Jewish sources and Jewish learning. He laughingly wrote once that his friends had warned him that he would discover that the Jews of his day would not live up to his romanticized view of his Jewish heritage. But, in his experience, ordinary people who started as reluctant recruits or status seekers ended by becoming dedicated synagogue builders.[6]

On more than one occasion, Goodman expressed his credo in words such as the following:

If God created man in His own image then man fulfills his godliness in so far as he is creative. To create means to make a new thing not seen on this

5   Rachel Wischnitzer-Bernstein, "The Problem of Synagogue Architecture," *Commentary* 3.3 (March 1947), 233–41. See also the final chapter of her *Synagogue Architecture in the United States* (Philadelphia: Jewish Publication Society, 1955), pp. 135–85; Percival and Paul Goodman, "Creating a Modern Syn-

agogue Style," *Commentary* 3.6 (June 1947), 537–44; idem, "Modern Artists as Synagogue Builders," *Commentary* 4.1 (January 1949), 524–30.
6   Percival Goodman, in *Recent American Synagogue Architecture* (New York: Jewish Museum, 1963), p. 20 ff.

PERCIVAL GOODMAN'S SYNAGOGUES   47

Fig. 3. Synagogue exterior, Congregation B'nai Israel, Bridgeport, Connecticut.

earth before. "Sing," as the Psalm says, "a new song unto the Lord."[7]

As he became aware of Jewish traditions they influenced his views on the design of the synagogue's interior. He had a strong preference for the center *bima*, which was installed in the two Orthodox synagogues he planned, the Fifth Avenue Synagogue in New York City and the Great Neck Synagogue on Long Island. However, he was unable to persuade American Conservative and Reform congregations to accept it.[8] Since the Torah ark and *bima* were combined, he always tried to bring the congregation as close as possible to this focus of the service, frequently by using a broad semi-circular seating plan. He felt very strongly that the most creative effort should be expended on that which received the most frequent use — not, as he put it, on decorative columns but on the Torah ark.[9]

This conviction was linked with Goodman's special feeling for the wilderness Tabernacle, the *Mishkan*, to which he was drawn by his interest in beginnings, in "first causes". He felt that the portable sanctuary which accompanied the children of Israel in their wanderings was a fitting metaphor, even in brick and stone, for much of Jewish history.[10]

Consequently, in many of his buildings from the very productive decade, 1953 to 1963, there is a suggestion of a tent-like structure. The chapel of Fairmont Temple in Cleveland (1956) has such a pavilion roof (Fig. 2), and the tent form is even more pronounced in synagogues at Bridgeport, Connecticut (1958) (Fig. 3) and Springfield, Massachusetts (1953) (Fig. 4). This plan also makes possible striking clerestory windows that link the interior with the natural light of the heavens rather than the surrounding urban scene. Goodman wrote appreciatively of the "functional

[7]   Ibid., p. 21. Goodman also chose this verse as his theme for the Shabbat sermon he delivered during the dedication weekend at Congregation Beth Shalom, Oak Park, Michigan, 10 April 1965.
[8]   Percival Goodman, "The Sanctuary," in *The American Synagogue: A Progress Report*, eds. Myron E. Shoen and Eugene

Lipman (New York, 1958), p. 134.
[9]   Percival Goodman, *An American Synagogue for Today and Tomorrow*, p. 103.
[10] Mrs. Naomi Goodman, personal interview, 5 March 1991.

Fig. 4. Temple Beth El, Springfield, Massachusetts. The sculpture is Ibram Lassaw's "Pillar of Fire." (After Avram Kampf, Contemporary Synagogue Art.)

Fig. 5. The exterior of the synagogue of Congregation B'nai Israel in Millburn, New Jersey. (After Avram Kampf, Contemporary Synagogue Art.)

analysis of the structure'', as he put it, that is found in the description of the building of the *Mishkan* in Exodus, Chapters 25 to 27.[11] He admired the careful emphasis on the use of fine and appropriate materials and especially the priority given to the Ark of the Covenant, to which he responded as to a work of modern sculpture.

Small wonder, then, that Goodman's favorite themes for the design of the Torah ark and its appurtenances had their origin in the biblical description of the *Mishkan* and of other aspects of the sacred presence in the wilderness like the Pillar of Cloud and the Pillar of Fire. Goodman and the artists he commissioned produced a rich body of creative variations on these motifs. In some cases, the traditional

[11] It is noteworthy that Goodman made this statement in the early 1947 *Commentary* article, p. 544.

6

8

7

Fig. 6. *The Torah ark in Temple Bet Emet, Albany, New York, its dimensions closely approximating those of the biblical Ark of the Covenant.*
Fig. 7. *The interior of the sanctuary of North Suburban Beth El Synagogue in Highland Park, Illinois.*
Fig. 8. *The aron kodesh of Temple Aaron, Saint Paul, Minnesota, with the ark curtain designed by Helen Frankenthaler. (Courtesy of Temple Aaron).*

elements are relatively obvious. In others, the older forms are translated into striking modern idiom.

The Ark of the Covenant, transmuted into the Torah ark, the *aron kodesh*, was often Goodman's point of departure. He liked the clear statement of the box-like container form. In one of the first synagogues that he designed, for Congregation B'nai Israel in Millburn, New Jersey (1951), the *aron kodesh* projects onto the exterior, the rectangular shape a reference to the Ark of the Covenant. Herbert Ferber's *Burning Bush* was the first work of abstract sculpture ever placed on a synagogue façade (Fig. 5).

For Temple Bet Emet in Albany, New York (1957), Goodman designed an *aron kodesh* based very closely on the shape and dimensions of the Ark in the *Mishkan* (Fig. 6). In Highland Park, near Chicago (1964), the Torah ark similarly alludes to the Ark in

the wilderness, here adorned by a fine example of Ludwig Wolpert's modern Hebrew calligraphy (Fig. 7).

Goodman also found the idea of the guardian wings of the cherubim especially intriguing. He frequently shaped the upper portion of the ark to suggest their form, sometimes by two strong triangles, sometimes with a gentle slant. At Temple Aaron in Saint Paul, Minnesota (1957) the powerful abstract wings add to the dominating presence of the *aron kodesh*, gold-toned like the Ark of old (Fig. 8).

At Temple B'nai Israel in Bridgeport, the architect's skill in creating a beautifully proportioned and harmonious space is evident. The slant of the open Torah ark hints at the cherub's wings, and is repeated in the uneven placing of the Torah scrolls. The rhythm is picked up in the pattern of the surrounding ladder-

Fig. 9. The eastern wall assemblage at Temple B'nai Israel, Bridgeport, Connecticut.

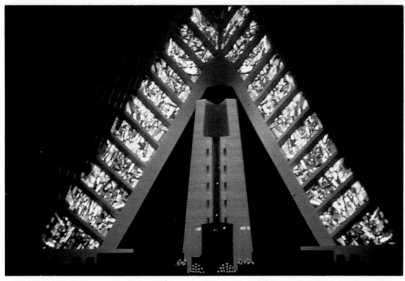

Fig. 10. The towering east wall of the main sanctuary of Temple Shaare Zedek in Southfield, Michigan.

Fig. 11. The Bet Midrash, the weekday chapel, at Shaare Zedek.

Fig. 12.   The courtyard at Shaare Zedek with the chapel at the right.

like screen, which highlights the centrality of the ark (Fig. 9).

In other instances, variations on the theme of the wings of the cherubim were used by artists such as Ibram Lassaw and Seymour Lipton to enfold the *ner tamid*, the eternal light, which is an integral part of the Torah ark assembly. They used the wings to form a protective shield for the glow that, in the rabbinic view, is the light Israel casts on the world. At Temple Israel in Tulsa, as part of Lipton's outstanding sculptural group, the eternal light is sheltered by powerful metal wings of textured nickel silver (see Fig. 1).

The scope of Goodman's creative interpretations on the wilderness theme is most apparent in one of the major structures he designed, the synagogue complex of Congregation Shaare Zedek in Southfield, Michigan (1963). For the interior of the main sanctuary Goodman felt that the desert motif should expand from the tent to Sinai and the Giving of the Law (Fig.

10). Within the assemblage, the ark is subordinate to Robert Pinart's complex abstract vitrage, its glorious color rising to a flaming climax.

In the Bet Midrash, the chapel for weekday prayer, the shape of the Torah ark is derived from the horned incense altar, another of the furnishings of the *Mishkan*. Again the building is tent-like and the triangular tracery of the windows sounds a modest echo of the great window of the sanctuary (Fig. 11). Outside the chapel is the courtyard, typical of the outdoor spaces Goodman deliberately included in his synagogue plans to emulate the *hatzer*, the sacred courtyard area which surrounded the wilderness Tabernacle (Fig. 12).

Goodman also used curtains and draperies in a conscious reference to the colorful fabrics of the *Mishkan*, not only for the *parochet*, the Torah ark curtain, but also to set off other areas. At Temple Beth El in Providence, Rhode Island, additional seating space for

Fig. 13.   A view of the side of the sanctuary at Temple Beth
El, Providence, Rhode Island, showing the hangings.
Fig. 14.   Adolph Gottlieb's parochet for Temple B'nai Israel
in Millburn, New Jersey.

the holidays was screened by hangings of blue, scarlet
and purple as listed in the Book of Exodus (Fig. 13).
Rather than attempt to rework the traditional motifs
used in *parochet* designs for centuries, he encouraged
artists to create new interpretations of the elaborately
worked hangings of the *Mishkan*.

One example is in the synagogue in Millburn,
where Adolph Gottlieb designed an ark curtain of
brilliantly colored silk velvet and appliqúe work. Gottlieb used the grid pattern and primitive, ethnic motifs
he favored in that period, but here in a Jewish
context (Fig 14). He incorporated abstract and stylized
elements such as the Torah crown, the lion's mane,
the twelve tribes and more familiar items like the
menorah and the Tablets of the Law. In Millburn,
the splendid hand-work was executed by the women
of the congregation, supervised by Gottlieb's wife
Esther, herself a talented needlework designer. They
regarded themselves as following the precedent set by
the biblical women whose weaving and embroidery
beautified the Tabernacle.

The *parochet* for the ark at Temple Aaron was
designed by the distinguished painter, Helen Frankenthaler. It is her interpretation of the Pillar of Fire and
the Pillar of Cloud, her only design for a textile on

Fig. 15.   A view of the Torah ark at Temple Beth El in Providence. Ibram Lassaw's "Pillar of Fire" is at the right.

a Jewish theme. The abstract yet suggestive work is densely hooked in high relief, giving an impression of power and sweeping vitality (see Fig. 8). A second curtain, made with a white background for the High Holydays, is equally effective.

For his *aron kodesh* at Beth El in Providence, Goodman chose works of art that combined the motifs he favored (Fig. 15). The scarlet and gold *parochet* was designed and woven by Dorothy Liebes, a top-ranking American weaver. It is flanked by the two great Lassaw sculptures, the Pillar of Fire and the Pillar of Cloud, which are an integral part of the ark assemblage.

Lassaw formed his abstract, bio-morphic columns by welding and brazing gold-toned bronze to which he added touches of colored alloys. Open and webbed, as in his other work, they are here most appropriate forms

for expressing a non-earthly presence. The Pillar of Cloud was chosen by the Museum of Modern Art to represent the United States at the 1954 Venice Biennale as the outstanding American sculpture of the year. The Pillar of Fire was exhibited at the Chicago Art Institute.

To complete the *aron kodesh* installation, Goodman always included a carefully chosen menorah. He preferred the single seven branched candelabrum of the Tabernacle to the more balanced pair which had become customary. Those he commissioned from Seymour Lipton, Herbert Ferber and Martin Craig were startlingly different from the traditional many-branched candlestick. Instead, their designs often stemmed from the plant origins attributed to the menorah form.

Figs. 16. & 17. The menorahs designed by Seymour Lipton for Temple Beth El, Gary, Indiana (1954) at left and Temple Israel, Tulsa (1955) at right. (After Avram Kampf, Contemporary Synagogue Art.)

At Tulsa, in Gary, Indiana and elsewhere, Seymour Lipton created several menorahs that are true pieces of contemporary sculpture. He broke with all precedents to fashion them as trees bursting open with life, full of an exuberant energy which surges up through the branches (Figs. 16, 17).

One senses in the work of all these men and women the profoundly creative impulse that Goodman articulated when he wrote of the artist's attempt to compose a new song before the Lord. Yet there remains an underlying irony in the ready acceptance by so many congregations of Goodman's frequent allusion to the Tabernacle in the wilderness.

The people for whom these synagogues were built were established second- and third-generation Americans, successful in business and the professions, seemingly secure in their place in society. Why were they so content with motifs that reflected transiency and wandering? One cannot help but think of an earlier ironical situation, that of the nineteenth-century German Jewish burgers who proclaimed that they were Germans like everyone else but built Moorish-style temples that displayed their difference.

In truth, with the spread of urban blight even to areas of second and third settlement and to the suburbs, the transient sanctuary has continued as a reality in American life, though it was not yet so obvious when these synagogues were built. Perhaps

too, there was a warm response to Goodman's portable *Mishkan* because, even in the *goldene medina*, the American promised land, there lurks a hidden uncertainty about the permanence of the Jewish community being built there. In any case, Goodman struck the right note. He succeeded in integrating very well-planned modern structures with a meaningful ancient source.

THE GOLDEN VINE, THE SANCTUARY PORTAL, AND ITS DEPICTION ON THE BAR-KOKHBA COINS*

Joseph Patrich

Fig. 1. Didrachm (sel'a) of Bar-Kokhba (courtesy of the Authority of Antiquities and Museums).

The Second Temple consisted of three parts: the Porch, the Sanctuary, and the Holy of Holies. Two portals led into the Temple: that of the Porch and that of the Sanctuary. A recently discovered silver coin of Bar-Kokhba (Figs. 1 and 2), in a denomination of two drachmas (half a sel'a),[1] displays the portal of the Porch.[2] A staircase leads to the portal; its door posts look like two columns and its lintel is cut diagonally at each end. It has been suggested, quite convincingly, that the object standing in the middle of the portal is the width view of the Table of the Shewbread.[3] I would like to suggest that the second portal, leading into the Sanctuary, whose holiness was greater than that of the Porch, is depicted on the silver tetradrachms (four drachms) of Bar-Kokhba (Figs. 3 and 4).[4] The artist-engraver forewent displaying the door posts, and instead depicted the narrow, length view of the Table. However, he did engrave the portal arch above the Table, flanked by two columns on either side as an impressive architectural frame. The very existence of these columns on either side of the portal is corroborated by the description of the golden vine and the posts upon which it intertwined over the portal of the Sanctuary. This description is preserved

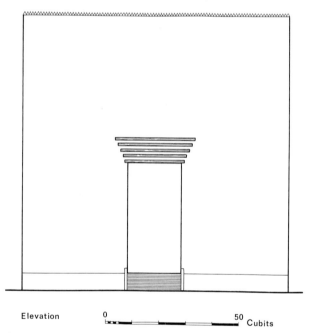

Elevation   0   50 Cubits

Fig. 2. Reconstruction of the Temple façade with the Porch portal in its center.

---

* Based on a lecture delivered in Hebrew at the Tenth World Congress of Jewish Studies, Jerusalem, 16–24 August 1989. Translated by Yonatan Nadelman.

1 L. Mildenberg, "The Bar Kokhba Didrachm," *Israel Numismatic Journal* 8 (1984–1985), 33–36, pl. 28; D. Barag, "The Shewbread Table and the Façade of the Temple on the Bar Kokhba Coins," *Qadmoniot* 20. 77–78 (1987), 22–25 (Hebrew).

2 Ibid., p. 25; J. Patrich, "The Structure of the Second Temple: A New Reconstruction," *Qadmoniot* 21.81–82 (1988), 35 (Hebrew); idem, "Reconstructing the Magnificent Temple Herod Built," *Bible Review* 4.5 (October 1988), 20.

3 Barag, "Table." A similar interpretation was also suggested for the object standing between the columns on the Bar-Kokhba tetradrachms (Fig. 3). The arched lines at the top of this object

are generally drawn as continuous lines, whereas the other lines of the object are drawn as a series of dots. This seems to suggest that the arched lines do not belong to the Shewbread Table but rather to the Sanctuary portal. An arch or conch above the Sanctuary portal is hinted at in the drawing above the Ark in the Dura Europos synagogue (see below, notes 36 and 37). This is probably the origin of the arch in Avi-Yonah's reconstruction (see below, note 27). Moreover, this arched line does not appear in the graffiti depicting the Shewbread Table in the Jewish Quarter of the Old City in Jerusalem, or in what was presumably engraved in relief on Titus's Arch in Rome.

4 I made this suggestion already in the articles mentioned in note 2 above (p. 36 in the Hebrew article, and pp. 21, 24 in the English one). Here I wish to display in detail the entire argument in favor of this interpretation.

Fig. 3. Tetradrachm of Bar-Kokhba.

Fig. 4. Reconstruction of the Sanctuary portal. The four columns supported the golden vine which was entwined on poles above the capitals.

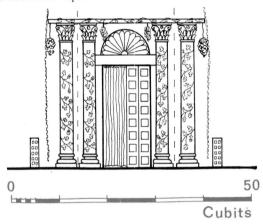

only in the Latin version of Josephus Flavius's *Jewish Antiquities* XV:394–395:[5]

ianuas autem introitus et superliminaria nec non et uela iuxta templi magnitudinem uario ornatu decorauit et aureos flores ambientes columnas fecit super quorum capita uitis tendebatur botryones aureos habens pendentes.

He [Herod] decorated the doors of the entrance and the sections over the opening with a multi-colored ornamentation and also with curtains, in accordance with the size of the Temple, and made flowers of gold surrounding the columns, atop which stretched a vine from which golden clusters of grapes were suspended (translation by Leah Di Segni).

It is clear that tall columns are referred to, since the height of the portal was twenty cubits (approximately ten meters). The vine itself was large and heavy and it had several clusters, as is indicated in Josephus's *The Jewish War* V, v, iv 210: "[The opening of the Sanctuary] had above it those golden vines, from which depended grape clusters as tall as a man" (translated by Marcus, Loeb Classical Library).

Additional information on its size and method of suspension can be found in *Mishnah Middot* 3,8:
A golden vine stood over the entrance of the Sanctuary, trained over posts; and whosoever gave a leaf, or a berry, or a cluster as a freewill-offering, he brought it and [the priests] hung it thereon [translated by H. Danby].

The posts mentioned in this tractate, around which the vine intertwined, were stretched horizontally between the columns, resting on their capitals. This method is similar to the hanging of vines in a vineyard. The columns' trunks were decorated with gold flowers which entwined them. Such a decorative system can be seen on a number of Roman wall paintings from Herculaneum[6] and Boscoreale.[7] Columns with similar decorations are also depicted on a bronze coin minted at Sidon.[8]

---

[5] The Greek version is corrupted in this passage, so that here, as in other places, the Latin version should be preferred, despite its being a translation from the Greek. On the inferior textual tradition of the Greek manuscripts, see B. Niese (ed), *Flavi Josephi Opera*, I (1887), pp. xxvii–xxix; F. Blatt, *The Latin Josephus* I, introduction, Aarhus 1958 (= *Acta Jutlandica* 30, I), pp. 17–26. Here is the Greek text for *Antiquities* XV, 394–395 which is evidently corrupted:
θύρας δὲ ἐπὶ τῆς εἰσόδου σὺν τοῖς ὑπερθυρίοις ἴσον ἐχούσας τῷ ναῷ ποικίλοις ἐμπετάσμασιν κεκόσμητο, τὰ μὲν ἄνθη ἀλουργέσιν, κίονας δὲ ἐνυφασμένους. καθύπερθε δ' αὐτῶν ὑπὸ τοῖς τριχώμασιν ἄμπελος διετέτατο χρυσῆ τοὺς βότρυας ἀπαιωρουμένους ἔχουσα, θαῦμα καὶ τοῦ μεγέθους καὶ τῆς τέχνης τοῖς ἰδοῦσιν, οἶον ἐν πολυτελείᾳ τῆς ὕλης τὸ κατασκευασθὲν ἦν.

[6] A. Maiuri, *The Great Centuries of Painting: Roman Painting* (Geneva: Skira, 1953), p. 48.

[7] Ph. W. Lehmann, *Roman Wall Paintings from Boscoreale in the Metropolitan Museum of Art* (Cambridge, Mass., 1953), p. 84, fig. 51; p. 152, fig. 75 (Pompeii); pls. XI–XX, XXXIII. See also E.R. Goodenough, *Jewish Symbols in the Greco-Roman Period*, vol. 4 (New York, 1954), ill. 41.

[8] M.J. Price and B. Trell, *Coins and their Cities: Architecture on the Ancient Coins of Greece, Rome and Palestine* (London and Detroit, 1977), p. 13, fig. 277 and pp. 156–157. The coin is from the reign of Elagabalus (218–222 C.E.) and shows the *temenos* of Ashtarta-Europa in Sidon. See also C.M. Kaufmann, *Handbuch der Christlichen Archäologie*, 2nd. edn. (Paderborn, 1913), pp. 483–484.

The number of columns which supported the golden vine is not mentioned in the quoted passage in *Antiquities*. If only two columns flanked the portal of the Sanctuary, it would surely bring to mind the two famous columns — *Yakhin* and *Boaz* in Solomon's Temple, columns which Josephus mentions when he describes the Solomonic Temple (*Antiquities* VIII, 77–78). Considering the silence of both the Mishnah and Josephus on this point, it seems better to reconstruct two columns on either side of the portal. The space between the Sanctuary portal and the wickets to its north and south (Fig. 4) conveniently affords room for two columns on either side of the portal.[9]

The golden vine above the entrance of the Sanctuary was not an innovation introduced in the Herodian Temple. It already existed in the Hasmonean Temple, as is indicated by Florus and Tacitus, writing at the end of the first and the beginning of the second century C.E. describing the occupation of Jerusalem by Pompey in 63 B.C.E.[10] At that time the façade of the Temple was narrower and lower than the Herodian construction, and the portal of the Porch was probably open wider to show the vine and the curtain below it. Both are mentioned by Florus as the most outstanding features on the Temple's façade. It is not impossible that already then the vine was twined over four columns which flanked the Sanctuary portal. Moreover, it is quite possible that a model was sent as a gift by Aristobulus to Pompey in order to earn his support. This vine was valued at 500 talents. Strabo calls it a

"vine" or "garden" (εἴτε ἄμπελος εἴτε κῆπος) and says that the Jews call this art work τερπωλή — a term which means delight, and according to Marcus's commentary to the English translation, its Hebrew name might have been ʿeden (עדן). Strabo, who saw this vine in Rome, in the temple of Jupiter Capitolinus, says the inscription "From Alexandrus King of the Jews" was attached to it (*Antiquities* XIV, 34–36). This inscription indicates that Aristobulus looted this exemplar from the treasury of the Temple in Jerusalem, where it was kept, to which it was donated as an offering by Alexander Jannaeus.[11]

The columns which supported the golden vine of Herod's Temple served at the same time as a magnificent architectural frame to the Sanctuary portal. Although these columns stood within the Porch, the priests were not the only ones to enjoy them. On special occasions the lay people were also permitted into the priestly court and even to the Porch itself, so that the Sanctuary portal with its decorations and columns were well known and admired by contemporaries.[12]

As was suggested above, the tetradrachm artist's intention was to represent the portal of the Sanctuary with the two pairs of columns on either side. The golden vine itself was not depicted above the columns on these coins, although it is not impossible that the wavy line appearing above the columns on coins of the third year of the revolt do refer to the golden vine.[13] It is quite possible that the artist refrained from an exact

9   In my reconstructions (Figs. 4 and 5), drawn with great skill by Mr. Leen Ritmeyer, the lower diameter of the columns is two cubits — a diameter that fits 20 cubits height, and they are placed at a distance of 1.5 cubits from the Sanctuary wall. Thus the columns take up 3.5 cubits of the entire east-to-west depth of the Porch which measures 11 cubits. The space between the columns is three cubits. See my "The *Mesibbah* of the Temple according to the Tractate *Middot*," *Cathedra* 42 (1987), 39–52 (Hebrew); *Israel Exploration Journal* 36 (1986), pp. 215–233. In the Hebrew article (p. 40), which appeared before the English one, the four columns are drawn without the flower decorations, since at that time I was not yet aware of the Latin version of *Antiquities* XV 394–5.

10   Florus, *Epitoma* I:40:30; Tacitus, *Historiae* V:5:5.

11   Josephus refers to Strabo. See Marcus's comments in his edition and English translation (Loeb Classical Library). Goodenough suggested that an earlier version of the golden vine of the Temple is described in this passage (*Antiquities* XIV, 34–36), and that Herod's vine was a substitute for this vine. See Goodenough, *Jewish Symbols*, vol. 5 (New York, 1956), p. 102. However, as stated, a golden vine also hung above the Sanctuary's portal at the time of Pompey's conquest. This means that Aristobulus's present was not the hanging vine, but its smaller version, since it

was donated to Pompey while he was still in Damascus, previous to the conquest of Jerusalem. See also K. Galling, "Die Terpole des Alexanders Janneaus," *Festschrift für O. Eissfeldt. Zeitschrift für die Alttestamentliche Wissenschaft* 77 (1958), 49–62. For donations of golden vines in Greek literature, see A.B. Cook, *Zeus* II.I (Cambridge, 1925), pp. 281–282.

12   Mishnah, *Kelim* 1:8, states: "The Court of the Priests is still more holy, for Israelites may not enter therein save only when they must perform the laying on of hands, slaughtering, and waving" (translated by H. Danby). S. Safrai, *Pilgrimage at the Time of the Second Temple* (Tel Aviv, 1965), p. 191, says that Israel are permitted in procession around the altar on Sukkot; see idem, "The Ritual in the Second Temple," in: M. Avi-Yonah (ed.), *Sepher Yerushalayim* I (Jerusalem and Tel Aviv, 1956), pp. 371–372; he says that the representatives of Israel (*ma'amadot*) assist in the worship near the priests.

13   This suggestion, put forth by Sporty, was totally rejected by L. Mildenberg, *The Coinage of the Bar-Kokhba War* (Aarau, Frankfurt, Salzburg, 1984), pp. 44 note 98, who interprets it as a crenelation. See L.D. Sporty, "Identifying the Curving Line on the Bar-Kokhba Temple Coin," *Biblical Archaeologist* 46 (1983), 121–123; Barag, "Table," p. 25 and fig. 1, explains it in a similar manner.

representation of the columns with the entwining flowers and with the vine above (*Antiquities* XV) not only because these features were not essential for the representation of the Sanctuary portal, but also because a prohibition against an exact depiction of the Temple, its components, and its vessels prevailed at that period.[14]

A cluster of grapes and a vine leaf are prominent motifs on Bar-Kokhba coins of lesser denominations.[15] The cluster has three lobes, as was common in Jewish art since the Herodian Period.[16] These motifs in the Bar-Kokhba coinage may be related to the golden vine which hung above the portal of the Sanctuary.[17] In the biblical period the vine represented the People of Israel.[18] A similar concept prevailed also in Rabbinic literature.[19] This is the symbolic meaning that should be attributed to the golden vine of the Temple.

As was suggested above, two portals of the Temple are depicted on the Bar-Kokhba coins: that of the less sanctified Porch is depicted on the two-drachm (half-*sel'a*) coin, and that of the more sanctified Sanctuary is depicted on the four drachms (*sel'a*).[20] In the center of each portal the Table of the Shewbread was

represented, as was suggested by Barag, once on its widthwise and once lengthwise. Both types refer to the Temple and presumably express a hope to rebuild it. Other motifs of Bar-Kokhba coinage, such as the Four Species, the trumpets, the grape cluster and the vine leaf, and the jug, are all closely connected to the Temple and to the religious ceremonies conducted in it.

Up until now, numismatists and historians of Jewish art had difficulty explaining the depiction on the tetradrachms and consequently various suggestions were raised.[21] It is the four pillars which supported the veil before the Holy of Holies in the Tabernacle,[22] or in Solomon's Temple,[23] or an architectural frame to the Holy Ark of a Synagogue.[24] The first two suggestions were the results of the identification of the object between the columns as the Ark of Covenant, which was not among the holy vessels of the Second Temple. The situation is different in the case of the Shewbread Table. Such an identification of the object between the columns negates the first two explanations, and negates any basis for the third. A further explanation was to identify it with the mag-

---

[14] *The Babylonian Talmud, Menahot* 28b (The Soncino Press, *Seder Kodashim*, vol, I, p. 184): "A man may not make a house after the design of the Temple, or a porch after the design of the Temple porch, or a courtyard after the design of the Temple court, or a table after the design of the table [in the Temple] or a candlestick after the design of the candlestick [in the Temple]. He may, however, make one with five, six or eight [branches], but with seven he may not make one, even if it be of other metal." See also parallels: *Rosh Hashanah* 24a: *Avodah Zarah* 43a. The archaeological remains indicate that between the end of the first century C.E. and the middle of the second century C.E. the Jews strictly refrained from representing a seven-branched menorah. See Varda Sussman, *Ornamented Jewish Oil-Lamps: From the Destruction of the Second Temple Through the Bar-Kokhba Revolt* (Jerusalem, 1972), pp. 39, 59–61; L.Y. Rahmani. "Depictions of Menorot on Ossuaries," *Qadmoniot* 13.51–52 (1980), 114–17.

[15] Y. Meshorer, *Ancient Jewish Coinage*, II (Dix Hills, 1982), pp. 138–152, 218–219, notes 31–62; Mildenberg, *The Coinage of the Bar-Kokhba War*, pp. 31–47; A. Kindler, "Coins of the Bar-Kokhba War," in: A. Oppenheimer (ed.), *The Bar-Kokhba Revolt (Issues in Jewish History* 10) (Jerusalem, 1980), pp. 162–3 (Hebrew).

[16] Meshorer, *Ancient Jewish Coinage*, p. 143, note. 46.

[17] Such is also Meshorer's opinion, ibid., p. 143. Mildenberg, however (*Coinage*, pp. 46–7), sees these motifs as symbols of fertility of the land, like the vine that the spies brought Joshua.

[18] See Jeremiah 2:21: "Yet I planted you a choice vine, wholly of pure seed. How then have you turned degenerate and become a wild vine?" (RSV). Cf. Psalms 80:9–12; Ezekiel 17:5–8.

[19] Goodenough, *Jewish Symbols*, vol. 5, note 12, pp. 102–3, sees the appearance of the vine in minor Jewish art as well as the golden vine above the Sanctuary portal as an expression of the ritual of imbibing wine which is central in Judaism. See also vol. 6 (New York, 1956), pp. 126–217.

[20] Mildenberg, "Bar Kokhba Didrachm," suggested that the number of columns on each of the two types indicates its denomination: two drachms and four drachms. However, in the period under discussion coin denominations were not marked thus.

[21] For the various interpretations in the research, see B. Kanael, "Altjüdische Münzen," *Jahrbuch für Numismatik und Geldgeschichte* 17 (1967), pp. 256–72: "Symbolik"; A. Muehsam, *Coin and Temple: A Study of the Architectural Representations on Ancient Jewish Coins* (Leiden, 1966); Meshorer, *Ancient Jewish Coinage*, pp. 138–40, notes 31–37 on pp. 218–9; Mildenberg, *Coinage*, note 16, p. 33, note 80.

[22] This suggestion was already raised in 1855 by Cavedoni and was adopted by Reifenberg, *Coins of the Jews* (Jerusalem, 1947) pp. 31–32 (Hebrew). Goodenough interpreted the object displayed between the columns as a Torah shrine and the architectural envelope as an expression of the centrality of the Torah in Judaism. *Jewish Symbols*, vol. 1, p. 277 and vol. 4, p. 114. For further bibliographical references, see Kanael, "Altjüdische Münzen," nos. 24, 95, 96, 269, 283.

[23] For complete bibliographical references see ibid., nos. 272, 46, 261, 295, 298. This suggestion was originally raised by Rogers (1911) and was adopted by Hill (1914), Lambert (1932), Romanoff (1944), and Roth (1955).

[24] So Rosenau (1936), Wendel (1950), and Kanael (1960). For complete bibliographical references see ibid., nos. 296, 278, 55.

nificent gate to the Second Temple, namely Nicanor Gate.[25]

Only a few scholars adopted the idea that these coins display the Temple which was destroyed by Titus.[26] The prominent representative of this idea was the late Professor Michael Avi-Yonah who promoted it widely, not only in his writings but also in his reconstruction of the Second Temple in the model at the Holyland Hotel in Jerusalem.[27] The four columns shown on the coin are definitely not a *prostyle* of a *pronaos*, which was a characteristic feature of contemporary Hellenistic-Roman temples, but lacking in the Jewish Temple.[28] A *pseudo prostyle* was the favorite opinion. Accordingly, Avi-Yonah and other scholars reconstructed in the corners of the façade two attached pilasters and between them and the Porch portal two attached half columns. Recently Barag repeated this view, with minor alterations concerning mainly the shape of the Porch portal, as suggested by the depiction on the didrachm of Bar-Kokhba.[29] However, the literary sources describing the Second Temple's façade do not mention any attached pilasters or half columns, so that there is no textual basis for such an interpretation.[30] Indeed, Vincent, Busink, and Eybeschuetz, adhering to the sources, reconstructed the Temple with a plain façade, refraining from these additions.[31] Such is also my suggestion (Figs. 2 and 5), as well as Avi-Yonah's in an earlier stage of his research.[32] As stated above, only a minority among the numismatists adopted the opinion that the depiction on the tetradrachms is the façade of the Temple destroyed by Titus. Meshorer preferred the suggestion that the depiction on the coin symbolizes the *concept* of the Temple rather than its actual shape.[33] In light of all this, the suggestion that the façade of Herod's Temple was depicted on the tetradrachms should also be rejected, in preference to my own interpretation: the tetradrachms show the portal leading into the Sanctuary.

On the coins of the Second Year an element was added under the columns, which may be a balustrade, emphasizing the sanctity of the construction above it.[34] In the coins of the Third Year, a wavy line was added above the construction, which may stand for the golden vine training above the columns.[35]

The depiction on these coins resembles the drawing above the Torah niche in the synagogue of Dura-Europos, and should be similarly interpreted.[36] The portal in Dura Europos, between two columns, is displayed with the wings of the doors shut, and above them an arch or rather a conch. The vine of an earlier phase, drawn as a tree with branches in the panel

25 This was Cavedoni's first interpretation and it was adopted by F.W. Madden, *Coins of the Jews*, 2nd edn. (London, 1881), pp. 202–3; and see Meshorer, *Ancient Jewish Coinage*, p. 139, note 32. See Muehsam, *Coin and Temple*, pp. 26–33.
26 This suggestion was raised in the last century by Levy and Merzbacher. See Reifenberg, *Coins of the Jews*, p. 31.
27 M. Avi-Yonah, "The Façade of Herod's Temple — An Attempted Reconstruction," in: J. Neusner (ed.), *Religions in Antiquity: Essays in Memory of E.R. Goodenough* (Leiden, 1968), pp. 327–35. Mildenberg, *Coinage*, p. 37, also sees the representation on the coins as the Temple's façade.
28 See numerous examples in Price and Trell, *Coins and their Cities*. Such temples also had gabled roofs, an element missing from the coins under discussion. Colonnaded structures with flat roofs are often identified in numismatics as gates to temple courtyards (p. 21, ill. 16; p. 30, ill 38; p. 86, ill. 152; p. 134, ill. 238); altars (p. 58, ill. 105; p. 104, ill. 188); or Phoenician temples: B. Trell, "Architectura Numismatica Orientalis: A Short Guide to the Numismatic Formulae of Roman Syrian Die-Makers," *Numismatic Chronicle*, 7th Series, 10 (1970), p. 38, fig. 74.
29 Barag "Table," figure on p. 25. Even though the door posts of the portal are represented on the coins as two columns (or two pilasters), I prefer in my reconstruction (Figs. 2 and 5) to adhere to the written descriptions (see following note), which do not mention door posts with such a shape. It is reasonable to assume that in this case, as in others, the artist refrained from a precise representation of the Porch portal (see note 14 above).
30 Mishnah, *Middot* 2:3; 3:7; *Wars* V, v, iv; vi (208–213; 222–227). See Patrich, "The Structure," pp. 32–40 (Hebrew); "Reconstruct-

ing," pp. 16–29 (English).
31 L.H. Vincent, "Le Temple Herodien d'apres la Michna," *Revue Biblique* 61 (1954), 5–35, 398–418; L.H. Vincent and A.M. Steve, *Jerusalem de l'Ancien Testament*, II–III (Paris 1956), pp. 432–525. T.A. Busink, *Der Tempel von Jerusalem*, II (Leiden, 1980). E. Eybeschuetz, "The Sanctuary and the Porch in the Second Temple: An Examination and Clarifications of the Rabbinic Sources," *Sinai* 87 (1980), 226–237 (Hebrew).
32 See my articles, note 2 above. Avi-Yonah, "The Second Temple," in: *Sepher Yerushalayim*, I, pp. 392–418 (Hebrew). This article presents two different suggested reconstructions of the Temple's façade. On p. 408, fig. 8, a plain façade is represented: yet a reconstruction different from these two was published later. See note 27 above.
33 Meshorer, *Ancient Jewish Coinage*, p. 140.
34 I do not mean the balustrade which divided the outer and inner courts. Also Mildenberg, *Coinage*, p. 42 and note 94, sees this element as a balustrade. Y. Meshorer, *Jewish Coins in the Second Temple Period* (Tel Aviv, 1966) (Hebrew), p. 121, coin number 179, and Barag, "Table," figure on p. 25, refer to it as the foundation of the Temple. For the display of balustrade grills in a similar manner on coins of the temple of Pan in Panias and the Zeus and Heracles *temenos* in Selge, see Price and Trell, *Coins and their Cities*, p. 20, ills. 10–11; p. 144, ill. 262.
35 See note 13 above.
36 Wendel was the first to notice this resemblance. See Wendel, *Der Thoraschrein in Altertum* (Halle, 1950). In both cases he believed that the descriptions refer to the Solomonic Temple.

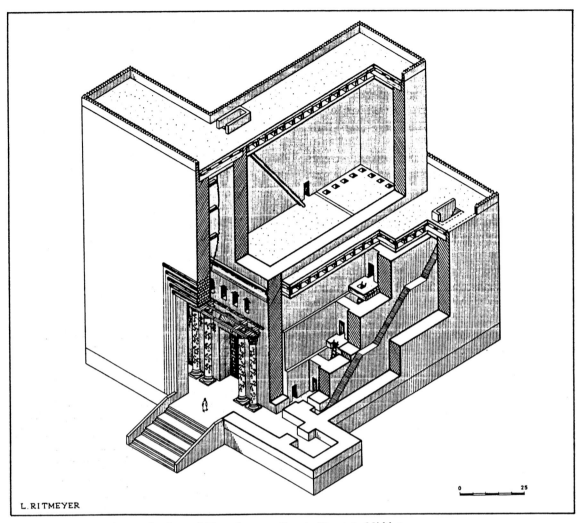

Fig 5.   Reconstruction of the Second Temple according to Tractate Middot.

above,[37] adds validity to my interpretation: it is the Sanctuary portal, with two columns on either side.

It may have served as a source of inspiration for the fashioning of Torah arks in later synagogues.[38]

[37] Comte du Mesnil du Buisson, *Les peintures de la synagogue de Doura Europos* (Roma, 1939), pp. 27–28, fig. 23 and p. XXIII.; C.H. Kraeling, *The Excavations at Dura-Europos, Final Report* VIII, 1: *The Synagogue* (New Haven, 1956), pp. 62–65, pls. XVII, LI; Goodenough, *Jewish Symbols*, vols. 5 and 9 (New York, 1964), pp. 78–82; volume 11 (New York, 1964) pls. I, III, ills. 66, 73, 74, 76, 93. Kraeling interprets the drawing as a tree of life rather than as a vine, while Goodenough interprets it as a tree-vine. According to H.F. Pearson the drawing depicts a vine, see *Guide de la synagogue de Doura Europos* (Beyrouth, 1940) pp. 22–23.

[38] R. Hachlili, "The Niche and the Ark in Ancient Synagogues," *BASOR* 223 (1976), 43–54; she shows a frieze from Kochav

Hayarden (fig. 4); a relief from Beit She'arim (fig. 6); a mosaic from Horvat Susiya (fig. 8). In these representations a distinction should be made between the Holy Ark which is furniture, possibly of wood, with two doors, and the architectural decorations which surround it, including the niche in which it was placed. This may have been inspired by the Sanctuary portal, with two pairs of columns on either side. An aedicule with a niche flanked by two columns on either side is depicted on several Palestinian oil lamps from the late Roman period, and the windows of the Capernaum synagogue were similarly decorated. See Goodenough, *Jewish Symbols*, vol. 3, ills. 286–288, 293, 462–463.

JOHAN LUND, SEINE "ALTEN JÜDISCHEN HEILIGTÜMER" UND DIE VORSTELLUNG VOM SALOMONISCHEN TEMPEL

Ralf Busch

Abb. 1. Portrait von Johan Lundius, vor dem Frontispiz in der Ausgabe seiner "Alten Jüdischen Heiligtümer" von 1722.

Seit der Darstellung von Helen Rosenau, die 1979 umfassend über die Vorstellungen vom Salomonischen Tempel im Judentum und Christentum berichtet hat, scheint dieses Thema erschöpfend behandelt zu sein, aber dennoch sind Anmerkungen und Ergänzungen möglich. Einige sollen hier nachstehend gegeben werden.

Das Modell des Salomonischen Tempels aus Hamburg ist zuletzt durch Gisela Jaacks und auch in älterer Literatur häufiger behandelt worden.[1] Wahrscheinlich zwischen 1680 und 1692 entstanden, aber unvollendet geblieben, galt es damals schon bald als Hamburgs bedeutendste Sehenswürdigkeit.

Es war und blieb allerdings nicht das einzige Modell dieser Thematik. Populär war auch das ältere Amsterdamer Modell von Rabbi Jacob Judah Leon, das allerdings nur durch Kupferstiche überliefert ist. Den zahlreichen jüdischen und christlichen Autoren ging es um eine Visualisierung dessen, was die Bibel über Salomons Tempelbau berichtet, wurde darin doch wegen der göttlichen Anweisungen dieser als die Vollendung höchster Harmonie in der Architektur angesehen. Am ausführlichsten schildert. Könige 6 die Errichtung des Tempels durch Salomon.

In der Renaissance-und Barockzeit hat die wissenschaftliche Diskussion um die Rekonstruktion des Jerusalemer Tempels in der Theologie, aber auch in der praktischen Architektur einen breiten Raum eingenommen.[2]

Die Behandlung des Themas war nicht auf literarische oder graphische Darstellung beschränkt. Das ausgreifendste Modell blieb jenes von Hamburg. H. Reuther konnte ausführlich darstellen, daß der Erbauer dieses Werkes sich eng an den bildlichen Vor-

---

[1] Die wichtigsten Abhandlungen, jeweils mit weiterführender Literatur, sind: O. Lauffer, "Das Modell des Tempels Salomonis," *Jahresbericht des Museums für Hamburgische Geschichte für das Jahr 1910* (1911), 17–24; K.V. Riedel, "Das Hamburger Modell des Salomonischen Tempels," *Beiträge zur Deutschen Volks- und Altertumskunde* 11 (1967), 117–26; H. Reuther, "Das Modell des Salomonischen Tempels im Museum für Hamburgische

Geschichte," *Niederdeutsche Beiträge zur Kunstgeschichte* 19 (1980), 161–98; G. Jaacks, "Abbild und Symbol. Das Hamburger Modell des Salomonischen Tempels," *Hamburg Porträt* 17/1982; G. Jaacks in *Vierhundert Jahre Juden in Hamburg* (Hamburg, 1991), 70–72.

[2] H. Rosenau, *Vision of the Temple* (London, 1979).

lagen nach dem spanischen Jesuiten Juan Bautista Villalpando (1552–1608) orientierte.

Bald nach der öffentlichen Ausstellung des Hamburger Modells wurde dieses Thema erneut in Hamburg aufgegriffen. Der gelehrte Theologe Johan Lund (Johannes Lundius), 1638 in Flensburg geboren und 1686 in Tondern gestorben,[3] hatte ein Werk verfaßt, das erst nach seinem Tod an die Öffentlichkeit gelangte, bald aber durch mehrere Auflagen populär wurde. Seine "Ausführliche Beschreibung der Hütte des Stifts, wie auch des ersten und andern Tempels zu Jerusalem" erschien zunächst 1695 in Schleswig, dann aber in erweiterter und illustrierter Fassung in Hamburg 1701, 1704, 1722 und 1738. Eine holländische Übersetzung kam 1723 in Amsterdam heraus. Die am weitesten verbreitete Auflage scheint die von 1722 zu sein, die bei Fickweiler verlegt wurde, deren Titel nun lautet: "Die alten jüdischen Heiligthümer. Gottesdienste und Gewohnheiten."

Das damals viel beachtete Werk ist in der neueren Forschung nicht rezipiert worden, was einen Hinweis auf dieses rechtfertigt und geradezu nötig macht, wenn man die Breite der Diskussion um dieses Thema vor allem in der Barockzeit und der praktischen Architektur erfassen will.

Neben dem Portrait des Autors (Abb. 1) enthielt diese Ausgabe 30 Tafeln.[4] Die Tafeln sind von Johann Wilhelm Michaelis gestochen, der aus Wittenberg stammte, in Hamburg lernte, dann aber in Berlin und Stargard wirkte, wo er 1737 starb.[5]

Es ist nicht bekannt, nach welchen Vorlagen J.W.

Michaelis die Illustrationen für Lundius Werk schuf. Nur eine Tafel bei Lundius in der Auflage von 1722 stellt den Salomonischen Tempel, hier das Allerheiligste, so dar, daß wir nach Vergleichen zum Hamburger Modell fragen dürfen (Lund, nach S. 254).

Der Vergleich ist deutlich. Die Abbildung von J.W. Michaelis (Abb. 2) im Werk von J. Lundius kopiert nicht das Hamburger Modell (Abb. 3), das Michaelis gekannt haben wird. Die Unterschiede sind so auffällig, daß eindeutig eine unterschiedliche Auffassung erkennbar ist. Michaelis zu Lundius stellt vier Geschosse bei der Eingangsfassade dar, das Hamburger Modell kennt nur drei Geschosse. Übereinstimmungen im Detail sind zwar unverkennbar, aber nicht ausreichend prägnant, um eine Verbindung zwischen Modell und Abbildung bei Lundius herstellen zu können. Dieser Befund ist bemerkenswert, da J. Lundius ausdrücklich ein Modell nach R. Jacob Judah Leon erwähnt (S. 256), nicht aber das Hamburger Modell nennt. Dieses scheint er nicht gekannt zu haben, was verständlich ist, da er schon 1686 starb, wo das Hamburger Modell noch nicht annähernd erstellt war. Die späteren Redaktoren seines Werkes haben keine aktuellen Bezüge hergestellt, d.h. in aller Konsequenz, daß das Hamburger Modell trotz seiner Berühmtheit in das Werk von J. Lund keinen Eingang gefunden hat, obwohl die jüngeren Ausgaben sonst durchaus Erweiterungen erfahren haben.

Bemerkenswert ist, daß das Heiligtum des Hamburger Modells auch im Inneren fein und detailliert ausgearbeitet ist. Ein Blick in den Vorraum zum

[3] Zu seiner Biographie: Chr. G. Jöcher, Herausgeber, *Allgemeines Gelehrten-Lexikon* (Leipzig, 1750), Sp. 2602. ADB 19, 1884. *Dansk Biografisk Leksikon* 14 (Kopenhagen, 1938), 540–541. Ebd., 9 Bd., (Kopenhagen, 1981), 170–171.
[4] Johannes Lundius, *Die alten jüdischen Heiligthümer, Gottesdienste und Gewohnheiten*, 3. Ausgabe bei Johann Wolffgang Fickweiler (Hamburg, 1722). Die Abbildungen (Kupferstiche) stellen dar: Nach dem Titel: 1. Porträt Johannes Lundius, Kupferstich J.G. Mentzel; 2. Das irdische und himmlische Jerusalem. Vor S. 1: 3. Grund-Riß der Stifts-Hütter. Nach S. 2: 4. Abgedeckte Wohnung / oder die Wohnung der Stiftshütten, von J.W. Michaelis. Nach S. 6: 5. Die Wohnung der Stifts-Hütte, von J.W. Michaelis. Nach S. 30:6. Die Bundes-Lade, von J.W. Michaelis. Nach S. 114: 7. Leuchter, von J.W. Michaelis. Nach S. 120: 8. Schau-Brod-Tisch; 9. Schau-Brod-Tisch mit den Schau-Broden. Nach S. 122: 10. Schau-Brodte, von J.W. Michaelis. Nach S. 130: 11. Der Rauch-Altar / Das eherne Hand-Faß, von J.W. Michaelis. Nach S. 172: 12. Brandopfers-Altar, von J.W. Michaelis. Nach S. 202: 13. Der Schaubrodts-Tisch, von J.W. Michaelis. Nach S. 216: 14. Grundriß des Feld-Lagers der Kinder, von J.W. Michaelis. Nach S. 254: 15. Abriß des Salomonischen

... Tempels, von J.W. Michaelis. Nach S. 260: 16. Das Heilige; 17. Das Allerheiligste. Nach S. 302: 18. Grund-Riß des inneren Vorhofes, von J.W. Michaelis. Nach S. 306: 19. Das Eherne Meer, von J.W. Michaelis. Nach S. 310: 20. Abriß eines der 10. Keßel Salomons. Nach S. 418: 21. Der hohe Priester, von J.W. Michaelis; 22. Ein Genriner Priester, von J.W. Michaelis. Nach S. 426: 23. Zween Edelgesteine, von J.W. Michaelis. Nach S. 564: 24. Der Götze Moloch, von J.W. Michaelis; 25. Der Götze Moloch mit Räumen der Capellen. Nach S. 654: 26. Unterschiedliche Meinungen, wie die Priester beym Segen sprechen, von J.W. Michaelis. Nach S. 732: 27. Das Wappen von Jerusalem. Nach S. 796: 28. Ein Pharisäer in seiner Kleidung nach Epiphani; 29. Ein Pharisäer in seiner Kleidung. Nach S. 800: 30. Denck-Zettel am Haupt, von J.W. Michaelis; 31. Denck-Zettel am Arm, von J.W. Michaelis. Nach S. 868: 32. Die Stadt. Die Ausgabe von 1701, die 1991 das Antiquariat Stenderhoff im Katalog 459 angeboten hat, enthält zusätzlich drei Palästina-Karten, die sonst nicht nachgewiesen sind.
[5] H. Vollmer, Bd. 24, 507.

Abb. 2.   Das Allerheiligste nach J.W. Michaelis, Lundius nach S. 254.

Abb. 3.   Das Allerheiligste nach dem Hamburger Modell.

Allerheiligsten läßt die ornamentale Wanddekoration erkennen, die vollständig vergoldet ist (Abb. 3a). Die Ansicht der Türwand zum Allerheiligsten (Abb. 3b), von schräg oben gesehen, zeigt eine ähnlich kostbare Gestaltung. In den Schnittpunkten des rhombischen Gitterwerkes, das die Wände überzieht, sind rote und grüne Glassteine eingelassen. Davor stehen die ebenfalls vergoldeten Cherubinen. Aber auch hier zeigt sich im Vergleich zu Lund (bei ihm die Tafeln nach S. 260), daß die Modell-Darstellung ganz eigenständig ist und einmalig bleibt.

Das Frontispiz hat das irdische und himmlische Jerusalem zum Thema (Abb. 4). Hierbei ist der Tempelberg dargestellt, in einer sehr vereinfachten Form, die auf die Rekonstruktion von Jacob Judah Leon von 1642 zurückzuführen ist.[6]

Das Tempelmodell des aus Hamburg gebürtigen Rabbi Leon, das dieser in Amsterdam fertigen ließ,[7] war Lundius nicht bekannt. Er erwähnt ihn zwar, schreibt aber über dessen 1642 erschienenes Werk "Obs heraus gekommen, weiß ich nicht, habe auch, da ich diß (Anno 1678. 19. Sept.) schreibe, nichts davon erfahren können."[8]

Was Lundius nicht kannte, hat sein späterer Il-

---

6   H. Rosenau, wie Anm. 2, 133.
7   Th. A. Busink, *Der Tempel von Jerusalem* (Leiden, 1970, 1980),

Bd. 1, 44–45.
8   J. Lundius, 1722, 256.

3a

3b

4

Abb. 3a. Blick in den Vorraum des Allerheiligsten vom Hamburger Modell (Foto Museum für Hamburgische Geschichte).

Abb. 3b. Ansicht der Wand zum Allerheiligsten im Hamburger Modell (Foto Museum für Hamburgische Geschichte).

Abb. 4. Frontispiz zu J. Lundius, Hamburg 1722.

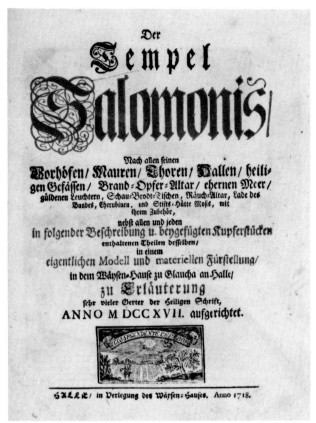

*Abb. 5. Titelblatt der Beschreibung des
Halleschen Modells, Halle 1718.*

*Abb. 6. Frontispiz zu der Veröffentlichung
des Halleschen Modells, Halle 1718.*

lustrator Michaelis in diesem Fall doch für seine
Abbildung im Frontispiz herangezogen.

Nachwirkung hat das Werk von J. Lundius, der
sich weniger an bildlichen Rekonstruktionen, sondern
schriftlichen Quellen der Bibel orientierte, dennoch
gefunden. Das 1717 errichtete Hallesche Modell[9] wurde
ein Jahr später in einem Buch erläutert (Abb. 5), dem
6 Kupferdrucke beigegeben sind.[10] Dieses Werk ist als
ein Führer zum Modell in Halle angelegt und bisher
in der neueren Literatur unbeachtet geblieben.

Hierin heißt es in der Vorrede:

"Lundius aber in denen Jüdischen Heiligthümern
scheinet, als sey er eigentlich um unsers Vorhaben
willen so bemüht gewesen, alle Ellen und halbe Ellen

zu determinieren, damit man bey dem Bau-Wesen
dieses kleinen Tempels allenthalben desto gewisser
fussen, und alle Mauren und Gegenden desto glück-
licher anlegen könte; Der führet den Maaß-Stab und
die Bleywage in der Hand; wir gehen ihm auf allen
Tritten nach, und ist er vor andern unser Bau-Direktor
gewesen."[11]

Das illustrierte Werk[12] zeigt im Frontispiz den
Tempelberg (Abb. 6) in noch vergröberter Fassung,
als wir es schon bei Lundius sahen. H. Reuther[13] hat
bemerkt, daß das Hallesche Modell "wesentlich puri-
tanischer wirkt in seiner architektonischen Durchbil-
dung fast schon primitiv."

Dabei greift er allerdings auf eine undeutliche

9 H. Reuther, wie Anm. 1, 185 und Anm. 48; in Ergänzung hierzu
   verweisen wir in Anm. 10 auf die Erstveröffentlichung.
10 *Der Tempel Salomonis, Halle in Verlegung des Wäysen-Hauses,
   Anno 1718*; ausführlicher Titel vgl. Abb. 5.
11 *Der Tempel Salomonis*, wie Anm. 10, 6.
12 Die beigegebenen Abbildungen sind: 1. Frontispiz, David präsentiert seinem Sohn Salomon ein Bild des Tempels. 2. Delineatio
   Palaestinae sive Terrae Sanctae, von J.J. Püschel; vgl. Anm. 13.

3. Grund-Riß von dem Modell des Salomonischen Tempels,
   J.F.D. 4. Scenographie des eigentlichen Tempels von J.F.D. 5.
   Profil des Tempels auf der Nordischen Seiten, von J.F.D. 6. Der
   Tempel Salomonis wie er sich rückwärts und auf der Abendseite
   präsentiert, mit sechs Rundbildern. 7. Scenographie des Modells
   vom ganzen Hierosolymitanischen Tempel.
13 Zu den Palästina-Karten von J.J. Püschel vgl. E. Laor, *Maps of
   the Holy Land* (New York und Amsterdam, 1986).

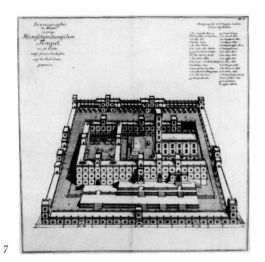

7

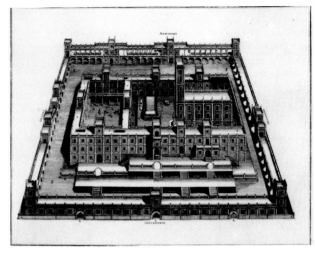

8

9

Abb. 7. Gesamtansicht des Halleschen Modells, Halle 1718.
Abb. 8. Abbildung des Halleschen Modells nach J.A.
Friedrich (wie Anm. 15).
Abb. 9. Das Heiligtum des Halleschen Modells, Halle 1718.

Abbildung zurück,[14] die wir hier um die aus der Veröffentlichung von 1718 ergänzen können (Abb. 7), die eine Gesamtansicht zeigt. Sie deutet doch eine bessere Durchformung der architektonischen Details an, die in einer weiteren Abbildung des Halleschen Modells von J.A. Friedrich[15] ihre Bestätigung findet (Abb. 8). Bemerkenswert ist, daß der viergeschossige

Turm des Allerheiligsten auf beiden Abbildungen einen waagerechten Abschluß zeigt, im Gegensatz zu Lundius und dem Hamburger Modell, die einen Giebel zeigen.

Nun ist aber der Beschreibung des Halleschen Modells von 1718 eine weitere Abbildung beigegeben, die nur das Heiligtum selbst zeigt (Abb. 9). Hier findet sich nun doch der erwähnte Giebel dargestellt. Die architektonische Gliederung ist dem Hamburger Modell durchaus vergleichbar und viel detaillierter dargestellt als in der Gesamtansicht. Die Pilaster und ihre korinthischen Kapitelle sind ähnlich geformt, wogegen jedes dekorative Beiwerk, das wir aus Hamburg kennen, hier fehlt. So bestätigt sich durch diesen Vergleich die herausragende Bedeutung des Hamburger Modells in seiner weitergehenden Detailfreude auf anschauliche Weise.

Zusammenfassend zeigt sich, daß das Hamburger Modell, populär und an mehreren Orten gezeigt, keine Nachwirkung hatte, wogegen Lundius nachhaltig auf das Modell von Halle einwirkte. In einer Bibelausgabe von 1716, gedruckt in Minden, finden sich Kupferstiche von J.F. Esau, die die Illustrationen von Michaelis aus dem Werk von Lundius genau übernehmen.

[14] H. Reuther, wie Anm. 1, Abb. 25.
[15] Als Illustration zu 1. Kön. VI.; Jacob Andreas Friedrich d.Ä. (Nürnberg 1684 — Augsburg 1751), Kupferstecher. Die Tafel stammt aus: Scheuzer, Johann Jakob, *Physica Sacra Johannis Jacobi Scheuchzeri, Medicinae Doctoris, & Math. in Lyceo Tiguri no Prof. .... Iconibus Aeneis illustrata procurante & sumptus suppeditante Johanne Andrea Pfeffel, Augustano, Sacrae*

Caesaareae Majestatis Chalocographo aulico. Kupferbibel in welchen die Physica sacra oder geheiligte Naturwissenschaft derer in heil. Schrift vorkommenden natürlichen Sachen deutlich erklärt und bewährt (Augsburg und Ulm: Christian Ulrich Wagner, 1731–35). Zu diesem Werk vgl. *Architekt und Ingenieur*, Ausstellungskataloge der Herzog August Bibliothek Nr. 42, 1984, 133–134.

68

EZEKIEL'S PLAN IN AN EARLY KARAITE BIBLE*

Yaffa Levy

Among the early Bibles in the Second Firkovitch Collection at the State Public Library in St. Petersburg[1] is a decorated parchment of two leaves, from the opening of an unknown Near Eastern biblical text, probably from the tenth century.[2] The quire consists of one blank page (fol. 1r), two facing carpet pages with verses from the Psalms (fols. 1v–2r), and a fourth page showing a gabled Temple (fol. 2v).[3] I believe that the combination of these phrases from the Psalms followed by a Temple plan derives from a Karaite world-view, and was probably intended to transmit the tenets of Karaite belief and theological opinion, as well as its messianic aspirations. It may therefore serve as important evidence of the Karaite origin of the biblical manuscript from which this quire came.

The verses on fols. 1v–2r are written in monumental mid-Eastern script, in spared ground technique on a gold ground, seven lines per page (Figs. 1–2).[4] The first three are:

The Lord is great in Zion; and He is high above all the people [Ps. 99:2]. Blessed be the Lord God of Israel from everlasting, and to everlasting. Amen, and Amen [Ps. 41:14]. For the word of the Lord is right; and all his works are done in truth [Ps. 33:4].[5]

The last word of this inscription appears on the facing page, where four more verses are written, all from Psalm 119:

Thy word is true from the beginning; and every one of thy righteous judgments endureth for ever [119:160]. Thou hast commanded us to keep thy precepts diligently [119:4]. Blessed are Thou, O Lord, teach me thy statutes [119:12]. Thou art good, and dost good; teach me thy statutes [119:68].

The three verses on fol. 1v first appeared as a benediction in the *Book of Precepts* by Anan ben David, founder of the Karaite sect and its first legislator.[6] In his book Anan assigns a special chapter to the laws of benedictions and determined their

* This article is based on the findings of a survey of Hebrew illuminated manuscripts at the State Public Library in St. Petersburg. The survey was conducted in the summer of 1992 by an expedition from the Center for Jewish Art of the Hebrew University in Jerusalem. I am grateful to my colleague Simona Grunemann, who translated my paper into English and helped me to clarify my ideas.

[1] For detailed information about the Firkovitch collections see K.B. Starkova, "Les Manuscrits de la Collection Firkovič," *Revue des Études Juives*, 134 (1975), 101–17; idem, "Rukopisi Kollekdcii Firkovica," *Pis'mennye Pamjatniki Vostoka* (Moscow, 1974), pp. 165–92; A. Katsh, "Hebrew and Judeo-Arabic MSS in the Collections of the USSR," *Acts of the 25th International Congress of Orientalists* (Moscow, 1962, I, pp. 421–29; V. Lebedev, *Arabskie Socinenija V evreiskoj grafike, Katalogue rukopisej* (Publications of the Saltykov-Ščedrin State Public Library Leningrad 1987; P.B. Fenton, *A Handlist of Judeo-Arabic Manuscripts in Leningrad* (Jerusalem, 1991). A facsimile album with 27 plates of decorated folios from Bibles in the Fikovitch Collections was published by D. Günzburg and V. Stassoff, *Ornementation des Anciens Manuscrits Hébreux de la Bibliothèque Impériale Publique de Saint-Pétersbourg* (St. Petersburg, 1886; Berlin, 1905). Henceforth Günzburg, *Ornementation*. All the plates were published again in a facsimile edition by B. Narkiss, *Illuminations from Hebrew Bibles of Leningrad with Hebrew and English Introduction and New Descriptions* (Jerusalem, 1990). Henceforth Narkiss, *Hebrew Bibles*.

[2] At present it is placed together with two other biblical fragments: A single page with decorated massoretic lists from one manuscript, and a quire of nine text pages with the beginning of Genesis from another manuscript. All three are shelfmarked by the Library as Firk. Hebr. II B 49. In his Hebrew Bibles (pp. 60–61) Narkiss calls them the "Firkovitch Compilation."

[3] The pages are almost square (418 x 373 mm), thus fitting the size of most mid-Eastern biblical codices written in the ninth to eleventh centuries. See M. Beit-Arié, *The Making of the Medieval Hebrew Book, Studies in Palaeography and Codicology* (Jerusalem, 1993), pp. 116–17. The decorated space measures: fol. 1v — height 359 mm. (386 mm. with extended palmette), width 330 mm. (380 mm. with palmette on the right hand side). Fol. 2r — height 356 mm. (380 mm. with palmette), width 350 mm. Fol. 2v — height 390 mm., width 323 mm.

[4] Partial facsimilies of fols. 1v–2r, were published by Günzburg, *Ornementation*, pl. X,2,3. On plate X,2 are depicted the two last lines of fol. 1v. On plate X,3 is the letter "Tet" from the lower corner of fol. 2r. For a full picture of fol. 1v see Narkiss, *Hebrew Bibles*, fig. 12.

[5] The letter *heh* written at the end of the second row and the incomplete letter *shin* at the end of the fourth row serve as line fillers. For similar fillers in the Damascus Pentateuch (Palestine or Egypt, ca. 1000 C.E.), see Beit-Arié, *Medieval Hebrew Book*, pp. 119–21, especially paragraphs 1 and 3.

[6] Anan came to Babylonia from the East, probably from Persia. His appearance occurred during the Caliphate of Ga'far al-

Figs. 1–2. Carpet pages with verses from the Psalms in monumental script from the Firkovitch Compilation. Egypt, late tenth century. St. Petersburg Public Library, Firk. Hebr. II B 49, fols. 2r–1v (after Narkiss, Hebrew Bibles, fig. 12).

precise versions, of which the main characteristic is the consistent use of recitations from the Psalms.[7] He also determined that Zion and Jerusalem should be mentioned in every blessing: before and after the reading of the Torah, before performing a mitzvah and before and after meals.[8] The Grace before and after meals begins: "Blessed be the Lord of Zion, who dwelleth at Jerusalem. Praise ye the Lord" (Ps. 135:21), while the Torah and the mitzvah benedictions begin: "The Lord is great in Zion" (Ps. 99:2), identical with the opening verse in our quire.[9]

Anan's requirement to remember Jerusalem and the destruction of the Temple in every precept, together with his personal tendency to seclusion, asceticism, and excessive discipline, are an outcome of the messianic tendencies in his own teachings, and which were

Manzur (754–775). See L. Nemoy, *Karaite Anthology: Excerpts from the Early Literature* (New Haven, 1952), p. 3. Most excerpts from Anan's *Book of Precepts* were published in Aramaic with Hebrew translation by A.A. Harkavy, זכרון לראשונים, מחברת שמינית, השריד והפליט מספרי המצות הראשונים לבני מקרא: לענן נשיא, בנימין נהאונדי ודניאל אלקומסי, Studien und Mitteilungen, VIII (St. Petersburg, 1903). Other passages were published in S. Schechter, *Documents of Jewish Sectaries* , vol. II, קונטרסים מספר המצות לענן (Cambridge, 1910); shorter passages were published by J. Mann, M.N. Sokolov and N. Epstein. See R. Mahler, *ha-Qara'im* (Merhaviah, 1949), p. 133; henceforth Mahler, *Karaites*.

7 Harkavy, *Anan*, pp. 17–21. In his edition Harkavy mentions that even those prayers formulated by Anan which have not been preserved were supposed to be excerpted from Psalms (ibid., p. 203, note to p. 39). In the book *Kitab al-Anwar wa-l-Marakib* (Book of Lights and Watchtowers), the Karaite scholar Jacob al-Qirqisani, a contemporary adversary of R. Saadyah Gaon, probably quotes the latter as saying that the early Karaites prayed only from Psalms and that only in a much later period did they start including hymns and benedictions in the Rabbinical fashion. See B.M. Lewin ed., *Otzar ha-Gaonim* (Thesaurus of

the Gaonic Responsa and Commentaries) (Haifa, 1928), vol. I, pt. 1, p. 142.

8 About other innovations in Anan's method, see Mahler, *Karaites*, p. 124–73.

9 However, in Anan's version of the Torah Benedictions other phrases were added, and only in his Mitzvot Benediction all three appear in full. These three verses are found also in the Karaite Siddur, where it opens the reading of the Torah on Shabbat by the Cohen in the synagogue. See *Prayer Book According to the Karaite Rite* (Ramleh, 1971), vol. I, p. 107. It is reasonable, therefore, to assume that the excerpts from the Psalms on our quire may have served originally in connection with the public reading of the Torah performed in the tenth-century Karaite synagogue. It should be noted, however, that the verse "Blessed are Thou, O Lord, teach me thy statutes (119:12), appears also in the Gemarah, in some versions of the Torah benedictions (*Berakhot* 11b), but is not included in the Rabbinic Siddur. See J. Heinemann, *Prayer in the Period of the Tanna'im and the Amora'im: Its Nature and its Patterns* (Jerusalem, 1978), p. 105, note 14 (in Hebrew).

developed by his Karaite followers.[10] The verses on the quire could, therefore, attest the longing for national redemption and for the return to Zion through the Karaite belief.

The importance of these phrases to the Karaites of the tenth century is further substantiated by the fact that they can be found on carpet pages of three other biblical fragments from the same period — two single leaves from the Second Firkovitch Collection, and a third loose leaf found together with the Moshe ben Asher Codex of the Prophets in the Karaite Synagogue in Cairo. An examination of the two first leaves shows that one of them (Firk. Hebr. II B 270) actually belongs to the famous First Leningrad Pentateuch written in 929 in Palestine or Egypt.[11] The measurements and layout, as well as the style of script and decoration of these leaves, are similar to the dedicatory carpet pages of Avraham and Ẓaliaḥ, the sons of Maimon, patrons of the First Leningrad Pentateuch (Fig. 3).[12]

As for the second leaf (Firk. Hebr. II B 263, Fig. 4),[13] Bezalel Narkiss has already established that on stylistic grounds it is close to the dedicatory carpet pages of Aharon ben Avraham — a patron of another biblical manuscript of which only two leaves, both carrying the patron's name, have survived (Fig. 5).[14] Narkiss also noted the resemblance of the latter to those of Avraham and Ẓaliaḥ, the sons of Maimon (Fig. 3).[15]

To this type of decorated carpet page belongs the third single page attached to Ben Asher's Codex (Fig. 6).[16] It resembles particularly the leaf in Fig. 4

Fig. 3. Dedicatory carpet page of Abraham and Ẓaliaḥ sons of Maimon, patron of the First Leningrad Pentateuch, Palestine or Egypt, 929 C.E. St. Petersburg Public Library, Firk. Hebr. II B 17 (after Günzburg, Ornementation, plate IV).

Fig. 4. Carpet page with verses from the Psalms in monumental script from "Aharon ben Avraham Leaves." Palestine or Egypt, mid-tenth century. St. Petersburg Public Library, Firk. Hebr. II B 263.

[10] See Mahler, *Karaites*, p. 225.
[11] The leaf (395 x 348 mm) was first identified as having originally belonged to the First Leningrad Pentateuch (Firk. Hebr. II B 17) by Michal Spielman-Sternthal, a member of the 1992 CJA expedition to St. Petersburg.
[12] Günzburg, *Ornementation*, pl. IV.
[13] See Narkiss, *Hebrew Bibles*, pp. 58–59 and fig. 11. Partial facsimile of this leaf, see Günzburg, *Ornementation*, pl. X,1, where part of the two last lines on the page is shown. Its measurements (322 x 284 mm) do not correspond to the original ones since most of the margins were cropped.
[14] Narkiss, *Hebrew Bibles*, pp. 58–59; Günzburg, *Ornementation*, pl. IX,1–2. The large fragment in this plate (IX,1) contains the patron's full name, Aharon ben Avraham, whereas the small fragment (IX,2) contains only "ben" — part of the patron's name appearing on the second leaf. These two leaves are shelfmarked in the Library as Firk. Hebr. II B 267.
[15] Narkiss, *Hebrew Bibles*.
[16] L. Avrin, "The Illumination of the Moshe Ben Asher Codex of 895 C.E.," Ph.D. Dissertation (University of Michigan, 1974) (University Microfilms, Ann Arbor, 1975), pp. 205–206, pl. 74;

Fig. 6. Carpet page with verses from the Psalms in monumental script. Moshe Ben Asher Codex, Tiberias, 895 C.E., Cairo, Karaite synagogue (after Avrin, Moshe Ben Asher Codex, plate 74).

Fig. 5. Dedicatory carpet pages of "Aharon ben Avraham Leaves." Palestine or Egypt, mid-tenth century. St. Petersburg Public Library, Firk. Hebr. II B 263 (after Günzburg, Ornementation, plate IX, 1).

in its bold display script, the composition of bands connected to each other by fillets, and the ground decoration.

The similarity between the carpet pages from these manuscripts led to the conclusion that they originated in the same school of illumination, probably active in Palestine or Egypt in the mid-tenth century.[17] But whereas the inscription in our quire (Figs. 1–2) is close to these fragments, it differs in having less space between the lines, as well as in the thinner shape of the letters. The side palmettes are somewhat similar to the decoration of the Leningrad Codex from Fustat of ca. 1009 (Firk. Hebr. II B 19a). A later date, possibly the end of the tenth century, could therefore be suggested for our quire.[18]

The three other single leaves mentioned above have other features in common. For one, they contain two of the verses appearing in our quire: "The Lord is great in Zion," etc. (Ps. 99:2) and "The word of the Lord is right," etc. (Ps. 33:4). Moreover they are written on one side of the page leaving the other side blank. It is quite possible that each of these three once constituted the first leaf of a bifolium, with the blank side forming a protective cover on its recto. It is furthermore likely that each of these proposed opening quires was inscribed by additional verses from the Psalms, whose content could have resembled the verses on fol. 2r of our quire.[19]

The verses on our second folio (Fig. 1) add to the Karaite's messianic idea, their views about the Torah. To the blessings of Zion and of the greatness of the Lord they added phrases containing a wish that the Lord, who commanded them to keep the Torah "diligently," will teach them to comprehend its ways. It ends with the twice repeated request: "Teach me thy statutes."

R. Yosef Algamil, תולדות היהדות הקראית (The History of the Karaite Jews) (Ramleh, 1981), v. II, pl. 37, the left figure.

[17] Narkiss, *Hebrew Bibles*, p. 59.

[18] Narkiss, *Hebrew Bibles*, p. 61, suggests dating the quire to the end of the tenth century mainly because of the similarity between the structure and density of our gabled carpet page (fol. 2v) and some of the carpet pages in the Leningrad Codex of ca. 1009 from Fustat.

[19] R. Yosef Algamil the Karaite teacher of Ramlah told me about a single leaf containing another verse "O magnify the Lord with me, and let us exalt his name together" (Ps. 34:4).

The conceptual connection between Torah and redemption is a familiar motif in Karaite writings. One of the sermons of the Jerusalemite tenth-century Karaite Sahl ben Maẓliaḥ says not only that the return to the Written Law hastens Israel's redemption, but the task of doing so is laid upon the shoulders of the Karaites themselves.[20] In a similar way the Karaite scholar Yefeth ben 'Ali (Jerusalem, second half of the tenth century) alludes in his Commentary on the book of Daniel to the time when it will be known to all those loyal to the Rabbanites that the truth is with the Karaite sect and that only this sect can bring the Redemption.[21] These ideas are consistent with the Karaite denial of any religious tradition other than the Bible. Their contention contradicts the Talmudic tradition, according to which the Oral Law is essential for the understanding of the scriptures and that the authority of the Bible depends on it.

This difference from the Rabbinic tradition is deeply rooted in the Karaite sect. One generation after Anan, the Karaite commentator Daniel al-Qumiṣi (Jerusalem, end of the ninth century), in his Commentary on the Minor Prophets (Malachi 2:8–9), admonishes the leaders of the Diaspora that by exchanging Moses' Written Law with the Oral Law they have diverted from the way of God and failed the people of Israel.[22] Like Daniel al-Qumiṣi, Salmon ben Yeruḥim (Jerusalem, mid-tenth century) argues against the Rabbanites that the belief that the Oral Law was given to Moses on Mount Sinai together with the Written Law is essentially a misconception.[23] His complaint is directed particularly at R. Saadyah

Gaon, the Karaite's chief adversary, that he and his laws diminish the people's hope for redemption, thus impeding the rebuilding of the Temple.[24]

There was also a point of contention between the Karaites and the Rabbanites over the question of vocalization and intonation of the signs of the Bible. The Karaites believe that a strict adherence to the Torah includes keeping the rules of vocalization and notation, which were given to Moses on Mount Sinai, and are hence as sacred as the Torah itself. The Karaite Yehudah Hadassi, in his comprehensive law book *Eshkol ha-Kofer* (Constantinople, 1148) claims that God handled the Tablets of Covenant to Moses already vocalized and accentuated and therefore, in his opinion, Torah books that are written unvocalized are lacking and imperfect, since it is written "the commandment of the Lord is pure, enlightening the eyes" (Ps. 19:8).[25] We may thus assume that the biblical text which contained our quire originally included all the vocalizations, notations and the whole Massoretic compendium.

The Karaite practice of manifesting their views through biblical quotations is further expressed in the choice of verses, which they repeatedly copied in micrographic script in numerous decorated carpet pages; for example on the carpet page with the depiction of the Temple in our quire (Fig. 7).[26] In this carpet page the outline of the small triangle surmounting the gable consists of the words "The Lord is great in Zion; and He is high above all the people" (Ps. 99:2), and "Blessed be the Lord God of Israel" (Ps. 41:13). The small lozenge in the upper left corner is

[20] Sahl ben Maẓliaḥ, ס׳ תוכחת מגלה לר׳ סהל הכהן (An Epistle to Jacob ben Samuel, pupil of Saadyah Gaon), in S. Pinsker, לקוטי קדמוניות: להורות דת בני מקרא והלטעראטור שלהם; *Lickute Kadmoniot* (Wien, 1860, Jerusalem, 1968), Appendix II, p. 36: כי לא נראה מלכות בית דוד ע״ה (עליו השלום) כי אם בשובנו ובהשיבנו את ישראל אל ה׳ אלהיהם, כי לא תהיה לנו תקוה ולא נראה ישועה כי אם בתשובה שלמה, ולא תהיה לנו תשובה כי אם על ידי גיבורי התורה והמקרא.

[21] Quoted by S. W. Baron, *A Social and Religious History of the Jews* (Philadelphia, 1958), VI, p. 509.

[22] Daniel al-Qumiṣi, פתרון שנים עשר *Commentarius in Librum Duodecim Prophetarum*, ed. I.D. Markon (Jerusalem, 1948), p. 78: יואתמ׳ יא (הוי) כהני בית שני ורועי הגלות ׳סרתם׳ מדרכי ה׳. הכשלתם רבים בתורה, כי שמתם מכשול לפני ישראל בחלוף המצות, ותאמרו: זאת מן התו׳ (התורה). על כן ׳שחתם׳ והפרתם את ׳ברית הלוי׳, וגם אני שמתי פני אתכם ׳נבזים ושפלים׳ בעיני הגוים, יען כי נשאתם ׳פנים בתורה׳, שאתם הרימותם את הפירושים (הבלתי צודקים, אלגוריות) בתורה, כי אמרתם, כי יש ארבעים ותשע פנים (ירושלמי סנהדרין פ״ד ה״ב) בפתרון התורה.

[23] Salmon ben Yeruḥim, ספר מלחמות ה׳, *Book of the Wars of the*

Lord, ed. I. Davidson (New York, 1934), Part 1, pp. 37–38: לתורת הכתב נאמין באמונה, כי באמת מימין שדי נתונה, כעדת כל עדת שושנה (הוא כינוי לקראים) המפוזרת בכל מדינה ומדינה... צור נתן שתי תורות כאמרתכם, אחת בכתב ואחת בפיהם, אם הוא כדבריכם, נמצא שקר ומרדות במעשיכם.

[24] Salmon ben Yeruḥim, *Wars*, Part 11, pp. 96–97: שועת בת עמי בכח קולה, לא די לה כובד עלה, עד שבאת גם אתה לסכסך בתוך קהלה, ולפתותה בחקקי און להמעיד רגלה. תקוה עדת ישראל כלם, תשועתם ועזרתם ונהולם, ובנין המקדש וההיכל ואולם, לעכב באת ולהזניחם כצדיקיהו וכאחאב מלך אשר קלם.

[25] Yehudah Hadassi, *Eshkol ha-Kofer, Cluster of Henna. Encyclopedia of Karaite Lore Arranged According to the Decalogue* (Gozlow, 1836), p. 60b, Alphabet 163: כי כן היו גם לחות הברית ננקדין בנקוד ובטעמים, כי אם אינם באות לא יכולנו להבין עבר ועתיד ועומד ויוצא ומצדד... וכל ספרי תורה ככה ראויים להיות בנקוד וטעמים, כי בלא הם לא נתנם האלהים. וככל הספרים הנכתבי׳ ולא ננקדים חסרים הם ולא תמימי׳ כצווי נותן תעודה, ככתוב: תורת ה׳ תמימה משיבת נפש (בכתוב: נפש — תהלים יט ח).

[26] Günzburg, *Ornamentation*, pl. XI.

outlined by: "Thou art good, and doest good; teach me thy statutes" (Ps. 119:68), and the vertical rectangle underneath is surrounded by: "Blessed art thou, O Lord; teach me thy statutes" (Ps. 119:12). The remnant of the rectangle on the right is likewise surrounded by: "Thou hast commanded us to keep thy precepts diligently" (Ps. 119:4).[27] The outline of the Temple itself consists of recitations from the book of Proverbs.

An assemblage of quotations from Psalms and Proverbs are repeated also in a carpet page from the Fragments of Mevorakh ben Ẓedaqah (Fig. 9).[28] The micrography of the upper curved line of the gate (lower right) repeat Ps. 99:2 and 33:4, while the continuation of the arch consists of other citations from Psalms and Proverbs. In the same way the outer frame of a carpet page from the Second Leningrad Pentateuch (Fig. 10),[29] likewise consists of verses from Ps. 119 in micrography, while in the spandrels and inside the tympanum of the gate appears the verse from Ps. 99:2.[30]

Another example is a carpet page from "Firkovitch's Eight Leaves," in whose outer frame (read from the upper right hand corner) appear the verses from Ps. 99:2, 41:13 and 33:4. The rest of the inscription is defaced and only the words "teach me thy statutes" (Ps. 119:68) can be deciphered.[31]

From the foregoing examples we must conclude that the repetitive use of the same verses, so conspicuously integrated in the decoration of these carpet pages, testify that they originated from Karaite Pentateuchs that were written and illuminated by Karaites and for Karaites. At this point we may summarize Nehemia Allony's ideas, who regarded the compiled, vocalized

and accentuated codices, such as the First Leningrad Pentateuch, as proper Karaite books, designated for reading in the Synagogue. He maintains, moreover, that while the Rabbanites object to the reading of the Torah from a vocalized and notated book, the Karaites object to public reading from an unvocalized scroll of the Torah. The Rabbanites' decisive objection to a vocalized and notated codex was the result of the Karaites' total rejection of the Mishnah, the Talmud, the Aggadah and the Midrash.[32]

Considering the above, the carpet page with the gabled structure in our quire (fol. 2v, Fig. 7) should now be examined for Karaite characteristics aside from the content of the inscriptions.

It has been observed by art historians that this gabled structure reveals shapes familiar from a pictorial tradition that prevailed after the destruction of the Second Temple, for example in clay oil lamps from the second and third centuries C.E. and in gold glasses from the fourth century. Likewise, a certain formal resemblance is found between our structure and Torah Arks on mosaic floors.[33] The most famous example is that on the floor of the Beit Alpha synagogue from the sixth century (Fig. 11). In both depictions there is a gabled rectangular structure, embellished with geometric and floral motifs.[34] But it seems that most early Jewish depictions contain some added objects or architectural elements belonging to the Temple and its implements. Furthermore, it is not always clear whether the depiction pertains to the façade of an ark or of a temple. Thus, for example, scholars differ in their interpretations of a structure painted on a well-known gold glass in the Vatican (Fig. 12).[35]

---

[27] There are many more verses in the decoration of this page, for example from Ps. 119: "The law of thy mouth is better unto me than thousands of gold and silver" (v. 72); "Thy righteousness is an everlasting righteousness, and thy law is the truth" (v. 142).

[28] Günzburg, *Ornementation*, pl. XIII,1. This is a second leaf out of six originating from two separate biblical manuscripts (Firk. Hebr. II B 262). In the center of this page appears a dedicatory inscription of the patron Mevorakh ben Ẓedaqah. See Narkiss, *Hebrew Bibles*, pp. 61–63. After our examination of this leaf (395 x 348 mm.) in the St. Petersburg Public Library we realized that it undoubtedly belongs to the Pentateuch Firk. Hebr. II B 10, written probably in the middle of the tenth century, in Palestine or Egypt. Mevorakh is probably the patron of the B 10 Pentateuch. Narkiss connects B 10 mistakenly with the Natan'el Pentateuch (I B 111); see ibid, pp. 53–56.

[29] Günzburg, *Ornementation*, pl. XVI,1. The Second Leningrad Pentateuch (Firk. Hebr. II B 8) was copied in 951 in Palestine or North Africa. See Narkiss, *Hebrew Bibles*, pp. 64–67.

[30] It is written by a different hand. Narkiss discovered that on the other side of this page appears the beginning of the book of Genesis (*Hebrew Bibles*, p. 66 and fig. 18). It is likely, therefore, that the Second Leningrad Pentateuch originally contained at its beginning pages with monumental inscriptions, which were later lost, and someone copied the first verse from Ps. 99:2 onto the extant carpet page now opening the Pentateuch.

[31] Narkiss, *Hebrew Bibles*, pp. 56–58 and fig 8.

[32] N. Allony, רמב״ם בן אשר ובן בויאאע משמשים כתר ארם צובא, *Tarbiz*, Jubilee Volume (Jerusalem, 1981), I, pp. 369–70.

[33] E. Revel-Neher, *L'arche d'alliance dans l'art juif et chrétien du second au dixième siècle* (Paris, 1984), pp. 137–38, fig. 53.

[34] See also the gabled structures in the mosaic floors of Hammath-Tiberias, fourth century C.E. (ibid. fig. 48), and Beit She'an, fifth century C.E. (ibid., fig. 50).

[35] See A. St. Clair, "God's House of Peace in Paradise: The Feast of Tabernacles on a Jewish Gold Glass," *Journal of Jewish Art* 11 (1985), 6–15, and Figs. 1–2.

Fig. 7.   Ezekiel's Temple Plan. Egypt, late tenth century. St. Petersburg Public Library, Firk. Hebr. II B 49, fol. 2v (after Günzburg, Ornementation, plate XI).

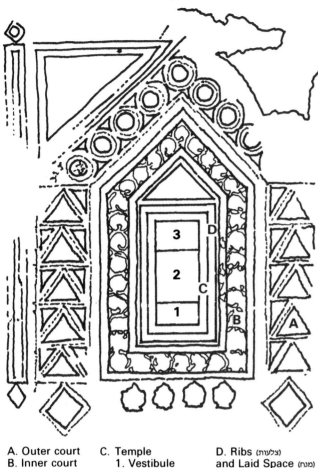

A. Outer court   C. Temple   D. Ribs (צלעות)
B. Inner court   1. Vestibule   and Laid Space (מנה)
               2. Temple hall
               3. Holy of Holies

Fig. 8. Diagram of Ezekiel's Temple plan from the Firkovitch Compilation (fol. 2v).

In any case, the singular depiction of the structure in our quire incorporates particular formal elements

that distinguish it from the earlier examples, and should therefore not be considered just a continuation of the old pattern. The main difference lies in the medium. This carpet page, probably from the beginning of a Pentateuch, was made in a novel technique, using micrography to outline the decoration. Consisting of verses that reflect the association made by the Karaites between the Bible and the Temple, the micrographic decoration may thus suggest the depiction of a temple rather than an ark. The fact that the verses in the outlines of the structure itself are from Proverbs which, according to chapter 25:1 was written by Solomon, the builder of the first Temple, may help to identify it as a temple.

Support for this assumption is found in some Karaite literary sources, which express their attitudes concerning the ark and the Temple. Daniel al-Qumiṣi, in his Commentary on Hosea (3:4) and Micah (5:12) admonished the Jewish practice of worshiping the Torah Ark by bowing to it, claiming that it follows the customs of idolaters, in contrast to the words "And thou shalt no more worship the work of thy hands" (Micah 5:12).[36] It seems plausible that the Karaites by that period would have refrained from drawing the ark as a single image in their Pentateuch.

The Karaite's attitude toward the Temple is elucidated in other literary sources, indicating that the messianic Temple will be the one in Ezekiel's vision rather than the edifices which were actually erected in Jerusalem — neither the First Temple, and certainly not the Second Temple, neither the one built by Zerubabel nor its replacement by Herod.[37] Yehudah Hadassi explains this position by arguing that none of the rewards promised to the people of Israel — the coming of the Messiah, the rebuilding of the temple

---

36   Daniel al-Qumisi, *Commentarius*, Hosea 3:4, p. 5: (הרבניים) והם הציבו מצבות בבתי כנסיותיהם וישימו את ארון והיא מצבה והם משתחוים לו, כי לא יבינו. ובזאת תדע כי כן, כי לא היה בכל גבול ישראל (לפני חורבן הבית) ארון להשתחוות לו, כי אם ארון ברית ה', והם שמו בכנסיותיהם במדינות רבות בכל כניסה וכניסה (כנסיה וכנסיה) ארון. וכתי ויאין אפוד ותרפי'. Later in the same context (on Micah 5:13), p. 46, he expatiated more fully on the opposition to use of the Ark made by the Rabbanites: איה היום מצבות בין ישראל חוץ מן התבות אשר בכל כנסיות בגלות, ומציבים לנגדם להשתחוות לפניה וקוראים בשם ארון. וגם בימי חג הסכות לוקחים לולב ומסובבים סביב וגם נשאים (כנראה את ספרי־התורה) על כתפם בהודות והלל סביבות הכניסת במועדים... ולא תשתחוה עוד למעשה ידיך', כי הם משתחוים היום לספר התורה בהוציאם מן הבית (אולי ר"ל: מן התיק שהספר מונח בו), וגם משתחוים לארון.

37   The essence of their contradicting views regarding the Second Temple and its spiritual world is brought by the Moslem writer

al-Makrizi (1364–1442), whose words, according to Pinsker, (*Lickute Kadmoniot*, v. I, pp. 7–8), are based on the Karaite sources themselves: אמנם הרבניים... מגדילים מעלת בית שני, שבנו שנית אחרי שובם מהגולת והחריבו טיטוס, וחשבוהו בקדשה ובמעלה ובחשיבות כמו הבית האי שהתחיל בבניינו דוד, ושלמה ע"ה השלימו ונבוכדנצר החריבו, ונעשה כאילו נקראו בעלי דת שניה, וזאת הכת (!) היא שהיתה נוהגת עפ"י מה שבמשנה, שנכתבה בטבריה אחר חורבן הבית ע"י טיטוס וסומכת במצות התורייות על מה שהוא בתלמוד עד זמנם זה... ואמנם הקראים והם בני מקרא, כלומר הקוראים, והם אינם סומכים כלל על בית שני כ"א (כי אם) על מה שהיה המנהג בבית ראשון, וכאילו נקראים בעלי דת הראשונה, אין מכירים אלא נוסח התורה, ואינם שמים לב לדעת מי שמתנגד לה ועומד על פשט התורה זולת הקבלה מן הקדמונים, וביניהם ובין הרבנים שנאה גדולה עד שאינם משתדכין ביניהם ואינם משיחין זע"ז (זה עם זה), ואינם נכנסין אלו לאלו בבי"הכ (בבתי הכנסת) שלהם, וכו'.

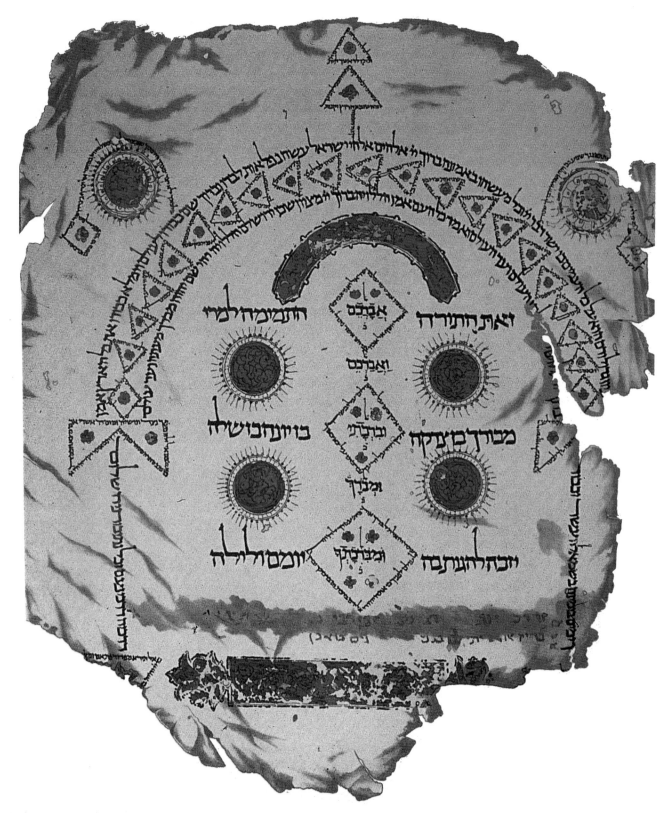

Fig. 9.   Dedicatory carpet of the original patron of "Mevorakh ben Zedaqah Fragments," with biblical verses in micrography. Palestine or Egypt, mid-tenth century. St. Petersburg Public Library, Firk. Hebr. II B 262, fol. 2r (after Günzburg, Ornementation, plate XIII, 1).

Fig. 10.   Dedicatory carpet page of the Yeshuʻah brothers, with biblical verses in micrography outlining the gate, and display script in the tympanum and the spandrels, Second Leningrad Pentateuch, Palestine, 951 C.E. St. Petersburg Public Library, Firk. Hebr. II B 8, fol. 1r (after Günzburg, Ornementation, plate XVI, 1).

Fig. 11.   Gabled Torah Ark, mosaic floor, Beit Alpha synagogue, sixth century, upper register (after E.L. Sukenik, The Ancient Synagogue of Beth Alpha, Jerusalem, 1932).

Fig. 12.   Gold glass fragment (drawing), fourth century. Vatican City, Museo Sacro (after De Rossi, Archives de l'orient latin, II, 1884, plate facing p. 439).

and the repatriation of Israel — were fulfilled during the Second Temple.[38]

This Karaite view contradicts Rabbinical tradition in which the Second Temple occupies a central position. Mishnah *Middot* describes the last Temple in detail: the measurements, shape, buildings and gates, chambers and cells. In the Babylonian Talmud (*Sukkah* 51a) it is said, moreover, that whoever did not

[38]   Hadassi, *Eshkol ha-Kofer*, p. 93a, Alphabet 223: יען כי כלל הבשורות
והנחמות וההבטחות לא נתקיימו בבית שני לנו. לא ביאת אליהו ז"ל ולא ביאת
משיחנו, ולא ביאת כבוד אלהינו בבית מקדשנו (על־פי יחזקאל, מג ב ואילך)
ולא רוח הקדש ולא ארון ה' ולא כרוביו, ולא כלים הגנוזים כלי מקדשנו
בית תפארתנו ולא כהנים באורים ותומי' (על־פי עזרא ב סג; נחמיה ז סה)
וכלל הבשורות ברכות של ארצנו, ולא כל קבוץ מוגלינו, ולא בנין מקדשנו
בפרך וספירים (על־פי ישעיהו נד יא) ולחומת אש סביב עליו (על־פי זכריה
ב ט) כנבואת יחזקאל (!) נביאנו, ולא המעיין מבית ה' יצא לשעשועינו,
ככתוב ינהר פלגיו ישמחו (תהלים מו ה') וגו', ולא שבת אחים גם יחד כל
אי ואי (אחד ואחד) שבט בנחלתנו. לכן לא סרו הצומות והאבלות ממנו,
ובעת שיתקיימו לנו אז יוסרו כל עניי אבלות גלותך. Z. Ankori, in
Karaites in Byzantium: The Formative Years, 970–1100 (New
York-Jerusalem, 1959), p. 28, says that Hadassi's *Eshkol ha-*

Kofer is perhaps the most widely quoted manual of Karaite ways and beliefs. It was long acclaimed as an inexhaustible treasury of early texts and discussions and as the definitive record of spiritual achievement by four centuries of Karaite endeavor. Pinsker in *Lickute Kadmoniot*, vol. I, p. 223, notes that Hadassi's book was composed in keeping with the book ביתן המשכילים of Nissi ben Noah (probablly 11th century) and borrowed from writings of the early Karaites. Pinsker adds that in Hadassi's polemics against the Rabbanites he repeats the words of Salmon ben Yeruḥim, Yefeth ben 'Ali, Sahl ben Maẓliaḥ, Ḥassan ben Mashiaḥ and others. I therefore assume that Hadassi's messianic writings quoted in this paper follow those of his predecessors.

see the Temple built by Herod did not see a beautiful building in his life.

It is true, however, that the Rabbis of the Mishnah refer to Ezekiel's building as the future messianic Temple.[39] Rashi too, in his Commentary on Ezekiel (Chapters 40–48), writes more than once that the future Temple is that which the prophet drew in his vision.[40] Nevertheless, the Talmudists studied the measurements of the Second Temple, as explained by Maimonides, in order to know how to build the future Temple, since the book of Ezekiel is not explicit enough.[41]

Although the messianic content of the aspiration for the repatriation of Israel and for the rebuilding of the Temple is similar in both Karaite and Rabbinical faith, the main disparity is about the shape of the future Temple. Already at the beginning of the tenth century Salmon ben Yeruḥim, from the Jerusalem Karaite school, expressed the opinion that the Third Temple will be the visionary and not the historical one. In his poetic epistle against Rabbanism (Saadyah Gaon), *Book of The Wars of the Lord*, he quotes the common arguments against Talmudic tradition and ends the book with rhymes expressing his hope for the rebuilding of the Temple and the renewal of its rituals in times to come. The biblical recitations given

in these rhymes reveal that he meant Ezekiel's Temple.[42] In the second half of the tenth century, Yefeth ben 'Ali, in his hitherto unpublished Commentary to the Book of Ezekiel, called the prophet's Temple בית עתיד (future Temple).[43]

The Karaites did not agree about the future Temple. In the fringe areas of the Karaites' dispersion it was thought that a new temple would never be rebuilt. In the introduction to his *Book of Lights*, the Karaite Jacob al-Qirqisani tells that some of the Karaites of Khurasan and Gibal (Elam and Media east of Persia) believed that the Messiah, whose coming had been promised, had already come and that the only Temple was the one built by Zerubabel.[44]

A clear opposition to such opinions may be found in Hadassi's *Eshkol ha-Kofer*. While recounting the fifty-four wonders that God will perform for his people in the days of the Messiah, he says in the second wonder that God will gather the People of Israel from four corners of the earth and will not leave a single person in the Diaspora as prophesied by Ezekiel (39:28). Hadassi then argues once again that this could not have happened during the time of the Second Temple because then only "forty and two thousand three hundred and threescore" people gathered in Jerusalem (Ezra, 2:64).[45] In his fifteenth

---

[39] For example *Middot* 2:5, dealing with the shape of the Women's Chambers, says: ולא היו מקורות (מקורות) וכך הן עתידות להיות (בימות המשיח), שנאמר (יחזקאל מו כא-כב), ...מקצוע החצר חצרות קטרות. ואין Likewise *Middot* 2:6, dealing with קטרות אלא שאינן מקרות, וכו' the "Water Gate": ולמה נקרא שמו שער המים? שבו מכניסין צלוחית של מים של נסוך בחג. רבי אליעזר בן יעקב אומר: ובו המים מפכים ועתידין להיות יוצאין מתחת מפתן הבית (על-פי יחזקאל מז א-ב).

[40] Commenting on "ורחב הצלע ארבע אמות" ("and the breadth of every side-chamber four cubits," Ez. 41:5), Rashi writes: ושל בית שני היה שש (אמות). ועל כרחך בית זה לעתיד לבא. שהרי בית שני לא היתה חומה מפסקת לבית קדש הקדשים. See also his Commentary on Ez. 40:48; 41:3,5,6,12; 43:14,15; 44:2.

[41] Maimonides, *Mishneh Torah* (Rules of the Temple), 1:4: וכן בנין העתיד להבנות, אף-על-פי שהוא כתוב ביחזקאל — אינו מפרש ומבואר. Also in his introduction to the Mishna he explains the need for the measurements of the Second Temple as given in the tractate *Middot*: והביא אחר 'תמיד' — 'מידות': ואין בו ענין אחר אלא סיפור, שהוא זוכר (מתאר) מידת המקדש וצורתו ובנינו וכל ענינו. והתועלת שיש בענין ההוא, כי כשיבנה במהרה בימינו, יש לשמור ולעשות התבנית ההיא והערך ההוא (הגדול היחסי), מפני שהוא ברוח הקודש.

[42] Salmon ben Yeruhim, *Wars*, Part 17, pp. 130–31: ברוך תמים דעים שהבדילנו מן התועים (כוונתו לרבניים) ונתן לנו (הקראים) תורתו שעשועים, וחיי עולם לעמו הנעים. ירחם ביתו הנאדר בגבורותיו, ויחיש לנו עם בשרותיו, ויבנה ביתו וישכלל חומותיו, כנס (או כנם) בצורת הבית בתרותיו. רצפה (יחזקאל מ יז-יח) ואולם וחצרות (שם, מא טו ואולמי החצר), ושתי לשכות האמורות (שם, מב מב ה-ו), אשר ביופוי ונאי נהדרות, וגדרת הגינה (שם מב יב), גבים ושדרות (מלכים א, ו ט). ואולם והיכל המפורשים (בספר יחזקאל), יפדה מצרימו חבושים, ובני צדוק הכהנים הקדושים, אשר שמרו את משמרת

[43] A fifteenth-century copy of Yefeth ben 'Ali's Commentary exists in the British Library, Or. Ms. 5062; and a microfilm in the Institute of Microfilmed Hebrew Manuscripts of the Jewish National and University Library in Jerusalem, no. 6455. I wish to express my gratitude to Professor Haggai ben Shammai, who kindly furnished this additional information.

[44] Jacob al-Qirqisani, *Book of Lights*. Quoted by Ben-Zion Dinur, ישראל בגולה מימי כיבוש ארץ-ישראל על-ידי הערבים עד מסעי הצלב (Tel Aviv, 1961), vol. I.2, p. 267: ומן הקראים של חיוראסאן ואל-גיבאל [יש] מי שסוברים, כי המשיח, שבואו הובטח, כבר בא, ושבית-המקדש הוא [רק זה] שבנה אותו זרובבל ולא נשאר זולתו.

[45] Hadassi, *Eshkol ha-Kofer*, p. 153a, b, Alphabet 377, wonder 2: כי יוציאם ה' מגלותם ויקבצם מד' כנפות הארץ ולא ישאיר בגולה עד אחד, כתוב וכנסתיו על אדמתם ולא אותיר עוד מהם שם' (יחזקאל לט כח) איש. אם כן על זה וכמוהו אם יטען טוען ויאמר כי זה נהיה בבית שני, אין כדבריו. כי בבית שני לא נקבצו בירושלי' כי אם ארבע רבו ושני אלפים, שנאמר 'כל הקהל כארבע רבוא וגו' מבחור זקן וישיש' (על-פי עזרא ב סד; נחמיה ז סו)

התורה אל ה' הנגשים (על-פי יחזקאל מד טו). חגים וזבחים וכל קרבנות, יקריבו בשירים וזמירות וגגינות, והלוים בשרותם קול אחד הוגים ברננות, ושרים כחוללים כל מעיניו (תהלים פז ז). ישיב שבות אהלי יהודה וישראל כבתחלה, ויהיו לאחדים ולא יחצו עוד לשני גוים, גוי אחד עם סגולה, ונבנתה העיר על תלה (ירמיה ל יח), ויקיים 'הנני מרביץ בפוך אבניך' (ישעיהו נד יא) אל נורא עלילה. מלך ביפיו תחזינה עיניו, ואליהו תשבני נביאנו, וישיב לב אבות על בנים בימינו, ולב בנים על אבות ליתורת ה' תמימה' (תהלים יט ח), תורה אחת היא לכלנו כדמותינו. Also according to Ezekiel (44:15; 48:11) only the sons of Zadok will be allowed to serve as priests and to enter the Temple, to approach the altar and offer sacrifices.

13   *14*

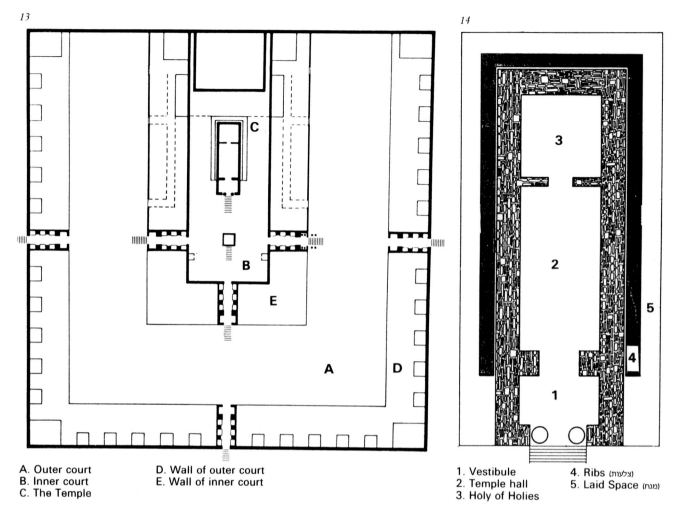

A. Outer court   D. Wall of outer court
B. Inner court   E. Wall of inner court
C. The Temple

1. Vestibule   4. Ribs (צלעות)
2. Temple hall   5. Laid Space (מנח)
3. Holy of Holies

Fig. 13.   *Plan of Ezekiel's Temple and courts (after Haran, Ezekiel, plate on p. 217).*
Fig. 14.   *Plan of Ezekiel's Temple (after Haran, Ezekiel, plate on p. 213).*

wonder he continues the prophetic vein and states explicitly that the Temple will be built as explained by Ezekiel (40–48).[46]

In view of the above cited sources it may be assumed that the gabled structure in our quire (fol. 2v in the Firkovitch Compilation, II B 49) is based on Ezekiel's Temple (Fig. 7). While there is still a difference between the general messianic contents to a pictorial description of Ezekiel's Temple with all its details, it is quite possible that there was an immediate Karaite source, whether literary of visual, from which

the artist of this "Firkovitch Temple Plan" borrowed his depiction. In any case, by studying ground plans for the reconstruction of Ezekiel's Temple provided by modern research, one may discern in our illumination some basic forms that follow the description in Ezekiel 40–48.

I shall now compare the Firkovitch Temple plan (Figs. 7 & 8) to some of these reconstructions, focusing mainly on the plans drawn by Menahem Haran to elucidate his commentary on Ezekiel (Figs. 13–14).[47] Plans by other researchers will likewise be considered,

[46]   Hadassi, *Eshkol ha-Kofer*, p. 153b, Alphabet 378, wonder 15:
כי בית המקדש יבנה עוד ביופיו ותכונתו ומוצאיו ושעריו וקדושת מקומותיו כאשר הוא מבואר ע״י יחזקאל נביאנו ע״ה. Compare Ez.
43:10–12: אתה בן אדם הגד את בית ישראל את הבית, ויכלמו מעוונותיהם ומדדו את תכנית. ואם נכלמו מכל אשר עשו, צורת הבית ותכונתו ומוצאיו ומובאיו וכל צורתו ואת כל חקתיו וכל צורתו וכל תורתו הודע אותם וכתב לעיניהם וישמרו את כל צורתו ואת כל חקתיו ועשו אותם. זאת תורת הבית

וכו׳.

[47]   M. Haran, *The World of the Bible Encyclopedia: "Ezekiel"* (Jerusalem, 1984, in Hebrew), pp. 204–18 and plans on pp. 213 and 217. While explaining his plan, the precise location of each item will be pointed out by means of inserted lettering. I am grateful to Prof. Menahem Haran for his helpful comments.

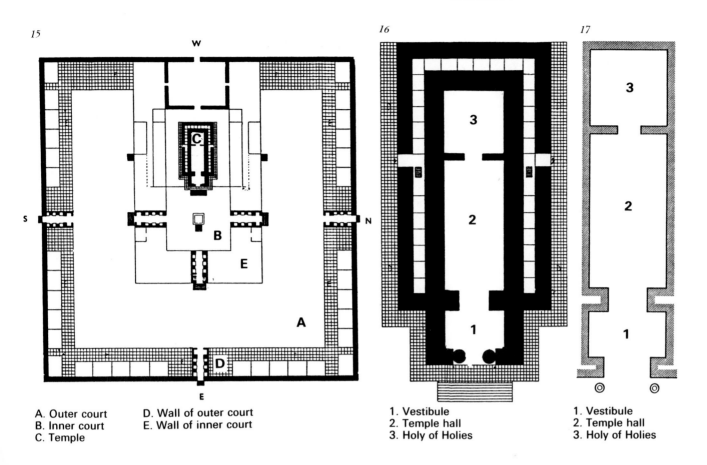

Fig. 15. Plan of Ezekiel's Temple courts (after Cooke, Ezekiel, fig. II, after fol. 541).
Fig. 16. Plan of Ezekiel's Temple (after Cooke, Ezekiel, fig. III, after fol. 541).
Fig. 17. Plan of Ezekiel's Temple (after Zimmerli, Ezekiel, vol. 2, fig. 5).

providing their features correspond to the Firkovitch Plan. It should be pointed out, however, that the scholars disagree on the interpretation of some obscure details from Chapters 40-48, and seek help in versions other than the Massoretic text of the book of Ezekiel, mainly from the Septuagint. There is no need to dwell here on the differences between them, as long as there is a similarity between their reconstructions and the most conspicuous forms of the stylized structure in our depiction, namely the division of the Temple area into three main zones and the shape of the Temple building in the center of the Firkovitch Plan.

According to Ezekiel's visionary plan, the Temple area is divided into three levels, one inside the other: the outer court, the inner court and the Temple. Each level rises above the one surrounding it. There are seven steps from the outer gates, eight from the gates

to the inner court, and the Temple itself is raised ten stairs.[48] The variable heights of the levels and the gates are not shown in the Firkovitch Temple Plan, but the three zones are clearly discernible and are distinguished by their color and decoration. Disregarding the gable on top of the Firkovitch Plan, the wide exterior band, decorated with triangles (A on Firkovitch Plan, Fig. 8), may correspond to the outer court (A on Haran's plan, Fig. 13); the inner band decorated with a palmette scroll (B on Fig. 8) may correspond to the inner court (B on Fig. 13), and the elongated rectangle at the center of the Firkovitch Plan (C on Fig. 8) may correspond to the Temple building reconstructed by Haran (C on Fig. 13, and Fig. 14). This division also agrees to

[48] Haran, *Ezekiel*, p. 205.

a large extent with other ground plans, such as those reconstructed by Cooke (Figs. 15, 16).[49]

The outer court (A in Haran's plan, Fig. 13) is in the shape of a square (five hundred square cubits, Ez. 42:17-20; 45:2), and is surrounded by a heavy wall (D on Fig. 13).[50] The wide outer band A in the Firkovitch Plan may perhaps depict the heavy wall around the court rather than the court itself, as previously suggested. Although it does not extend to the lower part of the Firkovitch Plan as the eastern side in Haran's plan or in Cooke's (Fig. 15), it is clearly based on the square shape of the Temple court.

The inner court according to Ezekiel (40:47) is also square (one hundred square cubits), but if it has to incorporate the Temple, Haran suggests that it must have been an elongated rectangle extended further to the west (B on Fig. 13) and surrounded by a thick wall (E on Fig. 13).[51] It is therefore interesting to find in the Firkovitch Temple Plan that the inner court (B on Fig. 8) is also elongated rather than square, and here also it may represent the wall rather than the court.

The resemblance between the interior of the Temple building in the Firkovitch Plan and in Haran's plans is more convincing. Ezekiel's building is divided into three: the Vestibule (1 on Fig. 14), the Temple Hall (2) and the Holy of Holies (3).[52] According to Ezekiel the length of the Vestibule is twenty cubits and it is twelve cubits wide. The Temple Hall measures 40 x 20 cubits and the Holy of Holies 20 x 20 cubits.[53] These proportions of the Temple's three parts are reflected in the reconstructed plans as well as in the Firkovitch Temple, where the Hall, a dark rectangle in the center (2 on Fig. 8), is larger than the Vestibule below it (1) and the Holy of Holies above it (3). Furthermore, the size of the Holy of Holies, being square, is larger than the rectangular proportions

of the Vestibule. It should also be compared to a reconstruction of the Temple building in Zimmerli's exegesis to Ezekiel (Fig. 17, nos. 1,2,3), showing the same proportions.[54]

Other features in the Firkovitch Plan probably follow Ezekiel's text: there are doors at the entries to the Vestibule and to the Holy of Holies, and the doors have two leaves (Ez. 41:23-24). It seems that in the Firkovitch Plan the door to the Temple Hall is depicted in the central rectangle (2 on Fig. 8), with two webbed leaves.[55]

In addition, the outside of Ezekiel's building is decorated with wooden "ribs" (צלעות, Ez. 41:5-9) probably serving as panelling.[56] The inside is likewise panelled with wood, and is carved with Cherubim and palm-trees (Ez. 17-20). On the outside, along the ribs, the Temple is surrounded with "laid space" (מנח, Ez. 41:9, 11), probably a pavement or a high platform five cubits wide (4 and 5 on Fig. 14).[57] It is suggested that the three thin bands in the Firkovitch Plan, surrounding the Temple building from the outside (D on Fig. 8), depict the ribs and the laid space: two inner bands for the ribs and a third one, on the outside, for the laid space. However, contrary to the text in Ezekiel, which says that only the ribs were decorated, here the laid space is decorated as well. Similarly, instead of the Cherubim and palm-trees there are floral and geometric motifs: a foliate scroll for the inner band, a guilloche motif for the middle band and a double chain for the outer band with a stylized flower in each of the four corners.

The floral motifs, here as well as in the decoration of the inner court and in the spandrels, may perhaps hint at the palm trees in Ezekiel. It is also possible that the absence of Cherubim in the Firkovitch Plan reflects the Karaite way of implementing the Second Commandment, "Thou shalt have no other gods be-

[49] G.A. Cooke, *A Critical and Exegetical Commentary on the Book of Ezekiel* (Edinburgh, 1970), figs. II and III on page 542.

[50] Haran, *Ezekiel*, p. 205. Both Haran's and Cooke's plans indicate three gates on three sides of the wall — north, east and south. Since these gates, both here and in the inner court, do not appear in our illumination, I shall not refer to them, although it should be mentioned that in place of the eastern gate (always closed according to Ez. 44:2), four palmettes are depicted here. Haran also mentions that along the wall "by the side of the gates over against the length of the gates" (Ez. 40:18), is a stone pavement and on it are built thirty chambers, probably ten

along each of the court boundaries (D in Fig. 13). These too do not exist in our illumination.

[51] Ibid. p. 211.

[52] Compare 1, 2 and 3 on Fig. 16, Cooke's plan.

[53] Haran, *Ezekiel*, p. 206.

[54] W. Zimmerli, *Ezekiel* (Philadelphia, 1983), vol. 2, fig. 5 on p. 357.

[55] Haran, *Ezekiel*, p. 206; Zimmerli, *Ezekiel*, v. II, p. 388.

[56] Haran, *Ezekiel*, p. 206.

[57] Ibid.

fore me" (Ex. 20:3). The latter is exemplified in Nissi ben Noah's extremely severe interpretation which is extended to include any form.[58] This may explain why the artists here refrained from painting any image of the Cherubim. It should further be noted that in the First Leningrad Pentateuch the Cherubim flanking the Ark of the Covenant may be represented by two large leaves (Fig. 18).

Other elements of Ezekiel's Temple do not appear in the Firkovitch Temple Plan. Such details as the division of the Temple ground into elevated levels, the plan of the gates and the form of the large altar in the inner court, constituting an important part in the description of Ezekiel's Temple, are missing in the illustrated plan. In addition, the formal deviation from the square form, as implied in the previously shown plans of modern scholars, should also be mentioned. It seems, therefore, that despite the similarity in the shape of the courts and the sanctuary, there is a basic difference in the overall form, namely in the gable given to the west side of the Temple.

The gable is made in a unique way, consisting of three triangles one inside the other. The inner triangle appears on top of the "sanctuary" itself (C on Fig. 8), the middle one continues the wall of the "inner court" (B), and the outer triangle continues the wall of the "outer court" (A). This gable is not likely to be a roof over the Temple's façade, since the roof of the edifice is never mentioned in Ezekiel's plan. This gable resembles most closely the conventional edifice or gabled Ark prevalent in Late Antiquity, and is what caused most scholars to refer to the Firkovitch Plan as the Ark of Covenant or the Ark of the Law. Could the Karaites have used this ancient motif as a model for their messianic Temple Plan?

A gable is also found in one of the Temple plans of the First Leningrad Pentateuch (fol. 5, Fig. 18). It would need further study to discern the similarity between the two Temples, and the other Temple in the First Leningrad Pentateuch (fol. 4v, Fig. 19).

It would thus seem that the elements of the Temple in the Firkovitch Plan suggest a depiction of a ground plan for Ezekiel's Temple. This observation is as yet a supposition, which may be proven by a pictorial or textual model in Karaite sources yet to be found. Nevertheless the faithfulness of the Firkovitch Plan to the text of Ezekiel in depicting the Temple and its courts may suggest that it is based on early exegeses to Ezekiel, possibly accompanied by suitable drawings, which could have inspired this painting.[59]

---

[58] Nissi ben Noaḥ, פירוש לעשרת הדברים (Commentary on the Ten Commandments) in Pinsker, *Lickute Kadmoniot*, Appendix II, p. 6: הדבור השני ׳לא יהיה לך אלהים אחרים — אלה הדברים וחלופם כל עול ורשע ...ואפוד ותרפים ואלילים ופסילים ומצבה ומסכה וגלולים ועצבים ומפלצות... ובעל ועשתרות ובמות ואשרות ותמונות כל סמלות ודמותות ותבניתות. Compare Hadassi, *Eshkol ha-Kofer*, p. 42a, Alphabet 101: ואל מי תדמיון אל וגו׳ למי תדמיוני ותשוו ותמשילוני ונדמה ...דברו הנצב לעולם היא תורתו התמימה הישרה מחכימת פתי (על־פי תהילים יט ח) ...לכן כל סריס ושטים מחקה נחשבים כעוברים במצוה ׳לא יהיה לך אלהים אחרים על פני ואני ה׳ אלהיך׳ מכליל כל צורה: לא פסל ולא סמל ולא תמונה ולא כוכב מכוכבים לצייירה, ולא שמש ולא ירח שם ברקיעך, זכרון ואבן משכית ואלילים וגלולים, ושקוץ מואב ובשת ובעלים, ועצבים והבלים ושקר ועץ אבן דומם ומפלצת לאשריך, וכי.

[59] One such possible Karaite source may be the 15th century copy of Yefeth ben ʿAli's Commentary on Ezekiel, written in the second half of the tenth century. However, further research is needed to tell whether that commentary can yield data for the reconstruction of such a plan. It should be noted that in the British Library copy is a simple drawing (fol. 182) of three rectangles, one inside the other, probably denoting the altar (Ez. 43:13–17) or the "Ariel" (Ez. 43:15,16) — see above, note 43. This line drawing suggests the possibility that diagrams were integrated into Karaite biblical commentaries. The use of diagrams is a feature of many medieval writers, e.g. Saadyah Gaon (892–942 C.E.), Rashi (ca. 1030–1105 C.E.), and Maimonides (1135–1204 C.E.); see Mayer I. Gruber, "Light on Rashi's Diagrams from the Asher Library of Spertus College of Judaica," *The Solomon Goldman Lectures*, vol. VI (Chicago, 1993), pp. 73–85.

Fig. 18. Plan of the Temple. The First Leningrad Pentateuch, Palestine or Egypt, 929 C.E. St. Petersburg Public Library, Firk. Hebr. II B 17, fol. 5r (after Günzburg, Ornementation, plate III).

Fig. 19. Plan of the Temple. The First Leningrad Pentateuch, Palestine or Egypt, 929 C.E. St. Petersburg Public Library, Firk. Hebr. II B 17, fol. 4v (after Günzburg, Ornementation, plate II).

SCRIBES, PATRONS AND ARTISTS OF ITALIAN ILLUMINATED MANUSCRIPTS IN HEBREW*

Luisa Mortara Ottolenghi

Over the last two decades, historians have repeatedly focused great attention upon the vicissitudes of Jews in Italy during the Middle Ages and the Renaissance. Monographs, papers, meetings, conferences, and source publications have followed in quick succession, providing a far more varied and complex overall view of the events than could have been imagined even in the recent past.

The bibliographies edited first by Attilio Milano and later by Aldo Luzzato and Moshe Moldavi bear witness to this activity.[1] These bibliographies show that as many works were published between 1970 and 1980 as between 1900 and 1970, and that the trend continues; and many of these latter works completely overturn certain deep-rooted opinions, such as that posited by Attilio Milano, that Lombardy had a small Hebrew population in the fifteenth century.[2] The four volumes of documents, *The Jews in the Duchy of Milan*, edited by Shlomo Simonshon, demonstrate that there were a great many towns, suburbs and even small villages in the Duchy of Milan where Jews resided permanently.[3]

In the same way, recent works by Ariel Toaff show that the banker was not always the absolute leader of community life; that Jews handled money in the marketplace, in shops, in factories and in fairs, and not always as pawnbrokers; that Jews in Italy — from at least the late thirteenth until early in the sixteenth century — lived and worked as an accepted minority within the Christian majority in a network of close relationships in all spheres, that they developed a capacity for adaptation to varying circumstances, learning to endure and survive, safeguarding their principles, their own culture, and their religious observances.[4]

In the context of this new approach to the study of the Jewish world in Italy, manuscripts have received new attention. Important catalogues, such as the ones edited by Colette Sirat and Malachi Beit Arí on material characteristics of codices, help to explain methodologies and techniques of manuscript compilation, thus improving locating and dating.[5] Research by many scholars in libraries and collections around the world has uncovered an unexpected trove of Hebrew codices illuminated in Italy; at the same time, several new and valuable works have provided more thorough and documented knowledge of illuminators and schools of illumination previously absent from the history of Italian art.[6]

All these developments have facilitated our study

---

* I wish to thank Anthony Shugaar and Marzia Branca for revising and editing this paper.

[1] A. Milano, *Bibliotheca Historica Italo-judaica* (Florence, 1954); A. Milano, *Bibliotheca Historica Italo-judaica* , Supplement (Florence, 1964); A. Luzzato and M. Moldavi, *Bibliotheca Italo-Ebraica*, ed. D. Carpi (Rome, 1982); A. Luzzato, *Bibliotheca Italo-Ebraica* (Milan, 1989).

[2] A. Milano, *Storia degli ebrei in Italia* (Turin, 1963), p. 205 (henceforth Milano, *Italia*).

[3] S. Simonshon, ed., *The Jews in the Duchy of Milan* (Jerusalem, 1982–1986) (henceforth Simonshon, *Milan*).

[4] A. Toaff, *Il vino e la carne* (Bononia, 1989), passim (henceforth: Toaff, *Il vino*).

[5] C. Sirat, M. Beit Arié, eds., *Manuscrits médiévaux en charactères Hébraiques portant des indications de date jusqu'a 1540* (Paris and Jerusalem, I, 1972; II, 1979; III, 1985) (henceforth Sirat & Beit Arié; M. Beit Arié, *Hebrew Codicology* (Jerusalem, 1981); idem, "Paleographical Identification of Hebrew Manuscripts. Methodology and Practice," *Jewish Art* 12–13 (1986–87), 15–44.

[6] Valentino Pace has done important work on Roman illumination in the thirteenth century: "Codici miniati a Roma al tempo del primo giubileo," in M. Fagiolo and M.L. Madonna, eds., *Roma 1300–1875. L'arte degli anni Santi* (Milan, 1984), pp. 318–322. Alessandro Conti has worked on 14th-century illumination in Bononia: *La miniatura bolognese 1270–1340* (Bononia, 1981). Sandrina Bistoletti Bandera discusses Bonifacio Bembo and Lombard illumination: "Documenti per i Bembo — una bottega di pittori, una citta ducale e gli Sforza," *Arte Lombarda* 80–81–82 (1987), 155–181. Anna Rosa Garzelli, *Miniatura fiorentina del Rinascimento 1440–1525* (Florence, 1985; henceforth *Miniatura*), has done an excellent job of completing the studies on Florentine 15th-century illumination begun by Paolo d'Ancona, *La miniatura fiorentina* (Florence, 1914), and Mirella Levi d'Ancona, *Miniatura e miniatori a Firenze dal XIV al XVI sec.* (Florence, 1962); and Giordana Mariani Canova has studied Venetian illumination: *La miniatura veneta del Rinascimento, 1450–1500* (Venice, 1969).

of manuscripts written in Hebrew characters and illuminated in Italy between the end of the thirteenth and the beginning of the sixteenth century. We have better knowledge of the historical context in which they were produced and of the cultural features of the Hebrew groups living in Italy; these and the relations — positive or negative according to the period — between the Hebrew minority and the Christian majority, all allow us to place these works of art in the context of the society that produced them, providing the various hypotheses set forth in the past with firmer foundations. Moreover, by virtue of civil documentary sources published over time and of the studies in Hebrew onomastics by Vittore Colorni,[7] the possibility of cross-identification of numerous scribes and patrons offers better knowledge of many personages whose names appear in colophons, about whom we have had little more than fanciful attributions to go on. A clearer view of economic roles in society also helps to explain the relations between the Jewish patrons and the Christian artists who, in most cases, saw to the painted embellishment of the codices and are now also better known to us.

The expansion of our knowledge of Hebrew manuscript production in the thirteenth, fourteenth and fifteenth centuries requires a reexamination of some of the issues discussed in previous articles. To this end I shall deal with the substantial group of Hebrew manuscripts written and illuminated in Rome between 1280 and 1320.[8] I will then describe the characteristics of a few scribes and patrons in the fourteenth century, and then cite examples of sumptuous North Italian and Florentine fifteenth-century manuscripts, closing this paper with the examination of a group of codices written in Hebrew for the cultured Christian humanist group of Medician Florence.

Hebrew Manuscripts from Rome

Considerable manuscript copying activity is documented in Rome, beginning from the early decades of the thirteenth century.[9] About the year 1280, it became fashionable to decorate the more important manuscripts with illuminations, often of great beauty, in line with customs previously established in other places of the Western Diaspora. The oldest known French illuminated manuscript with reliable dating and sourcing goes back to 1215.[10] The oldest illuminated manuscript in Germany is probably a commentary by Rashi and others on the Pentateuch (Munich, Bayerische Staatsbibliothek, Cod. Hebr. 5), dated 1233; and of somewhat later date are the splendid Ashkenazi Bibles and the great *mahzorim*.[11] In about 1260, illuminating was begun in the Sephardi realm.[12]

It has often been asked why it became fashionable for the Jews in Europe to embellish their books with paintings only in the first decades of the thirteenth century, while in the Christian world this practice had been in use for centuries. The reason may lie in the association of the Jews with book production which developed at that time around the universities, and resulted in the establishment of secular workshops to which the Jews had better access than to the great monastic institutions which previously held the monopoly in this field.

Patrons and Scribes

No less than twenty Hebrew manuscripts illuminated in Rome during the forty years between 1280 and 1320 have reached us. We know the names of numerous scribes and punctuators, of owners and patrons.[13] Among them Yoab bar Binyamin is outstanding. He was the patron of several of the most beautiful manuscripts in this group: the two-volume

7   V. Colorni, "La corrispondenza fra nomi ebraici e nomi locali nella prassi dell'ebraismo italiano," in *Judaica Minora* (Milan, 1983), pp. 661–825 (henceforth Colorni, *Judaica Minora*).

8   L. Mortara Ottolenghi, "Un gruppo di manoscritti ebraici romani del sec. XIII e XIV e la loro decorazione," in E. Toaff, ed., *Studi sull' ebraismo italiano* (Rome, 1974), pp. 141–158 (henceforth Mortara, "Manoscritti romani"); idem, "Miniature ebraiche italiane," in *Italia Judaica, Atti del I Convegno Internazionale* (Rome, 1983), pp. 214–220 (henceforth Mortara, "Miniature italiane"); idem, Manoscritti ebraici miniati nelle Biblioteche dell'Emilia Romagna," in A. Sacerdoti, ed., *Arte e Cultura Ebraiche in Emilia Romagna* (Milan, 1989), pp.

172–173, 186–187 (henceforth Mortara, "Biblioteche").

9   A. Freimann, "Jewish scribes in Medieval Italy," in *A. Marx Jubilee Volume* (New York, 1950), p. 340 (henceforth Freimann, *Scribes*).

10   The La Rochelle Bible, MS Vat. Heb. 468; see L. Mortara Ottolenghi, "La Bibbia di La Rochelle," in G. Dahan, ed., *Les juifs au regard de l'Histoire* (Paris, 1985), pp. 149–156.

11   G. Sed-Rajna, *Le Mahzor enlumiń* (Leiden, 1983).

12   *Keter of Burgos* , MS Heb. 4790 at the Jewish National and University Library in Jerusalem. See G. Sed-Rajna, "Toledo or Burgos?" *Journal of Jewish Art* 2 (1975), 6.

13   See note 8.

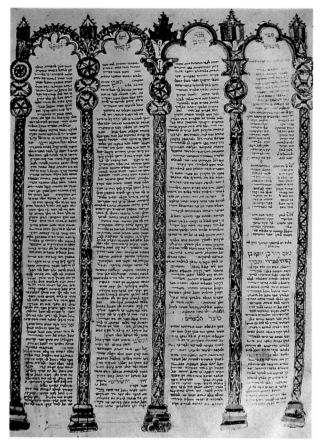

*Fig. 1.   Prophets and Hagiographa. Rome, 1325. Rome,
Biblioteca Angelica, MS Or. 72, fol. 80v.*

Bible in the British Library (Harley 5710/11), of which
he was probably the first owner, and the three-volume
Bible (MSS Parm. 2151–52–53 at the Parma Palatine
Library), dated Rome, 1304. In another manuscript,
now in the Ambrosian Library in Milan (G. 23 Sup.),
his full name appears, Yoab Fosco Bar Binyamin.[14]
This enables us to identify him as Fosco di Beniamino,
one of the lenders of the company that, coming from
Rome in 1284, had drawn up the *condotta* (charter)
with the city of Perugia and in 1292 with the city of
Todi.[15] Another partner in both these companies was
Sabato di Matassia de Urbe, known to us as Shabbatay
ben Mattatia,[16] another proud commissioner of im-

portant manuscripts such as the Bedell Bible (MS
1.1.5–7, at Emmanuel College, Cambridge) dated 1284,
the *Moreh Nevukhim* (BL Harley 7586), and a *Sefer
Mitzvot* by Maimonides (MS Parm. 2640) dated 1285.
Great bankers, men of great wealth, as patrons of
splendid works of art: this seems the general pattern
of the medieval world; that one of these men of finance
could have been a very capable scribe as well may
seem more unusual.

Manuello di Abramo was one of the partners of
almost all of the companies of bankers of Roman
origin which were active in Umbria and Tuscany
from 1285 until at least the end of the century.[17] In the
colophon of three manuscripts dated between 1319 and
1325, we find the name of the scribe Menahem Zemach
ben Abraham ben Binyamin ben Yehiel. According to
Colorni, Manuello corresponds to the Hebrew name
Menahem. If this identification is correct, we must
suppose that late in life (perhaps when he was about
sixty years old) the banker devoted himself to cultural
activities, producing — as a scribe — manuscripts of
great beauty such as MSS Parm. 3118–3126–3089, the
Miscellany (G. 3 Sup.) of the Ambrosian Library in
Milan and, above all, Prophets and Hagiographa, MS.
Or. 72, in the Angelica Library in Rome, a princely
codex which shows great skill in the composition of
the pages (Fig. 1).[18]

The embellishment of Roman Hebrew manuscripts
is of three types. Quill drawings of round arches with
characteristic roundel or palmette capitals (Fig. 1),
with few, very brilliant colors, probably executed by
the scribes themselves; drawings of great refinement,
also by quill and also by scribes, depicting animals and
monsters; and illuminations showing close affinity
with the best characteristics of the Roman school of
the period by various, probably Christian, artists who
worked alternately on the same codex.

The Fourteenth Century

We know the names of several Jewish fourteenth-
century scribes, for example, Yekutiel ben Shelomo
from Bononia, who in 1374 copied for Menahem ben

---

14   See   C.   Bernheimer,   *Codices   hebraici   Bybliothecae
     Ambrosianae* (Milan, 1933), pp. 25–26 (henceforth Bernheimer,
     Codices). The scribe, Jehiel ben Jekutiel Anaw, who copied
     this manuscript in 1284, was probably the son of the scribe of
     the Parma Palatine Library MS 2151–52–53, also commissioned
     by Yoab bar Binyamin.
15   A. Toaff, "Gli ebrei Romani e il commercio del denaro nei
     Comuni dell'Italia Centrale alla fine del Duecento," in *Italia*

Judaica: Atti del I Convegno Internazionale (Rome, 1983), p.
     194 (henceforth Toaff, *Commercio*).
16   Ibid. Cf. B. Narkiss, "Three Jewish Art Patrons in Medieval
     Italy," in *Festschrift to Reuben Hecht* (Jerusalem, 1984), pp.
     296–307.
17   Toaff, *Commercio* .
18   Mortara, "Manoscritti romani," pp. 153–155. Mortara, "Bib-
     lioteche," pp. 172 and 187. See also Colorni, *Judaica Minora* .

Fig. 2. Pentateuch. Pisa 1393, Perugia 1404. Venice, Museo Ebraico, fols. 19v–20.

Nathan the *Pisqei Isaiah of Trani* (BL MS Or. 5024), and the *Malmad ha-Talmidim* by Jacob Anatoli (MS Hebr. 401, Bibliotheque Nationale, Paris).[19] The scribe has been identified as Consiglio di Salomone who, in 1387, lived with his family in Bononia near the Cappella di San Bartolomeo at Porta Ravennate. The patron was the banker Emanuele da Rimini who, in

1392, left in his will, among other things, considerable legacies to the cities of Rimini and Rome.[20]

Another patron of illuminated manuscripts, Daniel ben Shemuel ha-Rofe bar Daniel Dayan from Bertinoro, was likewise active in finance in Pisa and Umbria, though not in a leading position but as a factor, from at least 1395.[21] This information, taken

19 L. Mortara Ottolenghi, "Manoscritti emiliano-romagnoli del XIV–XV secolo: un punto d'incontro tra miniatori cristiani ed ebrei?," in F. Parente, ed., *Atti del terzo Convegno...* (Rome, 1985), pp. 106–108 (henceforth Mortara, "Manoscritti emiliano-romagnoli"). See also Narkiss, "Three Patrons." Both Sirat & Beit Arí no. 50, and M. Garel, *D'une main forte* (Paris, 1991), p. 177, identify the scribe as Jehiel ben Salomon of Bevagna. The biographical data seems to confirm my reading of Bononia.

20 A.I. Pini, "Famiglie, insediamenti e banchi ebraici a Bologna e nel bolognese nella seconda metà del Trecento," *Quaderni storici* , 3 (1983), 791; Milano, *Italia*, p. 127; Freimann, *Scribes*,

p. 275; seven manuscripts were written by Yekutiel ben Shelomo in Bononia and Rimini.

21 Mortara, "Manoscritti emiliano-romagnoli," pp. 109–111, with bibliography. Particularly interesting is the Bible copied by Daniel (Pisa 1398 — Perugia 1405). The first 22 folios of the codex contain comparative massoratic tables typical of Sephardi Bibles of the time, and quite unusual in Italian Bibles. The refined illuminations of this part of the manuscript are due to a Christian artist, probably active in the town of Perugia. Cf. A. Toaff, *Gli Ebrei a Perugia* (Perugia, 1975), p. 36.

Fig. 3. Bible. Ferrara 1396. Florence, Biblioteca Mediceo-Laurenziana, MS Plut. 2/1 fol. 672v.

from the documents, confirms the dates (Pisa 1398 — Perugia 1404) in the colophon of the Bible, owned by the Jewish Community of Venice (Fig. 2).

A Sephardi scribe, Shlomo ben Hasday, copied in Ferrara in 1396 the most splendid manuscript produced in Italy during those years, a complete Bible with commentaries, now in the Mediceo-Laurentian Library in Florence (Plut. 2/1) (Fig. 3). The patron of this exceptional work of art, Binyamin ben Menahem from Corinaldo (Beniamino di Emanuele da Corinaldo), a very rich banker, was probably the most esteemed leader of the community of the Italian Jews in those years, and was well-connected with the Papal Court where he defended the rights of the Community. He was entrusted with this mission by the Congresses of the Italian Jewish communities of Bononia in 1416 and Forli in 1418.[22]

A little-known codex in the Ambrosian Library in Milan (A 192 inf.), a Rashi Commentary on the Pentateuch from the Bononian school of outstanding quality, merits closer examination. The manuscript was completed in 1401 by Shem Tov bar Shemuel Barukh: he was active in Bononia from 1399 until 1404. The patron, Shlomo Jedidia bar Mattatia (Salomone di Matassia di Sabato da Perugia) who was a banker in many towns of Central and Northern Italy, moved to Bononia in 1390 to continue his activity there.[23]

A Florentine Center

The documents published in recent years make it possible to identify the patrons of sumptuous Floren-

tine illuminated Hebrew manuscripts of the second half of the fifteenth century as well; they were rich bankers working in that city. The year 1441 was an exceptionally fruitful one. Two brothers, Jacob and David ben Shlomo from Perugia, entrusted to Itzhaq ben Obadja, the most famous scribe in Italy in those years, the task of copying a splendid *mahzor* in two volumes, now at the British Library in London (MS Add. 1944–45).[24] Jacob and David da Perugia, who probably came from Bononia, were among the most prominent Jewish bankers in Italy in those years: they had shares in the "Four Peacocks Bank" ("Banco dei Quattro Pavoni") in Florence since the very beginning of the *condotta* (charter) in 1437–38, and were also active in Fano from 1430, and in Borgo San Sepolcro in 1450; Jacob lived in 1461 in Siena. They entrusted the illumination of the *mahzor* to Zanobi Strozzi or to his workshop.

In the same year, 1441, a scion of another prominent family of bankers in Florence, Joseph ben Avraham of Tivoli, commissioned from a very capable scribe, Moses ben Avraham, the copying of another *mahzor*, now in the Schocken Library in Jerusalem (MS 13873). The illumination is once again by Zanobi. The scribe Moses was probably a member of the important Ashkenazi community, that of Treviso.[25] This may explain the use of Ashkenazi models by the Florentine illuminator Zanobi Strozzi, a rare example in the production of manuscripts in Italy (Fig. 4).

In 1467, Jacob Jacomo son of Rabbi Binyamin da Montalcino commissioned an anonymous scribe to do a small but beautiful manuscript (New Haven, Yale

22 L. Mortara Ottolenghi, "Alcuni manoscritti ebraici miniati in Italia Settentrionale nel secolo XV," *Arte Lombarda* 60 (1981), 42–43 henceforth Mortara, "Italia Settentrionale"). U. Cassuto, *Gli ebrei a Firenze nell'età del Rinascimento* (Florence, 1965, [1918], pp. 28–29, 358 (henceforth Cassuto, *Firenze*).

23 Freimann, *Scribes*, pp. 318–319. L. Mortara Ottolenghi, in V. Mann, ed., *Italya, Edizione italiana della mostra "Gardens and Ghettos,"* Ferrara, Palazzo dei Diamanti 18.3–17.6.1990 (Milan, 1990), p. 180, no. 43. See A. Toaff, "Convergenze nel Veneto di banchieri ebrei romani e tedeschi nel tardo Medioevo," in G. Cozzi, ed., *Gli Ebrei a Venezia* (Milan, 1987), pp. 604–606.

24 Jacob and David are the sons of the Shlomo Jedidia ben Mattatia mentioned above; see previous note, and M. Luzzatti, *La casa dell'Ebreo* (Pisa, 1985), p. 241 (henceforth Luzzatti, *La casa*). On Itzhaq ben Obadja, see Freimann, *Scribes*, p. 265. One must add to Freimann's list the *Arba'a Turim*, MS Ross. 555 of the Vatican Library, completed by the same scribe in Mantua in 1435 for Mordekhai ben Avigdor. There is no testimony on this patron in civil documentation. In the manuscript appear

the names of Abram b. Binyamin of Revere and Jacob ben Moses ben Avigdor: the first came from Perugia, the second from Urbino to Mantua, and were associated in the *condotta* of Mantua in 1444. Cf. S. Simonsohn, *History of the Jews in the Duchy of Mantua* (Jerusalem, 1977), pp. 204 and 655. See also Mortara, "Italia Settentrionale," p. 43.

25 B. Narkiss, *Hebrew Illuminated Manuscripts* (Jerusalem, 1968), p. 138; Th. and M. Metzger, *La vie juive au Moyen Age* (Fribourg, 1982), p. 306 no. 80. Narkiss considers this manuscript of Roman origin; the Metzgers suggest generically Central Italy. On the patron, Joseph ben Avraham of Tivoli, and his Florentine origin, see Cassuto, *Firenze*, p. 270. The scribe's name is recorded in a list of Jews living in Treviso in 1425. See L. Pesce, *Vita socio-culturale nella diocesi di Treviso nel primo Quattrocento* (Venice, 1983), pp. 48–51. See also A. Toaff, "Migrazioni di ebrei tedeschi attraverso i territori triestini e fruilani fra XIV e XV secolo," in *Presenza ebraica fra Trieste, Austria, Friuli ed Istria (sec. XIV–XIX)*, Acts of the Congress, to be published. Moses ben Avraham of Treviso is the scribe

Fig. 4.   Mahzor. Florence, 1441.
Jerusalem, Schocken Library of the Jewish
Theological Seminary of America,
MS 13873, fol. 76.

University Beinecke Library MS 409). It contains the Books of Psalms, Job and Proverbs (the so-called *Sifrei Emet*). The initial panels were beautifully illuminated by Mariano del Buono.[26] Jacopo was one of the sons of Guglielmo di Dattilo di Abramo da Montalcino,

an important money lender in Florence and in other centers of Tuscany, and identifiable as Binyamin, a scholar, liturgical poet, cabbalist and respected rabbi, not only in Florence, but probably also in Bononia.[27]

Another wealthy Florentine money-lender, Abramo

of the Parma Palatine Library cod. De Rossi 739 written in Fermo for Menahem ben Jehiel Gallico. He is probably also the Moses who completed in 1453 in Treviso (and not Tarvisio) the splendid siddur now in the Palatine Library of Parma (MS Parm. 2895) which had been started in Ulm and illuminated there in 1450. See B. Narkiss, "The Art of the Washington Haggadah," and M. Glazer, "The Ashkenazi and Italian Haggadah and the Haggadot of Joel ben Simeon," in Myron M. Weinstein, ed.,

The Washington Haggadah , Commentary volume (Washington, 1991), pp. 52, 93 (n. 65), 167 (n. 63).

26   E.M. Cohen, "Hebrew Manuscript Illumination in Italy," in V.B. Mann, ed., *Gardens and Ghettos* (Oxford, 1989), pp. 102, figs. 87 and 230 no. 40. See Garzelli, *Miniatura*, p. 208. The author reads the date wrongly.

27   Cassuto, *Firenze*, pp. 246–247. On the identity of Guglielmo as Benjamin see Lùzzatti, *La Casa*, p. 67, n. 15.

di Jacob da Siena or da Toscanella, who in 1471 was the main recipient of the new *condotta* in Florence, was the proud owner of a *mahzor* now in the British Library (MS Add. 16577). Perhaps he wished to consecrate the event of signing the charter by sponsoring this splendid work of art. Mariano was the possible illuminator.[28]

The *mahzor* of the Parma Palatine Library (MS Parm. 2738) was completed in Monselice in the Diocese of Padua in Veneto in 1489 for a member of the Finzi family.[29] The very rich borders and initial letters that embellish 225 pages of the volume are illuminated in a typical Tuscan style. This apparent contradiction can be solved by using documentary sources. In fact, Dolce or "Dulceta," the daughter of *Fincii de Finciis ebrei fili Beniamini habitatoris terre Monselexi* was, from 1477, the wife of Vitale (Jehiel) the son of Isaac of Pisa, the most affluent of the Tuscan Jewish bankers at the time.[30] The links between the two families can explain the fact that a Veneto manuscript was illuminated in Tuscany, perhaps in the workshop of Mariano del Buono.[31]

In 1492, Avraham ben Jehuda ben Jehiel of Camerino copied in Florence the Rothschild Mahzor now in the Jewish Theological Seminary Library in New York (Mic. 8892).[32] The patron was Elijah ben Joab of Vigevano of the Gallico family. The coat of arms of the Norsa family appears repeatedly in the manuscript. Elia di Dattilo of Vigevano (or of Cremona or of Mantua) was a partner not only in the Four Peacocks Bank in Florence, but was active in many other centers of Central and Northern Italy as well. Of particular interest in the case of the Rothschild Mahzor, is his association in the bank of Villafranca Veronese with the families Camerino (family of the scribe Avraham Jehuda) and Norsa.[33] The presence of Elia di Dattilo

in Cremona and his documented connections with Donato (Israel Nathan) Soncino[34] can explain the use, in a Florentine codex, of iconographic models drawn from the great Lombard Hebrew manuscripts of the time.[35] The most important illuminator was probably Mariano del Buono.[36]

Two years later, in 1494, one of the great Florentine artists, Attavante degli Attavanti, illuminated a Bible now in Parma Palatine Library (MS Parm. 2162).[37] The patron of this codex was Menahem ben Meshullam of Terracina, the scribe was Shimshon Zarfati ben Eliezer Halfon (Fig. 5). Manuele di Bonaventura da Terracina, the patron, was the brother of Solomon, owner of several banks in Tuscany and factor of Shemuel ben Jehiel — Simone di Vitale — of Pisa.[38] Shimshon, the scribe, was a member of a family of scribes active all over Italy. His brother Arieh ben Eliezer Halfon Zarfati,[39] copied a siddur in 1479 (MS Parm. 1754) in Cremona for Menahem ben Joab of Ascoli.

Two different scribes, also active in Cremona or its vicinity in Lombardy, in the years 1465–1480, copied two exceptional Hebrew manuscripts, which were illuminated in that town. One manuscript is a *Mishneh Torah* by Maimonides, now divided between two collections: a private collection in New York and the Vatican Library (Ross. 498). It was written by Nehemiah for Moshe ben Itzhaq — Mosdi Isacco known also as Angelo — who was a banker up to 1471 in Piacenza and Castelleone, then part of the Duchy of Milan. Cristoforo de Predis was probably the illuminator.[40]

Moses's widow, Allegra, later married Marco di Mosé Furlano di Consiglio Sacerdoti, a banker in Cremona. Marco's father was the patron of the Rothschild Miscellany, now in the Israel Museum in Jerusalem

28 Cassuto, *Firenze*, pp. 143–145; Luzzati, *La casa*, p. 240. G. Margouliouth, *Catalogue of the Hebrew and Samaritan Manuscripts in the British Museum* (London, 1899–1915), vol. II, no. 630; Garzelli *Miniatura*, pp. 11–15.

29 The arms illuminated on fol. 12 belongs to the Finzi family. F. Pisa, "Parnassim. Le grandi famiglie ebraiche dal sec. XI al sec. XIX," *Annuario di studi ebraici* 10 (1980–84), 358–359.

30 Luzzatti, *La casa*, p. 67.

31 Garzelli, *Miniatura*, pp. 210–215.

32 *The Rothschild Mahzor*. Introduction by E.M. Cohen and M. Schmelzer (New York, 1983).

33 Luzzatti, *La casa*, pp. 205, 220, 244, 263. A. Antoniazzi Villa, *Un processo contro gli ebrei nella Milano del 1488* (Milan, 1985), p. 44 (henceforth Villa, *Processo*).

34 Villa, *Processo*, p. 46. Simonshon, *The Jews*, pp. 142, 143, 358, 470, 481, 482, 849. L. Mortara Ottolenghi, "The Illumination and the Artists," in I. Fishoff, ed., *The Rothschild Miscellany* (Jerusalem and London, 1989), pp. 170–172 (henceforth Fishoff, *The Rothschild Miscellany*).

35 See Garzelli, *Miniatura*, pp. 210–215.

36 Mortara, "Biblioteche," pp. 173 and 187.

37 Cassuto, *Firenze*, p. 126.

38 Mortara, "Biblioteche," pp. 179 and 187. Freimann, *Scribes*, pp. 247–248. He is the scribe of at least six known manuscripts.

39 L.S. Gold, ed., *A Sign and a Witness* (New York and Oxford, 1988), p. 202, no. 69 (henceforth Gold, *A Sign*).

40 Mortara, "Miniature italiane," pp. 223–224.

Fig. 5. *Bible. Florence, 1494. Parma, Palatine Library, MS 2162.*

(MS 180/51). His name in Hebrew, Moshe ben Jekutiel ha-Kohen, was the key to the mystery that enveloped the "most precious of Hebrew manuscripts" until recently. He arrived in Cremona around 1465 probably from Pirano, a small port in Istria near Trieste, where the Sacerdoti family had been bankers since the end of the fourteenth century. Of Ashkenazi origin and linked with the town of Treviso in Friuli — as the nickname Furlano suggests — he possessed the qualities of culture, a deep sense of religious conformity and material wealth that were necessary for a patron of such an enterprise. The illuminations were probably executed by the workshops of Bonifacio Bembo and Cristoforo de Predis. The scribe's name was Abraham, but nothing else is known of him.[41]

Another unusual person among the Jews living in Northern Italy in the fifteenth century is Nethanel bar Levi Trabot: scribe, liturgical poet, and banker, he was successful in every one of those activities. He was the scribe of at least six codices of differing quality, the most important of which is the *Sefer ha-Mordekhay* (with other halakhic — legal — works) now in the Library of the Seminario Vescovile in Vercelli, completed in 1475 in Saluzzo or Savigliano, in Piedmont.[42] We know that much of his financial activity took place in villages of that region, beginning in Cuneo no later than 1445,[43] and that his civil name was Bellavigna Trevost.[44] He was also the patron of the beautiful wooden Torah staves now in the Gross family Collection in Ramat Aviv, Israel (Fig. 6).[45]

Around 1450 in Florence a cultural phenomenon of great interest began, absolutely unparalleled elsewhere: the copying and illuminating of precious biblical manuscripts in Hebrew, commissioned by erudite Christian Humanists. The most important ones are two Bibles in the Mediceo-Laurentian Library in Florence (Conv. Sopp. 268 and Plut. 1, 31), a Psalter in Berlin (Staatsbibliotek, Hamilton 547),[46] and perhaps also *Sefer Emet* (Psalms, Job, and Proverbs) (Israel Museum, MS 180/55).

We know that the Laurentian Bible Conv. Sopp. 268 was commissioned for the Convent of Saint Dominick in Fiesole,[47] and that the Hamilton Psalter has a crest of the Sassetti family.[48] It is also possible that the Israel Museum's *Sefer Emet* is related to the Medici family.[49] The most telling of those Humanist Hebrew manuscripts is the Laurentian Bible, Plut. 1,31 (Fig. 7), dedicated in Hebrew "to honor our

Fig. 6. Torah staves. Piedmont The Gross Family Collection.

Lord King Jesus Nazarenus King of the Jews... In the name of the Father, the Son and the Holy Spirit

[41] See M. Beit Arié, "A Paleographical and Codicological Study of the Manuscripts.," in Fishoff, *The Rothschild Miscellany*, pp. 111, 121–24; L. Mortara Ottolenghi, "The Rothschild Miscellany. Ms. 180/51 of the Israel Museum in Jerusalem: Jewish Patrons and Christian Artists," in *Resources in Hebraica* , Acts of the Congress, London SOAS 1990 (to be published); Mortara, in Fishoff, *The Rothschild Miscellany*, pp. 127–251 and especially pp. 246–250; for the connection between Bembo and the Jews, see Bistoletti Bandera, "Documenti per il Bembo," note 10 above.

[42] Freimann, *Scribes*, p. 307; Bernheimer, *Codices*, pp. 6–8; L. Mortara Ottolenghi, "Il manoscritto ebraico del Seminario Vescovile di Vercelli," in E.M. Artom, L. Caro, and S.J. Sierra, eds., *Miscellanea di Studi in memoria di D. Disegni* (Turin, 1969), pp. 153–165; Mortara in V. Mann, ed., *Italya*, p. 181, no. 52.

[43] R. Segre, *The Jews in Piedmont* (Jerusalem, 1986), vol. 1, pp. 182, 287, 293, etc.

[44] Colorni, *Judaica Minora*, p. 170.

[45] V.B. Mann, in *Gardens and Ghettos*, p. 265, no. 115.

[46] *Jüdische Lebenswelten, Katalog, Berliner Festspiele* (Berlin 1991), no. 20:1/26, p. 438. See also nos. 20:1/24–25, pp. 435–7.

[47] Mortara, "Miniature italiane," p. 226. M. Levi d'Ancona, "La miniatura a fiorentina tra Gotico e Rinascimento," in E. Sesti, ed., *La miniatura italiana tra Gotico e Rinascimento* , Acts of the Congress (Florence, 1985), vol. I, p. 464.

[48] Mortara, in Fishoff, *The Rothschild Miscellany* , p. 147; A.C. De La Mare, "The Library of Francesco Sassetti," in C.H. Clough, ed., *Cultural aspects of the Italian Renaissance* (Manchester and New York, 1976), pp. 160–201.

[49] Mortara, in Fishoff, *The Rothschild Miscellany* , pp. 146–147 and pl. 7. The crest on fol. 4v, which is partly erased could be connected with the Medici family. It should be noted that the iconography at the beginning of Psalms in the same page is typical of the Christian Book of Hours illuminated in Florence

Fig. 7. Bible. Florence, 1477. Biblioteca Mediceo-Laurenziana, MS Plut. 1,31, fol. 1r.

Amen.''[50] It bears no indication of who commissioned the Bible. The splendid decoration of these codices is due to the famous artists Beato Angelico and Francesco

Rosselli, who may have belonged to the patron's cultural milieu, and who inserted typical Christian iconography. Humanists at the time felt the need to

at the same period. The same subject illustrated on fol. 2 of the Yale University Beinecke Library MS 409 (see note 25) shows an iconography customary in Jewish art of the following centuries, David holding the enormous head of Goliath. A comparison between the scenes of the Judgment of Solomon on fol. 186v of the Jerusalem *Sefer Emet* and on fol. 153 of the Yale University manuscript, shows that the former presents a Christian Florentine iconography which includes a witness in the scene, while he is absent in the latter, following the Jewish tradition. Cf. G. Sed Rajna, *The Hebrew Bible in Hebrew*

Illuminated Manuscripts (Fribourg, 1987), fig. 150; V.B. Mann, *Gardens and Ghettos*, fig. 87. Garzelli, *Miniatura*, vol. II, figs. 718, 497, 580, 749, 763. On the iconography of David holding Goliath's head, cf. L. Mortara Ottolenghi, ''Tavole ebraiche,'' in *Midor Ledor* , Catalogue of the Exhibition (Bresseo di Teolo, 1989), pp. 68–69.

[50] The bibliography on this codex is abundant. Cf. Garzelli, *Miniatura*, pp. 184–185. The author, quite uninformed of the rich bibliography on Hebrew illuminated manuscripts, supposes a Jewish patron for this Bible. She dates it after 1477 and rightly

use original Hebrew texts for better comprehension of their meaning, although at the same time there were publications of anti-Jewish texts such as the *Contra Judeos et Gentes* by Giannozzo Manetti, the famous Florentine Humanist,[51] as well as organized debates between Jews and Christians at the homes of scholars with the attempt of converting the Jews to the Christian faith. These debates aroused interest in and a desire to acquire direct knowledge of Hebrew language and culture. The illuminated codices dealt with here were probably intended for that purpose, rather than being the expression of Judeo-Christian coexistence, as Cecil Roth would have it.[52]

We do not know who the scribes of these manuscripts were, if they were Orthodox Jews, Jews converted to Catholicism or Catholics proficient in Hebrew. It is still impossible to solve this problem, and more sophisticated research is necessary in order to reach a definite conclusion.[53]

attributes the illumination to Francesco Rosselli.

[51] R. Fubini, "L'ebraismo nei riflessi della cultura umanistica," in *Medioevo e Rinascimento* 2 (1988), 283–324 and especially pp. 284, 289, 295.

[52] C. Roth, "La decorazione dei codici ebraici biblici," in V. Antonioli Martelli and L. Mortara Ottolenghi, eds., *Manoscritti biblici ebraici decorati* (Milan, 1966), p. 23.

[53] Cassuto, *Firenze*, p. 192.

Fig. 1. End of Gotio Battaglias alleged letter and his coat of arms, 18th-century forgery, from the Garrett liturgical handbook, North Italy, end of 15th century. Princeton, University Library, Garrett MS 26, fols. 137v–138.

GIOTTO IN AVIGNON, ADLER IN LONDON, PANOFSKY IN PRINCETON: ON THE ODYSSEY OF AN ILLUSTRATED HEBREW MANUSCRIPT FROM ITALY AND ON ITS MEANING

Elliott Horowitz

On the first of May 1899, Sotheby's in London auctioned a manuscript entitled *La Guida dello Popolo de Israele* ["The Guide of the People of Israel"]. It was described in the catalogue as a fourteenth-century Hebrew manuscript on vellum of some 150 folios, including 27 miniatures (actually 28), which had been in the possession of the Earl of Ashburnham. The volume contained a letter of dedication, written in Italian and purportedly signed by Gotio (Gozio) Battaglia, the fourteenth-century cardinal whose family coat of arms adorns its top cover and folio 137v at the end of the letter (Fig. 1). The letter provided the title of the work and identified its author and illuminator.

According to the letter, which served as the basis for the description of the work in the Sotheby's catalogue and which was addressed to Battaglia's fellow churchman, Lord Galeotto de' Malatesta of Rimini, the guide "was written, with all possible care, by that great man and writer whose real name is Aramban the Hebrew, born in our native town of Rimini, and subsequently having gone to the school in Jerusalem.... who is now... First Rabbi in the city of Florence and enjoys the greatest reputation." So much for the author, although the (A)Ramban more generally known, that is Nahmanides, was Spanish rather than Italian, never served as chief rabbi of Florence, and died well before the beginning of the fourteenth century. As for the illustrator, Battaglia's letter reports that he was "that so famous man of outstanding merit and unique painter, Giotto of Florence, together with his most proficient pupil. As your excellency perceives," the letter continued, "he [that is, Giotto] has illustrated it in conformity with the text." The letter implies, we might note, not only that Giotto, in addition to his many other accomplishments, was able to illustrate a

Hebrew manuscript "in conformity" with its text, but that two fourteenth-century Italian churchmen would be able to appreciate his achievement.

One of those present at the 1899 auction was the noted scholar and collector Elkan Adler, who wrote about the manuscript in a brief article (in which he found room nevertheless to express his chagrin at having been outbid by a non-Jew "too wealthy to be a Hebraist") published later that year in the *Jewish Quarterly Review*.[1] The article was brief partly because Adler, whose father (Nathan) had been Chief Rabbi of the British Empire, and whose half-brother (Hermann) then occupied that position, had been permitted by Sotheby's to examine the manuscript only on the Saturday before its sale, and, as a Sabbath observer, he was therefore unable to take notes. Yet he was nevertheless able to determine that the catalogue description was imprecise. Adler recognized that the text of the manuscript could not actually have been written by Nahmanides; moreover, he had been assured by "great connoisseurs" that although the style of the miniatures was Florentine they could not be dated before the late fourteenth or early fifteenth century, which would exclude Giotto's participation. The text, Adler noted, despite the title attributed to it in the letter of dedication, had little in common with the better known *Guide of the Perplexed* by Maimonides. Rather, it consisted of "a compilation of various occasional prayers for all the events of life — Birth, Milah, Betrothal, Marriage, Travel, Burial, and so on." He found the pictures to be "characteristically Jewish," by which he seems to have referred to their content rather than style.

Despite his reservations, Adler concluded, somewhat surprisingly, that the description in the cat-

See E.N. Adler, "A Hebrew MS Illustrated by Giotto," *Jewish Quarterly Review*, 11 (1899), 679–682, who quotes from the Sotheby catalogue, and idem, *About Hebrew Manuscripts* (London, 1905), p. 107. On Adler see E. Marmorstein, *The Scholarly Life of Elkan Adler* (London, 1962), and on the degree of his loyalty to traditional Jewish practice, ibid., p. 11.

alogue, if less than correct, might be nearly so — that the work in question might have been "composed by the learned Ramban, and written for him by another learned Israelite," and that it might have been illustrated by one of Giotto's students even after the master's lifetime. One suspects that the prospect of a possible cultural link between Nahmanides and Giotto through senior members of the Church was too tempting for Adler to be able to dismiss it altogether. Had the directors of Sotheby's provided him with more favorable circumstances for examining the manuscript, Adler might have realized that it contained lengthy quotations from the *Zohar*, the kabbalistic classic Nahmanides never lived to see although he exerted considerable influence upon its author.[2]

Adler, in his brief notice, also commented on "the cordial relations between Jew and Christian in medieval Italy," which he found reflected in the circumstances under which the illuminated manuscript was created — a cardinal ordering a Jewish prayerbook to be illuminated for a fellow churchman by the finest artist of the day, and "the Jewish vagrant scribe discoursing to these great dignitaries of the Church on the glorious learning of his Rabbis."[3] This picture, or perhaps myth, as some might prefer to call it, of Jewish-Christian co-existence in Italy may have been implanted in Adler's mind not only by the Sotheby manuscript but by a book which had appeared only three years earlier and with which he was undoubtedly familiar — *Jewish Life in the Middle Ages* by Israel Abrahams, the noted Anglo-Jewish scholar and co-editor of the *Jewish Quarterly Review*. In that work Italy was often portrayed as the great exception to the usual hostilities which prevailed between Jews and Christians during the Middle Ages. In contrast to the rest of Europe, Abrahams wrote, "the priests in Italy were not fanatical instigators of the mob until the fifteenth century was all but passed"; and also

that "Italy... was the scene in all ages of close literary friendships between Jews and Christians, such as no other country could show in the same profusion."[4] Adler seems, then, to have been influenced, like others,[5] by this idealizing view of Jewish-Christian relations in Italy, and to have imposed it upon his reconstruction of the circumstances under which the curious illuminated manuscript offered at Sotheby's had been created. This may have blinded him to the fabricated character of the letter of dedication, supposedly written by the fourteenth-century Cardinal Battaglia. The forgery was later exposed by the great art historian Erwin Panofsky, who called it "one of the most curious mystifications in history."[6]

Adler was nonetheless sufficiently pleased with his little essay on the manuscript to incorporate it, some thirty-seven years later, in the longer article on "Jewish Art" which he submitted to the *Anniversary Volume* for Moses Gaster. He introduced only one change, which is worthy of notice. The original essay had concluded with a sad comparison between the appreciation of Jewish learning in medieval Italy and its appreciation among Adler's contemporaries. "Are we quite as broadminded nowadays?" he asked. "How many Jewish millionaires are there who would pay as much for a Bar Mitzvah present for their own son... or make so edifying a choice? How many Jewish bidders were there for this very little book?" The 1936 article concluded, however, on a less harsh note. The question of the number of Jewish bidders for the book was not left hanging rhetorically, but was now, belatedly, partially answered by Adler himself: "I daresay one of them was Dr. Gaster."[7]

Five years later Erwin Panofsky, who had evidently not seen either of Adler's above-mentioned articles, devoted to the manuscript the one article of his career connected with Jewish art. By then it had come into the possession of the American collector Robert Garrett

2   See, for example, fols. 30r–32v of the manuscript, now in the Princeton University Library, Garrett MS 26, which discuss the merits of the penitent, and compare *Zohar* I: 129a–b. For a translation of the Zoharic passage see I. Tishby, *The Wisdom of the Zohar*, trans. D. Goldstein (Oxford, 1989), vol. 3, pp. 1524–7. On the well known influence of Nahmanides on the *Zohar*'s author see, for example, G. Scholem, *Major Trends in Jewish Mysticism* (New York, 1946) pp. 173, 391 n. 79.

3   Adler, "A Hebrew MS," p. 682.

4   I. Abrahams, *Jewish Life in the Middle Ages* (Philadelphia, 1896), pp. 400, 419.

5   See, for example, C. Roth, *The History of the Jews in Italy* (Philadelphia, 1946), p. 156: "in no part of the world

did such a feeling of friendliness prevail as in Italy between the people and the Jews." For a cogent re-evaluation of this position see R. Bonfil, "The Historian's Perception of the Jews in the Italian Renaissance; Towards a Reappraisal," *Revue des Etudes Juives* 143 (1984), pp. 59–82; idem, "Società critiana e società ebraica nell'Italia medievale e rinascimentale," *Atti del VI Congresso internazionale dell' Associazione Italiana per lo Studio del Giudaismo* (Rome, 1988), pp. 231–260.

6   E. Panofsky, "Giotto and Maimonides in Avignon: The Story of an Illuminated Hebrew Manuscript," *Journal of the Walters Art Gallery*, 4 (1941) p. 35.

7   E.N. Adler, "Jewish Art," *Occident and Orient: Gaster Anniversary Volume* (London, 1936), p. 49.

of Baltimore, who shortly afterward gave it to the library of Princeton University, where I was graciously permitted to examine it under circumstances considerably more generous than those accorded Elkan Adler by Sotheby's in 1899.[8] If Adler suffered from the handicap of being unable to take notes, Panofsky, in examining the manuscript, suffered from the equally serious handicap of being unable, according to his own testimony, to read Hebrew. Yet, as a professor at the Institute for Advanced Study in Princeton he was able to draw upon the distinguished Ugaritic scholar Cyrus Gordon, who between 1939 and 1942 was associated with the Institute and taught Hebrew Bible at Princeton University.[9]

With his aid, Panofsky was able to determine that the volume was "not a philosophical or theological treatise, but a book for practical ritual use, the traces of which are all too evident in many of the miniatures."[10] Yet in assisting with the specifics of the text Gordon did not always measure up to the level of his own professional attainments, and his efforts seem, at times, to have been rather half-hearted. Thus in a miniature showing two boys and five girls in the section entitled *Seder Hatanim* ("Order of Bridegrooms"), the group is described by Panofsky as "setting out to meet the bridegroom" whereas the text beneath the illustration suggests that they are setting out to meet the bride. More serious, however, is the question of the identification of the biblical text to be read before the bride, which opens, in our manuscript, with the words *kumi 'ori ki va 'orekh* ("Arise, shine; for your light has come") (fol. 14, Fig. 2). Panofsky, undoubtedly on the basis of information received from the noted biblical scholar who assisted him, asserts that "the text belonging to the miniature alludes to the Song of Deborah" in Judges,[11] whereas those more familiar with the cycle of *haftarot* read in the synagogue would probably recognize it as the opening verse of Isaiah 60.

Panofsky nevertheless made some highly important observations about the manuscript and its illustra-

tions. Through shrewd detective work he determined that the 150 pages of the manuscript had been rearranged in order to accommodate the Italian dedication supposedly written by Cardinal Battaglia. Moreover, he showed that although both the alleged author and the purported recipient of the letter actually lived in the early fourteenth century, the letter's script and language indicated that it had been composed by an artful forger considerably later, probably in the eighteenth century. The errors in the coats of arms inserted inside the covers of the manuscript also pointed in a similar direction.[12]

Concerning the illustrations, Panofsky pointed out that Giotto, who was supposedly responsible for them, died two years before Battaglia, who supposedly commissioned them, became a cardinal. Yet their style, asserted Panofsky, "straightforward and at times amusingly naive, is definitely north Italian with some admixture of the Umbro-Florentine, and is reminiscent of the school of Ferrara." As for their date, they could not, in his view, "have been executed before the last two decades of the fifteenth century." The miniatures depicted "with rare completeness," Panofsky observed, "the religious life of the righteous from the cradle to the grave, and should thus be of considerable interest to students of Jewish history and customs."[13]

This, of course, was not an area in which Panofsky himself exhibited much interest, not only because it related to Jewish, as opposed to humanistic culture, but because he was concerned primarily with the symbolic meaning of pictures as opposed to what he called their "primary or natural subject matter."[14] The latter belonged to the "preiconographical description" of a painting, whereas Panofsky, who had just published his *Studies in Iconology: Humanistic Themes in the Art of the Renaissance*, focused on the two levels of interpretation which followed. These were iconographical analysis, which investigated the "secondary or conventional meanings" recoverable with the aid of literary sources; and iconological interpretation,

8 See now E.M. Cohen, "Hebrew Manuscript Illumination in Italy," in Jewish Museum, *Gardens and Ghettos: The Art of Jewish Life in Italy* (Berkeley, Los Angeles, Oxford, 1989), ed. V.B. Mann, pp. 100–101, and cat. no. 44. The bibliography provided there (p. 232) does not include, however, the two aforementioned articles of Adler.

9 See *Who's Who in World Jewry* (New York, 1955), pp. 281, 571; "Gordon, Cyrus Herzl" in *Encyclopaedia Judaica* (Jerusalem,

1970), 7: 793–94.

10 Panofsky, "Giotto and Maimonides," p.27.

11 Ibid., p. 30; MS Garrett, 14r. On this miniature see further below.

12 Panofsky, "Giotto and Maimonides," pp. 37–41.

13 Ibid., p. 28.

14 See M.A. Holly, *Panofsky and the Foundations of Art History* (Ithaca, 1984), p. 159.

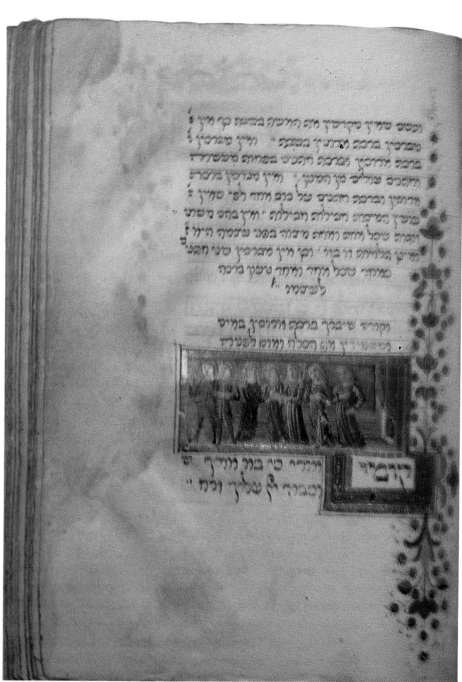

Fig. 2. Isaiah 60 to be read before the bride, from the Garrett liturgical handbook, North Italy, end of 15th century. Princeton, University Library, Garrett MS 26, fol. 14.

which went a step further and sought to uncover a picture's "intrinsic meaning or content."[15] Panofsky, therefore, was hardly interested in using paintings as a means of reconstructing life as it was actually lived in Renaissance Italy and was doubly removed from any effort to do so with regard to Jewish life, despite his own ethnic background (of which he must have been keenly aware in 1941, which may explain his rare

foray into the field of Jewish art). The manuscript he discussed in his learned article, and especially its miniatures, still awaits careful investigation by scholars of Jewish history and culture looking for windows on what I have elsewhere called "the way we were."[16] In what follows I shall make a brief preliminary attempt to demonstrate how this might perhaps done.

The Hebrew text of the fifteenth-century Princeton

[15] Ibid.

[16] E. Horowitz, "The Way We Were: Jewish Life in the Middle Ages," *Jewish History* 1 (1986): 75–90.

manuscript deals primarily, as noted above, with ritual aspects of Jewish daily life, and includes both prescriptions and prayers as well as theoretical disquisitions on some commandments (e.g. charity and prayer) taken from such sources as the *Zohar*. It could therefore be called the Garrett liturgical handbook. Its twenty-eight illustrations cover a broad range of topics, from birth and marriage to the interpretation of dreams, but, as Panofsky himself observed, the six devoted to the theme of death constitute by far the largest number belonging to a single subject (fols. 49r–60r). He did not attempt to explain this emphasis, but it may be noted that the French art historian Emile Mâle had pointed out that "in the fifteenth century the image of death is everywhere," and Panofsky's American colleague H.W. Janson had described that century's art as "preoccupied with the problems of death."[17]

Mâle, in his classic study of late medieval religious art, observed that it was "during the first half of the fifteenth century that death began to inspire the miniaturists," pointing to such works as the Rohan Hours, whose illuminator was "at once appalled and fascinated by death" and who devoted eight successive miniatures to the subject. These begin with a funeral procession and the digging of the grave, but more frightening scenes, such as the horrible visions of the dying, follow as well. By the end of the century the Dance of Death became a common motif in the art of Christian Europe. The first edition of a work in verse on this theme, illustrated with woodcuts, appeared in Paris in 1485.[18] The late fifteenth century also witnessed an enormous growth, throughout Europe, in the production of illustrated works on the art of dying, known generically as *Ars moriendi*. Beginning to appear in print from 1464, the *Ars moriendi*, as Roger Chartier has recently remarked, "was perhaps the most widely circulated woodcut book." At least seventy-seven (and perhaps as many as 97) incunabula editions of the work appeared, of which fourteen are north Italian — stemming, therefore, from the same general region as our manuscript. Of the two versions of the *Ars moriendi* to circulate in print, the longer one was divided into six "moments."[19]

These observations on the theme of death in late fifteenth-century art shed light on the decision of our artist (whether Christian or not) to devote *six* successive miniatures to the subject, although, as we shall see, there were differences between Christian and Jewish renderings of this theme. In the very first miniature, which appears immediately above the heading *'inyan 'avelut* ("the matter of mourning"), a young man is shown standing before a seated figure from whom he seems to be receiving instruction (Fig. 3).[20] According to Panofsky "these instructions concern the customs of mourning," an assertion which would appear to have been suggested by the heading, and which he buttresses by pointing to the cypress trees seen through the window.[21]

The cypress, it is true, had been associated with death in both pagan and Christian antiquity, whether because of its dark foliage or because once cut it never springs up again from its roots.[22] But the presence of the tree, even assuming that its symbolism in Jewish art coheres with the Christian tradition, does not necessarily point to mourning — it might suggest the theme of death in general. Panofsky's association of the scene with instruction in the laws of mourning would seem to be connected with the heading *'inyan 'avelut*. But if we look at the text which follows that

[17] E. Mâle, *Religious Art: From the Twelfth to the Eighteenth Century* (reprint, Princeton, 1982), p. 142; idem, H. W. Janson, "The Putto with the Death's Head," *Art Bulletin* 19 (1937), p. 427.

[18] Mâle, *Religious Art* pp. 141–145, and more extensively idem, *Religious Art in France: The Late Middle Ages*, ed. H. Bober (Princeton, 1986) pp. 320–32. The latter work is a translation of Mâle's *L'art religeux de la fin du moyen âge en France*, which first appeared in 1908.

[19] R. Chartier, "Texts and Images: The Arts of Dying, 1450–60," in idem, *The Cultural Uses of Print in Early Modern France*, trans. L.G. Cochrane (Princeton, 1987), pp. 34–41. Note also the earlier studies of A. Tenenti, "Ars moriendi, Quelque notes sur le probléme de la mort à la fin du XVe sïcte," *Annales: Écomonies, Sociétés, Civilisations* 6 (1951), 433–46, idem, *La Vie et la Mort à travers l'art du XVe sïcle* (Paris, 1952). On the influence of the *Ars moriedi* woodcuts in Italy see also Mâle, *Religious Art in France*, p. 349.

[20] MS Garrett, fol. 49r; Panofsky, "Giotto and Maimonides," p. 35. See the color reproduction in Jewish Museum, *Gardens and Ghettos*, p. 101, fig. 86.

[21] Panofsky, "Giotto and Maimonides," p. 34.

[22] See G. Ferguson, *Signs and Symbols in Christian Art* (Oxford, 1966), p. 30, and note also the excellent entry "Cypress" in the *Encyclopaedia Brittanica* (11th ed. Cambridge, 1910–11), vol. 7, p. 694, where Shakespeare's awareness of this tradition (in Henry VI) is noted. The Mediterranean tradition of the cypress as the tree of death was also later acknowledged by Van Gogh. See A. Boime, "Van Gogh's Starry Night: A History of Matter and a Matter of History," *Arts Magazine* 59:4 (Dec., 1984), pp. 96, 103.

Fig. 3. Instruction in "the matter of mourning," from the Garrett liturgical handbook, North Italy, end of 15th century. Princeton, University Library. Garrett MS 26, fol. 49.

heading we encounter not the laws of mourning but rather the opening words of the third chapter of *Avot*, the Ethics of the Fathers: "Akabya b. Mahalalel said 'Consider three things and thou wilt not fall into the hands of transgression. Know whence thou art come and whither thou art going, and before whom thou art about to give account and reckoning'." It should be noted that this passage also opens the section on 'inyan 'avelut in the first edition of the *Mahzor Minhag Roma*.[23]

These words from *Avot*, and especially those per-

taining to the importance of knowing "whither thou art going," would seem to constitute the subject in which the youth in our miniature is receiving instruction. The cypress trees seen through the window do indeed symbolize death, but they do not point to the laws of mourning. Rather, they seem to serve as a *memento mori* for which the skull was then becoming

---

23 *Mahzor Minhag Roma* (Soncino and Casalmaggiore, 1485–1486), vol. 2, p. 313. On further similarities between the Roman mahzor and our manuscript see below.

ויהי שביב ברע

ויהי מבותיכו הגמל לפני
תסלוחנו ומל תפכבלי
מתרתכתכ שריך נוכו עור פטט וקשי

Fig. 4. Confessional prayer, from the Garrett liturgical handbook, North Italy, end of 15th century. Princeton, University Library, Garrett MS. 26, fol. 50v.

the more conventional symbol in Renaissance art. Medieval art had used the corpse for this purpose, in order to frighten the onlooker, but Renaissance art, as Janson has noted, "sought to evoke a more pensive attitude."[24] The cypress trees, it would appear, were used by the illuminator of our manuscript in order to evoke such an attitude.

The next miniature in the series on death (fol. 50v)

depicts, according to Panofsky, "a sick man in bed confessing his sins to four relatives or friends" (Fig. 4).[25] Upon closer examination we can detect, however, that the individuals in question do not constitute a single group. Rather, three stand together at the right of the sick man's bed and one stands apart from them on the left, at the foot of the bed, reading from a small book which he holds in his hands. Neither

[24] Janson, "The Putto with the Death's Head," pp. 428–429.

[25] Panofsky, "Giotto and Maimonides," fig. 6, p. 34.

Panofsky nor Adler commented on this book nor speculated on its content, but one wonders whether the illustration may be self-referential and whether the book is intended to be our own manuscript, which was suitable, as we shall see, for use at the deathbed.

Although the three grouped to the right may well be friends or relatives, it is likely that the fourth person, on the left, has a separate and distinct identity. Whether or not he is an ordained rabbi, he would appear to be a specialist in the liturgy and customs of death, for the Hebrew text which follows the miniature alludes to such an individual. It opens with the confessional prayer known to us primarily from the Yom Kippur liturgy (*Elohenu...*) followed by the *'al het* confession arranged according to the order of the Hebrew alphabet (fols. 51r–52v). Only after these two passages do we encounter the words "and the sick man recites the following prayer" (fol. 53r) — suggesting that the previous material was not recited by the bedridden man, but by someone else on his behalf. Moreover, the passage assigned to the sick man himself for recitation is much shorter than the confessional prayers which precede it, consisting primarily of the forty-word confession (*modeh ani lefanekha...*) found, for the first time, in the *Torat ha-Adam* of the real "Aramban," that is, Nahmanides.[26]

After the short confession the sick man in our manuscript is instructed to recite two chapters from Psalms, after which, we are told: "The expert (*baki*) recites the *mi she-berakh* prayer on his behalf, and he promises to charity an amount of his choosing" (fol. 54r). Who is this expert? He would appear to be identical with the person who, according to our text, recites the long confessional on behalf of the sick man before the latter recites his own shorter version. And he would appear, furthermore, to be identical with the individual portrayed in our miniature with a book in his hands standing at the foot of the sickbed.

The same use of the term *baki* may be found in the first printed edition of the *Mahzor... Roma*, the Italian Jewish prayer rite, published in Soncino and

Casalmaggiore during the mid–1480s, and fairly contemporaneous with the miniatures of our manuscript. In that liturgical compendium there appears a service for changing the name of the seriously ill (*seder shinui ha-shem*) which is preceded by the following instructions: "Ten gather together and the expert (*baki*) among them grasps the Torah scroll and begins the prayer *mezalin anahna* [we pray]." The 1480 edition of the *Mahzor Roma* also contains a selection of Psalms to be recited by a woman in childbirth, before which appears a prayer to be recited on her behalf by the *baki* while holding a Torah scroll.[27]

The *baki* in these late fifteenth-century Italian sources would seem to refer not to a rabbi, for whom other terms were more commonly used,[28] but to a specialist in a particular area of liturgy or custom — a religious functionary rather than a scholar. The term may perhaps be compared to the Italian *maestro*, suggesting a degree of professional expertise in a particular sphere. This was indeed how the celebrated Hebrew poet Immanuel of Rome (d. ca. 1330) had earlier used the word *baki* in the ninth of his *Mahberot*, when engaging in a satire of the professions in the style of the Italian poet Ruggiero Apuliese.[29]

The professional sense of the term *baki* seems by the fifteenth century to have carried over to the ritual realm. Its use for the ritual manager of the deathbed may be explained not only by that century's obsession with death, referred to above, but by the gradual elaboration of the Jewish deathbed rite during the later Middle Ages in such a way as to render expert management necessary. The confessional prayer presented by Nahmanides in his thirteenth-century *Torat ha-Adam*, for example, was twice the length of the parallel formula included by Maimonides in his *Mishneh Torah* (*Teshuva* 1:1) during the preceding century. In the fourteenth century one Provençal scholar, R. Aaron ha-Kohen of Lunel, suggested that the dying man might recite the Yom Kippur confession in addition to the one provided by Nahmanides, and another, R. Yeroham b. Meshullam, presented a pre-

26 C.D. Chavel ed. *Kitvei ha-Ramban* (Jerusalem, 1964), vol. 2, p. 47.

27 *Mahzor Minhag Roma*, vol. 2, pp. 305–6. Note also the similarity between the two texts in another matter entirely — the placing of three drops of wine in the infant's mouth during the blessings following his circumcision which does not appear in the standard medieval guides to Jewish practice (ms. Garrett 4r; *Mahzor Roma*, vol. 2, p. 310). On the custom in Italy of bringing a Torah scroll into the presence of a woman in childbirth note the very interesting discussion in the *Responsa of R. Azriel Diena* (Hebrew), ed. Y. Boksenboim, (Tel-Aviv, 1977–79), vol. 1, nos. 8–10.

28 See R. Bonfil, *Rabbis and Jewish Communities in Renaissance Italy*, trans. J. Chipman (Oxford, 1990), index, s.v. "titles."

29 See D. Yarden, ed., *Mahberot Immanuel ha-Romi* (Jerusalem, 1957), vol. I, pp. 174–6. See especially lines 182–6, 190–206. On the similarity with the early thirteenth-century Sicilian poet Apuliese see Yarden, p. 174, notes to line 163. For the original of "Servento del maestro di tutte l'arti" see V. da Bartholmaeis, *Rime giullaresche e popolari d'Italia* (Bologna, 1926), pp. 17–20.

30 R. Aaron ha-Kohen of Lunel, *'Orhot Hayyim*, ed. M. Schlesinger (Berlin, 1901), vol. 2, pp. 559, 634.; R. Yeroham b. Meshullam, *Sefer Toledot Adam ve-Hava* (Venice, 1553), 230a–b.

death confession which was four times the length of that recommended by the latter. Qualitatively it differed as well in that included, apparently for the first time, a confession of faith in addition to the confession of sins.[30]

Alongside the quantitative and qualitative expansion of the confessional prayer we encounter a good deal of ritual elaboration in R. Yeroham's *Toledot Adam ve-Hava* as well. Prior to this point it would have been difficult to describe a distinctly Jewish ritual of dying but in the fourteenth century such a ritual begins to take shape. In his work R. Yeroham not only prescribes the washing of hands before the recitation of pre-death confession, but insists also that this be done with the ritual blessing. The dying Jew is also instructed to don his prayer shawl before reciting confession, thus heightening the ritual character of the act. Although the presence of a rabbi or ritual expert is not yet required by R. Yeroham, it is clear that we are on the way.

At the end of the fifteenth century, in 1490 we learn of an instance in Segovia, Spain, where a (non-converso) Jew who had been imprisoned by the Inquisition, and who was about to be executed, begged his physician "to send a rabbi who could administer to him the death-bed consolations of his religion."[31] His request undoubtedly reflects popular practice among some segments of Spanish Jewry at that time, and dovetails also with the repeated references to the role of the *baki* in the deathbed rites included in the *Mahzor Roma* published only a few years earlier in Italy. Yet some scholars have been loathe to accept the idea that the presence of a rabbi or religious functionary at the Jew's bedside during his recitation of confession could have been desirable or necessary, believing (apparently) that this smacked too much of Catholicism. Even a scholar of Panofsky's stature, after asserting that the four standing figures in our miniature were friends or relatives, saw fit to add: "characteristically, the presence of a Rabbi was not required, and was even deemed undesirable."[32]

As his source for this observation Panofsky cited, in addition to the turn of the century *Jewish Encyclopedia*, the now deservedly obscure work, *Jew-*

ish Institutions and Customs by Herbert Rosenau. There we read that "when the persons surrounding a patient notice that there is no hope for recovery and that death is a matter of only a very short time, they prevail upon the patient to make a confession of his guilt. For this purpose the Rabbi is not called in."[33] This may be acceptable as a guide to American Jewish practice in 1903, but it hardly reflects the customs of Mediterranean Jewry at the end of the fifteenth century. In the sixteenth and seventeenth centuries we know from such sources as the autobiography of Leon Modena that the summoning of a rabbi to hear confession was widely practiced — even by adolescent girls (such as Modena's first fiancee).[34] The miniature under discussion, together with its accompanying text, strongly suggest that a ritual expert, if not necessarily a rabbi, began to play an active role in the deathbed rites of Italian Jews as early as the fifteenth century, just as a similar development had evidently occurred among the Jews of Spain.

Although this may rightfully be seen as evidence of the influence of the constantly impinging Christian environment, it would also appear to be a response to the impact of internal developments. As the rites of the Jewish deathbed grew more elaborate in the later Middle Ages and its liturgy more expansive, it became increasingly necessary, especially before the widespread introduction of print, to receive personal guidance from an "expert" who had mastered the art of dying. Thus the prevalent Christian practice of having a religious functionary (i.e. priest) attend the deathbed and supervise the confession was not simply blindly imitated at some arbitrary moment, but adopted rather, largely for pragmatic reasons; as much, it might be said, despite the Christian practice as because of it. Not only were the artists of the fifteenth century, as mentioned above, "preoccupied with the problems of death," but the procuring of a "good death" was an important goal among the populace as a whole, Christians and Jews alike, and the presence of a ritual manager at the deathbed was seen by many as essential for achieving that goal.[35]

By contrast with the confession scene, in which our manuscript reflects common elements in Jewish

31 See H.C. Lea, "El Santo Niño de la Guardia," *English Historical Review* , (1889) 4p. 238. Note also I. Loeb in *Revue des Etudes Juives* 15 (1887), pp. 218-19, 221, and Y. Baer, *A History of the Jews in Christian Spain* (Philadelphia, 1961), vol. 2, pp. 399-400.

32 Panofsky, "Giotto and Maimonides," p. 35.

33 H. Rosenau, *Jewish Institutions and Customs* (Baltimore, 1903),

p. 177.

34 See M.R. Cohen, trans. and ed., *The Autobiography of a Seventeenth-Century Venetian Rabbi: Leon Modena's Life of Judah* (Princeton, 1988), pp. 91, 165, 175.

35 On the perceived importance of a ritual manager at the deathbed for procuring a "good death" see R. Trexler, *Public Life in Renaissance Florence* (New York, 1980), pp. 199-205.

Fig. 5. Funeral procession, from the Garrett liturgical handbook, North Italy, end of 15th century. Princeton, University Library, Garrett MS. 26, fol. 57.

and Christian practice, the scene of the funeral procession (Fig. 5)[36] points to at least one significant difference. Torches or tapers do not yet appear; which suggests that their controversial though limited use in the 1509 funeral of R. Judah Minz in Padua was indeed as innovative as some members of the community then claimed. Elijah Capsali, who was present, reports that at the outset "forty enormous torches of white wax... were brought out and distributed to all the rabbis and notables and to the distinguished students of the academy... and we positioned ourselves around the coffin and then lit them." Although the torches were deliberately not carried in procession,

[36]   MS Garret, 57r, reproduced in T. and M. Metzger, *Jewish Life in the Middle Ages: Illuminated Manuscripts of the Thirteenth to Sixteenth Centuries* (New York, 1982), fig. 109.

Fig. 6. Meeting the bride with candles, from the Garrett liturgical handbook, North Italy, end of 15th century. Princeton, University Library, Garrett MS. 26, fol. 15v.

being extinguished after the first series of eulogies and then rekindled only upon arrival at the cemetery (where Minz was eulogized again), their use clearly provoked considerable controversy. Capsali reports further that immediately after R. Abraham Minz had been installed as his father's successor "he delivered an address in the synagogue to stifle the voices of those who criticized the custom he had instituted of having the torches lit, objecting that... this was something practiced by the gentiles.''[37]

In the wedding scenes included in our manuscript, however, torches are amply present, and are carried by youths escorting the bride and groom (fols. 14r, 15v

[37] See E. Capsali, *Seder Eliyahu Zuta*, ed. A. Shmuelevitz et al. (Tel Aviv, 1975–77), vol. 2, pp. 254–5.

Fig. 7. The bride on horseback, leading the bridal procession, from an Italian mahzor, Reggio, Emilia, 1465. London, British Library, Harley MS 5686, fol. 27v.

— Fig. 6 — and 20v).[38] Their use in Jewish weddings can be traced, as Panofsky noted (on the basis of Matthew 25:1), back to New Testament times,[39] but

it is worth noting the parallel late fifteenth-century evidence as well. In his 1488 letter to his father from Jerusalem, R. Obadia of Bertinoro recorded his

[38] Reproduced in Panofsky, "Giotto and Maimonides," figs. 9, 10, 14. Note also T. and M. Metzger, *Jewish Life*, p. 233.

[39] Panofsky, "Giotto and Maimonides," p. 30. See also Abrahams, *Jewish Life*, p. 195. On the use of torches at weddings note

also J.Z. Lauterbach, *Studies in Jewish Law, Custom, and Folklore* (New York, 1970), pp. 7–8; T.H. Gaster, *The Holy and the Profane: Evolution of Jewish Folkways* (New York, 1980), pp. 109–110.

impressions of a wedding he had recently witnessed in Messina, Sicily: "After the seven blessings had been repeated, the bride was placed on a horse, and rode through the town. The whole community went before her on foot... and before the bride... youths and children carried burning torches and made loud exclamations, so that the whole place resounded."[40] From Obadia's letter alone it might have appeared that the use of torches at weddings was common among Sicilian Jewry but not to be encountered among the Jews to the north, from whence he had come. The miniatures in our manuscript suggest, however, that their use, in contrast to that of funerary torches, was a fairly widespread phenomenon among Italian Jewry

of the late fifteenth century. An Italian mahzor from Reggio, Emilia of 1465 depicts a bride on horseback leading the bridal procession (Fig. 7).[41]

We have seen, then, through this manuscript, some examples of how Jewish art, when properly illuminated with contemporary texts and contexts, can serve as a valuable source both for the history of Jewish life and for the history of Jewish death. It can also help us to expand our imagination concerning the range of practices which were considered normative in past Jewish societies. Sometimes our vision is enhanced by standing on the shoulders of giants, but sometimes, too, by gazing through the prisms of the jewels that have fallen through their fingers.

[40] A. Ya'ari, ed., *Letters from the Land of Israel* (Hebrew) (Ramat Gan, 1971), p. 108. For the English translation see *Miscellany of Hebrew Literature* (London, 1872), p. 118 [= E.N. Adler, *Jewish Travellers* (London, 1930), p. 241]. Obadia's letter is not mentioned by any of the authorities mentioned in the previous note. On its value as a historical source see E. Horowitz,

"Religious Practices among the Jews in the Late Fifteenth Century — according to the Letters of R. Obadia of Bertinoro" (Hebrew) *Pe'amim* 37 (1988): 31–40.

[41] London, British Library, Harley MS 5686, fol. 27v. See Metzger, *Jewish Life* fig. 343, pp. 228–29, 233.

112

1

2

3

Fig 1. Abu-Gosh, Crusader Church, Crucifixion Detail: Synagogue and Angel (after the restoration works carried out in autumn 1993 by the firm Maul & Beumling, Cologne. Photo Maul & Beumling).

Fig 2. Abu-Gosh, Crusader Church, Crucifixion Detail: Synagogue (after the restoration works carried out by the firm Maul & Beumling, Cologne. Photo Maul & Beumling).

Fig 3. Abu-Gosh, Crusader Church, Crucifixion Detail: Synagogue and Angel. Watercolor by Piellat. (Photo G. Kühnel).

THE PERSONIFICATIONS OF CHURCH AND SYNAGOGUE IN BYZANTINE ART: TOWARDS A HISTORY OF THE MOTIF[1]

Bianca Kühnel

On the southern wall of the Crusader basilica in the Arab village of Abu-Gosh, identified by the Crusaders as Emmaus, is depicted a personification of Synagogue being driven away from the Crucified Christ by an angel (Figs. 1–3). Both the personification of the Synagogue and the angel appear as half figures, corresponding to the half figures of Ecclesia and the angel approaching the cross from the left (Fig. 4). The Crucifixion wall painting, like all the other paintings in the church, is only partially preserved. Fortunately, the Abu-Gosh wall paintings were copied in watercolor at the beginning of this century by Comte de Piellat, and were studied and published several years ago by Gustav Kühnel.[2] The style of the wall paintings and the iconography of the separate scenes are Byzantine, attributable to the "dynamic phase" of the Comnenian art, i.e. to the third quarter of the twelfth century.[3]

A Crusader figure of Synagogue, holding a broken spear, pushed away from the Cross by an angel, and looking back regretfully, brings to mind the waves of anti-Jewish persecutions and the massacre of European Jewish communities committed during the Crusades. The liberation of the holy places was also accompanied by massacres of non-believers, occupants of the Holy Land, like Jews, Muslims, and even Eastern Christians. Synagogues and mosques were destroyed, and the Muslim and Jewish survivors fled the cities and took refuge in villages.[4] This was

Fig 4. Abu-Gosh, Crusader Church, Crucifixion. Watercolor by Piellat. (Photo G. Kühnel).

particularly so with regard to Jerusalem, the capital of the Latin Kingdom, from which Jews and Muslims were barred forever. This meant that even when the first wave of hatred and massacres passed and a return to the cities was possible, Jerusalem remained closed to the Jews until 1187, when Saladin put an end to the Crusader Kingdom of Jerusalem.[5]

[1] This is an extended version of a lecture delivered at the 28th International Congress on Medieval Studies in Kalamazoo, in May 1993. I would like to thank Bezalel Narkiss for reading a first draft of the article and making valuable suggestions.

[2] G. Kühnel, *Wall Painting in the Latin Kingdom of Jerusalem* (Berlin, 1988), pp. 149–80 (Frankfurter Forschungen zur Kunst, 14).

[3] The program, however, has some unique features and accents

resulting from the unconventional location of several scenes. See ibid., esp. pp. 177–80 (style and dating) and pp. 173–77 (the program).

[4] J. Prawer, *The Latin Kingdom of Jerusalem: European Colonialism in the Middle Ages* (London, 1972), esp. ch. 13, pp. 236ff.

[5] J. Prawer, "The Settlement of the Latins in Jerusalem," *Speculum* 27 (1952), 77ff.

Taking this background into consideration, together with the fact that Abu-Gosh lies only a few miles from Jerusalem, it may seem obvious that the figure of the expelled Synagogue should be seen also as a presentation of the Jews, exiled from Jerusalem, the place where Christ was crucified. The personification of Synagogue in Christian art as a hooded woman with a fallen crown and a broken scepter was shaped according to the canonical Christian interpretation of Lamentations 5:16–17: "The crown is fallen from our head: woe unto us, that we have sinned! For this our heart is faint; for these things our eyes are dim."[6] The Crusaders, as liberators of the Holy Places from the unbelievers, could be expected to emphasize their victory by showing the defeated Synagogue as an expression of their anti-Jewish attitude.

However this reading, despite its seeming plausibility, is not entirely correct.[7] The major historical studies and collections of sources regarding Jewish life under the Crusaders show unmistakably that after the first wave of massacres and persecutions the Crusader Kingdom changed its attitude towards the unbelievers.[8] Ten years after the establishment of the Crusader Kingdom Jews, Muslims and Eastern Christians found a`modus vivendi with the Latin Europeans. They returned to the cities from which they had fled, though Jerusalem continued to remain closed to Jews and Muslims. The Jews developed strong communities in the Galilee, where they settled some two dozen villages. The coastal cities, especially Ascalon and Tyre, which offered no resistance to the Crusaders, did not suffer destruction and brought no persecution on their original citizens even in the earliest stages of the Crusader conquest. Jewish pilgrimages continued and even increased during the twelfth century, being no longer limited to Jews from the Muslim Near East. Famous pilgrims such as Benjamin of Tudela and Petahiyah of Regensburg took the newly opened pilgrimage roads from the West. Benjamin of Tudela wrote that a few Jews were allowed to live in Jerusalem, under royal tolerance, near the citadel.[9]

From a legal point of view, the Latin masters of the Crusader Kingdom made no discrimination between Jews and other minorities like Eastern Christians, Muslims and Samaritans. All those who did not obey Rome were considered a single class according to the law, and they were all allowed to practice their faith. The Crusaders never turned into a missionary establishment in the East, seeking the conversion of individuals. For the most part they were indifferent to the problem and in some cases even opposed to conversion.[10] From William of Tyre, the chronicler of the First Crusades, we get some intimation of the occupations of the Jews and the high esteem they enjoyed among the Crusader ruling class. William complains that the Crusader princes preferred Jewish and Muslim doctors to Christian ones, though William's critical tone may be an expression of anti-Semitism and this may color his report.[11] There thus seem to be two ways of accounting for representations of Jews and of Synagogue in the art of the time, depending on whether one accepts the alienation of the Jews from the Crusader government or sees them functioning within the restrictions of that administration. It seems to me that accounting for the representations in the Abu-Gosh wall paintings by an anti-Jewish theory may be successfully countered by means of art-historical reasoning. The iconographical evidence and its theological and liturgical backing are

6   P. Weber, *Geistliches Schauspiel und kirchliche Kunst in ihrem Verhältnis erläutert an einer Ikonographie der Kirche und Synagoge* (Stuttgart, 1894); K. Künstle, *Ikonographie der christlichen Kunst* vol. 1 (Freiburg, 1928), pp. 81ff; A. Raddatz, "Die Entstehung des Motivs 'Ecclesia und Synagoge'; geschichtliche Hintergründe und Deutung," Diss. (Berlin, 1960).

7   A. Weyl Carr, "The Mural Paintings of Abu-Gosh and the Patronage of Manuel Comnenus in the Holy Land," in J. Folda, ed., *Crusader Art in the Twelfth Century* (Oxford, 1982), pp. 215–44 (BAR International Series, 152).

8   S.D. Goitein, *A Mediterranean Society*, 3 vols. (Berkeley, 1967–1978); id., *Palestinian Jewry in Early Islamic and Crusader Times in the Light of the Genizah Documents*, ed. J. Hacker, (Jerusalem, 1980), in Hebrew; E. Ashtor-Strauss, *History of the Jews in Egypt and Syria under the Mamelukes*, 3 vols. (Jerusalem, 1944–1970), in Hebrew; B.Z. Kedar, "On the History

of the Jews in Palestine in the Middle Ages," *Tarbiz* 42 (1973), 401–18 (Hebrew with English summary); J. Prawer, "The Jews in the Latin Kingdom of Jerusalem," *Zion* 11 (1946), 38–82 (Hebrew with English summary); id., "The Jews," in *The Latin Kingdom of Jerusalem*, pp. 236ff; id., "Social Classes in the Crusader States: The ¨Minorities," in *A History of the Crusades*, vol. 5: *The Impact of the Crusades on the Near East*, eds. N.P. Zacour and H.W. Hazard (Madison, 1985), esp. pp. 94ff.

9   *The Itinerary of Rabbi Benjamin of Tudela*, ed. and trans. M.N. Adler, vol. 1 (London, 1907), p. 35.

10 Such was the case of James of Vitry, cf. Prawer, "Social Classes," p. 112f, note 210.

11 William of Tyre, *Historia rerum in partibus transmarinis gestarum, XVIII, 34, RHC, Hist. occid.*, vol. 1, pp. 879–81; Prawer, "Social Classes," p. 95f.

much more conclusive than any speculation on the social, religious, and moral relationships between the Latin masters and the Jewish minority in the Crusader Kingdom of Jerusalem.

The iconography of Ecclesia and Synagoga has received much attention in comprehensive books, specialized articles, and separate entries in various lexicons and encyclopaedias.[12] A striking feature common to almost all these studies and expositions is that the Byzantine branch of this iconography — to which the representation in Abu-Gosh clearly belongs[13] — is generally disregarded.[14] In those few cases where Byzantine representations are considered, the main question posed by scholars is whether the theme made its first appearance in the West or in the East. This of course is not the only interesting question to be asked, especially when one observes that the Western and the Byzantine representations of Ecclesia and Synagoga in Crucifixion scenes belong to two distinct iconographic types whose beginnings are at a distance of some two hundred years from each other. The first Western representations date from the Carolingian period,[15] while the earliest Byzantine representations are from the eleventh century. Moreover, the Western iconography shows a great variety and an inner evolution, significantly dependent upon and reflecting the attitude of the Christians towards the Jews at different stages, while the Byzantine iconography is static, mainly of a liturgical and theological nature, and so consistent that it seems impermeable to historical changes in the relationships between Jews and Christians.

The first stage in the evolution of the Western iconography of Church and Synagogue in their association with Crucifixion scenes is richly documented in Carolingian manuscripts and on ivories. In the first extant Carolingian representation, an initial illustration on folio 43v of the Sacramentary of Drogo in Paris (Bibliothque Nationale lat. 9428), the personification of Ecclesia is paired not by Synagoga, but by the prophet Hosea, both facing each other from the two sides of the cross, in a visual translation of the *Concordia veteris et novi Testamenti*.[16] A later ivory binding from the same Carolingian school, Metz, also in Paris (BN lat. 9383), probably hints to the same concord when it shows Ecclesia and a heavier seated personification of Synagogue-Tyche on Christ's left side, facing each other.[17] The even later Nicasius dyptich in Tournai pairs the inscribed personifications of "Sca Ecclesia" with "Sca Iherusalem," both standing in identical positions facing the cross. The differences between them are stressed by the respective buildings behind the figures: a proud basilical church on the left, a building in decay on the right.[18] These examples illustrate the beginnings of the Western iconography of Ecclesia and Synagogue, when the theological concept of continuity between the Old and the New Testament was backed by an harmonious coexistence of the Jews among the Gentiles under Charlemagne and Louis the Pious.[19] Things began to change already in the second half of the ninth century, when a growing opposition of the church against the civil legislation, favorable to the Jews, took shape. Indeed, late Carolingian and Ottonian ivories document the change faithfully. Ecclesia and Synagoga do not face each other any more, the personifications are strongly differentiated in size, expression and position in relation to the cross: the personification of Ecclesia is taller and more dignified, usually collecting Christ's blood in a chalice, while Synagoga is personified as defeated, ashamed, running away from the cross, with no intervention of angels. Such is the representation on an ivory in London (Victoria and Albert Museum, Inv. no. 250.67) from

[12] In addition to the bibliography in note 6, see M. Schlauch, "The Allegory of Church and Synagogue," *Speculum* 14 (1939), pp. 448–64; A. Mayer, *Das Bild der Kirche: Hauptmotive der Ekklesia im Wandel der abendländischen Kunst* (Regensburg, 1962); W.S. Seiferth, *Synagogue and Church in the Middle Ages: Two Symbols in Art and Literature* (Munich, 1970 [1964]); A. Linder, "Ecclesia and Synagoga in the Medieval Myth of Constantine the Great," *Revue Belge d'Histoire et de Philosophie* 54 (1976), pp. 1019–60; O. von Simson, "Ecclesia und Synagoga am südlichen Querhauptportal des Strassburger Münsters," in *Wenn der Messias kommt; das jüdisch-christliche Verhältnis im Spiegel mittelalterlicher Kunst*, eds. L. Ḳtzsche and P. von der Osten-Sacken (Berlin, 1978), pp. 106–25.

[13] G. Kühnel, *Wall Painting*, pp. 166–71, pls. LV/98, LVI–LVIII.

[14] The Byzantine iconography of Church and Synagogue is briefly discussed in Weber, *Geistliches Schauspiel*, pp. 133–36; A.K. Orlandos, *E architektonike kai ai byzantinai toichographiai tes mones tou theologou Patmou* (Athens, 1970), pp. 213–15.

[15] Raddatz, "Die Entstehung des Motivs 'Ecclesia und Synagoge'," pp. 5ff.

[16] Künstle, *Ikonographie*, p. 81; Raddatz, p. 5, fig.1.

[17] A. Goldschmidt, *Elfenbeinskulpturen der karolingischen und ottonischen Zeit*, vol. 1 (Berlin, 1914), p. 47.

[18] Ch. de Linas, "Le dyptique de Saint Nicaise," *Gazette archéologique* 10 (1885), 308)16, pl. 36.

[19] Raddatz, "Entstehung," esp. pp. 30 ff.

around the year 900.[20] These relatively early depictions already contain the foundations of the late medieval, essentially antagonistic, monumental representations in the cathedrals of Bamberg and Strassburg. Like their Carolingian and Ottonian predecessors, these are also explained through specific historical relationships between Jews and Christians at the time.[21]

In Byzantium, Ecclesia and Synagoga at the Crucifixion occur only in the eleventh century. The representations are limited to a certain type of manuscript and to monumental painting, and are much more consistent in their appearance and meaning.[22] The first extant Byzantine representation of a Crucifixion with Ecclesia and Synagoga impelled by angels in opposite directions appears on folio 59 of the famous Greek Gospel manuscript in Paris (BN gr.74) from the third quarter of the eleventh century (Fig. 5).[23] On folios 58v and 59v of the same manuscript, two additional Crucifixions are depicted, without those personifications. The three representations illustrate three different moments of the Crucifixion story according to Matthew.[24] On the basis of several other details, not directly related to our topic, Kurt Weitzmann observed that the Paris Gospel gr. 74 was heavily influenced by a Lectionary, in which, for example, all four consecutive lections of the Passion had a title miniature of the Crucifixion.[25] The appearance of Ecclesia and Synagoga, not backed by the Gospel text, in a Crucifixion scene of this manuscript, is probably also to be explained by the influence of illuminated liturgical texts.

Significantly it is also in the eleventh century that the pair Church and Synagogue appeared in the illu-

Fig 5. Paris, Bibliothèque Nationale, Ms. gr. 74, fol. 59: Crucifixion. (H. Omont, Evangiles avec peintures byzantines du XIe siècle, vol. 1, Paris 1907, pl. 51).

minations to the *Homilies* of Gregory Nazianzenus.[26] In the eleventh century the *Homilies* underwent a textual recension. A selection of sixteen homilies was made, out of the original forty-five known from the two ninth-century copies: the one in Paris (BN gr. 510), and the other in Milan (Ambrosianus 49–50).[27] The sixteen selected homilies were arranged to be read in the liturgical order of the feast days. For example: the Easter Homily became the first Homily, placed at the beginning, and illustrated by the Anastasis. The second Homily, read on the first day after Easter, was appropriately illustrated with a theophany of Christ since the text speaks of Christ riding on the clouds and having the countenance of an angel, as a vision, by Habakuk.[28]

20 Goldschmidt, *Elfenbeinskulpturen*, vol. 1, fig. 85; Raddatz, p. 9f, fig. 32.
21 Simson, "Ecclesia und Synagoge;" id., "Le programme sculptural du transept méridional de la cathédrale de Strasbourg," in id., *Von der Macht des Bildes im Mittelalter, Gesammelte Aufsätze zur Kunst des Mittelalters*, new edn. by R. Haussherr (Berlin, 1993).
22 I will not deal here with the Italian representations of Church and Synagogue, such as the Exultet Roll in Monte Cassino and the ivory in Berlin, which have a place of their own between the Western and the Byzantine iconography of the scene. For the Berlin ivory, see H.L. Kessler, "An Eleventh-Century Ivory Plaque from South Italy and the Cassinese Revival," *Jahrbuch der Berliner Museen* 8 (1966), 66–95.
23 H. Omont, *Evangiles avec peintures byzantines du XIe siècle, Reproduction des 361 miniatures du manuscrit gréc. 74 de la Bibliothèque Nationale*, vol. 1 (Paris, 1907), pl. 51 and p. 8; B. Brenk, "Die Anfänge der byzantinischen Weltgerichtsdarstel-

lung," *Byzantinische Zeitschrift* 57 (1964), 106–26, esp. pp. 114–15 (mid-eleventh century); V. Lazarev, *Storia della pittura bizantina* (Turin, 1967), p. 187.
24 Omont in *Evangiles*, p. 8, describes the scenes thus: "Jésus est crucifié," for the representation on fol. 58v (pl. 50); "Jésus expire sur la croix," for the representation on fol. 59 (pl. 51); and "Jésus mort sur la croix," for the representation on fol. 59v (pl. 52).
25 K. Weitzmann, "The Narrative and Liturgical Gospel Illustrations," in id., *Studies in Classical and Byzantine Manuscript Illumination*, ed. H.L. Kessler, with an Introduction by H. Buchthal (Chicago, 1971), p. 265, figs. 254, 256 (originally published in 1950).
26 G. Galavaris, *The Illustrations of the Liturgical Homilies of Gregory Nazianzenus* (Princeton, 1969) (Studies in Manuscript Illumination, 6).
27 Ibid., pp. 4f.
28 Ibid., pp. 120–25.

Fig 6. Mount Athos, Dionysiou monastery, cod. 61, fol. 17: St. Mamas, Church and Synagogue. (G. Galavaris, The Illustrations of the Liturgical Homilies of Gregory Nazianzenus, Princeton, 1969, fig. 358).

The third homily, to which the visual representations of Ecclesia and Synagoga are attached, is read on New Sunday, the first Sunday after Easter, commonly known as Thomas' Sunday. This homily speaks of "the old dispensation, succeeded by a new life, which was derived from Christ's death and resurrection."[29] The homily is not exclusively illustrated by one scene, as in the case of the previous two homilies, but with a choice of different scenes, that of Church and Synagogue being but one of them. The different illustrations appear alternatively or in groupings of two or three. The homily opens with a reference to the Feast of the Consecration of the Church (Encaenia), which was originally the Feast of the Dedication of the Holy Sepulcher (14 September) and became generalized as representing the institution of the Church, as well as of any other church building. The Orthodox Church observes the Feast not only on 14 September but also on the eighth day after Easter. These two liturgical themes, namely the consecration of any church, and the Consecration of the Church of the Holy Sepulcher, which appear in this homily, inspired three different illustrations which occur either separately, or, rarely, in combinations of two in the same frame. A good example appears in Codex

61 in the Dionysiou monastery on Mount Athos, on folio 17 (Fig. 6). The panel depicts St. Mamas twice, once standing in the center and once milking a hind, while in the background are two angels pushing Ecclesia and Synagoga, appearing on top of two buildings. Mamas' connection to this homily is based on the concluding text of the Homily, where Gregory mentions "the famous Mamas, the shepherd and the martyr," in whose church near Nazianzus this sermon was delivered, possibly on the occasion of the transfer and deposit of the saint's relics.[30]

Besides St. Mamas and the personifications of Church and Synagogue, the third scene accompanying this homily on New Sunday in some other manuscripts is the anointing of the altar column, a rite characteristic of Encaenia celebrations to this day.[31] In manuscripts of the eleventh and twelfth centuries this scene appears mainly as a marginal illustration.[32] The connections and interchangeability between these three scenes point toward their common origin, the consecration of a church, as implied by the text. It also enables us to perceive the three degrees of liturgical symbolism in the text: the consecration of a new church, commemorating the consecration of the Church of the Holy Sepulcher, and of its predecessor, the Jewish Temple.[33] The three different illustrations correspond to the three degrees of symbolism: the depiction of St. Mamas refers to the actual consecration of a particular church in Nazianzus, the anointing of the altar column corresponds to the liturgical act of consecration of the Church, while Ecclesia and Synagoga illustrate the theological aspect of the homily, seeing the Church as the replacement of the Jewish Temple, as "new life succeeded the old dispensation," and the New Covenant succeeded the Old Covenant. The emphasis here is decidedly more on the continuity and legitimacy of the Church, rather than on an antithetical approach. Although the superiority of the "new" over the "old" is stressed, it is clearly not done antagonistically.

Apart from these three scenes relating directly to the content of the third homily, two other scenes occur in connection with it. One is St. Gregory teaching,

29   Migne, *PG*, vol. 36, cols. 608ff; Galavaris, p. 96.
30   A. Marava-Chadjinikolaou, *O Agios Mamas* (Athens, 1953), p. 59; Galavaris, p. 39.
31   Ibid., pp. 38ff.
23   E.g. Sinai, codex 339, fol. 42v; Moscow, Historical Museum 146,

fol. 23v; Turin, University Library C.I.6, fol. 16.
33   M. Black, "The Festival of Encaenia Ecclesia in the Ancient Church with Special Reference to Palestine," *Journal of Ecclesiastical History* 5 (1954), 78–85; Galavaris, p. 39.

BIANCA KÜHNEL

Fig 7. Paris, Bibliothèque Nationale, Coislin 239, fol. 22: Church and Synagogue. (Galararis, fig. 195).

Fig 8. London, British Library, Add. Ms. 24381, fol. 2: Church and Synagogue. (Galavaris, fig. 94).

as an illustration to all the *Homilies*, and the other is Doubting Thomas, reflecting the additional event commemorated on the same day.

The implicit intrinsic parallelism between Church and Temple, on one hand, and Ecclesia and Synagoga, on the other, is demonstrated visually by the equation made in most of the illustrated Gregory manuscripts between the personifications and the buildings or altars. For example, in a manuscript from the Bibliothèque Nationale in Paris, Coislin 239, on folio 22, behind Synagoga driven away by an angel there is a square building with a round tambour and dome possibly representing the Temple in Jerusalem (Fig. 7), while Ecclesia, who contributes to the expulsion of Synagoga, demonstratively holds in her outstretched arms a model-like basilica. The half-figure of Ecclesia's angel floats in the sky exactly above the basilica, thus conferring heavenly patronage upon it, as against the "terrestrial" group of Synagogue, her angel and the Temple. On folio 2 of an eleventh-century Gregory manuscript in the British Library (Add. Ms. 24381), the two symmetrical groups of personifications and angels appear behind different altar screens (Fig. 8). The altar screen of Ecclesia on the left is more elaborate, and has a ciborium behind it. In the above-mentioned Dionysiou codex 61 from Mount Athos, the two pairs are placed on top of two tower-like buildings, the one on the right being larger and more convenient for the personages than that of Synagogue on the left (Fig. 6). The fact that the differences between Ecclesia and Synagoga in these manuscripts are also stressed by differences in the shape of the ecclesiastical buildings

accompanying them is an expression of the implicit identity between the personifications and the church buildings. This valuable indication of their meaning supports the overall interpretation of Gregory's third homily. It seems that the depiction of contrasting new and old buildings is a symbolic representation of Church and Synagogue, and it antedates the depiction of the personifications. For instance, in codex Iviron 27 from Mount Athos, consisting of the complete range of Gregory's *Homilies*, from before the eleventh century, the homily on New Sunday is illustrated by a square structure, on top of which is depicted a three-aisled basilica.[34]

The same phrase in Gregory's New Sunday homily, which generated the visual translation of the "new" and the "old" into the personifications of Ecclesia and Synagoga, also specifies the events making the succession possible. Christ's death and resurrection is regarded as a condition by which the Old will become the New Israel, as Gregory put it: "the old dispensation succeeded by a new life, which was derived from Christ's death and resurrection." The introduction of the Crucified Christ between Ecclesia and Synagoga is the perfect compositional achievement, in which the movement initiated by the angels behind the personifications becomes meaningful, by creating an axis. And inversely: the introduction of Ecclesia and Synagoga into the traditional Crucifixion

[34] K. Weitzmann, *Die Byzantinische Buchmalerei des 9. und 10. Jahrhundert* (Berlin, 1935), pl. XVIII/100; Galavaris, p. 95, n. 236.

Fig. 9.   Greece, Kastoria, Panaghia Mavriotissa: Crucifixion. (S. Pelekamidis, M. Chatzidakis, eds., Kastoria, Athens, 1984, fig. 12).

added a new liturgical and theological dimension to the representation. The coincidence in dates, the fact that the first extant Church and Synagogue representations in both the homily on New Sunday and the Gospel (BN. gr. 74) Crucifixion scene are from the eleventh century is most telling. It means that the representations of Ecclesia and Synagoga with and without the Crucifixion carried, originally at least, the same theological and liturgical meaning. It is indeed very probable, as Weitzmann has suggested, that the manuscripts of Gregory Nazianzenus and the Gospel manuscripts had a common source and were largely dependent upon Lectionaries, although the earliest extant Lectionary with a Crucifixion accompanied by the two personifications dates from the thirteenth century.[35] The common visual source may be proven by the similarity between the first representation of the

personifications, in the framework of a Crucifixion, that in the Paris manuscript gr. 74 (Fig. 5), and in certain *Homilies* manuscripts: the figures of Ecclesia and Synagoga are full-length, while the angels are half-length.[36]

What is important in the connection between the depictions of Ecclesia and Synagoga and these manuscripts is that it proves the origin of the motif and its association to the Crucifixion in the eleventh century, on a wide theological and liturgical basis.[37] It means, accordingly, that the wall paintings of the twelfth century need not have been an invention of the Crusaders. If we accept the early dating of the Crucifixion with Ecclesia and Synagoga in Panaghia Mavriotissa at Kastoria in Greece (Fig. 9) by Ann Wharton Epstein, this may be the monument bridging the gap in time between the manuscript illustrations

35   Weitzmann, "The Narrative and Liturgical Gospel Illustrations," in *Studies in Classical and Byzantine Manuscript Illumination*, esp. p. 264f. For the thirteenth-century Syriac Lectionary in the British Library, Add. 7170, fol. 151, see G. de Jerphanion, *Les miniatures du manuscrit syriac de la Bibliothèque Vaticane* (Vatican City, 1940), fig. 46.

36   For example, their representation on folio 22 of the eleventh-century Homilies manuscript in Paris, Bibliothèque Nationale,

Coislin 239 (Fig.7). See Galavaris, fig. 195.

37   The liturgical foundation of the theme in Byzantine art is backed up not only by Gregory's homily on New Sunday, but also by certain other liturgical texts, such as hymns of the Triodion, or the Great Canon of Andrew of Crete. See Galavaris, p. 97, n. 243; see below, note 39; Migne, *PG*, vol. 97, col. 1352 (Andrew of Crete).

Fig. 10.   Cyprus, Enkleistra of St. Neophytos near Paphos, Naos: Crucifixion. (Photo G. Kühnel).

of the eleventh century and the wall paintings of the twelfth century.

The traditional dating of the Mavriotissa wall painting in the late twelfth-early thirteenth century by Lazarev, Chatzidakis, Demus, Velmans, Djuric, Hadermann-Misguich, Mouriki, and recently Skawran,[38] was challenged by Ann Wharton Epstein, who moved it to the end of the eleventh century, in "a

[38] V. Lazarev, "Macedonian Painting During the 11th and the 12th Centuries," *Actes du XIIe Congrès International d'Études Byzantines, Ohrid, 1961*, vol. 1 (Belgrade, 1963), pp. 105–34, esp. p. 132, n. 111; M. Chatzidakis, "Rapports entre la peinture de la Macédoine et de la Crete au XIVe sicle," *Actes du IXe Congrès International d'Études Byzantines Salonica, 1953*, vol. 1 (Athens, 1955), pp. 136–48, esp. p. 137; O. Demus, "Die Entstehung der Paläologenstils in der Malerei," *Berichte zum XI. Internationalen Byzantinisten Kongress, München, 1958* (Munich, 1960), pp.

1–63, esp. p. 26, n. 106; T. Velmans, *La peinture murale byzantine à la fin du Moyen Age*, vol. 1 (Paris, 1977), p. 143f; V. Djuric, "La peinture murale byzantine: XIIe et XIIIe siècles," *Rapports et Co-Rapports du XVe Congrès International d'Études Byzantines*, vol. 3, *Art et Archéologie* (Athens, 1976), p. 196, esp. p. 61f; L. Hadermann-Misguich, "La peinture monumentale tardo-comnène et ses prolongements au XIIIe siècle," ibid., pp. 97–128, esp. pp. 108, 126; D. Mouriki, "Stylistic Trends

*Fig. 11. Studenica, Church of
St. Mary: Crucifixion.
(Photo G. Kühnel).*

speculative attempt to use the fresco program of the
Mavriotissa monastery as a historical document.''[39]
Wharton Epstein interprets Ecclesia and Synagoga in
the Crucifixion scene on the West wall of the church as

an expression of the anti-Semitic feelings of the local
population stirred up by the Crusaders who passed
through Kastoria in the wake of the First Crusade,
in 1096.[40] The situation of the Jewish community

in Monumental Painting in Greece During the Eleventh and
Twelfth Centuries,'' *Dumbarton Oaks Papers* 34–35 (1980/1981);
K.M. Skawran, *The Development of Middle Byzantine Fresco
Painting in Greece* (Pretoria, 1982), p. 180.

[39] S. Pelekanidis, *Kastoria* (Thessalonica, 1953, in Greek) is the only
one to allow a relatively early date for the earliest Mavriotissa frescoes, pp. 1120–30; id., ''Kastoria,'' *RbK* (1978), cols. 1190–1224;
A. Wharton Epstein, ''Middle Byzantine Churches of Kastoria:
Dates and Implications, With an Appendix on the Frescoes of

the *Mavriotissa Monastery*,'' *Art Bulletin* 62 (1980), 190–207,
esp. p. 206; id., ''Frescoes of the Mavriotissa Monastery near
Kastoria: Evidence of Millenarianism and Anti-Semitism in the
Wake of the First Crusade,'' *Gesta* 21 (1982), 21–29; id., *Art of
Empire, Painting and Architecture of the Byzantine Periphery;
A Comparative Study of Four Provinces* (University Park and
London: The Pennsylvania State University Press, 1988), pp.
115f.

[40] Epstein, ''Frescoes.''

in Kastoria before and after the Crusader invasions
serves as evidence for the anti-Semitic interpretation
of this and another motif apparent in the Mavriotissa
Koimesis, i.e. the apocryphal episode of Jephonias the
Jew according to the Greek account of the Virgin's
Dormition attributed to St. John.[41] In fact, the anti-
Jewish interpretation of the Abu-Gosh wall paintings,
by Annemarie Weyl Carr, depends exclusively on an
analogy with the Mavriotissa Crucifixion.[42] I do not
intend to argue here against the interpretation of the
Mavriotissa wall painting, but I am definitely opposed
to the kind of connection established between Abu-
Gosh and Kastoria on historical grounds. Even if both
monuments relate to the Crusades, they belong to two
completely and significantly different locations and
periods of Crusader history: the relevant Mavriotissa
wall paintings, the Crucifixion and the Koimesis, were
allegedly executed in the late 1090s, and are located
on one of the roads taken by the Crusaders on their
way to liberate the holy places, while the Abu-Gosh
decoration was made in the late 1160s in the Latin
Kingdom of Jerusalem. As we saw at the beginning,
the situation of the Jews in the Crusader Kingdom
during its most stable and flourishing period cannot
be compared to that of the Greek Diaspora Jews in
the path of the Crusader movement towards the Holy
Land. In view of the fact that the geo-historical conditions are not the same, the analogy, which is based
only on geo-political grounds, is untenable.

The only feature in common between the Crucifixion in Kastoria and that in Abu-Gosh is the iconography; this feature is in fact common to several other
monumental representations of the Crucifixion with
Ecclesia and Synagoga from the second half of the
twelfth century and the beginning of the thirteenth,
such as at Hagios Stratigos in Mani,[43] the Refectory of
the Monastery of St. John the Theologian in Patmos,[44]
the *naos* of the Enkleistra of St. Neophytos near Paphos
(Fig. 10),[45] and the Church of St. Mary in
Studenica (Fig. 11).[46] The Enkleistra of St. Neophytos
and Abu-Gosh have more than iconography in common: the figure of John the Evangelist from an earlier

*Fig. 12.   Cyprus, Enkleistra of St. Neophytos near
Paphos, Cell, Crucifixion Detail: St. John the
Evangelist. (Photo G. Kühnel).*

Crucifixion in the cell (Fig. 12) can be compared with
one of the best preserved figures of the Koimesis in
Abu-Gosh, on the north wall, opposite the Crucifixion
(Fig. 13). The folds and loops of the apostle's garment
in Abu-Gosh as well as the colors and shadows are
similar to those of John the Evangelist in Cyprus.
The style of the Crucifixion wall painting in Abu-
Gosh clearly associates it with the same group, as
demonstrated by a relatively well preserved figure
of an angel hovering above the cross (Fig. 14). The
Neophytos wall painting is dated to 1183,[47] while the
Abu-Gosh frescoes must have been done before 1187,

[41]   M.R. James, *The Apocryphal New Testament* (Oxford, 1924),
p. 208, ch. 46.
[42]   Weyl Carr, "The Mural Paintings of Abu-Gosh".
[43]   Skawran, p. 173f.
[44]   A.K. Orlandos, "Fresques byzantines du monastère de Patmos,"
Cahiers Archéologiques 12 (1962), 285–302; id., *The Architecture
and the Frescoes of Patmos* (Athens, 1970) (Greek, with French

summary).
[45]   C. Mango, E.J.W. Hawkins, "The Hermitage of St. Neophytos
and Its Wall Paintings," *Dumbarton Oaks Papers* 20 (1966),
149f, figs. 32, 33.
[46]   V.J. Djuric, *Byzantinische Fresken in Jugoslawien* (Herrsching,
n.d.), pp. 42ff.

Fig. 13. Abu-Gosh, Crusader Church, Koimesis Detail: Apostle. (Photo G. Kühnel).

Fig. 14. Abu-Gosh, Crusader Church, Crucifixion Detail: Angel (Photo G. Kühnel).

probably twenty years earlier.[48] The similarity in style between the two, therefore, indicates either a common source, or even direct influence, which can be extended to the iconography as well.

The appurtenance of the Crucifixion wall painting in Abu-Gosh to a well defined branch of Byzantine iconography, with a clear start in Byzantine liturgy, and a consistent development in manuscript illumi-nation and wall painting, works against an ad hoc invention of the motif out of a specific historical event or situation. If there are some anti-Jewish accents in the visual motif of Church and Synagogue in Byzantine art, they should be sought in their common textual and liturgical background, and not specula-tively and separately in the historical conditions of one or another monument.

[47] Mango and Hawkins, ''The Hermitage of St. Neophytos,'' p. 177f (the Crucifixion); pp. 193ff (the chronology of the paint-ings).

[48] Kühnel, *Wall Painting*, pp. 177ff.

PAGAN IMAGES IN JEWISH ART

Mira Freidman

Many scholars have discussed the use of pagan motifs in Jewish art. Among the images widely dealt with is the representation of Orpheus playing in front of the animals, depicted above the Torah niche in the synagogue of Dura Europos.[1] Orpheus was identified as King David when a mosaic floor was unearthed in the synagogue at Gaza, showing the image of the musician identified by the inscription "David".[2] Apparently, the Jews did not hesitate to borrow the pagan image of Orpheus, the mythological Thracian poet and musician. The Jews introduced new meanings into the image and represented it as King David.[3]

There is a similar use of clearly pagan motifs on the mosaic floors of ancient synagogues in Israel. The artists and those who commissioned the works, as well as the worshipers, did not feel any constraint in

depicting the figure of Helios, the sun god, riding his fiery chariot in the center of the zodiac.[4] Unlike King David, identified by an inscription, there are no inscriptions on the floors of the synagogues showing the image to be a personification of the sun, rather than a pagan god. However, we can put aside any connotation of idolatry in these images. The literary image of the sun, described as it rises in its chariot in the sky, appears already in Jewish commentaries, the *Midrash*.[5] These are not the only pagan images in early Jewish art.[6]

Because of the large number of these images in Eretz Israel, we can dismiss the theory interpreting their appearance as indiscriminate or unconscious borrowing from pagans.[7] We can further question the opinion, mainly set forth by Goodenough, that

[1]   E.R. Goodenough, *Jewish Symbols in the Greco-Roman Period* (New York, 1953), IX, 89–104; X, pl. IV, figs. 74, 77.

[2]   M. Avi-Yonah, "An Old Synagogue in Gaza," *Bulletin of the Israel Exploration Society* 30 (1966), 221–23 (in Hebrew).

[3]   The two surviving findings of David in the image of Orpheos are from the third and sixth centuries C.E. — in the Dura Europus synagogue in Syria, and at Gaza. We may thus assume that they were not isolated incidents and that there was a tradition of such representations in the Holy Land and beyond it. The image of King David playing to the animals appears again in illustrations in Byzantine psalters of the 10th to the 12th centuries, thought to be derived from early Christian sources. See e.g. Paris, Bibliotheque Nationale, gr. 139, fol. 1; H. Buchthal, *The Miniatures of the Paris Psalter: A Study in Middle Byzantine Painting* (London, 1938), pp. 13–17, pl. 1 and figs. 19, 20–23; K. Weitzmann, *Greek Mythology in Byzantine Art* (Princeton, 1951), pp. 67–68, figs. 82–86.

[4]   See e.g. the mosaics in the synagogues at Hammath-Tiberias and Beit Alpha; see M. Dothan, "The Synagogue at Hammath-Tiberias," in Lee I. Levine (ed.), *Ancient Synagogues Revealed* (Jerusalem, 1981), pp. 66–67; E.L. Sukenik, *The Ancient Synagogue at Beth Alpha* (Jerusalem & Oxford, 1932), pl. X.

[5]   "The Sun rides in a chariot and rises crowned like a bridegroom and he goeth forth and rejoiceth as a strong man, as it is said, 'which is as a bridegroom coming out of his chamber to run his course'"; see *Pirke de Rabbi Eliezer* (*The Chapters of Rabbi Eliezer the Great*), trans. G. Friedlander (New York, 1965), chap. 6. See also *Num. Rabbah*, chap. 122 (on Song of Songs 3:10).

[6]   See e.g. the mid-fifth-century mosaic of Odysseus and the Sirens

at the House of Kyrios Leontis at Beth She'an, which is, however, a private home. See N. Zori, "The House of Kyrios Leontis at Beth She'an," *Israel Exploration Journal* 16 (1966), 128–130; Lucille Roussin, "The Beit Leontis Mosaic: An Eschatological Interpretation," *Journal of Jewish Art* 8 (1981), 12–18. On mythological images on sarcophagi at Beth She'arim, see N. Avigad, "The Seventh Season of Excavations in Beit She'arim, 1955," in *Eretz Israel* 5 (1958), 180, 185–87, pl. 20 (in Hebrew); N. Avigad, "Excavations at Beth She'arim 1958," *Israel Exploration Journal* 9 (1959), 211–12. Jews from the Holy Land were familiar with Homer, and did not see any idolatrous act in reading his works; according to the *Jerusalem Talmud*, Sanhedrin, chap. 10,1, those who read the Apocrypha, have no part in the world to come, "But as to the books of Homer and all the books written henceforward — he who reads in them is tantamount to one who (merely) reads a letter": *The Talmud of the Land of Israel*, trans. J. Neusner (Chicago & London, 1984), vol. 31, Sanhedrin, X. It is possible that depictions of mythological images were not forbidden to the Jews. Thus the image of Leda and the Swan from Beit She'arim, considered to be an isolated example contrary to the spirit of Judaism (Goodenough, "Pagan Symbols in Jewish Antiquity," *Commentary* 23, 1957, 77), might not be so isolated. On this and on pagan remnants of a later period, see Th. H. Gaster, "Pagan Ideas and the Jewish Mind, Japhet in the Tents of Shem," *Commentary* 17 (1954), 185–90.

[7]   See H.H. Kitchener, "Synagogues of Galilee," *Palestine Exploration Fund Quarterly and Statement*, 1878, p. 129; H. Kohl and C. Watzinger, *Antike Synagogen in Galiläa* (Leipzig, 1916), pp. 202–3.

Fig. 1. Hanukkah lamp. Italy, 16th century. Paris, Muśe Cluny.

sees them as expressions of a gnostic Judaism or of mystic, Hellenized Jewish sects, as opposed to normative rabbinical Judaism and Jewish Law (*Halachah*).[8] Art, including figurative art, was part of the lives of pious Jews, devout and faithful to their religion and its customs. Figurative art was a usual component of synagogue decoration. Pagan motifs, stripped of all idolatrous connotations, developed new meanings which in no way violated basic Jewish precepts.[9]

The borrowing of pagan and mythological motifs in Judaism is not limited to the first centuries of the Christian era, a period when the new artistic language was still in its early days and when one could see in it a heritage of classical art and a continuation of old traditions. The same use of pagan and mythological motifs may be seen in Renaissance Jewish art, mainly in Italy but also in other areas of Europe, where pagan and mythological motifs, such as centaurs, sirens or gorgons are quite frequent.[10] We will not dwell on the abundant representations of Victories and cupids turned into angels which appear profusely throughout Jewish art, even in Eastern Europe. They are depicted in various types of art and are even used to decorate the holiest of ceremonial objects. For instance, on an early eighteenth-century German Torah shield, among the motifs most frequently used to decorate ritual objects — the two columns and three crowns of Torah, Priesthood and Royalty — a naked cupid stands on the top of each column, two clothed angels stand at either side, and below the columns

8 Goodenough, *Jewish Symbols*, I, pp. 70, 250, 256–7; II, pp. 3f, 28; VIII, pp. 202, 215, passim. See also idem, "Pagan Symbols," pp. 74–80; J. Neusner, "Jewish Use of Pagan Symbols after 70 C.E.," *Journal of Religion* 43 (1963), 285–94.

9 N. Avigad, *Beth She'arim*, vol. 3, *The Archaeological Excavations During 1953–1958* (Jerusalem, 1971), pp. 201–8 (Hebrew); E.E. Urbach, "The Rabbinical Laws of Idolatry in the Second and Third Centuries in the Light of Archaeological and His-

torical Facts," *Israel Exploration Journal* 9 (1959), 149–245.

10 See M. Narkiss, *The Hanukkah Lamp* (Jerusalem, 1939), pp. 12–24, pls. IX–XX (Hebrew); Chaya Benjamin, *The Stieglitz Collection, Masterpieces of Jewish Art* (cat.) (Jerusalem, The Israel Museum, 1987), nos. 120–26, 188, 215–18, 280; B. Narkiss, *Hebrew Illuminated Manuscripts* (Jerusalem, 1978), pl. 58; J. Gutmann, *Hebrew Manuscript Painting* (New York, 1978), pl. 36. Many of the works mentioned also include nude cupids.

are heads of putti or cherubs.[11] Sometimes even nude female angels are depicted, even on ritual utensils and holy vessels.[12]

One example of the use of mythological images that seem to be foreign to Judaism is a sixteenth-century Italian hannukah lamp (Fig. 1). At its center is the head of a Medusa, flanked by two centaurs, with a nude female riding each of them. The top center depicts a phoenix, a frequent image in Christian art, where it represents the Resurrection.[13] The image originates from the bestiaries, the zoology books of the Middle Ages, based on the *Physiologus*.[14] The decoration of the hannukah lamp derives with some minor changes from an early sixteenth-century Paduan jewelry box.[15] We may assume that the centaurs and the Medusa, though having clear significance in ancient times and even in the Middle Ages, may be solely decorative motifs in the Renaissance.[16]

This is not so in the case of the phoenix. Its image was linked to one of the cornerstones of Christianity, and most prevalent in the Christian art of the period. In spite of this, it was adopted by the Jews.

It is hard to imagine the adoption of such a deeply significant Christian image in a purely decorative manner, without giving it new meaning. The fact that the decoration was adopted by Jews proves that they did not see it as heretical. The reference to the phoenix in the *Midrash* enabled it to be used in Jewish art, despite its blatantly Christian significance: according to the *Midrash*, the phoenix won eternal life when it refused to eat the fruit of the Tree of Knowledge in the Garden of Eden, as opposed to other living creatures,[17] and because it was not a burden on Noah in his Ark, as it ate nothing.[18] It was even adopted by the Jewish community of Amsterdam as its coat of arms, possibly signifying the martyrdom of the Maranos and the rebirth of Judaism among them. In 1743, the Amsterdam Jewish community changed its arms, replacing the phoenix with the pelican, whose origin was also in the bestiaries and the *Physiologus*. The Christians saw in it the image of Jesus and his sacrifice, his crucifixion and resurrection, as it is described and thus depicted as feeding its young on its own blood. The image was likened to the blood

[11] Paris, Cluny Museum, inv. no. 12259, don. Rothschild, coll. Strauss, no. 26. V. Klagsbald, *Catalogue raisonée de la collection juive du Musée de Cluny* (Paris, 1981), pp. 106–7, no. 145. It is similar to the Torah shield in the Jewish Museum, New York. See S. Kayser and G. Shoenberger (eds.), *Jewish Ceremonial Art* (Philadelphia, 1955), no. 44.

[12] See e.g. in a 19th-century paper Mizrach, New York, Jewish Museum, Harry G. Friedman coll.; see A. Kanof, *Jewish Ceremonial Art and Religious Observance* (New York, n.d.), p. 203, fig. 214, and another Mizrach, presented to a German Synagogue in 1833 on the occasion of a wedding, Jerusalem, Israel Museum; see R. Posner, U. Kaplom and S. Cohen (eds.), *Jewish Liturgy* (Jerusalem, 1975), pl. between pp. 32 and 33.

[13] Paris, Cluny, inv. no. 12246, don. Rothschild, coll. Strauss, no. 11. See Klagsbald, *Catalogue*, p. 31, no. 19; M. Narkiss, *The Hanukkah Lamp*, no. 27. A similar lamp but without the top part decorated with the phoenix is in the Israel Museum, Jerusalem; Benjamin, *The Stieglitz Collection*, pp. 166–7, no. 126. Klagsbald mistakenly identifies the bird as a pelican. On the phoenix in Christian art, see Honorius of Autun, "Speculum Ecclesiae," 19, *PL* 172, 935 ff.; J. Kramer, "Phönix," in E. Kirschbaum, *Lexikon der christlichen Ikonographie* (Rome, 1971), III, cols. 390–1.

[14] The *Physiologus* was written originally c. 200 C.E.; P. Gerlach, "Physiologus," in Kirschbaum, *Lexikon*, III, cols. 432–36. It may also have had Jewish sources. See Emil Peters, *Der griechische Physiologus und seine orientalischen Übersetzungen* (Berlin, 1898), p. 9; Max Wellmann, "Der Physiologus," *Philologus*, Supplementband, XXII.I (Leipzig, 1930), p. 55. See also R. Wischnitzer, "The Unicorn in Christian and Jewish Art," *Historia Judaica* 13 (1951), p. 141.

[15] Benjamin, *Stieglitz*, p. 166, fig. 126.I; Klagsbald, *Catalogue*, p. 31, figs.

[16] The centaurs had a negative meaning, as did the gorgon since Antiquity. P. Gerlach, "Kentaur," in Kirschbaum, *Lexikon*, II, cols. 504–8; E. Psenner and E. Kirschbaum, "Sirenen," in ibid., IV, cols. 168–70; see also O. Seyffert, *Dictionary of Classical Antiquities* (New York, 1956), s.v. "Gorgo (Gorgons)." However, since the Renaissance, their frequent use in the decorative arts possibly lessened this meaning.

[17] "The word 'also' ["and she also gave some to her husband" (Genesis 3:6)] bears the force of a phrase of inclusion, meaning to encompass domesticated beasts, wild beasts, and fowl. Everyone obeyed her and ate of the fruit, except for one bird, which is called the phoenix. For it is written, "Then I shall die with my nest and I shall multiply my days as the phoenix" (Job 29:18). A member of the house of R. Jannai said: "It lives for a thousand years, and at the end of a thousand years a fire goes forth from its nest and burns it up and leaves an egg['s bulk of ash] which goes and grows limbs and lives on." R. Judah bar Simeon said: "It lives for a thousand years and at the end of a thousand years its body dissolves and its wings drop off, but an egg['s bulk] is left and it goes and grows parts and lives on'." *Genesis Rabbah*, XIX, 5; see *Genesis Rabbah, The Judaic Commentary to the Book of Genesis*, trans. J. Neusner (Atlanta, Georgia, 1985), I, p. 204.

[18] "As for the phoenix, my father [Noah] discovered it lying in the hold of the ark. 'Do thou require no food?' he asked it. 'I saw that thou wast busy,' it replied, 'so I said to myself, I will give thee no trouble.' 'May it be [God's] will that thou shouldst not perish!' he exclaimed, as it is written, 'Then I said, I shall die in the nest, but I shall multiply my days as the phoenix' (Job 29:18)." *Babylonian Talmud, Sanhedrin* 108b, trans. H. Freedman (London, The Soncino Press, 1935).

flowing from Jesus' breast wound, a source of life to believers.[19] Like the phoenix, the pelican received a new meaning in Judaism, and it also appears on various religious objects.[20] Here a similar process took place to that of the image of Orpheus. The latter was very widespread both in pagan art as Orpheus, and in Christian art as Jesus, while it was adopted by Jewish art as the image of David, king and future Messiah. In all these instances the Jews borrowed the iconographic scheme and even retained its meaning in a general sense, while giving it a Jewish content and removing from it all heretical associations which could offend against the Jewish religion.

The idea that the recurring pagan images appearing during the Renaissance and Baroque lost all symbolic significance does not seem valid. In addition, one cannot accept a view which does not allow that a blatantly Christian motif may be borrowed by Jewish art.[21] This can be seen in the case of the phoenix and the pelican. As in ancient times, new Jewish (and Christian) meanings were introduced into pagan images. Moreover, Jewish meanings were introduced even into the holiest of Christian images.[22]

In Italian marriage contracts, mainly from seventeenth-and eighteenth-century Rome, widespread use is made of allegorical figures and personifications, originally pagan, which adopted a clear Christian significance. One example is a 1797 Roman *ketubbah* decorated with allegorical figures, all of whom are identified in writing.[23] On the left are Justice, Modesty and Hope, and on the right, Fortitude, Victory and Temperance. These are personifications of the Virtues, with definite Christian significance. Similar allegorical figures were extremely frequent in contemporary Christian art, and we may assume that the Jews who ordered the *ketubbah*, as well as the artists, were familiar with their origins and their Christian significance. They borrowed the images as they were, but attributed them to the noble characters of the bride and groom.[24]

As mentioned, in quite a large number of Jewish objects, female figures, allegorical or otherwise, appear bare-breasted and even completely nude. Indeed, the figure of Beauty — *Bellezza* — shown nude, may sometimes be found among these images.[25] In marriage contracts in particular Adam and Eve are depicted naked.[26] Usually Eve is shown nude, with only her intimate parts covered. In a 1746 Italian *ketubbah* from Livorno, Adam and Eve are seen in a composition reminiscent of the painting by Tintoretto in the Academia of Venice, except that in the *ketubbah* the artist changed the figure of Adam to make the composition symmetrical.[27] Apart from Adam and Eve,

19 E. Kirschbaum, "Pelikan," in Kirschbaum, *Lexikon*, III, cols. 390–92.

20 The pelican in Jewish art represents the destruction of Zion, following Psalm 102:7: "I am like the pelican of the wilderness..." It is also the image of the Jewish mother, who like the pelican, watches over her young. See Rachel Wischnitzer, *Symbole und Gestalten der Jüdischen Kunst* (Berlin, 1935), p. 89, figs. 50, 51; Benjamin, *The Stieglitz Collection*, p. 62, no. 28, and figs. 28, 28 I, 28 II. In Jewish art the portrayal of the pelican feeding its young with its own blood is much rarer. The bird is sometimes shown with its chicks, but without the image typical in Christian art. See e.g. the double headstone of mother and daughter, dated 1868, of Basha, daughter of Mordeccai Ze'ev Ha'Cohen and her daughter, Liba, daughter of Yom Tov Lipman, in Monika Kraiewska, *Time of Stones* (Warsaw, 1983), p. 119. The pelican is also sometimes shown without its young. See also the *parochet* (ceremonial curtain covering the Holy Ark in the synagogue) from the Kassel Synagogue, c. 1730, donated by a mother on the occasion of her son's Bar Mitzvah in 1744, today in the Kassel Hessisches Landesmuseum. See R. Hallo, *Jüdische Kunst aus Hessen und Nassau* (Berlin, 1933), p. 2, no. 1, fig. A.

21 Goodenough, "Pagan Symbols," p. 75.

22 The unicorn, also a prominent Christian image representing the Incarnation, was also adopted by Judaism, which saw in it the biblical *re'em*, translated in the Vulgate as a unicorn. See Psalms 22:21 and the Midrash on Psalms for the same verse, and also the Talmud, *Zebahim* 113. See R. Wischnitzer, "The

Unicorn in Christian and Jewish Arts," *Historia Judaica* 13 (1951), 141–56.

23 Jewish National and University Library, Jerusalem, no. 331. See D. Davidovitch, *The Ketuba: Jewish Marriage Contracts through the Ages* (Tel Aviv, 1979), pl. III; S. Sabar, "The Use and Meaning of Christian Motifs in Illustrations of Jewish Marriage Contracts in Italy," *Journal of Jewish Art* 10 (1984), 53, fig. 5.

24 On Roman marriage contracts with allegorical figures of the virtues, see L. Grassi et al., *Italian Ketubbot, Illuminated Jewish Marriage Contracts* (Milan, 1984), nos. 25, 34, 43, 44, 45, 47. Also frequent in these marriage contracts are other allegorical figures, such as the Four Seasons, whose source is also pagan images adopted by Christianity.

25 See an 1806 Roman *ketubbah* of a bride named Bella Fiore, who is probably represented here by the image of Beauty; Rome, Archivio di Stato, Diplomatico, Appendice B: Documenti ebraici, cass. 264, perg. 2; and ibid, no. 43, pp. 132–33. See also two other marriage contracts, in which the name of the bride is Channa, where the figure of Beauty probably also represents the bride, as the Hebrew word Chen, i.e. beauty or grace; ibid., no. 25, pp 96–97; no. 44, pp. 134–135.

26 See e.g. Benjamin, *Stieglitz*, pp. 294–95, no. 198; pp. 356–57, no. 238.

27 Jerusalem, Israel Museum, 179/345, see Benjamin, *Stieglitz*, p. 324, no. 216. Tintoretto, *Adam and Eve*, Venice, Accademia, 1550–51; Hans Tietze, *Tintoretto: The Paintings and Drawings* (London, 1948), fig. 30.

this *ketubbah* depicts an abundance of winged, nude cupids. The portrayal of the pagan love god in a *ketubbah* does not signify heresy. The cupids are allegories of the love of the young couple. This *ketubbah* also shows two bare-breasted women supporting a family crest. In addition, among the Seasons — personifications whose origin is also in pagan art — shown in the margins of the *ketubbah*, Summer is depicted as a nude female, with only sheaves concealing her intimate parts.[28]

Another representation of nude females appears in a seventeenth-or eighteenth-century Esther Scroll, probably Dutch, now in the Jewish Museum in Amsterdam (Fig. 2).[29] The written text appears in roundels, with illuminations in the circles surrounding the text and in the spaces between the roundels. The illuminations in the circles include flowers, birds and animals, most of which do not appear to be linked to the content of the Book of Esther, as well as the wheel of the zodiac and some of the protagonists of the narrative. The illuminations between the roundels depict, in three registers, scenes almost all of which can be identified in the story. Among these are scenes of Ahasuerus's feast showing musicians, the hanging of Bigthan and Theresh, Haman meeting Ahasuerus, Haman falling on Esther's couch, the Jews vanquishing their enemies and so on. In the space following the first roundel

of text there are three scenes: Ahasuerus's feast; two string musicians, probably part of the depiction of the feast; and finally, in the lower register, four completely nude women sitting on a bench. At first glance they also appear to be part of the feast depicted above them and therefore may be illustrating the Jewish legend from the *Talmud*, which relates that Ahasuerus asked Vashti to appear naked at the banquet.[30] In the Duke of Alba's Bible, Vashti is indeed portrayed in the nude, with only a crown on her head, while the King orders her execution during the banquet.[31] However, in the Amsterdam scroll there are four naked women, as opposed to only one. The *Talmud* relates that the King asked Vashti to appear naked, because "The wicked Vashti used to take the Daughters of Israel and strip them naked." We could assume that the four nude women are Vashti and three of the Daughters of Israel, or perhaps four of the Daughters of Israel. Three of the women are holding what look like scepters, which upon further examination are seen to be distaffs. The depictions of nude women as spinners in a scroll may seem strange at first glance, but it is still possible that they are representations of Vashti and three of the Daughters of Israel, whom, according to another legend, she forced to beat wool and flax on the Sabbath while naked, resulting in her being ordered to appear naked before the King.[32]

28 See Kerber and Holl, "Jahreszeiten," in Kirschbaum, *Lexikon*, II, cols. 364–70. On the Seasons in Antiquity, see G.M.A. Hanfmann, *The Seasons Sarcophagus in Dumbarton Oaks* (Cambridge, Mass., 1951).

29 Amsterdam, Joods Historisch Museum, inv. no. 37. See *Joodse verluchte handschriften* (cat.) (Amsterdam: Joods Historisch Museum, 1961), no. 54 and pl. See also *Synagoga* (cat.) (Recklinghausen, Städtische Kunsthalle, 1960–61), no. B55 and pl.; *Synagoga* (cat.) Frankfurt a.M.: Historisches Museum, 1961), cat. no. 125, pl. 63. In the Recklinghausen catalogue, the scroll was attributed mistakenly to Salomo d'Italia and the 17th century. In the Amsterdam catalogue, it is attributed to 18th-century Amsterdam. However, the Frankfurt catalogue attributes it to Holland or France, c. 1700. A similar scroll in the Israel Museum (see below) is attributed to 18th-century Alsace.

30 *Babylonian Talmud, Megillah*12b: "Would you like to see her? They said, yes, but it must be naked...." See also "The Second Targum (Targum Sheni) to Esther," trans. P.S. Cassel and A. Bernstein, in *The Targum of the Five Megilloth*, ed. B. Grosfeld (New York, 1973), 1:11, p. 120: "Go and say to Queen Vashti: Arise from thy royal throne, strip thyself naked, put the crown upon thy head and thus appear before me...." See also *Midrash Esther Rabbah*: "To bring Vashti the Queen before the king with the crown royal (1:11)... they replied 'yes, but she must be naked'; 'very well,' he said to them, 'let her be naked.' R. Phinehas and R. Hama b. Guria in the name of Rab said: She asked permission to wear at least as much as a girdle, like a harlot, but they would

not allow her. He said to her 'It must be naked.' She said: 'If so, they will say 'She is a maid servant'.' Then she (a maidservant) might put on royal garments and enter. R. Huna said: 'A subject must not put on royal garments'. *Midrash Rabbah*, trans. M. Simon (1961 [1939]), III, 13. See also 'Midrasch Abba Gorion,' A. Jellinek (ed.), *Beit ha-Midrash* (Jerusalem, 1938), chap. 1, p. 4 (in Hebrew), which says also that she must be naked with only a crown on her head.

31 The Alba Bible, 1422–36, Madrid, the Duke of Alba collection, Palacio de Liria, fol. 390v. See C.O. Nordström, *The Duke of Alba's Castilian Bible* (Uppsala, 1967), pp. 196–98, fig. 115. The Duke of Alba's Bible is a Christian work, but it was translated by Rabbi Moses Arragel and illustrated under his guidance, with many references to Jewish legends. This illustration was done according to the legends quoted above.

32 "Said Ahasuerus to them... Would you like to see her? They said, yes, but it must be naked... This [remark] teaches you that the wicked Vashti used to take the daughters of Israel and strip them naked." *The Babylonian Talmud, Megillah*, p. 12b, trans. Maurice Simon (London: Soncino, 1938), p. 71. See also *The First Targum to Esther*, I:1, 11. "It happened during the days of the evil Xerxes... in whose days the work of [rebuilding] the house of our Great God ceased... upon the advice of the wicked Vashti... because she did not permit the [re-]building of the Temple, it was decreed concerning her that she be executed unclad... The king then ordered... to bring Queen Vashti unclad. Since she used to make Israelite girls work unclad and made

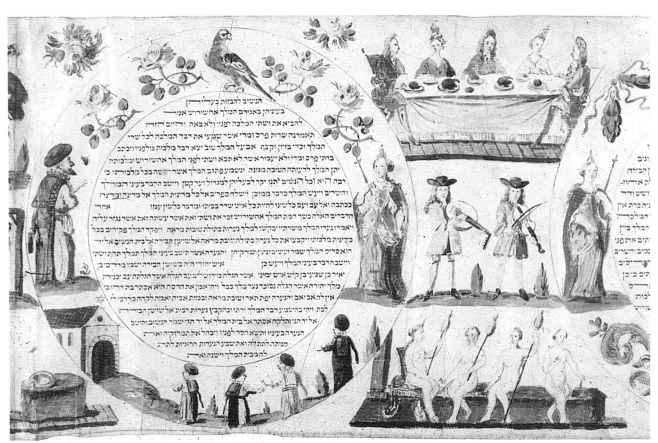

Fig. 2.   Esther Scroll. Holland, 17th or 18th century. Amsterdam, The Jewish Museum, inv. no. 37.

This could be an acceptable possibility and may have provided a source for the figures, despite the fact that the women are not beating wool and flax, but are spinning them. But there may be another interpretation: because mythological figures were not avoided in Jewish art, the three female spinners may be the three Moirae or Parcae, the goddesses of fate in ancient mythology, who spin the thread of life from birth, severing it at death, and who are often depicted

in ancient art.[33] This may seem a surprising image in an Esther scroll. However, the pagan goddesses of fate, may become the personifications of Fate when they appear in the scroll, and could represent the *pur* after which the festival of Purim is named, the lot that was cast to determine the time of the destruction of the Jews in the month of Adar (Esther 3:7). The three goddesses of fate may thus illustrate the casting of the *pur*, and possibly even represent indirectly the

them beat wool and flax for her on the Sabbath day, therefore it was decreed upon her to be brought unclad. However, the royal turban was on her head in recompense for the merit of her paternal grandfather Nebuchadnezzar, who dressed Daniel in purple. Therefore, it was decreed that she be brought before him with the royal turban to be seen by the nations and princes, since she was good looking." *The First Targum to Esther according to the Manuscript, Paris, Hebrew ms. 110 of the Bibliothèque Nationale,* trans. Bernard Grossfeld (New York, 1983), pp. 40, 42.

[33] S. Eitrem, "Moira," in G. Wissowa, *Pauly's Realencyclopädie der Classischen Altertumswissenschaft* (Stuttgart, 1932), XV/2, cols. 2449-2497. The three goddesses are Clotho, the spinner,

Lachesis, disposer of lots, and Atropos, inevitable or cannot be stayed (from severing the thread of life). See Seyffert, *Dictionary of Classical Antiquities*, p. 398, s.v. "Moira" Their names first appear in Hesiod's "Theogony," see Hesiod, *The Works and Days, Theogony, The Shield of Hrakles,* trans. R. Lattimore (Ann Arbor, 1970), vv. 217-18, 904-905, pp. 136, 177-78. The image of the Fates, spinning man's thread of life, appears also in Homer, *Iliad,* XX, 127; XXIV, 209; *Odyssey,* VII, 197 ff., etc. In the sarcophagi showing Prometheus as creator of man, the Parcae usually appear. However, only one of them, probably Clotho, is usually shown spinning. See e.g., the National Museum Naples, sarcophagus no. 6705, see C. Robert, *Die antiken Sarkophag-Reliefs* (Berlin, 1919), no. 357.

Festival of Purim. The association of fate, *pur*, and Purim, would be an easy one for a Jew to make, and it might thus be concluded that the artist was a Jew.[34]

In the Amsterdam Scroll to the right of the zodiac, in the space between it and the next roundel of text (next to the space where the Fates are depicted), there is a depiction of Haman pointing with a staff at the sign of Pisces, signifying the month of Adar, when the lot was cast.[35] The meaning of the zodiac, which appears frequently in marriage contracts, has already been discussed.[36] Some see it as a sign of good luck, and others saw its origin in the popular belief that the signs of the zodiac control man's fate. Its meaning is probably similar in the Book of Esther. Furthermore, in this context, the zodiac may refer to the word *pur* and the Festival of Purim.[37] None of these interpretations should be disregarded; they are all alluded to in the image. However here, where Haman is shown pointing to the sign of Adar, there is a clear indication that it refers to the lot that has been cast. In *Midrash Esther Rabbah* there is a detailed description of how the *pur* was cast and the reason the month of Adar was chosen. Haman cast lots in turn on all the months and all the signs of the zodiac, but they all seemed to have merits, until the lot fell

upon the month of Adar and the sign of Pisces in which he found no merits.[38] Hence the zodiac in the Amsterdam scroll might indeed describe the casting of the lot according to the *Midrash*.

Illustrations referring to the lot being cast are not frequent in Esther Scrolls, and therefore do not seem to have a traditional iconography. There are, for example some scrolls which show the casting of the *pur* as a game of dice.[39] In the Amsterdam scroll the casting of the *pur* is represented by two illustrations, one whose source is in the *Midrash* and the other based on mythology. It may be that the reason the three Fates are depicted naked in the scroll is in order to differentiate between them, as allegorical figures — personifications, with a mythological origin — and between the historical figures taken from the story of Esther.[40]

The depiction of the Fates spinning and even breaking the thread of life was not infrequent in late Italian Renaissance art and in the art of the Low Countries.[41] On a 1511 mural by Baldassare Peruzzi in the Villa Farnesina in Rome (Fig. 3), the Parcae appear as part of the painting of the Death of Meleager on a frieze in the Sala del Fregio.[42] According to the myth, on the seventh day after Meleager's birth, the

34   On the other hand, it should be pointed out that the zodiac shown later in the scroll goes in a clockwise direction, as in Christian art, rather than in an anti-clockwise direction, as a Jewish artist may have drawn it. See Landsberger, "Illuminated Marriage Contracts," *Hebrew Union College Annual* 26 (1955), 529.

35   See *Synagoga*, Frankfurt, no. 125, pl. 63.

36   Landsberger, "Illuminated Marriage Contracts," p. 528; I. Sonne, "Post Script to 'The Zodiac'," *Studies in Bibliography and Booklore* I (1953), 82; J. Gutmann, "Wedding Customs and Ceremonies in Art," in J. Gutmann (ed.), *Beauty in Holiness* (New York, n.d.), p. 320. See also Iris Fishof, "The Iconographical Origins of the Venetian Ketubbah," in Grassi, *Italian Ketubbot*, pp. 229–30.

37   Klagsbald, *Catalogue*, p. 68.

38   *Midrash Esther Rabbah* VII, 11: "In the first month, which is the month of Nissan (3:7). It was taught: When the wicked Haman determined to destroy Israel, He cast Pur, that is, the lot... When that miscreant saw that the lot would not help him to the right day, he tried months. He began with Nissan, and the merit of Passover appeared in it... When the month of Adar came up, he found no merit in it and he began to rejoice. He then turned to examining the signs of the Zodiac... On reaching the sign of Pisces which shines in the month of Adar, he found no merit in it and rejoiced saying: "Adar has no merit and its sign has no merit..." See also *The Second Targum to Esther*, 3:7.

39   See e.g. the *Megillah* from the Mrs. M. Morpurgo Collection, Sde Eliahu, on loan to the Israel Museum (no. 182/136; L78.31). Probably Venetian, attributed to the end of the 16th or beginning

of the 17th century. In the eleventh column, beneath the text which mentions the casting of lots, two figures are shown throwing dice, and between them the word "fate" (*goral*) is written. On their right another dice-throwing figure is seen. See Chaya Benjamin, "An Illustrated Venetian Esther Scroll and the Commedia Dell'Arte," *The Israel Museum News* 14 (1978), 50–59.

40   On allegorical figures in the *Megillah*, though not nude ones, see M. Metzger, "A Study of Some Megilloth of the Seventeenth and Eighteenth Century," *Bulletin of the John Rylands Library* 46 (1963), 116–21. Among them no representation of Fate is shown. See also a scroll from the Kaufmann Collection, Budapest, Academy of Sciences, MS 14. See D. Kaufmann, in D.H. Muller and J. von Schlosser, *Die Haggadah von Sarajevo* (Vienna, 1898), pp. 263–65.

41   It has already been noted that the Jewish artistic language of the Baroque period is a general European one, and that the art of Jewish illumination passed from Italy to Holland. On the similarity between the illuminations in the *ketubbah* and the *megillah*, probably done by the same artists, see Naményi, "La miniature juive," pp. 29, 31, 37; Landsberger, "Illuminated Marriage Contracts," pp. 540–41. The work of Salomo d'Italia, who was born and worked in Italy, and who later moved to Amsterdam, had a strong influence over *megillah* illumination; see S. Kirschstein, "Salom Italia," *Jüdische Graphiker aus der Zeit von 1625–1825* (Berlin, 1918), pp. 7–14; M. Narkiss, "The Work of Salom Son of Mordecai Italia," *Tarbitz* 25 (1956), 441–451; 26 (1956), 87–101 (in Hebrew).

42   Villa Farnesina was the home of the wealthy banker and merchant, Agostino Chigi. It was built by Peruzzi and decorated

Fig. 3. Baldassare Peruzzi, The Death of Meleager, 1511. Villa Farnesina, Sala del Fregio.

three Fates, weaving the thread of his life, appeared. They announced to his mother that the life of the newborn child would end when the log burning in the hearth was consumed by the flames. She immediately snatched the log from the fire and hid it. When, after the Calydonian hunt, Meleager quarreled with his mother's brothers and killed them, she was angry and burned the log, and so Meleager died a sudden death.[43] The painting depicts Meleager's mother throwing the log into the fire, while the spinning Fates stand next to her, one of them cutting the thread of life. The scene on the right shows the death and lamentation over Meleager. The painting was well known among

the artists of Rome; Benvenuto Cellini tells of his visits to the Villa where he and many others went to study and to copy the paintings of the famous artists that decorated the house.[44]

The image of the Fates cutting the thread of life, represented by a severed spindle, is well known also in the symbolic literature of the sixteenth century. It even appears as an hieroglyph, symbolizing death, in Horapollo's *Hieroglyphica*, as well as in Collona's *Hypnerotomachia Poliphili*. A similar image was also frequent in the Low Countries. In "The Triumph of Death" by Pieter Breughel, one of the Fates, holding a spindle in her left hand and a pair of scissors in

by various artists, among them Raphael. See C.L. Frommel, *Baldassare Peruzzi als Maler und Zeichner* (Vienna, 1967/68; Beiheft zum Römischen Jahrbuch für Kunstgeschichte), pp. 62–63, no. 18, pl. XIIa.

[43] Ovid, *Metamorphoses*, VIII, vv. 329–354. See also Robert Graves, *The Greek Myths* (Penguin, 1955), II, chap. 80, pp. 263–66.

[44] B. Cellini, *The Life of Benvenuto Cellini Written by Himself* (London, 1949), pp. 29–30.

Fig. 4.   The Triumph of Death over Chastity. Flemish tapestry, early 16th century. London, Victoria and Albert Museum.

Fig. 5.   The Triumph of Death over Chastity. French, 16th century, pen and wash drawing. Paris, Arsenal lib. MS 5066.

her right, ready to cut the thread of life, may be seen lying at the feet of the horse of Death.[45] Breughel's portrayal is not unusual and is borrowed from other depictions of the Triumph of Death, among them those derived from Petrarch's *I Trionfi*. A drawing of the Triumph of Death, attributed to the school of Pieter Coeke van Aalst (Alost), shows crowned Death, riding a chariot drawn by two bulls, while at his feet lie his dead victims, among them a king and a pope.[46] The three Fates are seated in the chariot. One holds a distaff and the other a spindle while the third cuts the thread.

The spinning female nudes in the Amsterdam *Megillah* are accompanied by a fourth nude who is not spinning. At first in ancient times, only one Moira was common, but they soon increased to three.[47] In the sixteenth century an additional figure sometimes appears beside the Fates. In some images derived from the Triumphs of Petrarch, showing the Triumph of Death over Chastity, the three Parcae are depicted trampling on the personification of Chastity lying at their feet, for example in an early sixteenth-century tapestry from the Low Countries, at the Victoria and Albert Museum in London (Fig. 4), and in a late

45   Keith P. F. Moxey, "The Fates and Pieter Breughel's Triumph of Death," *Oud Holland* 87 (1973), 49–50, figs. 1, 2. Horapollo, *Hieroglyphica* (Paris, 1551), p. 219; Francesco Colonna, *Hypnerotomachia Poliphili* (Venice, 1499), p. 111, according to the pagination system of Albert Ilg, *Ueber den Kunsthistorischen Werth der Hypnerotomachia Polphili* (Vienna, 1872). See also in Piero Valeriano, *Hieroglyphica* (Basel, 1556), Book XLIV, folio 356 v; see Moxey, 'The Fates,' p. 50, n. 3.

46   Vienna, Albertina, inv. 7965. See O. Benesch, *Die*

Zeichnungen der Niederlandischen Schulen des XV. und XVI. Jahrhunderts (Vienna, 1928) (in A. Stix, *Beschreibung des Katalog der Handzeichnungen in der Graphischen Sammlung Albertina*, Vienna, 1926 ff, Band II), no. 55, p. 9, pl. 17.

47   In Antiquity, sometimes only two of the three Parcae appeared. However, four Parcae appear only once, on the François vase from the first half of the 6th century B.C.E. found in Chiusi and today in Florence, Archeological Museum, see Eitrem, "Moira," cols. 2479, 2488.32.

sixteenth-century French manuscript, in the Arsenal Library in Paris (Fig. 5).[48] Both are very similar in their iconography. The Parcae, identified by inscriptions, are not all spinning. Only Clotho the spinner holds a distaff. Lachesis holds the thread and Atropos cuts it, and the spindle falls to the ground. The four figures are dressed according to the fashion of the period, their heads covered. The fourth woman in the *Megillah* may refer to the image of *Castitas*, who represents the innocent Jews. The position of the right hand of the fourth figure who is not spinning, covering her breast in a manner reminiscent of Venus Pudica, may also indicate her chastity. The representation of a nude figure is not opposed to tradition, and may even represent a virtue.[49] Such a figure appears in Giovanni Pisano's pulpit in the Pisa Duomo (1302–15), depicted as the classical Venus Pudica and representing one of the Virtues.[50] She supports the figure of the Virgin Mary, the Spousa-Ecclesia, and may represent Chastity, Temperance, or even Prudence.

Contrary to the French manuscript and the Flemish tapestry, the three Fates in the *Megillah* are all spinning and none of them cuts the thread of life. The tapestry and the drawing depict the Triumph of Death, and therefore emphasize the cutting of the thread of life. Though the Book of Esther tells of the intention to kill all the Jews, this threat was not carried out, and the thread of life was not severed. Therefore the figure identified as Chastity, or in our case, Innocence, is not trampled underfoot, but sits next to the Fates. This fourth nude woman may not even represent a specific Virtue, but virtue in a general sense, relating to the Jews. The fact that this figure is naked, like the Parcae, may also be an indication of its origin in Antiquity as an allegorical figure.

Perhaps the best explanation of the fourth figure is its mythological identification with Ananke, goddess of Necessity, who is also described as spinning with a distaff.[51] Plato, in the *Republic*, writes thus:

And from the extremities was stretched the spindle of Necessity, through which all the orbits turned... And the spindle turned on the knees of Necessity... And there were the other three who sat round about at equal intervals, each one on her throne, the Fates, daughters of Necessity, clad in white vestments with filleted heads, Lachesis, and Clotho, and Atropos... Lachesis singing the things that were, Clotho the things that are, and Atropos the things that are to be. And Clotho with the touch of her right hand helped to turn the outer circumference of the spindle, pausing from time to time. Atropos with her left hand in like manner helped to turn the inner circle, and Lachesis alternately with either hand lent a hand to each.[52]

The depiction of Ananke and her daughters also appears in art. In a mural of 1494–5 at the Castello di Bracciano (Fig. 6), among a series of paintings of female figures, there are four female spinners, identified as Ananke and the three Moirae.[53] The portrayal of Necessity and the Fates was well known and widespread, as can be seen from their depiction in Cartari's book (Fig. 7).[54] A wood-cut shows the four goddesses with an enormous distaff held by Ananke while the Moirae help her to spin; this is in accordance with Plato's description and explained in the text as relating to Plato's words.

The Amsterdam scroll has a "sister" scroll, at present in the Israel Museum. It is similar to the Amsterdam one in style and the way the text is written in roundels, as well as in many of its illuminations. The similarity is so great that the two scrolls might

---

[48] A.F. Kendrick, Victoria and Albert Museum, *Department of Textiles, Catalogue of Tapestries* (London, 1924), p. 29, pls. XV and XVI; Paris, Bibl. de L'Arsenal, MS 5066, early 16th century, pen and wash drawing.

[49] E. Panofsky, "The Neoplatonic Movement in Florence and North Italy," *Studies in Iconology* (New York, 1962), pp. 156 ff.

[50] M. Ayrton and Henry Moore, *Giovanni Pisano Sculptor* (London, 1969), fig. 172, cat. no. 313; see also P. Bacci, *La Ricostruzione del Pergamo di Giovanni Pisano nel Duomo di Pisa* (Milan and Rome, 1926), p. 63 ff. figs. 26, 27; Veritas (Truth) is usually also depicted nude, see Panofsky, "The Neoplatonic Movement," pp. 157–59.

[51] Wernicke, "Ananke," in Wissowa, *Pauly's Realencyclopädie*, I, cols. 2057–58.

[52] Plato, *The Republic*, trans. P. Shorey (London and Cambridge, Mass., 1956), II, Book X, vv. 615–18, pp. 501–5.

[53] Castello di Bracciano, belonging to the family of Orsini di Tagliacozzo. See Rosella Siligato, "Due cicli di affreschi nel Castello di Bracciano: ciclo delle figure femminili, ciclo di Ercole," in Anna Cavallaro, Almamaria Mignosi Tantillo, and Rosella Siligato, *Bracciano e gli Orsini nel '400* (cat.) (Bracciano, Castello Odescalchi, 1981, Roma, 1981), pp. 82–83, 92–93, fig. 15. I would like to thank my student Reouella Shahaf for drawing my attention to these paintings.

[54] V. Cartari, *Le imagini, con la Sposizione de i dei de gl'antichi* (Venezia, 1556), the edition of Venice 1647 with appendix of Lorenzo Pignoria, p. 302; See Cavallaro et al., *Bracciano*, fig. 25. The book was published in many editions and was very well-known.

Fig. 6. The Three Parcae and the Goddess of Necessity, 1494–95. Castello Odescalchi, Bracciano.

Fig. 7. The Three Parcae and the Goddess of Necessity. (V. Cartari, Le imagini con la sposizione de i dei de gl'antichi, p. 302.)

have been painted by the same artist.[55] In the Israel Museum version, however, the Fates are missing. In the Jerusalem scroll the pictures illustrating the texts are usually found next to the text roundel to which they refer. For example, the seven maidens given to Esther "out of the King's house" (2:9) are shown immediately after the text roundel which they illustrate. This is not so in the case of the Amsterdam scroll where the artist did not always place the illustrations next to their texts. Thus the seven maidens do not appear following their verbal description, but after the next roundel. Surrounding the fourth text roundel in the Jerusalem scroll is the zodiac, and on its left a depiction of Haman pointing to the sign of Pisces, representing the month of Adar. The text within the roundel does indeed refer to the lot according to which Adar was chosen for the Jews' destruction. In the Amsterdam scroll, however, the zodiac, with Haman pointing to Pisces, is shown in one roundel preceding the one containing the relevant text. The three Fates, allegorically illustrating the same event, are pictured even further away from the text describing the casting

of the *pur*, with two roundels between them and the text.

The fact that the text and the illustrations in the Amsterdam scroll do not correspond, proves that this was not the original scroll for which the illustrations were made. The illustrations and text in the Jerusalem version are almost always found next to each other, but some of the illustrations are missing. This suggests that the Jerusalem scroll is not the original either. The two manuscripts may possibly derive from a third, unknown manuscript, containing a larger number of illustrations, as does the Amsterdam scroll, but placed in the correct positions according to the written text.

To the two scrolls in Amsterdam and Jerusalem we may add a third, now in the Gross Family collection in Tel Aviv (Fig. 8).[56] This scroll however is different in its text layout, which is not in roundels but in irregular octagons, whose upper and lower sides are quite narrow. There are no illustrations or decorations around the text as in the Amsterdam and Jerusalem scrolls. The illustrations are limited to the spaces between the text "columns," which have thus

[55] Jerusalem, Israel Museum, 2390–12–52 (182/81). See K. Katz, P. Kahane and M. Broshi, *From the Beginning, Archaeology and Art in the Israel Museum* (London, 1968), pl. 176. The scroll at the Israel Museum is attributed to the 18th century, and contrary to the attribution of the Amsterdam scroll, to Alsace (see note 28 above). However, the two scrolls are so alike, that it is clear that

they have the same origin, though we do not wish to elaborate here on these problems.

[56] Gross family collection, 81.12.37. Elsace (?), c. 1700. See *Early Printed Books and Manuscripts, Christie's Auction Catalogue* (New York, 1 October 1980), lot 143, p. 127, fig. on p. 126.

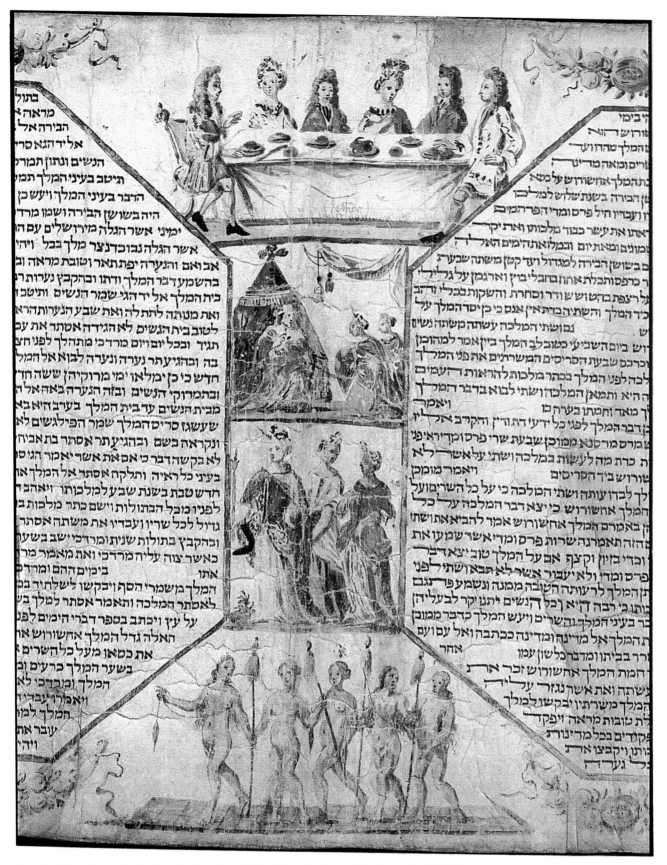

Fig. 8.   The Fates. Esther Scroll, Elsaß, c. 1700. Tel Aviv, Gross Family coll. 81.12.37.

the form of a column with wide triangular "base" and "capital." The composition of the illustrations however is similar to the two other scrolls, with two wide scenes below or above, and one or two narrower scenes in the middle.

Though the layout of the text is different, the composition of the illustrations, their style and iconography closely resemble those in the Amsterdam and Jerusalem scrolls. We might thus suppose that the same artist illustrated all three scrolls. Similar scenes are depicted with only small variety. For example in the Gross scroll there is no depiction of the hanging of Bigthan and Theresh, and the scene of Haman leading Mordecai's horse while Haman's daughter empties a chamberpot on her father's head is reversed.

The illustrations in the Gross scroll are sometimes next to the text columns, as in the scene of Haman pointing to Pisces in the zodiac wheel, or the scene of the Angel Gabriel giving the book of records of Chronicles to Ahasuerus. Some illustrations appear further away from the text they refer to, such as the scene with Haman leading Mordecai's horse. Besides the text illustrations the artist added garlands above and below the text columns, as well as one landscape scene with various animals, among them an elephant and a lion.

However the most important fact for us is that here we find also the spinning naked figures of the Fates, but in the Gross Esther Scroll there are five standing figures holding four distaffs (Fig. 8). The left figure holds a distaff in her left hand, together with the figure beside her, while in her right she holds the thread with the spindle at its end, whereas the other spindles are loose. The Fate holds the thread and does not cut it. The main problem here is that the scene shows five fates and not three or four. We do not know of any depiction with five fates. We might explain their number here by supposing that the original archetype illustration from which the

artist copied the scene might have had either three Fates or four, together with Ananke. The artist may not have grasped the importance of their number. On one occasion he painted four figures, and in another scroll, where he had a little more space, he painted five. The five naked spinning figures must represent Fates here as well, or the *pur* that was cast to determine the time of the destruction of the Jews. Since they point also to the association of Fate — *pur* — to Purim, they may be regarded as personifications of the Feast itself.

The appearance of the Fates, especially their nude portrayal in an Esther Scroll, a Jewish manuscript, should not be surprising. Figures of pagan goddesses can also be found in various marriage contracts. The relationship between the *Megillah* illustrations and those of the marriage contracts have already been pointed out. Some of these may possibly have been painted by the same artists.[57] In a 1690 Hamburg *ketubbah*, two figures stand on pedestals and are identified by inscriptions on both sides of the contract text: on the right, "Salvation" and on the left, "Love."[58] The latter is depicted as a bare-breasted Venus, holding the hand of a little winged boy, representing Cupid. The Jewish artist did not hesitate in borrowing the images of Venus and Cupid for a love allegory. In a 1790 Pisan *ketubbah*, in addition to six other semi-nude female figures, Venus appears at the top center of the manuscript.[59] The goddess is lying half-nude with a veil draped over her loins, while Cupid bends over and touches her exposed breast.[60] Here the artist and whoever ordered the *ketubbah* did not refrain from using the depiction of the almost nude pagan goddess of love. It contains no hint of heresy, in spite of its pagan origin, nor does the portrayal of the Fates in the *Megillah*.

In a 1739 Ferrara *ketubbah* several figures of pagan gods appear in pairs, with no attempt to disguise them as allegories. The upper part of the *ketubbah*, on both

57   E. Naményi, "La miniature juive au XVIIe et au XVIIIe siècle," *Revue des Etudes Juives* 16 (116) (1957), 36; Landsberger, "Marriage Contracts," pp. 540–1.

58   According to Rubens the *ketubbah* is in the possession of Mrs. Gomperts Teixeire de Mattos; see A. Rubens, *A History of Jewish Costume* (New York, 1967), p. 126, pl. 179; and according to C. Roth in the collection of the Ets-Haim Seminary of Amsterdam; see C. Roth, "The Sephardi Ketubah," *The Judaism Sephardi* 6 (1955), 258, 260.

59   Los Angeles, Hebrew Union College Skirball Museum, no. 34/111; see Shalom Sabar, "The Use and Meaning of Christian

Motifs in Illustrations of Jewish Marriage Contracts in Italy," *Journal of Jewish Art* 10 (1984), 47, 55, fig. 1. See also Landsberger, "Marriage Contracts," p. 533, 535, fig. 8 following p. 542.

60   Sabar, "Christian Motifs," pp. 47, 55–56, interpreted Venus here as a symbol of matrimony, following an article by Theodor Reff, "The Meaning of Titian Venus of Urbino," *Pantheon* 21 (1963), 359–60. Sabar does not see in Venus here, or in the other allegorical figure of a woman holding a dog, the image of Venus Pandemos, who rules over carnal love, but of Venus Urania, the goddess of noble love, culminating in marriage.

Fig. 9.   Apollo and Diana, Mars and Venus, detail of a ketubbah. Ferrara, 1739. Milan, coll. G.L. Luzzatto.

sides of the figures of the bride and groom, shows Apollo on the right, riding a horse-drawn chariot, while on the left is Diana riding a chariot drawn by dogs. Above them are Mars on the right and Venus on the left, both seated on clouds (Fig. 9).[61]

The three Fates in the Amsterdam scroll appear among the illustrations to the story because they refer to the casting of the lot. All the illuminations which appear in the spaces between the roundels in the manuscript illustrate the actual text of the Book of

Esther, or, in some cases, the text as interpreted in the *Midrash*, among them the depiction of Haman's daughter emptying a chamberpot on her father's head, mistaking him for Mordecai, and throwing herself out of the window *(Talmud, Megillah*16a; *Esther Rabbah* 6:11). The depiction of the Angel Gabriel giving the book of records to Ahasuerus when he can not sleep at night (6:1) is also according to the legend in the *Talmud (Megillah*15b).[62] In addition, the depiction of Haman pointing to the zodiac is

61   Milan, G.L. Luzzatto collection. See Grassi, *Italian Ketubbot,* no. 18, pp. 82–83.

62   On Jewish legends in the illuminations of the Book of Esther, see M. Metzger, "Die Illustration einiger Midraschim zum Buche Esther in der Jüdischen Kunst," *Das Neue Israel* 15 (1963), 563–567; R. Wischnitzer, "The Esther Story in Art," in P. Goodman, *The Purim Anthology* (Philadelphia, 1973), pp. 224–28. 'And proclaimed before him. Thus shall be done to the man whom the king delighteth to honour (Esth. 6:11). As he was leading him through the street where Haman lived, his daughter who was standing on the roof saw him. She thought that the man on the horse was her father, and the man walking before him was Mordecai, so she took a chamber pot and emptied it on the head of her father. He looked up at her and when she

saw that it was her father, she threw herself from the roof to the ground and killed herself'; *Babylonian Talmud, Megillah*16 a. On Gabriel, see 15b–16a: "On that night the sleep of the king was disturbed... he commanded to bring the book of records of the chronicles... and it was found [being] written — should it say a writing [ketav] was found? This shows that Shamashai kept on erasing and Gabriel kept on writing." Another version of the legend which might explain the figure of the angel in the same scene in other scrolls is found in the Second Targum *(Targum Sheni)* to Esther 6:1: "Sogleich ward der Herr der Welt... und befahl dem Engel, der über die Verwirrung eingesetzt ist, hinabzusteigen, dass er den Achaschwerosch beunruhige, so dass der Schlaf von ihm weiche..." See *Targum Scheni zum Buch Esther,* trans. A. Sulzbach (Frankfurt a.M., 1920), p. 79.

according to the *Midrash.* The artist derives his images both from Jewish legends and from the humanistic classical tradition.

This is not the only instance of such pagan figures in an Esther Scroll. A scroll in the John Rylands Library in Manchester, dated 1618, is one of the oldest Italian illuminated scrolls.[63] Among the text illustrations (Fig. 10), there is a nude figure, a thin veil covering her loins, holding a spindle and accompanied by yet another nude figure, also barely veiled.[64] They appear as part of the scene showing the Execution of Vashti. Vashti also appears nude, her severed crowned head lying beside her. The execution of Vashti is not mentioned in the Book of Esther, and her portrayal naked with a crown on her head when executed is according to the legend in the First Targum to Esther. The depiction here is similar to the one in the Alba Bible, where it forms part of Ahasuerus's and Vashti's banquet. The two naked females seen next to the execution of Vashti in the Manchester scroll could be based on the legend in the *Talmud* (*Megillah*12b) mentioned above. Alternatively, because of the distaff held by one of them, they could also be based on the story of the naked Daughters of Israel, forced by Vashti to card wool and cotton on the Sabbath. The artist might have shown them as spinners because of the link between the various processes of preparing the yarn. The spinning figure could also represent one of the Fates, as an allegory of the casting of the *pur*, though it is not depicted next to the relevant text. However, the figure might represent Fate at the moment when the life of Vashti ends. There is another nude female next to the spinning one, and in the margins of

the page, a third nude female. Together they may represent the three Fates in a more traditional manner, as an allegory of Death similar to the painting by Peruzzi in the Villa Farnesina or the Triumphs of Death after Petrarch in the Flemish tapestry and the French drawing, and even in Breughel's *Triumph of Death* and the drawing by Pieter Coecke van Aalst's school.

The figure in the margin, even though completing the number of the three Fates, does not actually belong to the narrative depiction which illustrates the text, or in this case the commentary to the text, and is separated from it by the frame. This nude figure keeps on appearing in the scroll. The scroll is made from ten skins with 29 columns of text (28 columns with the text of the scroll and a colophon). The columns are decorated on both sides and in the lower margins with plants, birds and animals. Above each column of text is a scene from the Esther story, in the seventh of which, with the scene of Vashti's execution, the nude spinning female is depicted. On both sides of each of the narrative scenes, a vase of flowers is shown, a purely decorative motif. However, at the beginning and end of each of the ten skins of the scroll, instead of the vase, a nude female is painted — two women, one on each side of the join — together a total of nineteen figures (the final figure is missing). The nude women stand on one foot on a round object, looking somewhat unsteady. In classical mythology, another Roman Fate, Fortuna, is associated with the Greek Moira or the Roman Parca. Her attributes are borrowed from Tyche, the Greek goddess, also originally a goddess of chance. The wheel or sphere upon which the Goddess stands are

[63]   Manchester, John Rylands University Library, Hebrew MS 22, formerly coll. of the Earl of Crawford and Balcarres. Mendel Metzger dates the roll to 1618, though the John Rylands Library catalogue dates it to 1511. See Metzger, "The John Rylands Megilla and Some Other Illustrated Megilloth of the XVth to XVIIth Centuries," *Bulletin of the John Rylands Library* 45 (1962), 166–71, pl. II; *Catalogue of Exhibition of Hebrew Manuscripts and Printed Books* (Manchester: The John Rylands Library, 1958), no. 7, pp. 10–11. The first date, 1511, is found in the colophon, which refers to the month of Adar of the year 5271 (1511 C.E.). Below it is another colophon which dates the scroll to 5368 (1618), seen by Metzger as the correct date, judging by the style of dress. In Metzger's opinion the upper colophon is probably a mistake. The 1618 colophon begins with the words: "Chance (*goral*) made it the property of my son Benjamin of Castelbolognese on the Day of Purim 5378." Metzger refers to the use of the Hebrew expression for chance as an allusion to its synonym Purim on p. 170. Rachel Wischnitzer

mentions an earlier scroll from 1616 from Ferrara, in a private collection, but does not give any details. Wischnitzer, "The Esther Story in Art," p. 231. Naményi, "La miniature juive," p. 73, mentions a 1567 scroll from Castelnuovo, mentioned also by G. Swarzensky and R. Schilling, *Die Illustrierten Handschriften und Einzelminiaturen des Mittelalter und der Renaissance in Frankfurter Besitz* (Frankfurt, 1929), p. 263. On both sides of the cartouche, above the colophon, there are two winged female heads. The cartouche shows the priest's blessing, and under it a lion standing by a palm tree (Metzger, "The John Rylands Megillah," p. 165, pl. II, c). There are no illustrations to the text in this scroll and Wischnitzer does not mention any scenes in the 1616 scroll, which makes the Manchester *Megillah*, dated 1618, the earliest illustrated Italian scroll, as Metzger notes, p. 171).

[64]   The picture is in the seventh column, at the beginning of the third skin of the scroll, above the text of 2:16–22.

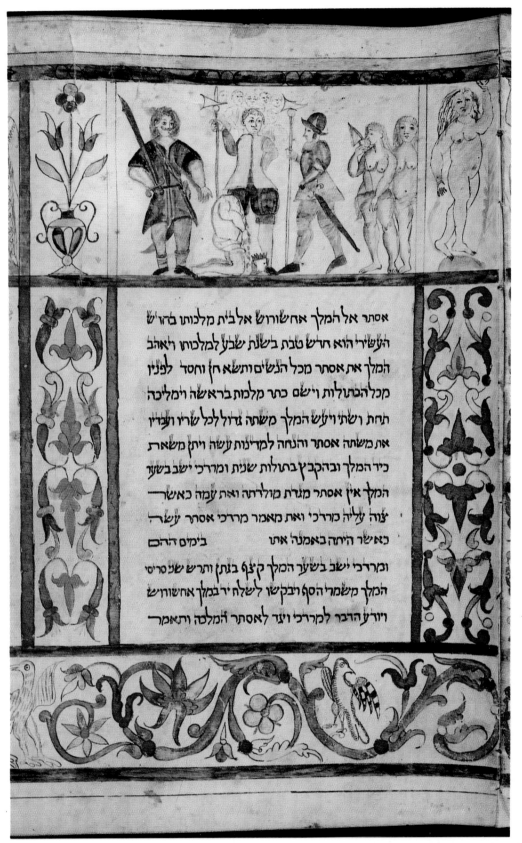

Fig. 10.   The Execution of Vashti. Esther Scroll, Ferrara 1618. Manchester, John Rylands Library, Heb. MS 22, col. 7.

Fig. 11. A. Dürer, Nemesis, or the Great Fortune, 1501–2.
Engraving.

Fig. 12. The Wheel of Fortune. In Boccaccio, Cayada
de Principes, Modena del Campo, 1552. Spanish, wood
engraving.

among Fortuna's attributes, illustrating her unstable
nature.[65] The image of Fortuna standing on a wheel
or a sphere is very widespread in art, for example
in Durer's etchings (Fig. 11).[66] The Manchester scroll
thus shows both the figure of the spinning Parca,
as well as Fortuna, standing unsteadily on a sphere.
The link between the Parca and Fortuna has already
been mentioned by Bocaccio in the Geneologia degli

Dei: "There are people who think that Lachesis is she
whom we call Fortuna."[67]

The nude females standing on both sides of the
seams in the skins in the John Rylands Megillah might
thus also be images of goddesses of Fate or Fortune.
However, while the nude woman spinning actually
illustrates the text, as in the Amsterdam scroll, not so
Fortuna balancing on a sphere reappearing repeatedly

65 The figure of Fortuna or Tyche appears on the ceiling of the
Jewish catacomb of the Vigna Randanini in room no. 2. See
Goodenough, Jewish Symbols, II, p. 18; III, figs. 738, 740, 748,
749. In the scroll only the upper part of the sphere or wheel
is visible, but the unstable posture of the figure confirms its
identity. As for the characteristics of Fortuna in this image, see
Cesare Ripa, Iconologia (1602; New York, 1970), s.v. "Fortuna,"
p. 169. See also Baroque and Rococo Pictorial Imagery: The
1758–60 Hertel Edition of Ripa's Iconologia (New York, 1971),
p. 152.
66 Nemesis called Das Grosse Glück (The Great Fortune) 1501–2;

see E. Panofsky, Albrecht Dürer (Princeton, 1945), I, p. 80 ff.,
II, p. 27, no. 184, fig. 15. See also Dürer's Small Fortune (Das
Kleine Glück), c. 1496; ibid, no. 185. See also R. van Marle,
Iconographie de l'art profane (New York, 1971 [The Hague,
1931]), II, pp. 178–202, esp. figs. 208, 211, 212, 214–16, 222. See
also G. Ristow and E. Kirschbaum, "Fortuna," in Kirschbaum,
Lexikon, II, cols. 53–4; J. Poeschke, "Rad," in Kirschbaum,
Lexikon, III, cols. 492–94; A. Doren, "Fortuna im Mittelalter und
in der Renaissance," Vorträge der Bibliothek Warburg (1922–3),
71–144.

in the margins as an isolated figure. She does not relate to the death of Vashti or to the casting of the lot, but represents a general allegorical personification, and might thus be the personification of the Festival of Purim. In the seventh column this personification of Purim joins the two Fates who are part of the story, to make the appropriate group of three Fates. The artist of the Manchester scroll may have known the significance of the number of the figures derived from classical mythology, and this confirms the assumption that the archetypical imagery of the Amsterdam and Manchester scrolls must have been the three Fates; whereas the artist of the Gross scroll was not aware of this iconographical tradition.

The recurring figure of Fortuna in the Manchester scroll suggests that the other two figures in the scene of Vashti's execution are indeed the Fates and not the naked Daughters of Israel. However, the artist or the patron may have known the *Midrash* and might even have been familiar with an unknown manuscript which showed the naked Daughters of Israel, and associated them with the spinning Moirae. There may thus be two levels of meaning in these images, that of the *Midrash*, and the mythological one. Another level of meaning may be added to the depiction of the severed thread of Vashti's life and the casting of the lot, as well as the personification of Purim, the festival of Fate or Fortune.

In Christian art Fortuna is also portrayed rolling the wheel of fortune, while various figures go up and down as their fates change. Fortuna is sometimes represented standing on a sphere while turning the wheel (Fig. 12).[68] The idea of Fate as a wheel is expressed in the *Talmud, Shabbath,* 151b: "The school

of R. Ishmael, taught: It is a wheel that revolves in the world..."; and also in *Exodus Rabbah* (chap. 31:3): "Because there is an ever rotating wheel in this world, he who is rich today may not be so tomorrow, and also he who is poor today may not be so tomorrow. One He casts down, and the other He raises up, as it says, For God is Judge; He putteth down one, and lifteth up another" (Ps. 75:8).[69]

The same idea is also expressed in Jewish art of the period we are dealing with, and as in the legends, Fortuna is not always referred to by name or depiction. This can be seen for example in a late seventeenth-century *memento mori* by an Italian Jewish painter, previously in the Neuheim Collection in Frankfurt.[70] Fortuna is not actually shown, but various allegorical images and scenes are portrayed in a circle. The inscription below the picture mentions the wheel of fortune several times, including "...suddenly the wheel revolves..."

A similar example can be seen in another Jewish *memento mori*, in the Jewish Museum in London, by the Amsterdam artist Benjamin Senior Godines, commissioned by Isaac son of Matatia Aboab.[71] The picture shows a man and boy, in the costume of the period, looking at a corpse next to which are scattered skulls and bones. Among the numerous texts expressing the same idea of transitoriness, we find: "He will turn the wheel upon the precious and will go on. He will turn, this one He will exalt and this one humble. Has He not caused this one to sit on the throne of a king? And even this one He will cause to fall to the depth of the pit of Sheol." Here also, however, Fortuna is not depicted or mentioned.

Fortuna in the Manchester scroll may also represent

67 R. Wittkower, "Chance, Time and Virtue," *Journal of the Warburg Institute* 1 (1937), 315, n. 4, mentions the French painter Jean Cousin, who calls the Fates the servants of Fortune; *Livre de Fortune* (1568), ed. Lalanne (1883), pl. 195.

68 van Marle, *Iconographie profane*, pp. 189–200, figs. 217–27. An image combining the two representations, Fortuna standing on a sphere and rolling the wheel, can be seen, e.g., in a woodcut in Boccaccio's book in Spanish, *Cayda de Principes* (Modena del Campo, 1522), see van Marle, *Iconographie profane*, pp. 191–2, n. 5, fig. 222.

69 My thanks to I.L. Rachmani, who brought this to my attention, See also *Exodus Rabbah* 31:14 on the same verse in Psalms: "To what is this world like? To a wheel [of a well] in a garden; the earthenware vessels attached to it ascend full from below and descend empty from above. Similarly not everyone who is rich today is rich tomorrow, and he who is poor today need not be so tomorrow. Why is this? Because there is a rotating wheel in

the world..."

70 Now at the Frankfurt Jewish Museum. See M. Narkiss, "Remember the Day of Death': On a Jewish Memento Mori in the Neuheim Collection," *Kiriat Sepher* 16, pp. 108–13, fig. b (in Hebrew).

71 Oil painting, commissioned between 1679 and 1681, the Jewish Museum, London. See A. Rubens, "Three Jewish Morality Pictures," *The Connoisseur* (August 1954), pp. 31–32, fig. 1; R.D. Barnett, *Catalogue of the Permanent and Loan Collections of the Jewish Museum London* (London, 1974), cat no. 895(1), pp. 154–56, color pl. 16 and pl. CLIII; Another copy is apparently in the Bibliotheka Rosenthaliana, Amsterdam, see M.H. Gans, *Memorbook: Pictorial History of Dutch Jewry from the Renaissance to 1940* (Baarn, 1971), p. 120. However there it is described as a print. Another copy is probably also mentioned in M. Grunwald, *Portugiesengräber auf deutscher Erde* (Hamburg, 1902), pp. 26–28, fig. p. 27.

the turn of Fate. The lot was cast to determine the day when the Jews would be destroyed. Through the turn of Fate, or in other words, when Fortune's wheel turned, the day became one of joy (9:1): "in the day that the enemies of the Jews hoped to have power over them it was turned to the contrary, that the Jews had rule over them that hated them." This reversal of Fate is, in fact, the core of the story of Purim, and it is illustrated by Fortuna, also representing Purim in the John Rylands or even perhaps in the Amsterdam *Megillah*.[72]

The representation of the Goddess of Fate in Jewish art in a different context, and with a somewhat different meaning, might also add another dimension to the meaning of the Fates in the Esther Scroll. On some marriage contracts — and we have already mentioned the link between these and the Esther Scrolls — Fortuna also appears balanced upon the unsteady wheel. A 1732 (5492) Paduan *ketubbah* (Fig. 13) shows Cupid on the right of the arch, blindfold, shooting his arrow, symbolizing the love which will blossom between the couple; and on the left, the allegorical nude figure of Fortuna, standing, or rather rolling on the wheel which is her attribute.[73] Similar figures can be found in a 1750 Venetian *ketubbah* and a 1733 Mantuan *ketubbah*.[74] In this context the figure appears to be a personification of good luck. It represents the good fortune of the groom, as quoted in Proverbs 18:22: "Whoso findeth a good wife findeth a good thing," a passage frequently quoted in marriage contracts. In addition, she might be interpreted as

a personification of the popular marriage blessing, *Besimana tava ubemazala malia*, "With good wishes and perfect fortune," also written in most marriage contracts.[75] This might be somewhat similar to the meaning of the zodiac, also depicted often in marriage contracts. In an 1809 Roman *ketubbah*, Fortune is depicted, possibly holding a spindle in her left hand, and a sail, or perhaps reins, in her right hand (Fig. 14).[76] She also appears here as the image of the bride, named in Hebrew *Mazal Tov* (Good Fortune), an equivalent of the Italian name Fortunata. Next to her, Jacob's Dream is portrayed, representing the name of the groom, Jacob. The parallelism between the depiction of Fortuna and the image of Good Fortune is very clear in this instance.

In Christian art, Fortuna sometimes has a negative meaning, because she indicates the randomness of chance, the fatalism that man gives in to without resistance, instead of seeking for the way to virtue.[77] However the positive portrayal of good fortune is not unusual. In Antiquity, Fortuna was also the goddess of good luck. She had many duties determining different fates, for example, as the goddess *Fortuna muliebris*, who determined the fates of women, and *Fortuna virilis*, determining the fate of married life. In fifteenth-and sixteenth-century art, Fortuna appears also as one of the virtues. Later she was popularised as a virtue by Alciati in his *Emblemata* (1531), and thus became well-known in artistic circles.[78]

Plays on words, like that which changes Fortuna to *Mazal Tov* — good fortune, or good luck in

[72] The representation of Fortuna is also frequent in Jewish books, as in the frontispiece of R. Moses Isserles's *Vezot Torat ha-Hata'im* (1599?), where, however, it is difficult to see a special meaning in the image. Narkiss, *The Hannukah Lamp*, p. 15, also mentions a figure of Fortuna which appears in Rabbi David of Lida's book, *Yad Kol Bo* (Frankfurt, 1722 [5482]), which I have not found. This book, or rather another edition, was probably published in 1727, in two editions, with only very few alterations, among them the front page. In the second edition, apart from a number of putti as decorations, the figure of a youth blowing bubbles appears on top, and lower down there is a similar figure, this time portrayed with wings. This is a typical representation of Vanitas.

[73] Jerusalem, Israel Museum, 179/290. My thanks to Iris Fishof, who drew my attention to this *ketubbah* before the publication of her article, "The Iconography of an Illuminated Italian Ketuba from Padua," *Israel Museum Journal* 15 (1989), 25–30, fig. 8. There is an artistic tradition of placing Fortuna and Cupid side by side. See Cesare Ripa, *Iconologia*, p. 170. Other illustrations in the *ketubbah* include a picture of the bride and groom and family coats of arms, as well as the Temple implements, Samson and the lion, Jonah in the belly of the whale,

Moses and Aaron, Abraham's sacrifice and Jacob's dream.
[74] Jewish National and University Library, 901 269; see Fishof, "Italian Ketuba," fig. 9; and see another *kettubah* in Grassi, *Italian Ketubbot*, no. 17, pp. 80–81.
[75] This passage is written in Aramaic as is the entire text of the *ketubbah* (other than the biblical quotations). See V. Colorni, "Historical and Legal Aspects of the Ketubbah," in Grassi, *Italian Ketubbot*, pp. 223–4.
[76] Due to the crude depiction it is hard to identify the attributes held by the allegorical figure. It is also possible that the inexperienced artist did not entirely understand what he was copying. Renato Menasci collection, ibid., no. 45, pp. 136–7.
[77] van Marle, *Iconographie profane*, p. 186.
[78] See Seyffert, *Dictionary of Classical Antiquities*, s.v. "Fortuna," pp. 239–40. Marsilio Ficino, in the famous letter "On Providence and Fate" which was sent to the Florentine merchant, Giovanni Rucellai: "The prudent man has power over Fortune but only if he understands the words of that Wise Man [Christ]"; see R. Wittkower, "Chance," p. 317, and n. 5. Paolo Giovio, *Raggionamento sopra i motti, et disegni d'arme, et d'amore* (Milan, 1569), p. 5v; see Wittkower, "Chance," p. 317, and n. 7.

Fig. 13. Fortuna and Cupid, ketubbah. Padua, 1732. Jerusalem, Israel Museum, 179/290.

Fig. 14. Fortuna — Mazal Tov (Fortunata), ketubbah. Rome, 1809. Coll. Renato Menasci.

Hebrew, or the Moira, the goddess of fate to the Hebrew meaning of lot casting (*pur*) and Purim, continue to occur in Jewish art, where pagan and mythological images have taken on Hebrew and Jewish meanings. In seventeenth-and eighteenth-century Italy and Holland there was a custom whereby poets would compose and present Hebrew poems for special occasions, such as the graduation of physicians and so on. It was most common to present epithalamia (nuptial poems) to brides and grooms on their wedding day, occasionally composed by famous poets.[79] The poems sometimes contain illustrations of different allegorical figures and also personifications. In one of the poems, *Nobilita* and *Gravita* are portrayed, illustrating the virtues of the bride, similar to the personifications in the various marriage contracts. Classical and mythological images are also depicted, such as nude cupids.[80]

These poems sometimes included various riddles which were also part of competitions held at weddings and other festivities, including Purim. The poetic rid-

dle was sometimes accompanied by a picture, an integral part of the riddle itself. These picture-riddles were passed around at competitions on single pages, sometimes handwritten and sometimes printed. Among them is the one by Yeshaiahu Carmi showing an etching of Fortuna balancing on the wheel (Fig. 15).[81] The solution to the riddle, in the words of the poem, in the use of letters as numerals, and in the picture, is *pur-zedek*, meaning just or righteous fate. The riddle was meant for a double wedding which took place on Purim, and its clues indicate a game of chance, luck, or fate, i.e. *pur*, and the fortunate lot of the couples, i.e. *Mazal Tov*. *Zedek* is both justice in Hebrew and the name of the planet Jupiter. A planet in turn is also called *mazal*, because it guides the fortunes of those born beneath it. Hence Fortuna in the picture represents both good luck in the nuptial context, and points to the link between Fortuna, *pur*, and Purim, similar to the depiction in the scrolls. The Jewish poet who composed the riddles saw no obstacle in using a personification derived from a pagan goddess. The

79 Naményi, "La miniature juive," p. 36; see p. 34 for the link between *ketubbah* illuminations and nuptial poems; Joseph B. Sermoneta: "Due canti nuziali di Rabbi Jaacov Joseph Caivano," in D. Carpi, A. Milano, U. Nahon, *Scritti in Memoria di Enzo Sereni* (Jerusalem, 1970) (in Hebrew); M. Bnayahu, "New Epithalamia of Ramhal (R. Moshe Luzzati)," *Hasifrut*) 24 (1977), 92–99 in Hebrew); idem, "R. Avraham ha-Cohen from Zanti and the Group of Physician-Poets from Padua," *Hasifrut* 26 (1978), 108–40 (in Hebrew).

80 The poem is in the possession of Prof. Joseph Sermoneta. See

"Due canti nuziali," pp. 189–90, 206–12, fig. facing p. 209. See also the poem by R. Shimshon Morpurgo to the president R. Shabtai Marini, Budapest, Kaufmann Coll., Kaufmann MS 580, fol. 21, c. 1710. See Bnayahu, "R. Avraham ha-Cohen," p. 111.

81 The riddle is *Re'im 'ad heker milati* (Friends, to the interpretation of my words), New York, The Jewish Theological Seminary, *Italian Broadsides, Occasional Poems*, Mic. 9027, vol. I, no. 43. The riddle was presented for a double wedding in Mantova. See Dan Pagis, *A Secret Sealed* (Jerusalem, 1986), pp. 81, 188, 200, fig. 31 on p. 161 (in Hebrew).

Fig. 15. Fortuna, nuptial riddle-poem. Etching, Italian. New York, The Jewish Theological Seminary, Italian Broadsides, Occasional Poems, Mic. 9027, vol. I, no. 43.

here according to the *Midrash* which says: "The sun rises in a chariot decorated like a bridegroom" and according to Ovid: "Ovid wrote... he had a chariot drawn by four horses..." Thus the poet is well aware of the classical source, which he takes for granted, and indirectly shows that the Jews of the period were familiar with the works of Ovid as well as with the Jewish *Midrash*. Furthermore, he does not see in this image an idolatrous pagan meaning, and at the same time gives it a Hebrew meaning according to the *Midrash*.

The awareness of the classical origins of the pagan images in Jewish art can be seen in another nuptial poem by Rabbi Jacob Josef Caivano, (Rome, 1721–2), where the Muses are depicted.[83] On the upper part of the page is a picture of three of the Muses — Calliope, Clio and Euterpe, each one depicted with her attributes. Their names are mentioned in the text. According to the poem, Melchizedek, "Father of the Muses," orders the "first three of his nine daughters" to attend the wedding, bringing their poems, songs and dances to the young couple. The Muses are described and depicted in their traditional classical functions. However, the Father of the Muses — Jupiter or Zeus in the classical tradition — is turned into Melchizedek. The identification of Jupiter with *Zedek*, the Hebrew name for the planet Jupiter, may be understandable. However the poet went even further and turned the figure into the biblical Melchizedek, thereby giving a Hebrew and biblical guise to the pagan god, Zeus, despite the fact that he calls the Muses by their original Greek names. It thus becomes clear that the poet was well aware of the classical and pagan origins of these images.

The changing of Zeus/Jupiter into the biblical Melchizedek, as well as the link to the planet *Zedek*, may explain the strange appearance of pagan sculptures in contemporary synagogues. The figure of a semi-nude Jupiter, with a cloth covering his loins, holding the thunderbolts, decorated a seventeenth-century candelabrum placed above the Holy Ark in the Altneuschul in Prague (Fig. 16). A similar seventeenth-century figure of Jupiter, with his eagle, also on a

use of personifications derived from pagan images appears in another picture-riddle by an anonymous poet, beginning with the words *Betoch hagan ani* (I am inside the garden), where there is a depiction of a chariot drawn by four horses, derived from the image of Helios.[82] In this case, as on the floors of synagogues a thousand years earlier, it is not the sun god that is shown, but the personification of the sun. The solution to the riddle is also preserved. The sun is painted

[82] The poet signed in initials only (Mordecai Tsoref?). Ink, Leeds University, The Brotherton Library, Cecil Roth coll. MSS. 103, fol. 45; 115, fol. 3b. See Pagis, *A Secret Sealed*, pp. 156–7, fig. 29.

[83] In the possession of Prof. Joseph Sermoneta. It was presented at the wedding of Manoach Haim ben Shabtai Serena (Tranquillo Vita Serena), to Fiore, daughter of Gavriel Ambron in 5482; see Sermoneta, "Due canti nuziali," pp. 182–212, fig. after p. 208. The Muses sometimes appear among *ketubbah* illuminations. See e.g. the 1806 Roman *ketubbah*, Rome, Archivio di Stato, Diplomatico, Appendice B: Documenti ebraici, cass. 264, perg. I.

Fig. 16. Jupiter, lamp decoration from the Altneuschul Synagogue in Prague. 17th century, copper, h. 15 cm. New York, the Jewish Museum.

Fig. 17. Jupiter (destroyed), lamp decoration from the destroyed synagogue of Worms.

candelabrum, was in the Rashi Synagogue at Worms, destroyed in 1938 (Fig. 17).[84]

Similar figures of Jupiter often decorated German, Dutch and Belgian candelabra in the seventeenth and eighteenth centuries, and were also used in churches. The figure of Jupiter holding thunderbolts is found on Roman oil lamps as a symbol of light, and this was the reason given by scholars for the use of the figure on the candelabra. However, nobody has accounted for the choice of this pagan figure in synagogue decoration.[85] Depictions of Jupiter are frequent among the illustrations accompanying the astronomic essay of the Hellenic poet and astronomer

Aratus (c. 315 240 B.C.E.) which were repeatedly copied. In the second half of the fifteenth century these illustrations reappear in their classical form. The image of Jupiter appears there in an almost identical manner to the figures on the candelabra in the synagogues, as in a manuscript from the second half of the fifteenth century in the Vatican Library (MS Barb. 76). (Fig. 18).[86] In the Aratean manuscripts, Jupiter does not appear as the mythological god, but as the planet named after him — Jupiter, or *Zedek* in Hebrew.

The inclusion of Jupiter in the synagogue may be understood in the same way as the inclusion of the

[84] Copper, c. 15 cm. diam. Formerly, Los Angeles, Siegfried Strauss coll., now in the Jewish Museum, New York. See G. Schoenberger, "A Late Survival of Jupiter Fulgur," in Lucy Freeman (ed.), *Essays in Memory of Karl Lehmann* (Locust Valley, N.Y., 1964), pp. 288–92, figs. 1 and 2.

[85] Schoenberger, ibid., thinks that the figures which were prevalent on the candelabra of the period were intentionally disfigured when used for synagogues, to avoid idolatry. This was, in his opinion, the reason for the damage to the nose of the figure from Prague, and also the explanation for the removal of Jupiter's

scepter. Afterwards, the entire figures were removed from the candelabra, leaving only the eagle. This is certainly an acceptable opinion, but it does not explain why a candelabrum with such a decoration was chosen in the first place. Jupiter still decorated the candelabrum of the Alteneuschul in the 1920s as can be seen from a photograph in R. Krautheimer, *Mittelalterliche Synagogen* (Berlin, 1927), fig. 26.

[86] Schoenberger, "Jupiter Fulgur," p. 291, fig. 8. Seznec mentions a number of other manuscripts; see *The Survival of the Pagan Gods* (New York, 1961), pp. 185, 186, fig. 71.

Fig. 18. *The Planet Jupiter. Aratos manuscript, executed for Ferdinand of Aragon, late 15th century. Vatican lib., MS Barb. lat. 76. (After Seznec, The Survival of the Pagan Gods, fig. 71.)*

classical Fates in Jewish manuscripts. The latter may be understood by their traditional meaning as Fates, as well as symbolizing *pur*, Purim, fortune, chance and good luck. Jupiter, occasionally represented as Melcizedek, became identified in the synagogues by his Hebrew name, *Zedek*, not only as the planet, symbolizing light, but also as the concept of Justice, appearing as its personification in a most fitting place — the synagogue.

In this survey we have discussed a number of images in seventeenth-and eighteenth-century Jewish art, derived from pagan sources. We can assume that they were mostly borrowed, not from their pagan origins — although with a clear awareness of them — but mostly from contemporary art. The Jewish artists and patrons, educated in the humanist environment of the period, were familiar with the classical origins of their images, but did not see in them any remnant of idolatry. They imbued the classical images with Jewish significance and adopted them for their purposes, as did their Christian colleagues who endowed the images with Christian meaning. The Jewish meaning of the pagan images is built on word games and thus become personifications of Hebrew concepts.

Characteristic of these images is the way the artists play with their various meanings. Thus they change the image of Jupiter, a pagan god, into the image of the planet Jupiter — *Zedek* — and hence to Justice. The image of the Fates, whether Moira, Parca or Fortuna, become personifications of fate, and then of *pur* and the personification of Purim. They also become images of luck — *mazal* — a star or planet as well as a sign of the zodiac, but also the personification of good luck — *Mazal Tov* — with all the significance of that accepted blessing.

148

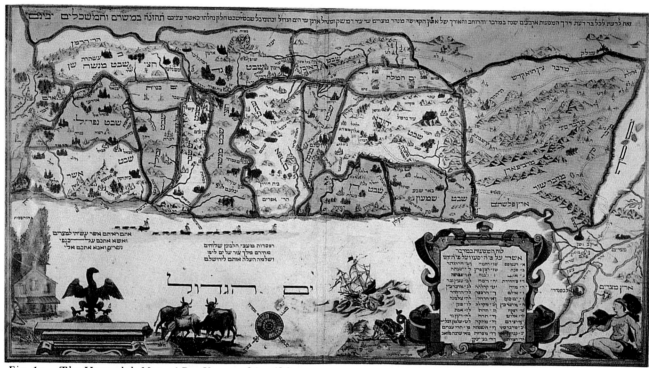

Fig. 1a. *The Haggadah Map of Bar Yaacov, 26 x 48.5 cm.*

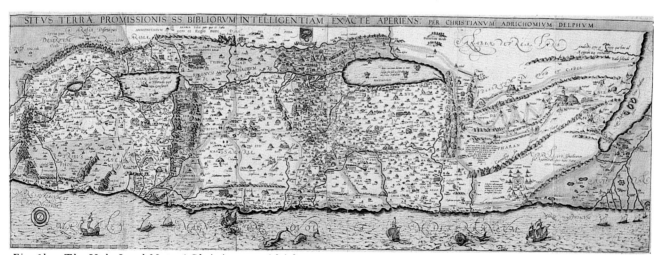

Fig. 1b. *The Holy Land Map of Christian von Adrichom.*

THE SEVENTEENTH-CENTURY HAGGADAH MAP OF AVRAHAM BAR YAACOV*

Harold Brodsky

The Amsterdam Haggadah of 1695 contains a fold-out Hebrew map showing the exodus from Egypt, the route of desert wandering and the Land of Israel divided into tribal territories (Fig. 1a). Although this map is now nearly 300 years old it was not the first printed Hebrew map. A more detailed and larger engraved Hebrew map was published seventy-four years earlier, in 1621, also in Amsterdam.[1] A woodcut from Mantua, dated from around 1560 is now believed to be the oldest printed Hebrew map.[2]

The geographic layout on bar Yaacov's 1695 map and the miniature biblical scenes on it were mainly derived from an influential Holy Land map by Christian von Adrichom (1590) (FIg. 1b). Other design elements on the Haggadah map are typical of seventeenth-century cartography: strapwork cartouches, masonry distance scales, sugarloaf mountains, and castles as symbols for cities.[3] Thus, bar Yaacov's map, like his other engravings in the Amsterdam Haggadah, contains material largely obtained from contemporary Christian sources.[4] These illustrations, nevertheless,

have become Jewish classics that continue to influence haggadah design.

The map appeared also in the 1712, 1781 and 1810 editions of this Haggadah.[5] Since then, the map has been photocopied and reprinted many times in various forms, even as decorative endpapers on the inside covers of a contemporary haggadah. Avraham bar Yaacov's success, therefore, lay mainly in his ability to adapt Christian biblical illustrations and maps for Jewish readers. His skill in doing so may be attributed, in part, to his unusual background. He was born a Christian, and for a time was a Pastor in the Rhineland. He moved to Amsterdam, became an engraver, and converted to Judaism in 1689 (six years before the publication of his illustrations in the Haggadah).[6]

It would be unfair, however, to say that bar Yaacov was merely a talented copyist. At least one of his haggadah pictorial engravings presents a theme that would not have been available to Christian illustrators. A figure shows Abraham smashing idols, which is

* I presented a version of this paper on 8 August 1991, as part of the Library of Congress lecture series highlighting a special exhibit of Judaic treasures, which included the Amsterdam Haggadah. I appreciate arrangements made for the lecture by Ms. Joan Hartman.

Dr. Michael Grunberger, Head of the Hebraic Section of the Library, helped me locate references. Shachar Iwanir, and Gidon Alster suggested several biblical citations, and Meir Katzper examined my Hebrew paraphrasing. Errors remain my responsibility alone.

1 Kenneth Nebenzahl, *Maps of the Holy Land* (New York: Abbeville, 1986). All the maps mentioned in this paper can be examined in recently published facsimiles. Nebenzahl's book contains the 1621 Hebrew map, pl. 40, p. 110; bar Yaacov's 1695 map, pl. 52, p. 138; Adrichom's 1590 map, pl. 35, p. 94; Visscher's 1659 map, pl. 49, p. 132; and Fuller's 1650 map, pl. 48, p. 128. Further details on the 1621 Hebrew map can be found in "Zaddiq's Canaan" by Kenneth Nebenzahl in *Theatrum Orbis Librorum*, ed. Ton Croiset van Uchelen, Koert van der Horst

and Gunter Schilder, (Utrecht: Hes Publishers, 1992), pp. 39–46.

2 Hans Jakob Haag, "A Map considered to be the oldest woodcut map of the Holy Land (around 1560)," trans. Eva Wajntraub, *Israeli Map Collectors Society Journal* 10 (Spring 1993), 40–41, and facsimile of the map on pp. 29a,b.

3 James A. Welu, "The Sources and Development of Cartographic Ornamentation in the Netherlands," in *Art and Cartography*, ed. David Woodward (Chicago: The University of Chicago Press, 1987), pp. 147–73.

4 Rahel Wischnitzer, "Von der Holbeinbibel zur Amsterdamer Haggadah," *Monatschrift für Geschichte und Wissenschaft des Judentums* 75 (1931), 269–86.

5 E. and G. Wajntraub, *Hebrew Maps of the Holy Land* (Vienna: Bruder, 1992).

6 Rahel Wischnitzer, "Zur Amsterdamer Haggadah", *Monatschrift für Geschichte und Wissenschaft des Judentums* 76 (1932), 239–41. Wischnitzer asked why bar Yaacov's name was not bar Avraham, which would be usual for a convert, but suggested no explanation. Perhaps his natural father was named Abraham.

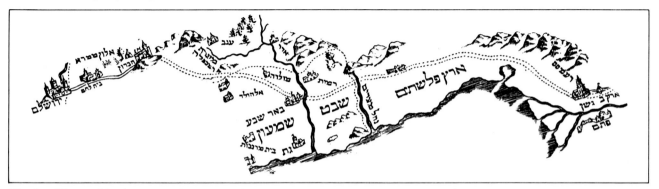

ין עד היה הגדול ובתוכו כל שבט ושבט חלק נחלתו כאשר עיניכם תֶּחֱזֶינָה בְּמֵישָׁרִם והמשכלים יבינם

Fig. 3.   The map superscription.

Fig. 2.   The road leads from Hebron to Goshen. Miniature scenes copied from Adrichom's map are: Abraham near Elon Moreh greeting the three men, and Hagar placing Ishmael a bowshot away under a bush.

derived from a talmudic Midrash (*Pes.* 118a).[7] In a similar vein the Haggadah map contains graphic details that are characteristically Jewish and especially appropriate for Passover.

For example, on his 1590 map, Adrichom shows several horse drawn wagons as well as figures of Mary and Joseph traveling along a coastal road on their way toward Egypt. An index number on the Adrichom map identifies Jacob in one of the wagons. However, Bar Yaacov on his map shows only a single wagon, and although the traveler is not identified, it can be none other than Jacob because, unlike the Adrichom map, this road begins at Hebron, passes through Beersheba and ends at Goshen (Genesis 46:1–28) (Fig. 2).[8] Thus, by selection and rearrangement, bar Yaacov emphasized an important part of the Passover story.

Not all of the graphics on bar Yaacov's map can be interpreted this easily. The first part of his superscription suggests that his map should be clear to almost everyone: "This is to make known to every reasonable person the journey of forty years in the

desert, and the breadth and length of the Holy Land from the River of Egypt to the City of Damascus and from the Valley of Arnon to the Great Sea, and within it the territory of each and every tribe." But the final part of the superscription is veiled and I have paraphrased the Hebrew: "... and when *looked at properly* (Psalm 17:2) *those who are knowledgeable will understand*" (Daniel 12:10) (Fig. 3).

Possibly the two italicized phrases, with slight changes, were derived from the Bible, as I have suggested. The underlined words are emphasized on the map by larger Hebrew lettering, which usually denotes a biblical quotation.[9] I think bar Yaacov may be hinting that the map goes beyond the obvious and contains subtle meanings available only to those who study the map carefully.

For example, let us examine the sailing ships tugging rafts behind them along the Great Sea from Tyre bound for the port of Jaffa (Fig. 4). From the Hebrew: "Rafts of the trees of Lebanon sent by Hiram King of Tyre on the sea to Jaffa; And Solomon had

[7]   Yosef Hayim Yerushalmi, *Haggadah and History* (Philadelphia: The Jewish Publication Society of America, 1975), pl. 67.

[8]   The biblical text does not specify that Jacob began his journey from Hebron but it is reasonable to assume that he did. The road continues on from Hebron to Jerusalem but appears to be paved (as suggested by solid rather than dashed lines), possibly in honor of David who began his rule in Hebron before moving

to Jerusalem (1 Kings 2:11).

[9]   The large letters also serve an additional function. The stressed Hebrew letters date the edition of the map. For example the three letters *tav, nun, hay* add up to the value of (5)455, which corresponds to the date 1695. *Tav, heth, zayin, nun, hey* and *beth* is stressed on the 1712 edition of the map corresponding to the Hebrew calendar year (5)472.

זאת לדעת לכל בר דעת דרך המסעות ארבעים שנה במדבר 'והרוחב והאורך של ארץ הקדושה מנהר מצרים עד עיר דמ

רפסדות מעצי הלבונך שלוחים
מחירם מלך צור על ים ליפו
ושלמה העלה אותם לירושלם

Fig. 4.   The four ships bound for Jaffa from Tyre towing thirteen rafts, the four cows and four points of the compass rose. The lone figure in one raft may reflect the verse: "And King Solomon fetched Hiram from Tyre ..." (1 Kings 7:13).

them brought up to Jerusalem" (ref. II Chron. 2:15). Bar Yaacov's illustration is hardly original since a similar miniature can be found on a map by Nicholas Visscher, published in Amsterdam in 1659. But on Visscher's map there are eight ships and flotilla of over twenty rafts. On bar Yaacov's map there are just four ships, and exactly thirteen rafts. Do these numbers have meaning?

Just below the four ships we see four cows, and close by, a compass rose with four directions. The number four is essential to the Passover Seder: the four questions, the four sons, and the four cups of wine — all related to the four expressions used in Exodus 6:6–7 to describe the deliverance of Israel. The thirteen rafts may also relate to the Passover Seder. The number thirteen appears near the end of the Amsterdam Haggadah in the song *"Echad Me Yodeya?"* (Who knows one?). This joyous song concludes on a triumphant, "Who knows thirteen? I know thirteen; thirteen are the attributes of God".[10]

Did bar Yaacov intend us to find numerical sym-

bolism on his map? Since bar Yaacov left no explanatory text (as did Adrichom) one cannot be certain. Any interpretation of symbolism, to be convincing, has to fit the purpose of the map and the style of the mapmaker. Concerning interpretation Gombrich has stated: "What matters here is surely that the work does not resist this particular projection of meaning."[11]

Use of Mistakes

The Haggadah map contains errors and possible mistakes. Errors are not relevant here, since they merely reflect geographic knowledge at that time: the Kishon river is shown connecting the Kinneret with the Great Sea, the Jabboc River is shown flowing into the Kinneret, Mount Gerezim is erroneously placed north rather than south of Mount Ebal, and so on. A major error (probably fortunate for the design of the map), is the foreshortened distance separating the Land of Israel from Egypt and the Sinai. Almost the entire Negev is missing.

Mistakes are another matter, they could have in-

10   E.H. Gombrich, *Symbolic Images* (Chicago: University of Chicago Press, 1972), p. 18.
11   I am indebted to Professor Jonas Alster, of the University of Tel Aviv, for suggesting this interpretation.
12   Mistakes can be made into a game and a learning experience.

In Jewish micrography, according to Meir Ronnen, it was a challenge to "catch the scribe out on omissions and errors." The Jerusalem Post International Edition, 22–28 March 1981, p. 18.

5a 5b

5c 5d

Fig. 5. Mistakes, or apparent mistakes: a) the short resh squeezed between Midbar and Paran, compare with Midbar Shur below it; b) tiny Jaffa lettering, compare with the lettering for Askelon, also near the shore, or any other city; c) Judah spelled with an aleph rather than a hey; d) Jezreel, with an aleph missing before the lamed.

terpretive value.[12] Bar Yaacov proofread his work. One can see a mistake where the letter *resh* was left out of Midbar Paran (Fig. 5a). To correct this, bar Yaacov squeezed in a *resh* as best he could. But why did he make the lettering of Jaffa small and obscure when he had more than adequate space for it on his map (Fig. 5b)? This city is mentioned in the transport of the rafts from Lebanon to Jerusalem, and in the story of Jonah, shown below it. Possibly, bar Yaacov made Jaffa difficult to find, so that a child would have to search carefully up and down the coast for it — a common pedagogical trick in geography.

Yehudah is spelled with an *aleph* at the end, which is unusual, since Yehudah is always spelled with a *hey* in the Hebrew Bible (Fig. 5c). However, a variant spelling with an *aleph* is known in the Talmud.[13] Perhaps bar Yaacov may be testing our knowledge, or being stylistic. (He preferred the name *bar*, which is Aramaic for "son of" — and has a Talmudic flavor — to *ben*, which is Hebrew). The spelling of Jezreelah, however, is incorrect. Bar Yaacov omitted an *aleph*, which may simply reflect a moment of carelessness. On the other hand, Jezreel was the infamous city where Jezebel lived (1 Kings 21:23) (Fig. 5d). Perhaps Bar Yaacov may have decided that *el* (a name of God) was inappropriate within this city name.

Only one city on this map is given two names, one right-side-up, and the other upside-down. Right-side-up, we find Beth El (literally "house of God"),

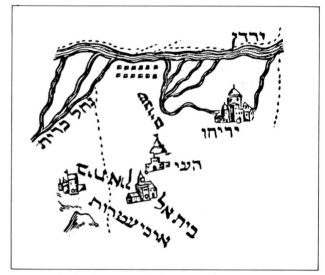

Fig. 6. Beth El appears right-side up, whereas Beth Aven is upside-down, both names on the map apply to the same city, a conflation as in Hosea 4:15.

the city that Abraham and Jacob visited. Upside-down we see Beth Aven, a sarcastic name (which can mean "house of iniquity") (Fig. 6). The prophet Hosea (4:15) used Beth Aven as a pejorative for Beth El because Jeroboam had set up a Golden Calf in Beth El to divert people from legitimate Temple service in Jerusalem. Actually, Beth El and Beth Aven are two

13 Marcus Jastrow, *A Dictionary of the Targum, the Talmud Babli and Yerushalmi, and the Midrashic Literature* (New York: Shalom, 1967).

nearby but entirely separate places (Joshua 7:2), and are shown that way on Adrichom's map. Bar Yaacov conflates the two names on his map, as does Hosea in his text, to express indignation at Golden Calf worship.

Jeroboam also set up another Golden Calf at Dan, near the headwaters of the Jordan (1 Kings 12:29). Significantly, bar Yaacov wants nothing to do with this city, since he does not even locate it on his map (though Dan is clearly located on Adrichom's map, and also on the 1621 Hebrew map).

The map cartouche contains a handy listing of the stations of the desert wandering (Fig. 7). Each is indexed by Hebrew numbering corresponding to places shown on the map. Only forty-one stations are shown although there are forty-two stations (Num 33:5–50).[14] A lack of symmetry shows up on the cartouche, which should have three even columns of fourteen names. Such an obvious mistake could not have escaped notice. The missing station is Iye-abarim (variously translated, if translated at all, as "ruins over there"). It should be placed between Oboth and Dibon Gad. According to Rashi, Iye denotes "wastes, or heaps", as in Psalm 79:1: "They have made Jerusalem into heaps of rubble" (Rashi's commentary to Num. 33:44). The "mistake" of leaving Iye-abarim off the map would bring the knowledgeable reader to this verse, and to Rashi's commentary on it. Thus, bar Yaacov would enable this reader to observe the *halachah* (tradition) of recalling the destruction of Jerusalem on a festive occasion.[15]

Geography in the Masoretic Text

During the period of the Protestant Reformation disputes arose among scholars about the accuracy of the Masoretic Hebrew Bible, as opposed to the Greek Septuagint (frequently used in the Catholic Church). For example, one textual problem concerns the delineation of the borderlines of the Tribe of Naphtali. According to the Hebrew text: "The border ... reached Zevulun in the south, Asher in the west, and Judah at the Jordan in the east" (Joshua 19:34). Scho-

Fig. 7. Cartouche with a listing of all the places along the journey from Egypt to the Jordan, with one notable omission.

lars have argued that reaching Judah from Naphtali makes no sense.[16] How could the territory of the most northern tribe reach down to the most southern tribe? Significantly, Judah is excluded from this verse in the Septuagint, which may suggest that the Septuagint is more accurate than the Masoretic Hebrew text.

The Vilna Gaon (1720–1797), the eighteenth century Jewish commentator, was puzzled by this problem and offered a solution. Since Naphtali borders on the headwaters of the Jordan it could claim rights to the entire river and consequently Naphtali's territory could literally extend to the territory of Judah along the Jordan.[17]

On his map bar Yaacov drew the border separating Naphtali from Menasheh east of the Jordan River, giving Naphtali control over these waters (Fig. 8). He then extended this dashed line east of the banks of the Kinneret and all the way down the Jordan to reach Judah at the Dead Sea. The territory of Naphtali

---

14   Bar Yaacov uses a final *kaph* for the number twenty. In Cabalistic calculations this letter had the value of 500, but in ordinary works it had the same value as the regular *kaph*. See G. Ifrah, *From One to Zero, A Universal History of Numbers* (Baltimore: Penguin Books, 1987), p. 256. However, bar Yaacov did not use a final *mem*, so he appears to have been inconsistent, which complicates interpretation.

15   I am indebted to Professor Yehoshua Ben-Arieh, of The Hebrew University in Jerusalem, for suggesting this interpretation.
16   R.G. Boling and G.E. Wright, Joshua, *The Anchor Bible*, vol. 6 (New York: Doubleday, 1982), p. 457.
17   Reuven Drucker, *Yehoshua* (New York: Mesorah Publications, 1982), p. 388.

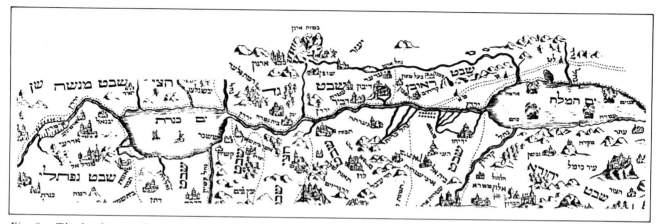

Fig. 8. The border of tribe of Naphtali shown by the dashed line. It continues along the east bank of the Jordan River until the tribal territory of Judah at the Dead Sea — in literal fulfillment of one interpretation of the Masoretic text (Joshua 19:34).

thus extends along the Jordan River to Judah — in literal keeping with the Masoretic text.

While the issue of Naphtali reaching Judah may appear trivial to a modern reader it did engage the attention of another, earlier, mapmaker, Thomas Fuller. On his 1650 engraved map of the Galilee he clearly shows a place called Judah in tribal Naphtali near the Jordan River. Fuller interpreted Judah in this verse to be a place name. Bar Yaacov, on the other hand, interpreted Judah as a tribal name. Both maps defend the literal accuracy of the Masoretic text. The Vilna Gaon is likely to have seen the Amsterdam Haggadah, and possibly his own defense was influenced by bar Yaacov's map. In any event, bar Yaacov's map is visually consistent with the interpretation of the Vilna Gaon.

Talmudic Interpretation

Hebrew lettering and exclusive reliance on the Masoretic text are characteristically Jewish, but Talmudic influence makes a work especially Jewish. Bar Yaacov seems to have been sensitive to this point since he included the figure of Abraham smashing the idols among his Haggadah illustrations. The loops drawn at the Red Sea provide a clear indication of talmudic influence on bar Yaacov's map (Fig. 9a). On Adrichom's map and on the 1621 Hebrew map only a simple crossover of the sea is shown. However, loops identical with those of bar Yaacov's are shown on the

Hebrew map prepared by Rabbi Aharon Ben-Hayyim in 1776.[18] Ben-Hayyim fortunately provides us with the talmudic reference to explain the basis for the loops (*Tosephta* to *Arikin* 15a) (Fig. 9b).

According to this Midrash, Israel lacked faith at time they crossed the Red Sea: "... Israel were rebellious at that very hour, saying: 'Just as we go up from this side, so will the Egyptians go up from the other side'" (*Arikin* 15a). The Tosephist comments here that Israel did not go directly across the Red Sea but made a semi-circle, entering and exiting on the same side of the sea. Consequently, the Egyptians could have overtaken Israel, either by following along the shore on the same side, or by entering the sea, crossing over, and outflanking them on the other side. The comment of the Tosephist allows bar Yaacov to draw a semi-circle for the movement of Israel. The straight line across the Red Sea may represent the path of the Egyptians.

According to the biblical description, the Egyptians pursued the Israelites into the midst of the sea. Since the pillar of cloud stood behind Israel when they entered the Red Sea, "the one came not near the other all the night" (Exodus 14:20). Bar Yaacov may be suggesting a Red Sea maneuver similar to a classic movie chase, where the hero takes advantage of a smoke screen to make an adroit left turn while the pursuers, unknowingly, hurl straight on to oblivion.

The Influence of Bar Yaacov's Background

Although bar Yaacov succeeded in creating a map with distinctive Jewish content, traces of his earlier Christian background may also be found in the map,

18 A variation of Ben Hayyim's Hebrew map is shown on page 123 of Eran Laor, *Maps of the Holy Land* (New York: Alan R. Liss, 1986).

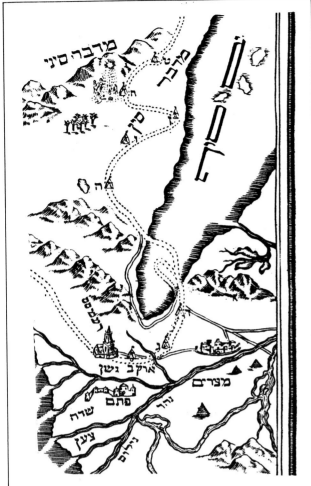

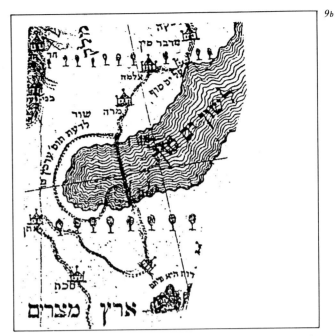

Fig. 9. The semi-circular loops across the Red Sea, possibly a reference to the circuitous journey.

Fig. 10. Lower right-hand corner of map. A nearly nude figure with parasol and barbed arrows, riding a crocodile.

just as they are found in his other engravings. One haggadah engraving by bar Yaacov shows King David kneeling before "the Holy Spirit." While there is nothing heterodox about the illustration, "the visual representation is entirely Christian in atmosphere."[19] Similarly, bar Yaacov's use of the term *Eretz ha-Kodesh* (The Holy Land) in the superscription of his map is characteristically Christian, even if it appears in Hebrew script. The term Holy Land never occurs in the Hebrew Bible or the Talmud. Only Jerusalem is called holy, and then obliquely (Joel 4:17, and elsewhere). This is not to say that Jews refrain from using the term Holy Land, or find it offensive. But when addressing a Jewish audience, the term Holy Land is not entirely appropriate, or usual, and never preferred. On the 1621 engraved Hebrew map the land is called *Eretz Zev* (Land of the Gazelle, or

figuratively, Beautiful Land). *Eretz Zev* is also used on Rabbi Ben-Hayyim's Hebrew map (1776).

The figure of the nearly nude woman at the lower right of the map is, at the very least, unusual for a seventeenth-century Jewish illustration (Fig. 10). True, the Prague Haggadah shows a nearly naked woman in its 1526 edition, but by 1603, in the Venice Haggadah, this illustration was altered as it was

19 Yerushalmi, *Haggadah and History*, pl. 61.

אתם ראיתם אשר עשיתי למצרים
ואשא אתכם על—כנפי
נשרים ואבא אתכם אלי

Fig. 11.   Jonah before and after his experience. Avraham bar Yaacov's name appears just below.
Fig. 12.   A pedestal topped by a scale in which each unit equals one parasang. There are twenty-eight units as indicated on the left. Bar Yaacov shows the bird above the pedestal clutching the carcass of a large animal, possibly a reference to nesher, a vulture (Ex. 19:4).

considered too immodest in its original form.[20] Bar Yaacov's seductive lady carries a stylish parasol in her right hand, but in her left are two barbed arrows, and she is riding on a crocodile representing Egypt: "the great dragon that lieth in the midst of his rivers" (Ezekiel 29:3).

Christian Holy Land maps in the seventeenth century commonly showed illustrations of Eve, nude or nearly so. Bar Yaacov would have seen many similar representations in Church art. The nude woman on his map was left unexpurgated by the first publisher of the Haggadah (1695) and by the later publishers, possibly for the same reason that the engraving of a kneeling David at prayer was retained. The illustration is not offensive, just a bit alien, and one does not embarrass a *ger zeddeq* (a convert to justice) by criticizing traces of his past.

Bar Yaacov's name is found on the map just below the figure of Jonah who is shown ejected on to the land by the big fish (Fig. 11). Illustrations of sailors tossing Jonah into the sea are frequently found on Holy Land maps of the seventeenth century, but in bar Yaacov's map Jonah is also shown safely on land. In this illustration, Jonah, on all fours, seems bewildered as he looks back toward the sea. But then bar Yaacov had also gone through an extraordinary personal experience. And what did bar Yaacov think of his adopted Jewish community?

On the left bottom corner of the map we are given some indication (Fig. 12). There on a masonry bench is a map scale in Persian parasangs. The Talmud mentions the parasang but rarely gives actual distances between places. A parasang is, more or less, equivalent to a league, or the distance one might walk in an hour, between three and four statute miles.[21] Precision is not important here since the map itself is not accurate. Bar Yaacov probably never intended anyone to use his scale for distance measurements. Usually scales have

[20] Ibid., pl. 41.

[21] R. Chardon, "The Linear League in North America," *Annals of the Association of American Geographers* 70 (1980), 129–53.

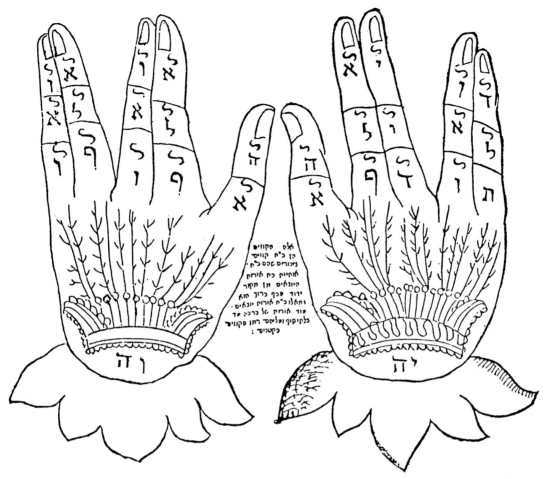

Fig. 13. A cabalistic illustration showing the hands divided into twenty-eight sections along the joints, signifying the Hebrew word koach, meaning strength. Shefa Tal, 1612. (Hebraic Section, Library of Congress, Washington, D.C).

convenient tick marks, and end at a round number such as thirty. Conventional map distance scales start on the left side of the map and increase to the right, using Arabic numbers. Bar Yaacov uses Hebrew numbers, and his scale starts on the right and increases towards the left. He marked his scale at *aleph* (1),

and ended it abruptly at *kaph heth* (28). The number twenty-eight is a meaningful Hebrew word meaning "power," as shown, for example, in a drawing taken from a 17th century Cabalistic work (Fig. 13). Bar Yaacov, in his own characteristically Jewish way, is wishing his haggadah readers strength.

THREE DESK SEALS IN THE JEWISH MUSEUM, LONDON*

L.Y. Rahmani

The Jewish Museum in London possesses a small but interesting group of Jewish seals, which have so far been published only as entries in the General Catalogue, edited by Richard Barnett.[1] Three of them are re-published here, with some amendments and further discussion.

1. The Western Wall Seal

The Western Wall Seal (cat. no. 1192, Fig. 1) is a desk seal with a plain, wooden handle 46 mm. high, with a matrix diameter of 19 mm. The matrix shows a schematic rendering of the Western Wall in Jerusalem, behind which are seen the tops of four cypress trees. A star above the center indicates the beginning of the Hebrew inscription, which surrounds the Wall.[2] The representation is very common on the seals of institutions or officials of the Jewish communities in Jerusalem from the eighteenth to the twentieth centuries.[3] The Western Wall appears also on private seals,[4] as well as on many Jewish ceremonial or other

objects, some serving as souvenirs of the Holy Places.[5] The inscription, יוסף בר חיים ז"ל מריוש "Joseph bar Hayyim of blessed memory MRIWS," ends with an ambiguous word. "Marius" is a very rare Jewish name,[6] so some other meaning may be possible. The first letter, *mem*, may be the prefix "from,"[7] which would be followed by a place name, possibly "Reusch," which may be a village in Bavaria, or two neighboring townlets in Moravia. One of the latter may fit this seal.[8]

* Thanks are due to the Director and Curator of the Jewish Museum in London, Mr. Edgar Samuel and to its Registrar, Alisa Jaffa, for enabling me to examine these seals at the Museum, supplying me with photos and permitting their publication here. My thanks are also due to R. Spiegel of the Central Archives for the History of the Jewish People in Jerusalem for permission to publish photo no. 255a of their Harburger Collection of Photos (no. P 160). The names given to the seals in this paper are mine. Figs. 1, 2, 4 and 5 represent the impressions of the seals.

1 R.D. Barnett, ed., *Catalogue of the Permanent and Loan Collections of the Jewish Museum, London* (London, 1974), pp. 183–84 (hereafter *Catalogue*).

2 *Catalogue*, no. 1192, pl. 206 shows this image upside-down and describes it on p. 183 as a "central rectangle with projecting spikes below star."

3 A. Wolf in *The Jewish Encyclopedia* (New York), s.v. Seal, p. 139 (hereafter Wolf). See also I. Shachar, *Jewish Tradition in*

Art, The Feuchtwanger Collection of Judaica (Jerusalem, Israel Museum, 1971), nos. 528–539, 549, 552–553 (hereafter Shachar).

4 E.g. Wolf, pl. II:31; Shachar, no. 554.

5 E.g. B. Narkiss and B. Yaniv, *Index of Jewish Art: The Gross Family Collection*, I (Jerusalem, 1985), pp. 115, 123, 219, 247, 299, 311. For a souvenir seal, which lacks a private name, see C. Benjamin, *The Stieglitz Collection* (Jerusalem, Israel Museum, 1987), no. 262.

6 But for Marösch in 1311, see L. Zunz, "Namen der Juden," *Gesammelte Schriften* II (Berlin, 1876), p. 33.

7 For the use of *mem* to refer to a Jew from abroad living in the Holy Land, see Shachar (seals nos. 613 and 640).

8 Cf. A. Starkendorf Ritter, *Geographisch-Statistisches Lexikon* (Leipzig, 1865). The first letter of the place-name might be read as a *dalet* and thus the word דיוש might refer to the town of Diosgyor, near Miskolci in Hungary. it was however designated by the Jews as דיא"ר; see A. Fuchs, *Hungarian Yeshivot* (Jerusalem, 1987), p. 191 (Hebrew) and thus must also be excluded.

Fig. 2.   The Speyer Seal. London, Jewish Museum, cat. no. 1203. Courtesy Jewish Museum, London.

2. The Speyer Seal

The Speyer Seal (cat. no. 1203, Fig. 2), is a silver desk seal with a handle 88 mm. high,[9] topped by a crest depicting a swan, 33 mm. high.[10] The slightly elliptic matrix measures 16 by 15 mm., depicting a standing female figure, carrying in its right a leafed branch and supporting with its left a crowned, oval shield, resting on a banderole; within the shield is a vigilant cock. The Hebrew inscription surrounds the seal and is framed by a line. It starts and ends with dots at the bottom right and left, reading: הדס א׳ ה׳ יוזפא

שפייאר ("Hadas[a] wife of Rabbi Yozpa Speyer"). The crest of the elongated, hollow handle in the shape of a swan may signify purity of heart, and might therefore have been chosen as a suitable emblem for a lady.[11] It could also have served as an allusion to the sign over the house of the owner. Such names of house-signs were often added to Jewish homes of Central Europe in the seventeenth and eighteenth centuries.[12]

The female figure in the seal itself clearly represents the zodiac sign of Virgo, usually shown as a maid carrying a leafy branch, representing the month of Elul.[13] Zodiac signs, indicating the month of the seal's owner's birth, appear regularly on Jewish seals from the mid-seventeenth century onwards. They replace the real coats-of-arms on seals of Christians, forbidden to Jews by the law of the land. The use of these signs, however, does not indicate belief in astrology.[14]

The dress in which the figure appears on the seal suits the last decades of the seventeenth or the first of the eighteenth century: a low-necked bodice, closely fitting and cut to a point in front, its full sleeves ending at the elbows in wide cuffs. The full skirt hangs in folds to the ground, covering the shoes completely.[15] The form of shield and crown also fit such a date.

The cock in Jewish tradition is a symbol of fruitfulness (*Babylonian Talmud, Gittin* 57a). The cock is also valued for its ability to foresee the coming of the light of day.[16] At an early stage, Jewish exegesis had interpreted the *sekhvi* in Job 38:36 as referring to the cock, who was thus imbued by the Lord with special wisdom (*BT, Rosh Hashanah* 26a; see also *Palestinian Talmud, Berakhot* 9:2). Accordingly, the Lord should be blessed for giving the rooster sense (*BT*

---

[9]   The *Catalogue*, no. 1203, p. 184, claims that this handle was designed as a corkscrew, which is unfounded.

[10]   My thanks are extended to Mrs. Haya Benjamin, Curator of Judaica at the Israel Museum, Jerusalem, for showing me a similar crest on the lid of a Nuremberg tankard (Israel Museum, no. 133/63) dated to the late 16th century. The motive appears throughout the 17th and well into the 18th century on various silver vessels of central European origin.

[11]   Cf. A. Henkel and A. Schöne, *Emblemata; Handbuch zur Sinnbildkunst des XVI und XVII Jahrhunderts* (Stuttgart, 1987), col. 817, citing J. Camerarius, *Emblemata* III (Nuremberg 1596), no. 22. It should be noted that a German translation of this book existed since 1661.

[12]   E.g. *zum goldenen Schwan* in the first half of the 17th century, at Worms: R. Reuter, *Warmeisa, 1000 Jahre Juden in Worms* (Frankfurt/Main 1984), pp. 96–99, or on the seal of Michel Herz, *zum weissen Schwanen*, where a swan is added to the zodiac sign of Scorpio: J. Taglicht, *Nachlässe der Wiener*

Juden im 17. und 18. Jahrhundert (Quellen und Forschungen der Juden in Deutsch-Österreich VII) (Vienna, 1917), pp. 10, n. 2, pp. 175–176, no. 106, dated 1707; see also Wolf (note 3 above), p. 140.

[13]   E.g. Wolf, ibid., pl. I:16; A.K. Klagsbald, *Jewish Treasures from Paris, from the Collections of the Cluny Museum and the Consistoire* (Jerusalem, 1982), no. 152.

[14]   As claimed by *Encyclopedia Judaica* (Jerusalem, 1971), 14, col. 1080, s.v. Seal. See, however, J.J. Schudt, *Jüdische Merckwürdigkeiten II: Frankfürter Judenchronik* (Leipzig 1714), Book VI, Chapter 12, para. 4, pp. 172–173; Chapter 15, para. 7, p. 262. See also M. Narkiss, "The Zodiac in Jewish Art," *Kiryat Sefer* 16 (1939–40), 513–519 (Hebrew).

[15]   J. Laver, *Costume Through the Ages* (London, 1964), p. 53.

[16]   For similar ideas in Greek and Roman thought and lore, see C. Nauerth in *Reallexikon für Antike und Christentum*, s.v. Hahn.

Ber. 60b); and indeed a benediction for the rooster's wisdom is included in the daily morning prayers.[17] Such a daily reminder immediately associates the cock with foresight and wisdom. Since the late third century C.E. the cock's ability to see even in darkness was linked with the coming of the messianic light of redemption (*BT Sanhedrin* 98b and Rashi's interpretation there). Eventually the cock was equalled to Israel in his fierceness and undauntedness (*BT Beiza* 25b; *Ex. Rabbah*, 42:9).

The cock was thus a Jewish symbol of wisdom and foresight, as well as of hope of messianic redemption, and may have been engraved by fourteenth-century German Jews on their seals to express thoughts which were to remain hidden to the hostile Christians, but clear enough to fellow Jews.[18] It is perhaps in keeping with these concepts that the cock was again depicted as armorial devices by Italian Jews from the seventeenth century onwards, serving at times as *armes-parlants* (e.g. with the Gallico family).[19]

The inscription contains two abbreviations; the first, *aleph*, standing for *eshet-*, "wife of", and the second, *heh*, for *harav*, Rabbi;[20] the inscription can thus to be rendered as "Hadasa, wife of Rabbi Yozpa Speyer."[21] It is true that in Jewish private correspondence of the seventeenth and eighteenth centuries a married woman would sign her name and her father's including his titles, rather than using the name and title of her husband;[22] she would, however, apply her husbands seal to close the letter.[23] Hadasa's seal reveals therefore that she is married or widowed.[24] As an independent business woman she may have had

Fig. 3.   The "Man with the Balance" Seal. London, Jewish Museum, cat. no. 1193. Courtesy Jewish Museum, London.

her own, personal seal, as would a man.[25] This seems to be the case with another woman, the owner of an eighteenth-century silver seal inscribed in Hebrew: "Zippora, daughter of R. Henich Nickelsburg, of blessed memory", carrying the device of a rampant lion within a crowned oval shield, framed by a wreath.[26]

[17]   See S. I. Baer, *Seder 'Avodat Yisrael* (Berlin 1939), p. 40 (Hebrew).

[18]   D.M. Friedenberg, *Medieval Jewish Seals from Europe* (Detroit, 1987), nos. 82, 90, 91, 100. This device should however, not be connected (p. 176) with ancient Jewish seals; see e.g. N. Avigad, "A Group of Hebrew Seals," *Erez Israel*, 9 (1969) 9, pl. II:21, or with Greek coins. Of the former the medieval Jews had no knowledge and about the latter they would care little; nor was "aggressive male vitality" (Friedenberg p. 202) a Jewish ideal during the Middle Ages, to be so expressed. One has also to reject a further claim by the *Encyclopedia Judaica* (note 14 above), col. 1979, that the cock on the seal of one of these Jews (identical with Friedenberg, ibid. no. 100) "points to a Christian seal maker."

[19]   C. Roth, "Stemmi di famiglie ebraiche italiane", in *Scritta in memoria di Leone Carpi* (Jerusalem, 1969), pp. 169–173; G.F. Pisa, "Parnassim — le grandi famiglie ebraiche italiane dal sec. XI al XIX", *Annuari di Studi Ebraici* X (1984), 291–491. See also: U. Piparno, "Il gallo nella tradizione Ebraica," *Annuario di Studi Ebraici* X (1984), 179–219. My thanks are due to Miryam de la Pergola of the Centro di Studi sull' Ebraismo

Italiano, Jerusalem, for having drawn my attention to these publications.

[20]   Cf. Klagsbald (note 13 above), no. 153: ב״ה — *ben harav*.

[21]   "Hadas" was a common name of Jewish women, as was "Yospa", a common form of Joseph, for men; see: Shlomo Ettinger, *Lists of Names of Frankfurt Jews* (Frankfurt/Main 1960), kept in the Central Archives for the History of the Jewish People, Jerusalem. My thanks are due to Hadassa Assouline of the Archives, for having drawn my attention to this important study.

[22]   A. Landau and B. Wachstein, *Jüdische Privatbriefe aus dem Jahre 1619 (Quellen und Forschungen zur Geschichte der Juden in Deutsch-Österreich* III) (Vienna 1911), p. xxv.

[23]   Ibid., pp. 14–15; 66.

[24]   Ibid., p. 25.

[25]   Taglicht (note 12 above) pp. 10–11, quoting, among others, several such cases in the wealthy Oppenheimer family, all of the 18th century.

[26]   Shachar (note 3 above), no. 637.

Fig. 4. The "Man with the Balance" Seal. London, Jewish Museum, cat. no. 1193. Courtesy Jewish Museum, London.

3. The Man-With-The-Balance Seal

The third seal is a brass desk seal (cat. no. 1193, Figs. 3 and 4), with a turned baluster handle, 70 mm. in height.[27] The matrix measuring 30 mm. in diameter depicts a standing man, facing left, holding a balance in his right hand while his left arm is held akimbo. Around the balance of large, equipoised scales, appear three stars. A Hebrew inscription surrounding the image, with dots between each word, starts above the man's head, reading: גדלי * בהרר * יצחק שליט * דורלך *. A German inscription contained within

a pearled frame surrounds the Hebrew one, starting above the first letter of the Hebrew name, with four additional points as space-fillers, reading: CATALIE * ISAC * FON * DURLACH * * * * . This type of desk seal with a baluster molding appears from the late sixteenth century until the nineteenth century, executed in different materials such as metal, wood or ivory; its moldings ranging from the elaborate to the plain.[28] The present specimen can be dated to the first decades of the eighteenth century.[29]

This date suits the dress of the man depicted on the matrix: he wears a long waistcoat, buttoned from neck to hem. Over this he wears a *justaucorps*, a kneelength collarless coat, worn open; its large, reversed cuffs are clearly shown, as is a row of elaborate buttons seen on the left. Full breeches emerge below this coat, reaching above the knees.[30] The head is wigless and is covered with an old-fashioned hat, its broad brim turned up and forwards, instead of the tricorn, which just came into fashion.[31]

The scene on this seal is similar to another contemporary Jewish seal, of which only a photo survives (Fig. 5).[32] The beveled rectangular matrix depicts a man holding an equipoised balance in his outstretched right hand, his left held akimbo. He stands in a relaxed position, his right leg bent behind his left. His dress may be similar to the man on the former seal, although less elaborate, and his head is covered with a barret. The Hebrew inscription starts at the bottom right, reading שמעון : בר : יעקב : שמעון : (Shimeon bar Ya'aqov Shimeon) and below the balance, the Latin letters S I. Under this appears a branch, ending at left with a round fruit.

The man's pose, curiously inappropriate to the act of weighing, seems influenced by contemporaneous paintings and etchings.[33] The appearance of a com-

27 The *Catalogue*, no. 1193, p. 183 erroneously describes the handle as made of wood.
28 M. Finley, *Western Writing Implements in the Age of the Quill Pen* (Wetheral, Carlisle, Columbia 1990), p. 182, fig. 319 (now British Museum, London, nos. 1982:7-1,1 and 7-1,2), and pp. 183-184, figs. 321–327.
29 My thanks are due to Prof. Dr. A. Dreier, former Director, Kunstgewerbemuseum, Berlin, for informing me that it should be dated to ca. 1700; and to Mr. A. North, Keeper of the Metalwork Department, Victoria and Albert Museum, London, for suggesting a probable date in the first quarter of the eighteenth century, comparing the workmanship to that of similar turned brass candlesticks in the Museum's collections, dating to 1699 and 1705/6 respectively.
30 Cf. C. Kohler, *A History of Costume* (New York, 1963), pp.

308–313; figs. 381; 385 (dated 1690); Laver (note 15 above), p. 53, nos. 1, 4; J. Laver, *A Concise History of Costume* (London, 1969), p. 121, Fig. 127 (all from the end of the 17th century); M. Sichel, *Costume Reference 3: Jacobean, Stuart and Restoration* (Boston 1977), p. 41, right (of ca. 1692).
31 Best exemplified in the confrontation of the Jewish merchant and the Gentile gentlemen in an Amsterdam etching of 1720: see M.H. Gans, *Memorbook, A History of Dutch Jewry from the Renaissance to 1940* (Baarn, 1971), p. 174, right. For Jewish dress of that period, see also: J.J. Schudt, *Neue Frankfurter Jüdische Kleiderordnung* (Frankfurt/Main 1716), frontispiece.
32 Harburger Collection of Photos, no. P. 160, Central Archives for the History of the Jewish People, Jerusalem.
33 See e.g. Watteau's *Recreation itallienne*, outer right and his *Les plaisirs du bal*, center right, in J. Sunderland and E. Camesasca,

Fig. 5.   The "Man with the Balance" Seal. Harburger Photo Collection, Central Archives for the History of the Jewish People, Jerusalem, no. P. 160:255a.

plete human figure upon a Jewish seal is somewhat surprising. There was no need to add a human figure in order to depict the zodiac sign of Libra, a pair

of scales would suffice.[34] Human figures of zodiac signs on Jewish personal seals usually appear when they are unavoidable as in Sagittarius, Gemini and Virgo.[35] A specific prohibition on depicting human figures on seals is based on the rulings of the Rabbis as early as the second century C.E. (*Tosefta, Avodah Zarah* 5:2;, repeated in *BT Avodah Zarah* 3 b; see also *Mishnah Avodah Zarah* 3:1). Foreign influences caused transgression or circumvention of such interdictions.[36] Thus human figured personifications, such as *Caritas*, appear on Jewish objects from mid-fifteenth-century Italy onwards, including personal seals. In such cases this personification must have been understood as charity (*zedaka*).[37]

The model of a man holding an equipoised balance on an eighteenth-century Jewish seal may be sought in earlier depictions of the zodiac signs. Depiction of the signs of the zodiac appear in books concerning the calculation of the Jewish calendar and intercalation on leap years, to corroborate between the solar year and the lunar Jewish year. One of the most popular intercalation books of the seventeenth and eighteenth centuries, which was often illustrated, is called *Sefer 'Ibronot* (from the term '*ibur*, literally "conception", i.e. the intercalation of an additional month of Adar in a leap year). The book is intended for practical

The Complete Paintings of Watteau (London, 1971), nos. 129, 164; available in engravings in the 18th century; see also such engravings as *Repas des Juifs pendant la Fête des Tentes* in B. Picart, *Ceremonies et coutumes religieuses de tous les peuples du monde* (Amsterdam, 1723). In the shape of its matrix, in the display of figure, in the inscription, as well as in its execution, this seal most resembles the seal in Klagsbald (note 13 above), no. 152.

34 E.g. *Catalogue*, no. 1198. See also Shachar, no. 636 and cf. Narkiss (note 14 above), p. 517. Libra, shown as a human figure holding a balance, appears in ancient representations, including Jewish ones (see e.g. M. Dothan, *Hammat Tiberias*, Jerusalem, 1983, p. 46, pls. 16:5; 33:1) as well as on more recent Jewish vessels — e.g. a silver Seder dish, first half of 19th century: H. Volavkova, *A Story of the Jewish Museum in Prague* (Prague, 1968), fig. 94; also in drawings, e.g. male half-figure: B.B. Levy, *Planets, Potions and Parchments — Hebraica from the Dead Sea Scrolls to the Eighteenth Century* (Montreal, Jewish Public Library, 1990), p. 127; such items are however unrelated to our present case, concerning seals.

35 Narkiss (note 14 above), 517–519. For Sagittarius one can now add an early 17th-century example: Landau-Wachstein (note 22 above), pl. VIII:29 and possibly also one of the last quarter of that century: Reuter (note 12 above), p. 138, though there the figure may represent the owner's house sign: *Zur Armbrust*.

36 For these interdicts in general, see E.G. Urbach, "The Rabbinical Laws of Idolatry in the Second and Third Centuries in the Light of Archaeological and Historical Facts", *Israel Exploration Journal* 9 (1959), 149–165; 229–245. For particular cases, see also

Y. Yadin, *The Finds from the Bar-Kokhba Period in the Cave of the Letters* (Jerusalem, 1963), pp. 118–121; L.Y. Rahmani, "A Jewish Rock-Cut Tomb on Mt. Scopus", *'Atiqot* (English Series) 14 (1980), 53–54, pl. VII: 5–7.

37 For the Jewish views on *Caritas*, see Narkiss's remarks on a 17th-century item, probably from Germany: M. Narkiss, *The Hanukka Lamp* (Jerusalem, 1939), p. 30; 91, n. 27 (English); pl. XXI:59. Friedenberg (note 18 above), p. 347, thought that this personification on a Jewish seal of 1462 (no. 172) was influenced by ancient Palestinian city-coins. In fact this too is a depiction of the image of *Caritas*, as developed in Italy and known eventually in the rest of Europe. For earlier types of *Caritas*, see R. Freyhan 'The Evolution of the Caritas Figure in the Thirteenth and Fourteenth Centuries,' *Journal of the Warburg and Courtauld Institutes* XI (1948), 68–86; see further M. Wellershoff-van Thadden, in O. Schmidt *et al.*, *Reallexikon zur deutschen Kunstgeschichte* III, s.v. Caritas, fig. 5, cols. 351–352. For the 'Filippo Lippi-Typ' see Guy de Tervarent, *Attributes et symboles dans l'art profane, 1450–1600* (Geneva, 1958), col. 175, fig. 33, left. For prints from the 17th century onwards, see Cesare Ripa, *Iconologia* (Rome, 1970, [1603]) ed. Mandowski, Hildesheim, p. 64. Additional images of *Caritas* in Jewish art may be found on an Amsterdam marriage contract of 1692, see M. Narkiss, "Aboab, a Non-Existent Jewish Copper Engraver," *Kiryat Sefer* 15 (1938–39), 488–490 (Hebrew); and on tombstones at Altona, dated 1716–17, see M. Grunwald, *Portugiesengräber auf deutscher Erde* (Hamburg, 1902), pp. 31, 91; nos. 253; 558; 1416.

*Fig. 6. The month
of Tishrei, a merchant
holding a balance, from
Sefer 'Ibronot, 1619.
The Jewish National
and University Library,
Jerusalem, Department of
Manuscripts and Archives,
MS Heb. 8° 3247, fol. 5v.*

reckoning of leap years, the new moon, as well as the different feasts, fasts and festivals. It is based on *Sefer Ha-'Ibur* by Abraham Ibn-Ezra (Spanish poet and astronomer, 1089–1164), which was also illustrated at times.

The page dealing with the month of Tishrei. which relates to the balance as its zodiac sign, usually depicts a pair of equipoised scales inscribed: "Scales of Justice to weigh the new moon." Two Ashkenazi manuscripts of this book contain a scene similar to that of the London seal. Both, however, modify the scene to depict an emblem of an honest merchant. The earlier of the two, dated 1619 (Fig. 6),[38] depicts

[38] Thanks are due to the Department of Manuscripts and Archives of the Jewish National and University Library for permission to publish here fol. 5v of their Heb. 8° 3247, written by Asher bar Shemuel Hacohen. For these books in general see Levy (note 34 above), pp. 101–103.

Fig. 7.   *A merchant holding a balance, from Sefer 'Ibronot, 1690(?). The Jewish National and University Library, Jerusalem, Department of Manuscripts and Archives, MS Heb. 8° 6678 fol. 22v. Photo: D. Harris.*

a bearded man facing left, holding an equipoised balance in his right hand, dressed in early seventeenth-century costume.[39] A second manuscript (Fig. 7) depicts the frontal view of a beardless and wigged youth, both feet turned to the left, a balance of equipoised scales in his right hand and his left arm akimbo.[40] The manuscript has been variously dated to 1640 or 1690;[41] the latter date is better suited the youth's dress.[42] A depiction of a wealthy Sephardi merchant from Amsterdam appears in a morality picture of 1681 similarly dressed, with an elegant wig.[43] Both pictures of the *Sefer 'Ibronot* illustrate the same topic of the balanced "Scales of Justice" (מאזני צדק) held by the figure of a man, symbolizing a just and honest merchant. A balance can be seen in another *'Ibronot* manuscript of Ashkenazi origin dated 1670. The scales are carried here by a pair of workmen (Fig. 8).[44] Another morality picture by Benjamin Senior Godines dated 1679 is a triptych depicting from left to right: the giving of alms, a palm tree bearing the ten commandments and a heavenly hand, holding a

pair of equipoised scales inscribed "Scales of Justice."[45] The use of scales in all these representations does not refer to the emblem of *Justice*, which is usually shown with a sword as well as a balance.[46] The scales here are an attribute of the honest merchant appearing in the image of *Aequitas*[47] as depicted in a popularized form in emblemata books.[48] Here too, many depictions make do with the image of a balanced pair of scales, under the eye of the Lord or together with the figure of a merchant carrying his tools.[49] The image of a man or woman with a balance became popular in seventeenth-century painting, especially in the Netherlands,[50] paralleled by the depiction of the Last Judgment, where the Archangel Michael weighs souls.[51]

The Jew with the balance, a symbol of falsehood and injustice fully deserving heavenly punishment, was part of antisemitic concepts concerning Jews and particularly Jewish merchants throughout the Middle Ages and the Renaissance.[52] The Jewish reaction to such prejudiced images can be found *inter alia* in

[39] See A. Rubens, *A History of Jewish Costume* (London, 1973), fig. 195 (dated to 1601), especially for the Jewish barret; for the lace-edged, upright band collar (the *golilla*) — see also Sichel (note 30 above), p. 15, dated c. 1612. For the hanging sleeve, ibid., p. 64. In general such a costume might still have been worn by a Jewish merchant ca. 1664 — see Rubens, fig. 200.

[40] The Jewish National and University Library, Jerusalem, Department of Manuscripts and Archives, MS Heb. 8° 6678 fol. 22v.

[41] See Y.L. Bialer, *Min Hagenazim*, I (Jerusalem, 1967), pp. 53–55 (Hebrew); also mentioned in Y.L. Bialer, *Jewish Life in Art and Tradition* (London, 1976), p. 141. The date תי׳ לפ״יק (A.C. 5400 = C.E. 1640) is challenged by A. David, in the Card Index of the Institute of Microfilms, Hebrew Manuscripts, The National and University Library, Jerusalem (no. 38483 ס׳), who reads the date as תי״ק לפי״ק (A.C. 5450 = C.E. 1690).

[42] E.g. P. Cunnington, *Costume in Pictures* (London, 1964), p. 72, right.

[43] Painted by Benjamin Senior Godines in 1681; see *Catalogue*, no. 895 (1), pl. 153. See also Grunwald (note 37 above), pp. 26–28; and A. Rubens, "Three Jewish Morality Pictures 1679–1681", *The Connoisseur*, Feb. 1954), 65–68.

[44] Thanks are due to E. Milano, Director of the Biblioteca Estense in Modena, for permission to publish here fol. 9r of manuscript 2802 = Gamma z.2.5, written by Moses b. Joseph at Dubno; see C. Bernheimer, *Catalogo dei manuscritti orientali della Biblioteca Estense (Modena)* (Rome, 1960), pp. 91–92, no. 17. For this image in early 19th-century *'Ibronot* manuscripts, see Levy (note 34 above) pp. 101–102, 124, cat. 143.

[45] See *Catalogue*, no. 895 (3), pl. 152, right; Rubens (note 43 above), p. 68, no. III. For his translation of the accompanying Hebrew inscription, see note 53 below. On another morality picture see M. Narkiss, "Remember the Day of thy Death: A Memento Mori in the Nauheim Collection," *Kiryat Sefer* 16 (1938–9), 108–113

(Hebrew).

[46] Cf. R. Kahsnitz in *Lexikon der christlichen Ikonographie*, s.v. Justitia; R. van Marle, *Iconographie de l'art profane au Moyen-Age a la Renaissance II: Allegories et symboles* (New York, 1971), s.v. Justice.

[47] See G.G. Belloni in *Lexicon Iconographicum Mythologiae Classicae* (Zurich, 1981), s.v. Aequitas.

[48] Henkel-Schöne (note 11 above), col. 1432, citing Petrus Costalius, *Petri Costalii Pegma* (Lyon, 1555), p. 89.

[49] Henkel-Schöne, ibid., col. 1436, citing J. Mannich, *Sacra Emblemata* (Nuremberg, 1625), p. 81, who emphasizes the Lord's will: "Recht Maß und Gewicht er haben will" and ends with a clear statement: that such just bearing will bring honor to the merchant.

[50] See E. de Jongh, concerning Salomon Koninck's *The Goldweigher* in *Tot Lering en Vermak — Betekenissen van Hollandse genrevorstellingen uit de zeventiende eeuw*, ed. S.H. Levie (Rijksmuseum, Amsterdam, 1976), pp. 138–141.

[51] E.g. Vermeer's *Woman, Holding a Balance*; see P.C. Sutton's remarks in *Masters of Seventeenth Century Dutch Genre Painting* (Philadelphia Museum of Art, Philadelphia, 1984), pp. 322–344.

[52] For representations of Jewish money-changers with a pair of scales out of balance, see e.g. the wall-painting in the lower church of Schwarzrheindorf, of before 1151; W. Messer, "Kölner romanische Kunst inter genera," in *Baukunst des Mittelalters in Europa — H.E. Kubach zum 75. Geburtstag*, ed. F.M. Munch (Stuttgart, 1988), p. 86, fig. 5. See also the caricature in the Tollage Roll from 1233, *Encyclopedia Judaica*, s.v. Caricature, cols. 171–172. Cf. F.M. Zafran, "The Iconography of Antisemitism: A Study of the Representation of the Jews in the Visual Arts of Europe 1400–1600" (Phd. Thesis) (New York University, 1973), pp. 221–222.

Fig. 8.   Workman carrying a balance, from Sefer 'Ibronot, Dubno 1670. Biblioteca Estense, Modena, MS 2802, Gamma Z.2.5, fol. 9.

the above-mentioned morality pictures, stressing the image of the "Just Scales" according to Jewish laws and mores. Like those in the Dutch Emblemata books, these morality pictures are accompanied by biblical quotations. In the Sephardi triptych from Amsterdam these inscriptions include Isaiah 5:16 and Amos 5:24 referring to justice and Isaiah 56:1 concerning the Last Judgment. These verses are framed by mundane advice: "If you wish to ascend on the wheel [of fortune], keep justice [equally] with poor and rich."[53]

The two seals depicting a man with a balance equally refer to the honest Jewish merchant who does

---

[53] I have to disagree with Rubens's translation of *galgal* as galaxy (note 43 above), p. 68. *Galgal* as the wheel of fortune is mentioned explicitly in the first morality picture, mentioned above in the *Catalogue*, no. 895 (1). The inscription on top right reads: "A wheel He turns on rich and poor/ It turns, uplifts one and one degrades/ Thus does He place one upon a royal throne/ And one down to the depth of netherworld does He throw." For the Wheel of Fortune in Jewish thought see *BT Shabbath* 151b (R. Ishmael, 2nd century C.E.); *Exod. Rabbah* 31:3; *Ruth Rabbah* 5:9; *Lev. Rabbah* 34:9 (4th century C.E.). See L. Ginzburg, *The Legends of the Jews* (Philadelphia, 1968), V, p. 291, n. 134. In 17th-century Gentile European art and literature the wheel of fortune, with or without Fortuna, was disappearing, see: K. Weinhold, *Glücksrad und Lebensrad* (Abhandlungen der königlich preussischen Akademie der Wissenschaften) (Berlin, 1892), p. 21.

follow justice and adheres to equity.[54] The addition of stars to the London seal may express the idea that the use of "Just Scales" takes place under Heavenly Law, as is more explicitly stated in contemporary emblems, morality pictures and their accompanying texts.[55]

The Hebrew inscription upon the London seal identifies its owner as "Gedali(e), the son of Rabbi Isaac, may he live for many good days; Durlach." The German inscription confirms the common pronunciation of the owner's name, Gedalie instead of the Hebrew Gedalia, and confirms his place of origin: from Durlach. The term "from" makes it clear that Durlach is no longer his place of residence, nor is it his surname. Durlach is a city east of Karlsruhe, which had been from the second half of the sixteenth century to 1715 the residence of the margraves of Baden-Durlach; but it was abandoned by Karl Wilhelm, who transferred his seat to the newly founded Karlsruhe. The destruction of Durlach by the French in 1689 diminished the Jewish community. By 1704 only five Jewish families remained in the town. Consequently Jews from Durlach and from other nearby cities gladly answered the call of the margrave, who encouraged the quick construction of his new residence town, and moved to Karlsruhe. At the time of Karl Wilhelm's death in 1738, the Jewish community in Karlsruhe numbered 67 families.[56]

The London seal probably belonged to a member of the Karlsruhe community, identifying himself by his place of origin. The emblem declares him an honest merchant, just and equitable. The years 1715–1720 seem particularly suitable for the making of such a seal, since Karlsruhe was at that time teeming with artisans and craftsmen, as well as with eligible customers.

Jewish seals during the seventeenth and eighteenth centuries were distinguished from others by their Hebrew inscriptions.[57] When borrowed from Gentile seals, motifs were modified to conform with Jewish traditions, ranging from Bible to Talmud and Midrashim, from prayerbooks to popular customs. The artisans who cut the seals may have been Jewish at times, mainly because of these Jewish modifications in the emblem of the seal, but also because of the accuracy of the Hebrew inscriptions as opposed to the German ones.[58]

---

54 The medieval Worms and Leipzig *mahzorim* depict a man with the balance as a money changer weighing the "half Shekel" as well as weighing souls. R. Wischnitzer, "The Moneychanger with the Balance, a Topic of Jewish Iconography," *Erez Israel* 6 (1960) in memory of Mordechai Narkiss, pp. 23*–25*. These and similar representations have, however, little to do with the emblematic figure of the honest merchant.

55 A swivel seal of Haim b. Nissan (*Catalogue*, no. 1198, pl. 207) depicts a balance on one side and a monogram with an anchor on the other, combined on both sides with a "Merchants Mark" (*qattre-de-chifre*), for which see also: C.C.Oman, *Catalogue of Rings* (Victoria and Albert Museum, London, 1930), p. 14; pl. 31:739. In this swivel seal all components need be no more than statements of its owner's occupation.

56 See B. Rosenthal, *Heimatsgeschichte der badischen Juden* (Buhl/Baden 1927), pp. 196–209.

57 Though not by "the absence of the human form" as stated in the *Encyclopedia Judaica*, vol. 14, col. 1079.

58 For the existence of Jewish seal makers during this period, see Schudt (note 14 above). It was still the case a hundred years later, see F. Pribram, *Urkunden und Akten zur Geschichte der Juden in Wien II, Quellen und Forschungen zur Geschichte der Juden in Deutsch-Österreich VIII, 2)* (Vienna 1918), p. 147, no. 322. For the correctness of the Hebrew inscriptions and mistakes in the German ones, see e.g. the second London seal depicting a man with a balance, where the name "Gedalie" was written faultily in German as "Cedalie"; and instead of "von", which for many centuries had been the usual German spelling, the seal has "fon", as pronounced. Cf. *Trübners Deutsches Wörterbuch*, ed. W. Mitzka (Berlin, 1956), s.v. "von".

Fig. 1.   Hanukkah lamp, silver gilt, made by Johann Valentin Schüler probably for a wedding in 1681 (Jüdisches Museum, Frankfurt am Main, JMF 87–79).

SPLENDID BRIDAL GIFTS FROM A
SUMPTUOUS WEDDING CEREMONY OF 1681
IN THE FRANKFURT JUDENGASSE

Annette Weber

The most notable group of ritual objects surviving from the Judengasse in Frankfurt on the Main comes from the workshop of the brothers Schüler: Johann Valentin (1650 1720) and Johann Michael (1658–1718), who were active in that city from 1680 up to 1720. Their relatives, Joh. Abraham Boller (1679–1718) and G. Wilhelm Schedel (1698–1762), continued the workshop until the second half of the eighteenth century.[1] The objects are lavishly decorated Hanukkah lamps, hanging lamps for Shabbat and festivals, and a series of Torah shields and candle holders for *havdalah*, representing the nucleus of the "golden age" of Jewish ritual silver from Frankfurt.[2] All these objects show elaborate decorations combining a complex cast open-work with castings of small animals and figures. The latter hold ceremonial objects or the attributes of biblical heroes.

This paper[3] presents an analysis of the iconography of the Hanukkah lamp in the Frankfurt Jewish Museum with the hallmark of the goldsmith Johann Valentin Schüler (Fig. 1).[4] It will thus be possible to reconstruct when the menorah was made, for which occasion and for whom. It will also enable to establish a relative chronology for the Hanukkah lamps and hanging lamps for Shabbat and festivals produced in the Schüler workshop. In addition it is possible to show that the iconographical program is based on a precisely worked out religious imagery.

Originally, the Frankfurt menorah was left to the Historical Museum of the city of Frankfurt in 1909 as a bequest of Franziska Speyer. She was the wife of Georg Speyer (1835–1901), who owned the Bank "Speyer Ellissen" in Frankfurt. Since the seventeenth century the Speyers were one of the richest, most important and famous families of the Frankfurt-Judengasse. Georg Speyer was among the notable benefactors to his native city. He bestowed a considerable legacy to charitable institutions as well as to research work and he made a very important contribution to the foundation of the Frankfurt University.[5] The menorah, a precious family heirloom, was donated by the Speyer family to the city of Frankfurt after being in the family's possession for a long time.[6]

From 1922 the menorah was exhibited in the "Museum Jüdischer Altertümer" and in 1938, after the sacking and destruction of the museum by the Germans, it was rescued by the director of the Historical Museum.[7] Since 1988 it has been in the Jewish Museum of Frankfurt. This upright candelabrum alludes to that of the Tabernacle as described in the

1. Wolfgang Scheffler, *Goldsmiede Hessens* (Berlin, 1976), p. 224 (J. Valentin Schüler) and p. 228 (J. Michael Schüler), notes the similarity between the work of the brothers and suggests that they worked in the same workshop. Vivian B. Mann, "The Golden Age of Jewish Ceremonial Art in Frankfurt," *Leo Baeck Institute Yearbook* 31 (1986), 395f., points to the parental links of J. Abraham Boller, who was the brother-in-law of the Schüler brothers, and Georg Wilhelm Schedel, who became Boller's father-in-law after his remarriage.

2. Mann, "Golden Age," attributes the following pieces to the workshop: 1. To Valentin and Michael Schüler: six Torah shields (p. 393, n. 25); three book covers (p. 394, n. 31); three Hanukkah lamps and one other lamp (p. 397, nn. 45, 49); three hanging lamps for Shabbat and festivals (p.398, n. 55); and one candle holder for *havdalah* (p. 399). 2. To J. Abraham Boller: a Torah shield (pp. 395–6, n. 37); two Hanukkah lamps (pp. 396,

398); two hanging lamps (p. 398, n. 55); and a candle holder for *havdalah* (p. 396). 3. To Georg Wilhelm Schedel: a Torah shield (p. 396, n. 42); and a hanging lamp (p. 399, n. 58). There is also an *etrog* box in the Jewish Museum of Frankfurt, JMF 87–110 (formerly Historisches Museum X 61:17).

3. I wish to thank William Gross and Rafi Grafman for their most useful suggestions and kind help in writing this article.

4. Jüdisches Museum, Frankfurt a.M. JMF 87–79, formerly Historisches Museum X 25 312.

5. Paul Arnsberg, *Die Geschichte der Frankfurter Juden seit der Französischen Revolution*, vol. III (Darmstadt, 1983), p. 447f.

6. Mitteilungen der Gesellschaft zur Erforschung jüdischer Kunstdenkmäler III/IV, 1903, fig. 9.

7. Felicitas Heimann-Jellinek in *Was übrig blieb...* (Frankfurt, 1988), p. 27f.

Fig. 2. Detail of the Frankfurt Hanukkah lamp; the animals above the oil fonts, right side of the stem: eagle, deer, pelican and squirrel.

Bible (Ex. 25:33) because the arms are decorated with flowers and calyces and each one of the eight arms is topped by an oil font. The central shaft rests on a rectangular base fenced by an openwork fleur-de-lis balustrade. Four rampant lions holding shields support this base, which shows four cast cherubs and four embossed representations of gates. Above the platform there are six arabesques mounted on the stem. Originally, they decorated a smaller rectangular platform framed with openwork fleur-de-lis as on a similar example from the Muśe de Cluny.[8] The central shaft is topped by a cast statuette of Judith, holding the head of Holofernes, standing on a small platform fenced by openwork fleur-de-lis. Below this platform on the central shaft, the fixed server (*shamash*) bears the cast statuette of a riding warrior, probably Judas Maccabeus. Each of the four fonts on either side are hung with a bell and covered by a plate surmounted

by four cast animals. Behind them, on the reverse of the plate, four little cast trees are set. The four cast animals are repeated on either side but in a different sequence. (Figs. 2, 3). On the left side of the stem are a squirrel, deer, eagle and pelican, whereas on the right are a squirrel, pelican, deer and eagle. Such animals characterize a group of three Hanukkah lamps created by J. Valentin and J. Michael Schüler and their brother-in-law J. Abraham Boller. One of them is the menorah in the Jewish Museum in Frankfurt (Fig. 1). Another, made by J. Michael Schüler, is in the possession of the Musée de Cluny, Paris (Fig. 6). The third, made by Abraham Boller, is part of the Goldschmidt Collection which is located in the Jewish Museum, New York (Fig. 7).[9] These menorot, which are similar in shape and decoration, show different ensembles of animals: only the deer is included on all three.

8   I am grateful to Rafi Grafman, who drew my attention to this problem. See also Victor Klagsbald, *Objets du Culte, Catalogue of the Muśee de Cluny* (Paris, 1981), cat. no. 26; H. Gundersheimer and G. Schoenberger, "Frankfurter Chanukkaleuchter aus Silber und Zinn," *Notizblatt der Gesellschaft zur Erforschung*

jüdischer Kunstdenkmäler 34 (1937), 25.
9   V. Klagsbald, *Objets du Culte*, no. 26, Inv. No. 12241; V.B. Mann, *Treasures of the Jewish Museum* (New York, 1986), p. 82, Inv. No. JM 1983–160.

Fig. 3.   Detail of the Frankfurt Hanukkah lamp; the animals above the oil fonts, left side of the stem: pelican, eagle, deer and squirrel.

These animals above the oil fonts seem to be the most puzzling element, since they follow neither an iconographical tradition nor a common pattern of decoration. The animals of the Cluny menorah have been discussed by G. Schoenberger and V. Klagsbald.[10] Schoenberger suggested that the deer and the eagle are symbols corresponding to the *Ethics of the Fathers* (V, 30), but the turkey and the crossbow are purely decorative elements invented by the goldsmith. In 1981, Klagsbald interpreted two animals and the crossbow of the Cluny Menorah as house signs in the Frankfurt Judengasse. For him the deer represented the first name "Hirsch." Through his interpretation he suggested that the owner might be Lazar Herz Wimpfen, a member of a wealthy and important family of court Jews in the Judengasse.[11]

The proposal to interpret the cast animals as house signs in the Judengasse is supported by comparing other small animals and symbols adorning ritual objects from Frankfurt, two richly engraved beakers once in the possession of the *hevrah kadisha* of Frankfurt and a third beaker, of the *hevrah kadisha* of Hanau.[12] According to the sources the three beakers were decorated with medallions enclosing house signs with the names of the members of each burial society. On a cooking pot probably from Frankfurt, at the Jewish Museum of New York, the schematic rendering of a ladder illustrates the name of the owner "Hirtz Propert's spouse, the daughter of Moses zur Leiter."[13] A Hanukkah lamp from Frankfurt, made by Conrad Hieronymus May in the second half of the eighteenth century, has a server formed like a stork, in all like-

[10]   Guido Schoenberger, "Johann Matthias Sandrart 1683–1750," *Schriften des Historischen Museums Frankfurt am Main* (Frankfurt, 1966), p. 160f.
[11]   Klagsbald, *Objets du Culte*, pp. 36–7. A. Dietz, *Stammbuch der Frankfurter Juden* (Frankfurt, 1907), p. 326f.
[12]   For the Frankfurt *hevrah kadisha* beakers, see Paul Ahron, *Die Inschriften der im Besitz der Chewra Kadischa Dekabranim zu*

Frankfurt am Main befindlichen silbernen Pokale (Frankfurt, 1925). Both beakers are dated to 1707/1708: R. Hallo, *Schriften zur Kunstgeschichte* (Kassel, 1983), p. 275. The beaker from Hanau shows the mark of Jeremias Zobel, master from 1701 to 1741 in Frankfurt.
[13]   Mann, *Treasures*, p. 36.

Fig. 4.   *Hanging lamp for Shabbat and Festivals, silver, made by J. Valentin Schüler probably for a wedding in 1681 (The Jewish Museum, New York, JM 37–52).*

Fig. 5.   *Copy of the kiddush beaker, silver gilt, Germany, first half of the 17th century, bequeathed to the Frankfurt Jewish Community by Michael Speyer in 1764. (The original is in the Israel Museum, Jerusalem.)*

lihood the house sign of the owner.[14] Since they do appear on so many Jewish ritual objects from Frankfurt, it seems reasonable to explain the small animals on the Hanukkah lamps as house signs as well.

Going one step further with Klagsbald's method of interpretation leads to the identification of the

families who ordered the Frankfurt menorah. Sources like tombstones and family documents collected by J. Ettlinger in his *Ele Toldot* and by A. Dietz[15] show that the squirrel, deer, eagle and pelican were signs of houses in the Judengasse when J. Valentin Schüler was active as a goldsmith during 1680–1720. The same

[14] Felicitas Heimann-Jellinek, *Was übrig blieb*, cat. no. 13.
[15] Samuel Ettlinger, *Ele toldot: Verzeichnis aller Juden von*

1241–1828 (Frankfurt, 1962) (Manuscript). Dietz, *Stammbuch*, Appendix with the list of the houses, p. 440ff.

sources enable us to identify the inhabitants of these houses: during 1680–1720, there existed one house of the Squirrel and one of the Pelican, two houses with the sign of an eagle (the Golden and the Black Eagle) and four houses with the sign of the deer (the houses of the Golden, the Red, the Black and the White Deer). These eight houses were inhabited by 23 families, revealing how overcrowded Judengasse was at that time.[16] As the menorah is a precious object made of gilded silver, it is likely that only a wealthy family, owning one of the largest and finest houses of the Judengasse, could afford to order it. The finest houses in the Judengasse were situated close to the synagogue. Of the eight houses mentioned, three were situated in the vicinity of the synagogue: the House of the Squirrel, the House of the Golden Eagle and the House of the Golden Deer. The House of the Pelican, adjacent to the Tanzhaus, was the largest house and one of the most splendid on the street. Among the owners of these houses, the Speyer family, former owners of the menorah, owned the house of the Golden Deer from 1642 until the destruction of the Judengasse in 1796 and then even after the year 1800.[17] It is therefore reasonable to suggest that the sign of the deer on the Frankfurt menorah as representing the house of this family.

If indeed the small animals adorning the Menorah represent the house signs in Frankfurt's Judengasse, the question arises as to the occasion on which the four signs, i.e. four families, would be represented on one object. It is highly likely that such an event is a wedding, at which time the two families of the groom are joined with the two families of the bride. According to A. Dietz, an important marriage within the Speyer family took place between 1680 and 1720. The annals of the Judengasse record a most sumptuous marriage between the *dayan* (rabbinical judge) Moses Michael Speyer of the Golden Deer and Scheinle Bing-Kann in 1681, an event which raised much notice.[18] According to Ettlinger's *Ele Toldot* the four families who joined in that marriage were related to four of the most important houses of the Judengasse, displaying the Golden Deer, the Golden Eagle, the Squirrel and the Pelican as house signs. The father of the groom was Isaak Michel Speyer, an important and rich

member of the community and a *dayan*. He founded the House of the Golden Deer and was married to Jütle Oppenheim in 1644, whose parents were from the house of the Golden Eagle ("zum Vogelgesang"). The father of the bride was Isaak Bing-Kann of the Golden Ewer from one of the oldest families with many branches on the Judengasse. His branch was apparently connected to the Bing family residing in the House of the Squirrel. He was married to a woman of the Oppenheim Family dwelling in the House of the Pelican. Isaak Bing-Kann is well recorded in the Annales of the Judengasse.[19] He was the wealthiest man of the community, who made a fortune in the silk and jewel trade. He acted as a financial advisor and court agent of many rulers such as the Great Elector of Brandenburg, the Marquess of Bayreuth, the Bishops of the cities of Trier and of Würzburg. As a rich court Jew of great influence he claimed the leadership of the community, which was then held by Aaron Drach who equaled him in wealth and power. Their rivalry led to a law suit before the imperial court. The trial ended with a judgment in 1687 against Isaak Bing-Kann, whose relatives had to pay the enormous fine of 100,000 guilders.[20] In the midst of this quarrel, Isaak Bing-Kann arranged a sumptuous wedding recorded in the annals for his daughter Scheinle. Among the guests are said to have been many noblemen, the clients of Isaak Bing-Kann, who attended the ceremony and were entertained at the climax of the festivities by a masquerade performed by Jewish actors. The wedding, which was held in disregard of contemporary luxury laws, provoked the council of the city to fine the father of the bride the sum of 1,000 guilders.[21]

Such a splendid marriage was enhanced by beautiful gifts and the Frankfurt Hanukkah lamp may have been such a wedding gift. Besides representing house signs, the animals afford two more indications that such a suggestion is correct: The first is supported by the different sequence of the animals on either side of the stem (Figs. 2, 3). Reading from right to left, like Hebrew, the different sequence of animals on each side of the stem represents the process of marriage, relating the four families. On the right side of the menorah there are first the house signs

[16] Ibid., list of the houses, Appendix.
[17] Ibid., p. 289ff.
[18] Ibid., p. 161.
[19] Ibid., no. 293, p. 159ff.

[20] Isidor Kracauer, *Die Geschichte der Juden in Frankfurt am Main*, vol. II (Frankfurt, 1927), pp. 50–72.
[21] Ibid., p. 58 and Dietz *Stammbuch*, p. 161.

of the parents of the groom, the eagle representing the house sign of the mother Jütle Oppenheim and the deer representing that of the father Isaak Speyer. Next to them but still separated are the house signs of the parents of the bride: the pelican and the squirrel for the Bing-Kann family. On the left side of the shaft the consummated marriage is indicated by the sequence of the signs of both families now combined: the house signs of both mothers — pelican and eagle — precede those signs of both fathers — the deer and squirrel.

The second indication that the menorah is a wedding gift is provided by a law passed by the Jewish Council of the Judengasse in 1715 which concerns the wedding ceremony. As Schudt relates in his book *Jüdische Merckwürdigkeiten*,[22] the Jewish Council prohibited the display of more than three silver objects at the *Spinholtz*, the solemn reception in the bride's house which was held on Friday afternoon before the day of the wedding ceremony. It seems that it was at this occasion, when the bride and the groom sat together for the first time, that the wedding gifts were presented. The three objects permitted by the 1715 law were a *leuichter*, a *lampp*, and a *becher*. The law apparently was passed following the disastrous fire of 1711, which destroyed the Judengasse, as a prohibition against display of private luxury in public. If, nevertheless, three objects were exempted from the regulation, they must have been regarded as basic objects necessary to a new household. One is tempted to identify these items as ritual objects used in every Jewish home. Thus the *leuichter* could be the Hanukkah lamp, the *lampp* is possibly the hanging lamp for Shabbat and Festivals, and the *becher* is likely to be the *kiddush* cup. The short text of the law seems to refer to the traditional custom of presenting the wedding gifts at the *Spinholtz*, a ceremony, which may well have been established in 1681. The lavishly decorated Frankfurt menorah may have been presented as a wedding gift at the *Spinholtz* of Scheinle Bing-Kann and Moses Michel Speyer in 1681.

Furthermore, in addition to this menorah, a *lampp* was also apparently presented at this spectacular wedding. It can be identified with another work of J. Valentin Schüler adorned with the same animals:

a hanging lamp for Shabbat and Festivals, given to the Museum Jüdischer Altertümer in Frankfurt by Mathilde Baroness Rothschild, but now housed in the Jewish Museum in New York (Fig. 4).[23] Following the previous considerations, they may represent the same families as those of the Frankfurt menorah. The animals stand on the upper part of the lamp, which is built like a roof on the fountain below: The deer, eagle, squirrel and the pelican seem to be cast out of the same moulds used for the Frankfurt Menorah, and they too appear twice on this lamp. Thus both the Frankfurt Menorah and the Rothschild Lamp of New York were made by J. Valentin Schüler as precious wedding gifts presented at the *Spinholtz* of Scheinle Bing-Kann and Moses Michael Speyer in 1681.

The third gift allowed to be presented at a wedding by law is a *kiddush* cup, and one is tempted to identify it, to complete the set. The cup could have resembled, or indeed be, the sumptuous golden beaker now in the Israel Museum, Jerusalem (Fig. 5), which was once owned by the nephew of our groom of 1681. According to the inscription, the beaker was bequeathed to the Frankfurt Jewish community after the owner's death in 1764.[24] The beaker is of the most common type used all over Germany for private and official occasions from the late sixteenth century to well into the eighteenth. Several of this type were used in the Frankfurt Judengasse.[25] Its decoration with the three cartouches in repoussé work surrounded by foliage scrolls and strapwork points to the late sixteenth or early seventeenth century, i.e. at least two generations before the wedding was held. This fact does not negate the possibility that the beaker was given as a wedding present in 1681, as it was customary to present objects of family heritage or even objects of old, non-Jewish provenance.

The knowledge of the proposed date of the Frankfurt menorah and of the Rothschild Lamp in New York (Figs. 1, 4) helps to establish a relative chronology of the menorot and hanging lamps for Shabbat and festivals produced in the Schüler workshop and their successors, J. Abraham Boller and Georg Wilhelm Schedel. In 1681, when J. Valentin Schüler produced both objects, he was first recorded as a goldsmith, so that these are among his earliest works. Schoenberger

[22] Joh. J. Schudt, *Jüdische Merckwürdigkeiten*, (Frankfurt and Leipzig, 1714). Part IV, Continuation III (Frankfurt, 1717), p. 84, providing the original text in Yiddish.
[23] Mann, *Treasures*, p. 80., Inv. No. 37–52.
[24] Eugen Mayer, "Historische Pokale der Frankfurter Juden,"

Archiv für Frankfurter Geschichte und Kunst 53 (1973), 64.
[25] See above, the *hevrah kadisha* beakers, note 12; and *Notizblätter der Gesellschaft zur Erforschung jüdischer Kunstdenkmäler 21.5 (1928), no. 61–XXVIII, P.2.*

has already suggested that the Frankfurt menorah is likely to be the oldest piece of the entire group.[26] This can be confirmed by the date and the style of the menorah. Its elaborate decor consists of many small cast elements like the four cherubs and the rampant lions which create the impression of solemn and sumptuous splendor, typical of the baroque period at its height. By comparison, the Cluny menorah (Fig. 6), made after 1684 by the younger brother, J. Michael Schüler, when he became a master himself, shows some differences in style which point to a later date. The massive, bell-shaped calyces of the Frankfurt menorah are replaced by elegant pierced oval knops. The central shaft is surrounded by a repousse wreath of twisted flutings, a typical ornament of the late baroque period of the end of the seventeenth and early eighteenth century. The menorah of the Frenkel Collection, where the small animals were apparently omitted, still has the calyces of the Frankfurt menorah, but the form of the base of the central shaft follows the Cluny menorah in a simplified version.[27] Therefore approximately the same dating for both seems reasonable.

An entirely new form of base is presented by the Goldschmidt menorah of New York (Fig. 7) made by Joh. Abraham Boller.[28] It is a rectangular domed form on four rampant lions, engraved with large acanthus leaves. The central shaft rests on a simple stepped platform. The smooth surface, enhanced by some fine engravings, points to a date in the first two decades of the eighteenth century. An innovative approach to this type of Hanukkah menorah is the Warburg menorah at the Jewish Museum in New York, also crafted by J. Abraham Boller.[29] The domed hexagonal base is engraved with large acanthus leaves and holds four enamel plaques with scenes from the life of Jacob. A rampant lion holding a shield forms the lower part of the central stem and the knops are made of enamelled filigree work. The new multicolored effects

achieved by using different materials accentuate the stylistic change from the massive baroque forms of the Frankfurt menorah to the more refined and elegant Warburg menorah.

Like the five menorot, the six hanging lamps for Shabbat and festivals of the same workshop form a closely related group.[30] The Rothschild lamp of New York (Fig. 4) which was most likely produced by J. Valentin Schüler for the wedding in 1681, probably presents the earliest example of this group, showing baroque baluster columns and a lower part which is decorated with large cast mascarons, lionheads and canons.[31] Like the Hanukkah menorot, which follow the model of the Menorah of the Tabernacle, the star-shaped hanging lamps also derive from an old type known from the thirteenth century.[32] The oldest examples show the center shaft as a multi-storied tower and this type was also produced by J. Valentin Schüler, Abraham Boller and Georg Wilhelm Schedel.[33] Apparently it was in use in various Jewish communities in the eighteenth century, as proven by the examples from Nürnberg, by Johann Friedrich Ehe, and from Offenbach, said to be from Metz around 1715.[34] Iconographically, the Rothschild lamp of New York, and another hanging lamp resembling it (Inv. no. F 2257) also in the Jewish Museum of New York, but made by J. Abraham Boller,[35] are notable exceptions to the tower-type, since both present the shape of a fountain. Schoenberger refers to this shape as an allusion to the term a "fountain of blessing" in the hymn "Lekhah Dodi" sung at the beginning of Shabbat.[36] According to Vivian B. Mann, the use of the fountain shape for the hanging lamps of Frankfurt might be related to the introduction of this hymn into the services of the Frankfurt community in the first half of the seventeenth century.[37] The exceptional form of the fountain type is enhanced by little figures, set between the columns, and carrying the specific ritual objects of the festivals. Apparently both types of

---

[26]   Schoenberger, "Sandrart," p. 160.

[27]   Ibid., fig. 11, p. 158, present location unknown.

[28]   Mann, *Treasures*, p. 82.

[29]   Ibid.

[30]   Mann, "The Golden Age," p. 398f.

[31]   Mann, *Treasures*, p. 80.

[32]   Fritz Landsberger, "Ritual Implements of the Shabbat," *Beauty in Holiness*, ed. J. Gutmann (New York, 1972), p. 175; H.G. Meyer, *Eine Schabbatampel im Erfürter Dom*, (Hildesheim, 1982), p. 96, dates the piece from Erfurt to the first half of the 13th century and refers to the lamp formerly in Dijon (pp. 105–110).

[33]   Valentin Schüler, New York, Jewish Museum, F2707; Los Angeles, Skirball Museum; J. Abraham Boller, New York Jewish Museum, F4400; C. Wilhelm Schedel, Paris, Consistoire.

[34]   For Nürnberg see *Synagoga* (Recklinghausen, 1962), cat. no. C284, fig. 107. C. Offenbach, *Jüdisches Lexikon* (Berlin, 1933), vol. 4/1, col.29.

[35]   Kayser and Schoenberger, *Jewish Ceremonial Art* (Philadelphia, 1959), cat. no. 72, pl. XXXVI.

[36]   Schoenberger, "A Silver Shabbat Lamp from Frankfurt on the Main," *Essays in Honour of Georg Swarzenski*, (Berlin, 1951), p. 157.

[37]   Mann, "The Golden Age," p. 399.

Fig. 6.   Hanukkah lamp, silver gilt, made by Johann Michael Schüler, ca. 1700 (Muśe de Cluny, Paris, Cl. 12241).
Fig. 7.   Hanukkah lamp, silver, made by Johann Abraham Boller, 1706–1732, (The Jewish Museum New York, JM 1983–160, gift of the Estate of Alice B. Goldschmidt).

hanging lamps were produced by the same goldsmith at the same period; but it seems that the tower was the traditional form, whereas the fountain seems a special order by wealthy Jews of the Frankfurt Judengasse.

The classical example of the tower shape is represented by J. Valentin Schüler as an originally four-storied tower with a pointed quadrafoil helmet.[38] The tower possibly symbolizes a fortress with barred windows and lions' heads and therefore could allude to the Tower of David. This suggestion is supported by the representation of the king on the thirteenth-century hanging lamps from Erfurt and Dijon.[39] J. Abraham Boller also produced the tower-type by following the model of J. Valentin Schüler, but he added six candle-holders and doubled the storeys of the helmet.[40] Georg Wilhelm Schedel almost literally copied the model of Joh. Valentin Schüler with his lamp, now in the Consistoire of Paris.[41] It seems that, in this case, J. Abraham Boller and Georg Wilhelm Schedel reused the moulds of J. Valentin Schüler, as all three lamps of the tower-type show the same barred windows, lionheads and fleur-de-lis galleries. But in the case of the fountain type J. Abraham Boller followed the model of J. Valentin Schüler only iconographically. Stylistically, he created new openwork forms. Both types of star-shaped hanging lamps demonstrate that on the one hand moulds and models were kept for generations in one workshop, with the result that some objects show little stylistic innovation at a period when strong stylistic development in general can be seen. On the other hand, the same master who produced the traditional forms, was also able to create a new style for the same type of ritual object.

The question is to what degree the goldsmiths were free to create the new forms and types of Jewish ritual objects. How much influence did the customer have on the process of creation? The involvement of the customer in the process of creation will be discussed below, as it is clear that the type of the Frankfurt menorah is the result of an elaborately worked out program of Jewish iconographical symbols and thoughts.

As mentioned above, the Frankfurt menorah reflects the form of the Menorah of the Tabernacle. Its reference to the Torah together with the cast statuettes of Judith and Judah Maccabee is a common iconography for Hanukkah menorot. Not so usual are the animals and the little trees as well as the four gates represented on the lower platform (Fig. 1). These gates together with the fence and the four cherubim around the central shaft suggest the idea of the Garden of Eden guarded by the four lions. As far as I know, the Frankfurt menorah is the first of its kind to show a fenced paradise on its base. It was subsequently repeated not only on the Schüler workshop Hanukkah menorot but also on others made in Berlin and for the Synagogue of Pohrebyszcze.[42]

If the menorah stands in the Garden of Eden, it represents the image of the Tree of Life and of the Tree of knowledge. R. Wischnitzer has pointed out that the menorah as the image of the Tree of Life serves also as a symbol for the Torah.[43] One could underline this idea by quoting the *Debarim rabbah*: "As the oil (of the menorah) gives life to the world, the words of the Torah bestow life to the world. As this oil lights up the world, the words of the Torah enlighten the world. The Torah is a Tree of Life and a Menorah."[44]

Presumably the small trees above the oil fonts also represent this image. Their oil gives light to the lamp as the Torah, the Tree of Life, nourishes and enlightens the people of Israel. Living and learning the Torah is represented by the small animals which are no longer mere house-signs of the Judengasse. The deer and eagle are mentioned in the *Ethics of the Fathers* as symbols of religious zeal (V, 30).[45] The squirrel and pelican are represented within an illuminated page of a talmudic manuscript at the Bibilothèque Nationale, Paris, (cod.hebr.418) as images of studiousness and religious zeal (Fig. 8).[46] The squirrel cracks the nuts of wisdom and the pelican feeds its young with its own blood as the Torah nourishes the people of Israel.

Such an elaborate iconographical program of religious symbols and thoughts is unusual for a

[38] Now in the Skirball Museum, Los Angeles. I am very grateful to Rafi Grafman for this information; he examined the lamp and discovered that one storey is missing.

[39] See note 32 above.

[40] See Kayser and Schoenberger, *Jewish Ceremonial Art*, cat. no. 198, pl. CII, Inv. No. F4400.

[41] Klagsbald, *Jewish Treasures of Paris* (Jerusalem: Israel Museum, 1982), cat. no. 67.

[42] See Vera Bendt, *Judaica: Catalogue of the Berlin Museum* (Berlin,

1989), cat. no. 168. Here the fence was removed because it was seen as a later addition, but it may have alluded to the Garden of Eden. For the piece from Lemberg, see *Beauty in Holiness*, ed. J. Gutmann, p. 308.

[43] R. Wischnitzer, *Gestalten und Symbole in der jüdischen Kunst* (Berlin, 1935), pp. 59–60.

[44] Ibid., p. 47–48.

[45] See Schoenberger, "A Silver Shabbat Lamp," note 10, in reference to the Cluny menorah.

[46] Wischnitzer, *Gestalten und Symbole*, fig. p. 58; Michel Garel,

Fig. 8.   Commentary of the Talmud, France, 14th century (Bibliothèque Nationale de Paris, cod. hebr. 418).

משרה נשים פטורות יכיותתן וירצות יכיחתתן ודן המלייטהו

יבריא רעודקן עכד הינה ות יולי רשמיע רקביה יהם מן על .

Hanukkah menorah. Certainly it is not the goldsmith who invented this program. In the case of the Frankfurt menorah the uncle of the bride, Isaak Bing-Kann's brother, a rabbi of great reputation in the Frankfurt community, may have been involved in the creation of the menorah.[47] The menorah would then be an emblem not only of great wealth but also of the high standard of Jewish learning of the Bing-Kann family. It is likely that the iconographical program invented by this rabbi led to the creation of a new type of lavish Hanukkah menorah by J. Valentin Schüler. In this case, the goldsmith would have received precise instructions on what to create and how to put it together. The menorah is an interesting example of how ideas of Jewish iconography can be predominant in the creation of a new type of a ritual object.

The iconographical analysis of the Frankfurt menorah suggests that its imagery is due to the patron's demands. Its purpose as a wedding gift determines the choice of symbols as well as allusions to religious thoughts.

As a wedding gift, the menorah forms a part of an ensemble completed by a hanging lamp for Shabbat and festivals and a beaker for *kiddush*. These objects are a unique document of the traditional wedding customs of the Judengasse in Frankfurt, and as such they shed light on the intense life of this important Jewish community. The fact that ritual objects were regarded as basic wedding gifts, necessary to set up house, points to a daily communal life guided by strict religious observance. This kind of life provides the base for widespread learning and teaching by famous rabbinic authorities, for which the Frankfurt Jewry was renowned.

As a result, the Frankfurt menorah and the other ritual objects made in that golden age owe their highly original forms to the patrons of the Judengasse, whose high standard of Jewish learning led to a close examination and alteration of traditional forms of Jewish ritual silver.

D'une main forte (Paris, 1992).
[47] Dietz, *Stammbuch*, p. 62.

180

Fig. 2.   Fredericus Becker, Senior, Torah shield, c. 1800 (Courtesy Gross Family Collection, Ramat Aviv).

THE BECKER FAMILY:
SILVERSMITHS OF BRATISLAVA

Ilona Pataky-Brestyánszky

Bratislava, Pozsony in Hungarian, Pressburg in German, is a bridgehead at the Austrian-Hungarian border and since 1920 the capital of Slovakia. Since the Middle Ages, the town has played a major role in the history of the Hungarian and the Central European Jewish populations. Starting with the Turkish occupation it was the capital of Hungary from 1514 to 1848, the residence of the government, palatine and Parliament, even the coronation of the Hungarian kings was held there. Already in the Middle Ages Pozsony was a flourishing commercial, industrial and cultural center. By the end of the thirteenth century the population spoke mostly German.

According to Hebrew chronicles Pozsony had Jewish residents already in the eleventh century.[1] Under the privileges granted to Pozsony by the Hungarian king Andrew III on 2 December 1291, the Jewish community received equal rights with resident Christians. During the thirteenth and fourteenth centuries the Jewish community flourished, and due to its wealth and prestige it played an outstanding role in the life of the entire Jewish community of Hungary. From the fourteenth century on the Jews lived in the old "Kalapos" and Hummel streets, where the synagogue was built in 1399. Many of the Jews expelled from Austria in 1421 and from Syria in 1496 moved to Pozsony.[2] However, after the battle against the Turks in Mohács in 1526 they were expelled from Pozsony as well. They found asylum on the large estates of the Crown and on those of leading landowners. The Jews of Pozsony fled to the estate of the counts of the Pálffy, situated at the foot of the castle of Pozsony,

in the area known as Schlossberg or Castlemount. The area expanded and joined neighboring Pozsony, together with the "Zuckermandel" quarter, the site of the old ghetto and the synagogue which had disappeared by now.

By the eighteenth century the community was flourishing again and became the spiritual center of Hungarian Jewry, for it did not come under Turkish rule. During this period it became the European center of rabbinical studies.

The national census performed in 1736 listed 120 heads of Jewish families.[3] Beyond Austria and Germany Jews immigrated mostly from Bohemia and Moravia.[4] The ghetto was established by Emperor Charles III in 1712. His successor, Empress Maria Theresa, separated the Jewish residential area by locked gates which were removed only by the rulings of the parliamentary sessions which introduced reforms in 1834/40.[5] Christians were prohibited from settling within the confines of the ghetto.

Pozsony had a renowned silversmith guild already in the Middle Ages. In the fifteenth century and the first quarter of the sixteenth, fourteen Christian silversmiths operated in the town.[6] The records were kept in German from 1575, and are accessible today at the Town Museum.[7] The Jewish silversmiths of the ghetto were excluded from the guilds — as was customary in those times in Central Europe, Bohemia, Moldavia and Poland, though by the eighteenth century they were admitted in some cases. By the nineteenth century they were listed as masters. The records often mention Jewish silversmiths working in Prague and in Poland,

[1] P. Ujváry, ed., *Zsidó Lexikon* (Budapest, 1929), pp. 718–19.
[2] Ibid.
[3] Ibid.
[4] János Kapossy, *Magyarországi ötvösök a XVIII–XIX. században* (Budapest, 1934); Janós Illésy, *Magyarországi ötvösök 1732-ben* (Budapest: Arch. Ért, 1904).

[5] Ujváry, *Zsidó Lexikon.*
[6] E. Köszeghy, *Magyarországi ötvösjegyek* (Budapest, 1936), p. 305; E.K. Winkler, *Pozsonyi ötvösjegyek* (Budapest: Muzeumi és konyvtári Ért, 1911), p. 155.
[7] J. Mihalik, *Háromszáz év a pozsonyi ötvösseg történe téböl* (Budapest: Muzeumi és konyvtári ért, 1911), pp. 85–155.

perhaps because these less expensive masters competed with the guilds.[8] A typical guild-admittance process exists in the records describing the case of Michael Weissmann between 1759 and 1780, who worked and lived in Castlemount and was probably a Jew, originally from Silesia. According to the guild records dated 29 July 1759 he "lived in Schlossberg and has been working undisturbed for more than nine years without being a guild member, thereby endangering the existence of silversmiths in the town."[9] But finally he "applied for admittance" which the guild was willing to grant but he refused to make a masterwork, failed to appear before the guild and attempted to sue it at the local council, who rejected his application. Finally he gained "the protection of a high-standing official and as a result his majesty the king sent a sharp ruling advising the guild to accept him".[10] This process was unique. Nevertheless, Weissman had to agree to be examined. Though he reported on 16 August 1759 on the creation of his masterwork, he failed to make the prescribed goblet and bought it instead. However, he did make the two other items of the masterwork, a ring and a seal. Despite having paid for the master's title he failed to file his birth certificate or apprentice certificate.[11] Following prolonged disputes he was finally accepted as master in the guild due to his high-standing protector, because on 28 April 1765 he already employed an apprentice on a five-year contract.[12] He served as deputy master of the guild from 1775 to 1780.[13] Unfortunately none of his work was preserved.

The silversmiths of Castlemount may be traced to the first half of the eighteenth century. There were four of them in 1732 according to comprehensive country reports.[14] One of the residents, Leo Hercz, of Silesian origin, studied in Poland and settled in Hungary 30 years earlier. As he was not a guild master he could not work with silver, but produced some gold rings for women. Otherwise he traded for a living. In the same house lived a woman, Borbal, the wife of a Viennese silversmith János Lörincz Jung, who had disappeared half a year previously.

The woman worked with an assistant producing gold jewelry for Jewish tradesmen. Another woman, the Silesian Regina, widow of Benjamin Engl, working with a Jewish assistant, Josef Duches, also produced gold jewelry. By 1838 there were already seven individuals working in this area.[15] They were continually harassed by the official guild.

Eighteenth-century liberalism led to the 1781 Acts released by Emperor Josef II, facilitating the situation and settling of Jews. Several Hungarian towns, especially Pozsony, protested against these acts because "non-guild members would settle on Castlemount, reducing the profit of the citizens."[16] On the basis of their application the settling of Jews was only granted individually despite the fact the Castlemount was the largest Hungarian Jewish community with 82 families.[17] Their right to form free settlements and to work freely in their trade was only granted 50 years later, by Section 29 of the Act of 1840.

The guild continued its fight against all non-guild members, including Jews. In 1826 it requested the City Council to prohibit the trade in gold and silver wares by all unauthorized individuals. On 23 August 1830 the Council authorized all guild members to denounce all Jews trading in gold and silver jewelry, and to confiscate their wares.[18] However a ruling of the Governor's Council on 18 November 1842 authorized the Jew Ignza Loeb to open a workshop.[19] Though the guild attempted to lodge an appeal with the king, this failed to attain its purpose. As late as 10 December 1854, the guild master, Josef Weinstable (1835–1866) applied to the town council requesting that it should prevent one of the Jewish silversmiths of Castlemount, who had a workshop opposite the former residence of Count Pálffy, from opening a shop at the side of the house.[20] The slow deterioration of the guilds continued despite the guild reform introduced by Emperor Frances I in 1804–5. Free enterprise undermined the guild monopolies and led finally to the collapse of the guild system.

The silversmiths in the town used the coat-of-arms of Pozsony as their hallmark: a town gate with

8   Ilona P. Brestyánszky, *A Tóra és díszei* (Sajtó alatt), p. 31; Mihalik, *Háromszázá*, p. 96; C. Schirek, *Punzierung in Mähren* (Brünn, 1902), pp. 28–30.

9   Kapossy, *Magyarországi ötvösöká*, p. 271; originated "ex Silesia loco Naürauen oriundus"; Mihalik, *Háromszázá*, p. 91.

10 Mihalik, *Háromszázá*, pp. 132–3.

11 Ibid.

12 Ibid.

13 Ibid.

14 Köszeghy, *Magyarországi ötvösjegyeká*, p. 307.

15 Ibid.

16 Ibid., p. 148.

17 Ujváry, ed., *Zsidó Lexikoná*, p. 719.

18 Mihalik, *Háromszázá*, p. 96.

19 Ibid.

20 Ibid.

three towers, the sign "13" representing silver purity, flanked by the date or by letters standing for it, and their initials.[21] Here, in accordance with German and Latin custom, which was followed in Hungary too, the first letter stood for the forename. The silversmiths of Castlemount observed fully the rules of the silversmith guild in Pozsony with regard to hallmarks, despite not belonging to a guild. However, sometimes the central of the three towers on top of the gates was crown-shaped or the lateral towers were at an angle. By 1813 the town gate was omitted, the number 13 indicating the purity of the grade of silver was placed within a circle with a small crown on top, and was flanked by two lines, sloping left and right, replacing the former towers. At the side were date and control letters. Though "12"-grade silver was used in 1776, this was indicated by a specific mark.[22] The guild documents of Pozsony state that there were two Castlemount masters in the eighteenth and two in the nineteenth century.

Fredericus Becker, Senior, the first in a dynasty of silversmiths, and Adam Renner, were outstanding silversmiths of Pozsony-Castlemount in the first part of the nineteenth century. Many of their works are missing, believed stolen. Adam Renner (1786–1837) was the more talented of the two.[24] I have found data on his activity in the guildbooks, but only a few items of his work are known, for many pieces disappeared during the war years. His masterpiece, the Torah shield made for the synagogue at Hunfalva in 1835 (Fig. 1) (Elemér Köszeghy's list, no. 1786) shows him to be a noteworthy artist.

Fredericus Becker, Senior, was a talented silversmith and the founder of a Jewish silversmith dynasty — unique in Hungary — which can be traced until the mid-nineteenth century, or to the dissolution of the silversmith guild. His works are documented from 1800 to his presumed death in 1827 or 1826, as he was not listed in the master-list of 1826.[26] His work came to light recently, when inventories were made at the Jewish Museum in Budapest, at the Hungarian National Museum, at the Town Museum in Pozsony and among the Jewish community in Pozsony, whose

archives were destroyed. Research has revealed some of the works made by Fredericus Becker and his family.

Nothing is known about the date of Becker's birth or where he studied. The shape of his pieces, and his repoussé technique suggest that he was trained in Vienna and Pozsony. He may have been familiar with works made in Prague, judging by the bold application of exceedingly large crowns on his Torah shields.

The earlier pieces listed by Elemér Köszeghy were lost during the upheavals of the past decades in Central Europe.[27] I could not locate any of the following items: a salt cellar on four trestles made in 1807, which was in a private collection; the chandelier of the Synagogue in Hunfalva from 1810; an engraved, garlanded goblet from 1810, which was shown at the Historical Hungarian Silversmith Exhibition in 1884; a round plate and a six-lobed spice dish of 1813, formerly the property of Dr. Béla Radvánszky; an engraved cup of 1807 listed in the Friedmann Collection; a cup of 1817; a goblet with cover which is in a private collection in Kassa; and cutlery of 1826–27 which is in private hands in Pozsony. Becker's art can only be reconstructed on the basis of pieces still available.

His earliest piece is a 22 cm. high Torah shield in the Gross Collection (Fig. 2).[28] It was probably made ca. 1800 because by 1810 he already attempted to add to Torah shields such innovations as a baldachin. Resembling those produced in Germany, Austria-Hungary, Moldavia, Bohemia and Poland, this Torah shield has an oblong form with an arched top, beautifully chased, and framed by foliage and a row of pearls motif. Following eighteenth-century tradition, two pillars emerge from two vertically fluted vessels. The pillars are relatively small and emphasize the two large heraldic lions, holding a large crown with their forefeet. An oblong calendar tablet is placed in the center of the field and is in harmony with the rim ornaments. On top is an elegantly fluted bowl with floral ornaments of marigolds and vines; and below it is a floral basket with the Decalogue. On top of the Torah shield is a cast double eagle, crowned

[21] Köszeghy, *Magyarországi ötvösjegyek*, pp. 305–307.
[22] Ibid.
[23] Ibid.
[24] Ibid., p. 301.
[25] Ibid.
[26] Ibid., p. 306.
[27] Ibid.
[28] *Sotheby's Judaica: Books, Manuscripts and Works of Art* (Jerusalem, 1988), no. 81.

Fig. 1.   Adam Renner, Torah shield, 1835 (Sotheby's Judaica Auction, N.Y. December, 1988, No. 274).
Fig. 3.   Fredericus Becker, Senior, Torah finial, 1810 (Budapest, Jewish Museum, Inv. No. 64.382.1–2).
Fig. 4.   Fredericus Becker, Senior, Torah finials, 1810 (Weinstein, fig. 96).

Fig. 5.   Fredericus Becker, Senior, Torah finial, 1810
(Budapest, Jewish Museum, Inv. No. 64.391.1–2).

Fig. 6.   Fredericus Becker, Senior, Torah finials, 1810
(Bratislava, Jewish Community, Inv. No. K.7–8).

Fig. 7. Fredericus Becker, Senior, Torah finials, 1816 (Bratislava, Jewish Community, Inv. No. K.5–6).

Fig. 8. Fredericus Becker, Senior, Torah finials, 1818, hallmark and mastermark (Bratislava, Jewish Community, Inv. No. K.25–26).

Fig. 9. Fredericus Becker, Senior, Torah shield, 1810 (Budapest, Jewish Museum, Inv. No. 64.403).

Fig. 10. Fredericus Becker, Senior, Torah shield 1813, and hallmarks (Budapest, Jewish Museum, Inv. No. 64.4).

and open winged, a characteristic feature of all Becker masterpieces. The mastermark "FB" is in an oblong field (Köszeghy, no. 1853).

According to his mastermark, a pair of finials (33.5 x 11.8 cm.) presented in 1833 by the leaders of the Bikur Cholim Association, now in the Jewish Museum in Budapest, was made in 1810 (Fig. 3) and has a Hebrew inscription. The influence of Viennese silversmiths is apparent and understandable, considering the proximity of Vienna and its leading role among contemporary European silversmiths. The raised round base is decorated with chased and engraved leaves. Its crown is a stylized filigree with a band of palmettes at its base, consisting of chased leaves. On top is a cast double eagle, crowned and open winged, which typifies all religious objects created by Becker (Köszeghy no. 1816).

A beautiful, large (height 33 cm.) pair of finials (Fig. 4)[30] was made around 1810, and is similar in composition of those at the Jewish Museum in Budapest (Fig. 3). The base is decorated with chased leaf ornaments. The cylindrical form of the base top confirms its early origin; this is also suggested by the crown of the Austrian emperor Frances I, and its decoration with a bank of ovals in the style of Louis XVI. The lacy collar with the small bells is a typical feature of the works by Fredericus Becker Senior, as is the crowned double eagle knop, which surmounts the finials. This eagle, the symbol of the German-Roman empire, was an ornament of choice used in similar forms by the silversmiths of the Austro-Hungarian Empire.

Another pair of finials (27 x 10 cm.) in the Jewish Museum in Budapest was created in 1830 (Fig. 5). Several variants are preserved by the Jewish community in Pozsony. The finials are of simple construction and decoration: the base is decorated with chased palmette-band ornament and the cylindrical shaft by engraved belts. The node is indicated only by two soldered wires. It is pierced, fitted at the base with a lacy collar, three bells and an arcade belt above it. Here too the crown is decorated by a band of ovals, and surmounted by a cast heraldic double eagle knop (Köszeghy, no. 1816; Pozsony-Castlemount no. 1853). This type of finials evolved also in Vienna, one

example of which, by J. Feyerabendt, of 1810, is at the Jewish Museum in Budapest.

In 1810 Fredericus Becker made a similar pair of finials (21 x 8 cm.) for the Jewish Community in Pozsony (Fig. 6). Its round base is decorated with a band of eggs between vertical chased lines. Rings are engraved in the cylindrical shaft, and its node protrudes slightly. The crown-like dome is fitted with a band of palmettes at the base and an eight-part, four-petaled rosette band on top. The entire finial is surmounted by the usual cast double eagle knop. At the base of the dome, at the stem of the three bells are Köszeghy's nos. 1816 and 1853 and the letters "FB."

A smaller pair of finials (18.5 x 8 cm.) by Becker (Fig. 7) made in 1816, is a variation on the former ones. It is also in the Jewish community in Pozsony. The date in the hallmark is unclear. There are chased and engraved palmettes on the round base and engraved belts on the shaft. The protruding node is separated from the shaft by a pearl belt. The dome is fitted with a lacy collar and a single bell, and the crown is decorated with a bank of arcades at the base and a motif of triple leaves on top. The top ornament is missing. On the shaft is the hallmark of Pozsony-Castlemount (Köszeghy, no. 1855).

Becker may have made another pair of finials (34 x 13 cm.) of similar form in 1818, now in the Jewish Community in Pozsony (Fig. 8). The decoration consists of a band on the raised round base, a vertically fluted shaft, and a node with cast palmette band. The crown-shaped dome is adorned at the base with a chased arcade band and foliage band and at the top with seven pearl bands. It is surmounted by the cast crowned double eagle knop. The hallmark on the band is of Pozsony-Castlemount (Fig. 8a) (Köszeghy, nos. 1820 and 1853).

The Torah shield (27.7 x 18.5 cm) of Fredericus Becker Senior was created in 1820 and belongs to the Jewish Museum in Budapest (Fig. 9). It has an oblong form, as was customary at the end of the eighteenth century throughout Germany, Austro-Hungary, Moravia, Bohemia, and Poland. The composition follows the scheme used in Austria-Hungary, with a baldachin knotted on top. The crown sur-

[29] Köszeghy, *Magyarországi ötvösjegyeká*, p. 309; I.P. Brestyánszky, "Kegyszerek," in Benoschofsky and Scheiber, *Budapestizsidó Muzeum* (Budapest, 1987), p. 71.

[30] J. Weinstein, *A Collector's Guide to Judaica* (New York, 1985), p. 89, fig. 96.

mounting the baldachin as well as the cast double eagle are missing. Three sides of the Torah shield are framed by a band of pearls and chased triangles. Mounted on the bottom frame are two small pillars, a typical Becker ornament, which are surmounted by two exquisitely chased heraldic lions, of a similar size as the pillars. The lions hold a crown on one raised paw and a large Decalogue on the other, filling a major part of the shield. There is no calendar table. The mastermark is "FB" (Köszeghy, nos. 1853 and 1817).

The other Torah shield (38 x 26.2 cm.) at the Jewish Museum in Budapest, a true masterpiece by Becker, was made in 1813 (Fig. 10) (Köszeghy, nos. 1814, 1854). The form is oblong, as is usual in his works. The top has a richly plaited baldachin knotted at both sides. The baldachin is surmounted by a closed, comparatively large crown and a cast, crowned double eagle knop with extended wings, a motif he used in the Torah finials. Two large lions, rampant, exquisitely chased, face outwards, each holding a crown and the Decalogue. They are placed on pillars, mounted on two highly chased plinths. Under the Decalogue is the square calendar tablet. The lateral frame of the shield is enclosed by chased floral ornaments, marigolds and vines. The elegant composition of the shield is dominated by the over-sized lions and the large crown.

This Torah shield as well as the finials show Becker to be a qualified Central European silversmith, skilled in all aspects of his craft. His designs and ornaments were commonly used by Viennese silversmiths, as for example in the Torah shield by Tobias Schmied, made in 1816 (Fig. 11), and that by Franz Lorenz Turinsky, made in 1806 (Fig. 12). These elements appear likewise in the objects of Pozsony-Castlemount, such as in the Torah shield of the Synagogue of Hunfalva, made by Adam Renner (Fig. 1). It was probably Turinsky who first introduced the motifs of lions and the double eagle knop.

The simple, small, truncated-pyramid shaped cup (6.2 x 2.8 cm.) with only two engraved lines around the rim, was made by Fredericus Becker Senior in 1813 (Fig. 13) at present in the Jewish Museum in Budapest (Köszeghy, mark 1907, no. 1853).

The funeral collecting box with a hinged door on one side has the Hebrew inscription "Righteousness delivereth from Death" and a donor's name. It is one of the simpler items of the master, made in 1815,

Fig. 11. *Tobias Schmied, Torah shield, Vienna 1816 (formerly Berger Collection, Vienna. Berger 1/6.1).*

Fig. 12. *Franz Lorenz Turinsky, Torah shield, Vienna 1806 (formerly Berger Collection, Vienna. Berger 1/6.9).*

Fig. 13.   Fredericus Becker, Senior, Cup, 1813 (Budapest, Jewish Museum, Inv. No. 64.153).

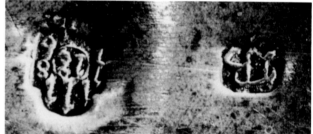

Fig. 14.   Fredericus Becker, Senior, Platter 1810, and hallmarks (Bratislava, Town Museum, Inv. No. U.85–48).

Fig. 15.   Fredericus Becker, Senior, Salt-cellar, 1825 (Budapest, Hungarian National Museum, Inv. No. 54.64).

Fig. 16.   Fredericus Becker, Senior, Candlesticks, 1826 (Budapest, National Museum, Inv. No. ö II.79.9).

Fig. 17.   Fredericus Becker, Senior, 18th-century Reliquary cross, and marks on the base, 1828 (courtesy J. Koday Collection, Bratislava).

Fig. 18.   Johannes Becker, Votive object, 1830 and hallmark (Bratislava, Town Museum, Inv. No. U.3982).

and now housed in the Hechal Shlomo Museum in Jerusalem.[31]

The high level of Becker's work is also demonstrated by the large plate (40.5 x 23.5 x 9 cm.) in the Town Museum in Pozsony (Fig. 14) made in 1830 (Köszeghy, a variation of no. 1816). The elegant oval plate is mounted on cast, dome-shaped supports of a classical style. The rim is formed from an arcade band, the two arched handles start from cast grapes with foliage. The hallmark has a silver grade — 13 — within a circle. Becker's initials are differently engraved.

[31]   Y.L. Bialer and E. Fink, *Jewish Life in Art and Tradition* (Jerusalem, 1980), p. 176.

Becker had many customers, including private citizens and even the Church. A salt cellar (5.5 x 5 cm.) standing on three cast palmette supports, made in 1825 (Fig. 15) is a representative example of the traditional Austro-Hungarian empire style. A simple and elegant pair of candlesticks (26 x 11 cm.) also in the typical style of the region, dates from 1826 (Fig. 16). In Pozsony an eighteenth-century reliquary in the shape of a cross is the private property of Mr. Juray Koday (Fig. 17). According to the hallmark and the letter "H", representing the year, Becker made a new base for it in 1828. He adapted the chased, oval base to the original style of the reliquary by embossing a garland on it in the style of Louis

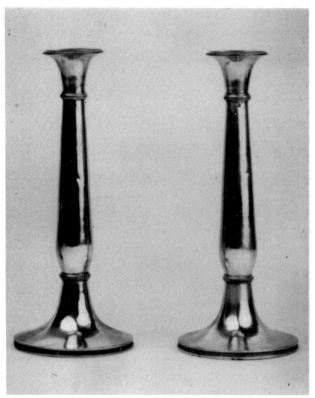

Fig. 19.   Johannes Becker, Candlesticks, 1830 (Budapest, Hungarian National Museum Inv. No. 1868.70.12).

Fig. 20.   Johannes Becker, Torah finials, 1826 (Budapest, Jewish Museum Inv. No. 54.10).

XVI, with chased, stylized floral ornaments at the intersection of the wave. Although the hallmark from 1828 says it was made by Becker, it could be that of his successor.

Fredericus's successor, Johannes Becker, is first mentioned in 1828. Cutlery made by him in 1830 is lost (Köszeghy, nos. 1831–1844). In the Town Museum of Pozsony there is a small, simple votive object (11 x 7 cm.) displaying a baby in an oblong, beaded frame (Fig. 18). Such objects were hung near the picture of a saint when a prayer was answered. The hallmark indicates that was made in 1830 (Köszeghy, no. 1829). Also from this year is a pair of candlesticks (28 cm.) with a shaft widening towards the round base (Fig. 19), bearing a band with a wasps' nest decoration in typical Austro-Hungarian style, in the Hungarian National Museum.

Johannes Becker was already working by 1826, according to a beautiful pair of finials (Fig. 20) which bear the Pozsony-Castlemount hallmark (Köszeghy, no. 1860). The inscription in Hebrew identifies them as belonging to the Hevrah Kaddisha in Budapest. The

round base of the relatively small (20 cm. high; base 5 cm.) finials are decorated with engraved vertical flutes, as is the shaft. The crown-shaped dome is formed of four bands with marigold and leaf ornaments, fitted at the bottom with an acanthus band. The finials are surmounted by a bud with a bell inside. This exquisite pair confirms the outstanding abilities of its maker.

The last traceable member of the family is Fredericus Becker, Jr., mentioned in 1845, but already working in the 1830s.[32] From 1831 to 1844 he was mostly known for his cutlery made for private owners. His master mark was a cursive "FB" in an oblong field, together with the Pozsony-Castlemount hallmark. His religious masterpieces, discovered recently, provide evidence that he was his father's apprentice before inheriting his workshop. A pair of finials (30 x 7.5 cm.) made in 1831 is now in the Jewish Museum in Budapest (Fig. 21). The inscription in Hebrew

---

[32]   Köszeghy, *Magyarországi ötvösjegyek*á, nos. 1863–65.

21   22   23

Fig. 21.   Fredericus Becker, Junior, Torah finials, 1831 (Budapest, Jewish Museum, Inv. No. 64.54.1–2).
Fig. 22.   Fredericus Becker, Junior, Torah finials, 1838 (Bratislava, Jewish community, Inv. No. K.1–34).
Fig. 23.   Fredericus Becker, Junior, Sugar shaker, 1833 (Budapest, Hungarian National Museum, Inv. No. 55.161).

engraved around the base contains a list of names of the Obuda Hevrah in Budapest, and the date, 1845. The shape of the round base and of the shaft is of two counterpoised cones, demonstrating that Fredericus Jr. observed the traditions established by his father. The node is fitted with a band of egg-shaped forms. The dome is crown-shaped, fitted at the bottom with a lacy collar surmounted by a band of arcades. The top is constructed of vertical bands flanked by branches engraved into oval fields. The top ornament is a cast, finely shaped bud.

Another pair of finials (26 x 5.5 cm.) made according to the hallmark in 1838 (Fig. 22), has a round chased base with a palmette band, and a list of donors engraved in Hebrew. The cylindrical shaft is surmounted by a dome fitted with indented, detached collar — as in the objects made by his father — and a bell. The node is beaded. There is a pierced pyramid band at the bottom and a six-band crown on top of the dome (Köszeghy, nos. 1863, 1832, and 1848).

Besides the ritual objects there were smaller commissions which formed much of the silversmiths' regular work. One example, in the Hungarian National Museum, is a sugar shaker (11.8 x 4.8 cm.) made in 1833 in the traditional design of the region (Fig. 23). It stands on a round, arched, support, fitted with a ring and two handles on the cylindrical body. It has a cap, decorated with pierced, engraved leaf ornament.

The Jewish silversmiths of Pozsony-Castlemount, among them members of the Becker family, belong to the qualified Jewish masters of Central Europe, as evidenced by the works bearing their hallmarks and master marks (Fig. 24). The quality of their work, especially that of Fredericus Becker Senior, is comparable to that of the Christian silversmiths in Vienna, Pozsony, Hungary and Prague.

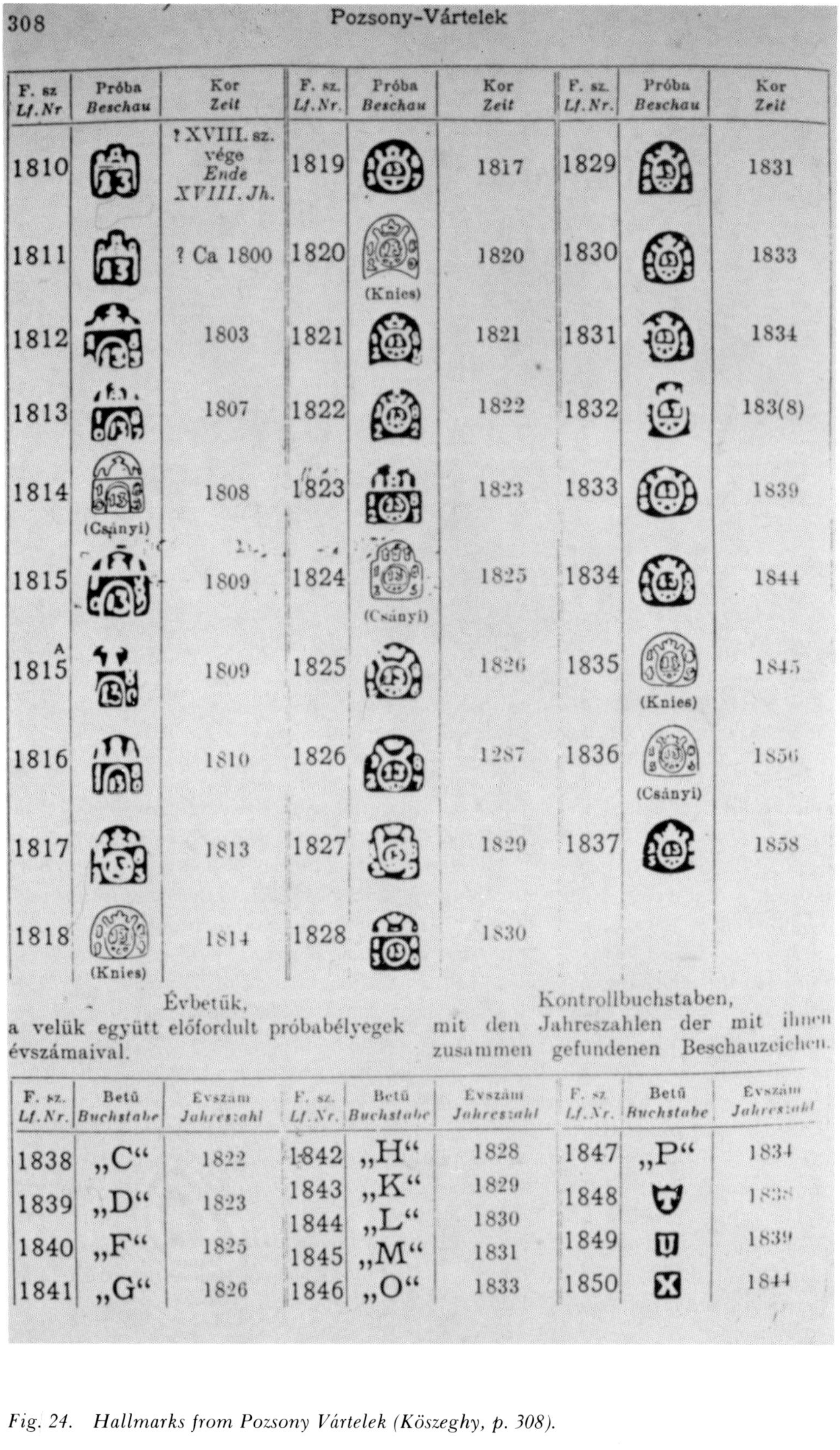

308 — Pozsony-Vártelek

F. sz Lf.Nr	Próba Beschau	Kor Zeit	F. sz. Lf.Nr.	Próba Beschau	Kor Zeit	F. sz. Lf.Nr.	Próba Beschau	Kor Zeit
1810		? XVIII. sz. vége / Ende XVIII. Jh.	1819		1817	1829		1831
1811		? Ca 1800	1820	(Knies)	1820	1830		1833
1812		1803	1821		1821	1831		1834
1813		1807	1822		1822	1832		183(8)
1814	(Csányi)	1808	1823		1823	1833		1839
1815		1809	1824	(Csányi)	1825	1834		1844
1815 A		1809	1825		1826	1835	(Knies)	1845
1816		1810	1826		1287	1836	(Csányi)	1856
1817		1813	1827		1829	1837		1858
1818	(Knies)	1814	1828		1830			

Évbetük, a velük együtt előfordult próbabélyegek évszámaival.

Kontrollbuchstaben, mit den Jahreszahlen der mit ihnen zusammen gefundenen Beschauzeichen.

F. sz. Lf.Nr.	Betü Buchstabe	Évszám Jahreszahl	F. sz. Lf.Nr.	Betü Buchstabe	Évszám Jahreszahl	F. sz. Lf.Nr.	Betü Buchstabe	Évszám Jahreszahl
1838	„C"	1822	1842	„H"	1828	1847	„P"	1834
1839	„D"	1823	1843	„K"	1829	1848		1838
1840	„F"	1825	1844	„L"	1830	1849		1839
1841	„G"	1826	1845	„M"	1831	1850		1844
			1846	„O"	1833			

Fig. 24. Hallmarks from Pozsony Vártelek (Köszeghy, p. 308).

Selected Bibliography

Altschuler, D. *The Precious Legacy: Judaica Treasures from the Czechoslovak State Collections*. Catalogue. New York, 1983.

A régi Buda és Pest iparmüvészetének kiállitása. Budapest, 1935.

Benjamin, Ch. *The Stieglitz Collection: Masterpieces of Jewish Art*. Jerusalem, The Israel Museum, 1987.

Benda, V. *Ars Judaica Bohemiae*. Bratislava: Vystavy Slovenského Národného Museum, 1968.

Berger, M., W. Häusler, E. Lessing. *Die Sammlung Berger, Kult und Kultur des europäischen Judentum*. Munich and Vienna, 1959.

Bialer, Y.L. and E. Fink, *Jewish Life in Art and Tradition*. Jerusalem 1980.

Budapest Müemlékei II. Budapest 1962.

Büchler, S. *A zsidók története Budapesten a legrégibb időktöl 1867-i* Budapest, 1901.

Grünwald, F. and S. Schiever. *Adalékok a magyar zsidóság településtörténetéhez a XVIII század elsö felében*. Budapest. Magyar Zsidó Oklevéltár. 1963.

Gutman, J. Ed. *Beauty in Holiness: Studies in Jewish Customs and Ceremonial Art*. New York, 1970.

Gutman, J. *Jüdische Zeremonialkunst*. Frankfurt am Main, 1936.

Ember, G. "A margyarországi Orsz. Zsidösszerirások a XVIII század elsö felében" in: *Magyar Zsidó Oklevéltár VII*. Budapest 1963.

Jakobovits, T. "Die Jüdischen Zünfte in Prag." In: *Jahrbuch der Gesellschaft für Geschichte der Juden in der czechoslovakischen Rep.* (1936), 57ff.

Judentum in Wien. Sammlung Max Berger. Ausstellungskat. Hist. Museum der Stadt Wien. 108. Sonderausstellung, 1988.

Landsberger, F. *A History of Jewish Art*. Cincinnati, 1946.

Lepszy, L. *Preszemysl Zlotniczy w Polsce*. Cracow, 1929.

Kaniel, M. *Judaism*. Dorset, 1979.

Kayser, S. and G. Schoenberger. *Jewish Ceremonial Art*. Philadelphia, 1955.

Knies, O. *Die Punzierung in Österreich*. Vienna, 1986.

K. Winkler E. *Pozsonyi tvösjegyek*. Budapest. Arch. Art. 1911, p. 43.

Krüger, R. *Die Kunst der Synagoge*. Leipzig, 1968.

Nahon, S.U. *Torah Scroll Ornaments*. Jerusalem, 1966.

Orsz. Levéltár. Budapest. Archivum Regnicolare, Lad AA-Lad KK. Orsz. összeir sok XVIII szd I.

Portisch, E. *Geschichte der Stadt Pressburg*. Bratislava, 1833.

Roth, C.B. *Die Kunst der Juden*. Frankfurt am Main, 1963.

Shachar, I. *Jewish Tradition in Art: The Feuchtwanger Collection of Judaica*. Jerusalem: The Israel Museum.

Scheiber, S. *Magyar Zsidó Oklevéltár* 7 (1963) 160 Budapest 1974.

Toranova, E. *Zlatnictvo w Slovacji*. Bratislava, 1983.

Venetianer, L. *A Magyar zsidóság története*. Budapest 1922.

Volavkova, H. *The Synagogue Treasures of Bohemia and Moravia*. Prague, 1949.

Wischnitzer, R. "Origins of the Jewish Artisan Class in Bohemia and Moravia, 1500-1648." *Social Studies* 16 (1954), 335-50.

Wischnitzer, R. *A History of Jewish Crafts and Guilds*. New York, 1965.

194

Fig. 1.   Raphael Soyer, Dancing Lesson, 1926 (collection of Renee and Chaim Gross).

"JEWISH" ART? THE CASE OF THE SOYER BROTHERS*

Milly Heyd and Ezra Mendelsohn

In his celebrated book *World of our Fathers* Irving Howe names four artists whose work, so he believes, can be considered "Jewish." Raphael Soyer is one of them, but this artist's reaction to being singled out in such a way reveals considerable ambivalence regarding any attempt to attach an ethnic label to his work. He writes that being put in this company "moved" him, but he adds: "Of the four artists whose work Irving Howe reproduced in his book, Max Weber, Ben Shahn, Abraham Walkowitz, and myself... I was the least involved with Jewish content in art. Weber purposefully depicted religious Jews in prayer and study; Shahn became interested in Hebrew calligraphy, and illustrated Haggadahs; Walkowitz published a book called *Ghetto Types*."[1]

In fact Raphael Soyer (1899–1987) adamantly refused to define himself, and objected to others defining him, as a "Jewish artist." He was an American artist, more specifically a New York artist, and took pride in remarking that he worked every day of the year, including Christmas and Yom Kippur — thus parading his intense devotion to his craft and his indifference to Judaism.[2] Nonetheless, despite the fact that, with a very few exceptions, his paintings do not deal explicitly with Jewish subjects, the authors of this article agree with Howe that his work, like that of his two brothers, Moses and Isaac, is intimately related to his Jewishness, and does shed light on certain aspects — sociological, political, and psychological — of modern Jewish life.

The Soyer brothers came to America shortly before World War I. Their parents hailed from the Lithuanian-White Russian region of the Pale of Settlement, but the family lived for some time outside the Pale and was at least to a degree Russified. In fact Raphael and Moses, his twin, liked to converse in Russian, and remained throughout their lives intensely interested in Russian culture and politics. This was not a typical Jewish immigrant family. The Soyers were poor but the sweatshop was not part of their experience. Their father, Avrom (Avraham) was an intellectual, who eventually gained employment as a teacher of Hebrew literature at the Teachers' Institute of the Isaac Elhanan Theological Seminary (later Yeshiva University). He was religious but no fanatic, a man of culture, a Hebrew and Yiddish writer, a well known member of the small, elite circle that promoted modern Hebrew in America. In Jewish politics he was a Zionist. Three of his children became artists, the remaining three teachers. All had knowledge of Hebrew and Yiddish but English, of course, became their main language. Of their parents' religiosity the children retained nothing, unless one considers the political radicalism they adopted a form of religion, and of the father's Zionism very little. One daughter spent a few years in Palestine and married a "Palestinian" (a Russian Jewish pioneer) with whom she returned to New York. If the Soyer family's combination of features typical of the Russian *intelligentsia* and of the *Haskalah* marked it off from most Jewish immigrants to America, the children's acculturation and rejection of religion was common enough.

1. Immigration and Acculturation

This process of acculturation is the subject of a well known early painting by Raphael Soyer, entitled *Dancing Lesson* (Fig. 1). The painting depicts two of the artist's siblings learning to dance American-style while another brother and the artist's parents look on. On the wall hangs a picture of the artist's

* We wish to record our thanks to Rebecca Soyer, Rebecca Beagle, Mary Soyer, David Soyer, Daniel Soyer and Daniel Beagle for their generous help. It goes without saying that the authors alone are responsible for the contents of the article.

[1] Raphael Soyer, *Diary of an Artist* (Washington, 1977), pp. 292, 290.
[2] Barbaralee Diamonstein, "Raphael Soyer," in *Inside New York Art World* (New York, 1977), pp. 367–380. I [E.M.] often heard the artist make this statement.

Fig. 2.   *Reuven Rubin, Dancers of Meron, 1926 (The Rubin Museum, Tel-Aviv).*

Fig. 3.   *Reuven Rubin, The Artist's Family, 1932 (Tel-Aviv Museum).*

grandparents. Here is Howe's perceptive analysis of this work:

> There is a painting by Soyer called *Dancing Class,* [*sic*] which shows in the foreground two rather awkward young people trying to dance while in the rear some elderly figures, obviously parents, are dozing off in their chairs. It would be idle to speak here of a Jewish style, since the formal means employed by Soyer are not distinctively "Jewish"; yet the picture communicates something about the immigrant experience through more than its declared subject. The postures of its figures are bent, a little fearful and clumsy; these immigrant postures, held through the decades, seem now to be shaping the very contours of the picture; and not to be aware of this is probably to miss something of the picture's aura. More than subject, less than style, is at stake here. One wants to speak of "aura," "tone," "posture," "inflection," — all admittedly vague and difficult terms, yet pointing to a felt reality... Some tonality of "Jewishness" may therefore inhere in Soyer's picture...[3]

Howe's analysis is based on an intuitive idea of what constitutes "Jewishness" deriving from his own past memories. He evidently believes that there is a sort of consensus on this subject, a consensus shared by Soyer in his presentation of the figures of his parents.

Howe does not discuss the importance of the fact that the artistic language of this early painting derives from naive primitivism. The choice of this language to depict the immigrant experience is paralleled in the work of another Jewish artist, much admired by Soyer — Reuven Rubin.[4] To compare the two cases

3   Irving Howe, *World of our Fathers* (New York, 1976), pp. 583–584. This picture is reproduced on the cover of the catalogue of the exhibition "Painting a Place in America," held in 1991 at the Jewish Museum in New York. See Norman L. Kleeblatt and Susan Chevlowe, eds., *Painting a Place: Jewish Artists in New York, 1900–1945* (Los Angeles, 1991), pp. See also Avram Kampf, *Jewish Experience in the Art of the Twentieth Century* (South

Hadley, Mass., 1984), pp. 82–83, and Ezra Mendelsohn, *On Modern Jewish Politics* (New York, 1993), p. 9.

4   See Milly Heyd, "The Uses of Primitivism: Reuven Rubin in Palestine," in Ezra Mendelsohn and Richard I. Cohen, eds., *Art and its Uses: Studies in Contemporary Jewry*, vol. VI (1990), pp. 43–70.

is to discover, however, that this experience is under-stood very differently and that the artistic language is used to different effect by these two artists from Eastern Europe, one of whom emigrated to New York and the other to Palestine.

The *Dancing Lesson* was painted in the very same year as Rubin's *Dancers of Meron* (Fig. 2) and may also be compared to Rubin's *The Artist's Family* (Fig. 3). It was around this time that the new American identity of the Soyers was being established. When they came to America their name, the Hebrew version of which was Sho'er, was apparently rendered by some family members as Suer — an obvious disaster in English. Eventually the artists and their parents adopted the name Soyer, which was used by Moses Soyer in his passport issued in 1926. This name recalls one of the great classics of American literature, *Tom Sawyer*, a book the Soyers claim to have read in Russia. Name changing as a means to and result of acculturation is described ironically in one of Avrom Sho'er's stories dating from 1920:

> Surely this Aharon-Leib has already changed his name to Irving or to Harold... he has got himself furniture for his library too, for he wants a respec-table collection of books at home. And among the works of Dickens, Shakespeare, Mark Twain, etc., there was no room for something like the old *Hok le-yisrael* [a traditional Jewish work]...''[5]

Indeed, Mark Twain may have served as a source of inspiration for Avrom's children's Americanized name, just as they were embarking upon their artistic careers.

Let us now compare how Raphael Soyer and Reu-ven Rubin deal with the subject of immigration and acculturation. For Rubin it is perceived as a liberating experience, in which dance is part of the integration with the new natural setting, with the "old-new land." The family portrait is set within a landscape. There is an obvious ideological, Zionist sub-text to these works. Raphael Soyer took note of this and compares Rubin to the Mexican muralist Diego Rivera: "Like the Mexican's, his subject matter became steeped in the new life and lore of the land and its people. He found a new style for this context, a kind of oriental neo-primitivism somewhat akin to Persian miniature, but on a mural scale."[6]

For Soyer, on the other hand, immigration is quite

a different matter. It is above all a constraining, restric-tive, urban experience. The somewhat shapeless plant depicted in *Dancing Lesson* belongs in an interior, in an apartment, while the one in Rubin's *Dancers of Meron* is more luxuriant and more definite. There is no rejoicing in the *Dancing Lesson*; on the contrary, the old people here seem rather depressed. We can interpret this painting as a portrayal of the difficult process of separation from Jewish traditional life, here represented by Beyla, the mother, who holds a Yiddish newspaper which appears to be called *Suer Tog* (instead of *Der Tog*, the well known New York Yiddish daily). Rubin perceives the Jewish tradition in a positive sense, as a means of dealing with the problem of immigration and coming to terms with his roots. His mother, also an orthodox Jewish woman, is placed in a central position in the family portrait. In the case of Soyer, however, one feels his desire to "dance away," forever, from this tradition.

Different artistic styles illustrate these very different attitudes. In Rubin's *The Artist's Family* realism is used to depict the mother's features, naturalism for the sister, a slightly African style for the brother, and a much more African one for Rubin himself. All this suggests that these figures are going through a period of transition in their integration into the new land of Israel. The most integrated, the artist himself, is depicted in the most primitivistic style. In the *Dancing Lesson* the parents, seated on the couch, are painted in the most primitivistic style, while the dancing couple is more naturalistic. For both artists, primitivism is the language in which new beginnings in new lands is depicted; it is used in a very positive sense by Rubin, the Zionist come to Palestine, but in a much less positive way by Soyer, for whom this new beginning is associated with the painful but inevitable process of separation from the old generation.

Irving Howe's reading of the *Dancing Lesson* is illuminating, but he has accepted uncritically a mis-interpretation by Harold Rosenberg of another of Raphael Soyer's works — *The Artist's Parents*, done both in oil and as an etching (Fig. 4). Rosenberg sees the scene in a romantic light: "The artist's parents [are] seated at the table after a Friday night supper. The candles are beginning to melt, and the middle-aged couple are also melting into half sleep. They look as though they have eaten a good deal — a

[5] *Ha-toren*, 7, 1920, p. 7. The story is called *"Ha-Kadishin."*

[6] Raphael Soyer, *Self-Revealment* (New York, 1967), p. 109.

Fig. 4.   Raphael Soyer, The Artist's Parents, 1932 (Metropolitan Museum of Art, New York City).

golden glow as of chicken soup permeates the picture. With the droopy, worn quality of the parents in the midst of the Sabbath haze, the scene is thoroughly authentic, and it is beautifully painted.''[7] Rosenberg is writing from memory — there are no candles in the picture. But he has also been carried away by the strength of his own idealization and has utterly missed the mood of the painting, which is again one of dejection. Despite the physical closeness each figure is gloomily set apart; the father is in a contemplative mood, the mother, her stare unfocused, is enclosed inwardly by the triangular setting of her pose. This setting may be contrasted to the picture of the mother and child in the background.

Rosenberg's nostalgic interpretation is all the more strange since he acknowledges that the painting is "a translation of a Jewish situation into French art" and

that "its style had no relation to the Jews or to the lower East Side."[8] Indeed, the painting is Raphael's variation of the Degas' *Absinthe Drinkers* adapted to his own family situation.[9] Raphael omits Degas' Japanese perspective, and sets the couple directly confronting the viewer; there is no absinthe, of course, and rather than show shadowy reflections in the mirror he contrasts the couple with the photograph of the new generation (the people shown in the photograph may be their son Moses' wife and her son, David). The cupped palms are a central means of expression, and the heavy Cézannesque cupboard blocks the interior. As for the mother, Raphael is on record as having said that: "The portrait of my mother as heavy and frustrated is the portrait of so many women immigrants."[10] It is the portrait of a woman who could not acclimatize and who remained shut up in her own world. As

7   Harold Rosenberg, "Is there a Jewish Art?," *Commentary* 42.1 (July 1966), 58; cited in Howe, *World*, p. 584.
8   Rosenberg, "Is There a Jewish Art?," p. 58.
9   Soyer, *Diary of an Artist*, pp. 219, 292.
10 Israel Shenker, "Raphael Soyer," *Art News*, Nov. 1973, p. 55.

Fig. 5.   Raphael Soyer, City Faces, 1958 (Louis Friedenthal Collection).

Fig. 6.   The Soyer Family in Russia (photograph, collection of Ezra Mendelsohn).

in the case of his *Dancing Lesson,* here too Raphael Soyer conveys to us through his art the difficulties of immigration to the new world, and in particular the high price paid by the older generation, who look out at their new surroundings with bewilderment, with incomprehension, with sadness.

If the members of the old generation are fated to suffer in the New World, as indeed they had in the inhospitable old country, and if the children are strenuously engaged in the bittersweet process of acculturation, the grandchildren, American-born, have it within their power to achieve true assimilation. Raphael Soyer depicts this optimistic vision in his painting *City Faces* (Fig. 5). Here the rather somber self-portrait of the artist and his wife, seen in the background, contrasts sharply with the portrayal of

the artist's daughter, Mary Ruth (in red), and a look-alike with whom she is twinned. Another group, composed of three figures (apparently artist friends) is in the background on the right. It is striking that Mary's features are those of the ideal young American of that time — no alienated Russian Jew she, but a healthy, optimistic, forward-looking young American.[11] The basic structure of this painting is similar to that of an early photograph of the Soyer family before the departure to America (Fig. 6). This photograph, apparently the only one of its kind from that period in the family's possession, served the artist as a point of reference, a dignified, static commemoration of the basic structure of the family. The trio on the right — Abraham and the twins — constitutes one unit. In the middle are the mother and daughter,

---

[11]   It is interesting that another of Raphael's portrayals of young American women, *Office Girls* (1936, Whitney Museum), was chosen by the *American Historical Review* (Oct. 1990) as the frontispiece for its issue on women on modern society. It

seems that the editors of this journal believed that Soyer's women epitomize the "new look" of the working women of the 1930s.

and on the left we see Fannie, the elder daughter, clasping the hand of the third brother, Isaac. Some fifty years later Raphael, in his *City Faces*, retained the basic compositional structure of the early photograph (groups of three, two, and two); in this case, however, the representatives of the American-born generation are in the forefront.

2. Universalism

Like so many members of their generation — immigrants or first generation American intellectuals reaching maturity in the 1930s — the Soyers identified with the left. Both Raphael and Moses were what came to be known as "fellow travelers" — highly critical of American capitalism, receptive to the great Soviet "experiment," willing to cooperate with the American Communist Party if not actually to join it. Moses was for a time the art editor of the pro-Communist intellectual journal *New Masses*.

For the Soyers, as for so many others, identification with the left was linked with a fierce reaction against the old Jewish world. Raphael's attitude to Judaism has already been mentioned. In place of the Jewish traditional world, characterized, so they believed, by narrowness, fanaticism, meaningless religious taboos, and hatred of the gentiles, the Soyers wished to play a role in building a new rational, secular world in which religious and ethnic differences would be minimized, perhaps even eliminated, along with the prejudices these differences engendered. The cosmopolitan left, for them, was the only force capable of defeating Nazism and fascism and combating the terrible poverty of the depression years, but it also signified an international sub-culture of growing power and influence where all prejudice, including, of course, antisemitism, had already been abolished — as it had been, so they believed, in the Soviet Union.[12]

Both Moses and Raphael identified not so much with the Jewish left, by which is meant specifically Jewish left-wing organizations, such as socialist Zionism, the *Arbeter ring* or the Jewish section of the American Communist Party, but with the general, American and international, universalist left. Thus Raphael was active in the John Reed Clubs, named after one of the founders of the American Communist Party. After all, adherence to the specifically Jewish left (Zionist, Bundist, or Communist) might well

imply a positive attitude towards the preservation and cultivation of Jewish culture, based either on Hebrew or Yiddish, and while the Soyer brothers knew these languages they certainly had little or no interest in cultivating them or passing them down to the next generation, to their children — who in fact grew up in a basically de-Judaized atmosphere lacking any kind of coherent Jewish content. Their radicalism was associated with a desire not only to change the "reactionary" Jewish ghetto of their parents but, it would seem, with a denial of the worth of the continued existence of any sort of separate Jewish world.

In this left-wing universalist scheme of things the "Negro question" took on special importance. Jews had long taken a great interest in American blacks, no doubt out of concern for the oppression they had suffered and were suffering but also because they believed that the kind of society they wished for in America — one in which diverse people, including Jews, could successfully integrate into American society — required the successful integration of blacks as well. It is well known that many Jews were active in assisting the black cause, and some even assumed leadership positions in the flagship organization working for black integration, the National Association for the Advancement of Colored People.

For radical Jews the plight of the American Negro symbolized the wickedness of American capitalism, which promoted economic exploitation and racial divisiveness. Clearly, no one was more oppressed than the Negro — indeed, as we see in a drawing by the Jewish pro-Communist artist William Gropper depicting a lynching, he was the very symbol of oppression (Fig. 7). But the existence of the Negro problem also represented a great opportunity for these radicals, for whom building bridges to the gentile world and making coalitions with other oppressed men and women to establish a prejudice free, color-blind society was invested with cosmic significance. If Jews and Negroes, so different in so many ways, could work together, then surely all groups could. Their brotherhood would be a powerful symbol of the victory of rationality and a harbinger of the much-to-be-desired fusion of different races and ethnic groups.

Since the ideal of Jewish-Negro cooperation within the framework of the left was particularly attractive

---

[12] On the link between the Jewish artists of New York, including the Soyers, and the left, see Matthew Baigell, "From Hester

Street to Fifty-Seventh Street: Jewish American Artists in New York," in Kleeblatt and Chevlowe, *Painting a Place*, pp. 50–62.

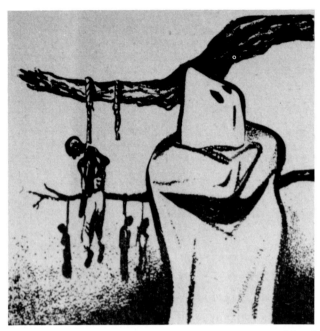

Fig. 7. William Gropper, Lynch. Wystawa rysunków i litografii Williama Groppera (Warsaw, 1949).

Fig. 8. Ben Shahn, Thou Shalt Not Stand Idly By, 1965 (Kenneth W. Prescott, Prints and Posters of Ben Shahn, New York, 1982, No. 40).

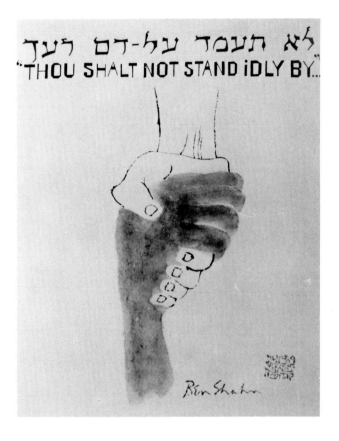

to radical Jews, it is hardly surprising that radical Jewish artists made it a theme of their work, as for example in the print by Ben Shahn depicting an interracial handshake (Fig. 8). Shahn has given this picture a title taken from a rather difficult passage in *Leviticus* 19:16, which the artist translates to mean that (white) men and women of good will must not "stand idly by" while their (black) brothers and sisters suffer.[13] Raphael Soyer also produced several works on this theme. His universalist vision is represented by the image of a white girl carrying a black child. He repeatedly depicted this theme in various media — a black and white drawing (Fig. 9), a lithograph, and as a detail in the oil painting *Village East Street Scene* (Fig. 10). In the black and white drawing the medium employed lends itself to a concise statement of an iconic nature, while in the oil painting the woman blends into the ecstatic frenzy of the street. She is placed among "the bearded, long-haired young

men; the loose haired, blue-jeaned girls with ecstatic faces."[14] The multi-ethnic street, which also depicts the artist himself, seeking his own identity, represents quite a contrast to the self-enclosed presentation of the artist's immigrant family.

Soyer has given us a graphic explanation of the importance of the image of the white woman and the black child:

> This is a young woman called Gypsy who had a child with a black man. I thought of this scene as mother and madonna. To me she signifies the madonna of our times. Instead of a halo she has the sign for an atomic fallout shelter.[15]

Particularly interesting, from our point of view, is another black and white version of this theme (Fig. 11) which bears the famous biblical quotation: "Are you not as the children of the Ethiopians unto me, O children of Israel?" (Amos 9:7). What fascinates here, as in the case of Shahn, is the artist's need

---

13 In the Jewish Publication Society translation of the Torah (1962) this passage is translated as "Do not profit by the blood of your neighbor." But Shahn's version is also to be found in the sources. See the discussion in the *JPS Torah Commentary, Leviticus*, commentary by Barukh A. Levine (Philadelphia, New York & Jerusalem, 1989), p. 129. Cf. the naive reading of this

painting in Jack Salzman, ed., *Bridges and Boundaries* (New York, 1992), p. 224.

14 Soyer, *Diary of an Artist*, p. 162.

15 Frank Gettings, *Raphael Soyer: Sixty-Five Years of Printmaking* (Washington, D.C., 1982), p. 64.

9

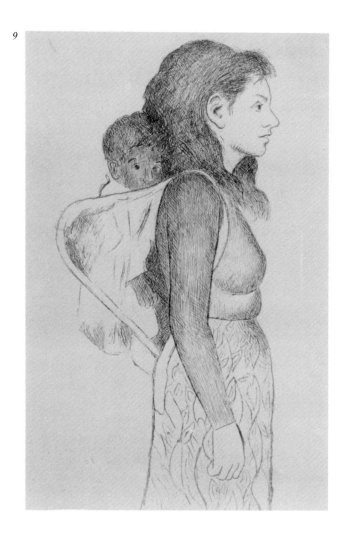

10

11

to buttress his universalist vision of the future with scriptural authority. Both he and Shahn go so far as to write the verse in Hebrew as well as in English, thus proclaiming their competence in this language. Why should a man of the left like Raphael Soyer, a man with contempt for Judaism, resort to such a strategy? The fact is that many Jews on the left, despite their much-heralded universalism, took intense pride in what they believed to be the universalist *Jewish* heritage, a heritage whose message they considered their own and regarded as a guide to action. It was the prophets — whose breadth of vision was, so they thought, the very opposite of the narrow, clannish, gentile-hating world of the Rabbis — who took pride of place in their pantheon of Jewish heroes. In their attraction to these figures Jewish artists like Soyer demonstrated that for all their desire to "merge" into the classless, denationalized and non-religious society of the future they were, nonetheless, despite everything, very much

Fig. 9.   Raphael Soyer, A White Woman Carrying a Black Child, c. 1960s (collection of Ezra Mendelsohn).
Fig. 10.   Raphael Soyer, Village East Street Scene, 1965/6 (collection of Joan and Lester Avnet).
Fig. 11.   Raphael Soyer, Amos on Racial Equality, c. 1960s (collection of Rebecca Beagle).

Fig. 12.   Raphael Soyer, Waiting Room, 1939/40, Corcoran Museum.

Fig. 13.   Isaac Soyer, Employment Agency, 1937 (Whitney Museum, New York City).

part of a defined Jewish tradition. In this sense they may be regarded as "non-Jewish Jews," in Isaac Deutscher's well known formulation.[16] Their pride in being Jewish could be legitimized by referring to the prophetic heritage of Judaism — as they interpreted it, of course.

Indeed, it may well be that Soyer (and Shahn) have incorrectly interpreted the true meaning of their Hebrew sources. Perhaps what the prophet is really saying is that his own children of Israel have so sadly declined in their moral behavior that they are no better than the wretched Ethiopians, low people on the totem pole of the ancient Near East. This hardly matters. What does matter is that left wing Jewish intellectuals like the Soyers believed in the existence of a powerful Jewish tradition that justified their intense dislike for the competing Jewish tradition of *ata behartanu*, the "chosenness" of the Jews. The Jewish God, who did not, of course, exist, agreed with the Communist Party that all men were equal, and that there were no essential differences among them.

The importance of the Black theme is evident in other works by the Soyers. Raphael's painting *Waiting Room* (Fig. 12), while inspired by Daumier's *Third Class Carriage*, is multi-racial. In Isaac Soyer's *Employment Agency* (Fig. 13) a black woman in a

contemplative pose, dressed in red and blue, is seen in the midst of three men in dark, almost subdued outfits. All share the same fate, epitomized by the harsh capitalist inscription: "All fees are payable. Cash in advance." In Raphael's *City Children* (Fig. 14) white children and a black boy are vertically facing the viewer, parallel to the vertical lines of the rails that set each one of them apart. In 1964 an exhibition devoted to the subject of "the portrayal of the Negro in American painting" was held in Maine, including Raphael's *City Children*. The artist urged that "such an exhibition ... should be circulated throughout the country," apparently because he thought it would improve race relations.[17]

Art, then, had its uses in the struggle to achieve a just society. It was not only in their depiction of blacks that the Soyers played their part in that struggle. They also fought for the right of black artists to exhibit. In 1926 the three Soyer brothers, along with Jack Levine, Chaim Gross, and the black artist Jacob Lawrence wrote to Abbo Ostrowsky of the Educational Alliance urging him to "hold on its premises an exhibition of the promising young Negro painter, Edward Strickland."[18]

The Soyers' political view of the world was also reflected in their aesthetic preferences. Their extreme hostility to abstract expressionism derived at least in

---

[16]   See Isaac Deutscher, *The Non-Jewish Jew and Other Essays* (London, 1968).

[17]   Soyer, *Diary of an Artist*, p. 135.
[18]   Archives of American Art, 1926–0597.

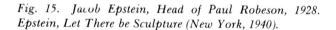

Fig. 14. Raphael Soyer, City Children, 1952 (collection of
L. Arnold Weissberger).

Fig. 15. Jacob Epstein, Head of Paul Robeson, 1928.
Epstein, Let There be Sculpture (New York, 1940).

part from their feeling that such art conveyed nothing
of importance to the viewer.[19] Moses' art criticism in
the New Masses, though certainly not of the vulgar
Marxist variety, upheld the idea that art should inspire
people with what would be called today "politically
correct" thoughts.[20] Consider the following, written
in 1944:

> The artists of New York will feel deeply the loss
> of the sculptor Adolph Wolfe. He was a gentle,
> kindly man, loved by his fellow artists and admired
> by many thousands of the working people whose

houses are decorated with his plaques of Debs,
Lincoln, Lenin, Stalin, and other beloved figures.[21]

Moses opposed "art for art's sake."[22] He also rejected modern surrealism's "ivory tower" aesthetics
and compared it unfavorably to the work of Breughel,
Bosch, Blake and Redon who were perceived as social
surrealists.[23] Exhibitions that included "progressive"
works were invariably given good reviews. For instance
in 1944 Moses wrote positively of a "Tribute to President Roosevelt" exhibition that included a work by
Richmond Barthe, especially singled out for praise,

19 See the "Statement" of a group of artists opposing "mere textural
novelty" in modern art and insisting on the position that the
purpose of art is "the depiction of man and his world" in
Reality, vol. 1, No. 1, Spring, 1953. The statement is signed by
Raphael and Moses.

20 His favorite words are "people" — "common people," "poor
people," "rising people," "plain people," "a people's art
gallery," etc., and "human" — "human experience", "more hu-

man," "inhumanity," etc.

21 New Masses, 23 May 1944, pp. 27–28.

22 New Masses, 1 May 1945, p. 29: "[William] Gropper need not
fear. His work, so vividly recording our time, will live longer
than the work of the highly praised and much sought after
exponents of art-for-art's sake."

23 New Masses, 9 Jan. 1945, p. 28.

Fig. 16. Moses Soyer, Eartha Kitt, 1964.

entitled "The Negro Looks Forward."[24]

Another review is illustrated by Jacob Epstein's *Head of Paul Robeson* (the great black singer and actor, and the Communist Party's most visible black supporter) that, as Moses puts it, "reveals strong, impressive character"(Fig. 15).[25] On the other hand he has little to say about Chagall: "I have space only for a mention of some of the other important shows... [including] the rather unusual exhibition of the Synagogue Paintings of Marc Chagall at the new Gallery of Jewish Art."[26] Moses by no means ignored Jewish artists, but those whom he praised were primarily concerned with "people's art." His own painting of a young Negress was warmly received by an art critic of the journal *Art Front* as possessing "a significance not to be overlooked." Unlike the expressions of "white superiority" to be found in the paintings of black people by Winslow Homer, for example, "the Negress represented by Moses Soyer has dignity and self-assurance — she is treated as an equal."[27] An examination of his portrait of another young black woman — the famous singer and actress Eartha Kitt — would seem to bear out the critic's remarks (Fig. 16).

[24]   *New Masses*, 7 Nov. 1944, p. 27.
[25]   *New Masses*, 20 March 1945, p. 27.
[26]   *New Masses*, 26 June 1945, p. 30.

[27]   Jerome Klein, "Twenty-one Gun Salute," *Art Front* 1.5 (May 1935), 4.

Fig. 17. Raphael Soyer, How Long Since You Wrote to Mother?, c. 1934 (collection of J. and R.S. Schafler).

One other work illustrates the Soyers' universalism and social criticism — *How Long Since You Wrote to Mother* (Fig. 17), also produced as a black and white lithograph entitled *The Mission*. Here the artist displays his identification with Walter Broe, a homeless man, who became his model. Broe, the man of the people, became Raphael's *alter ego*, a persona through which the artist's views on society and the human condition were expressed. Raphael has recorded how this painting came to be done:

> Walter Broe took me to a mission house where I saw homeless men drinking coffee from tin cups with pieces of bread in front of them... That's Walter Broe [on the far right, drinking coffee], and this is the Lithuanian who could hardly speak English [at the left, eating bread].'[28]

[28] Gettings, *Raphael Soyer: Sixty-Five Years of Printmaking*, p. 36.

How Long Since You Wrote to Mother is a protest picture based on the discrepancy between text and image. Five withdrawn men concentrate on eating and drinking. The composition is characterized by a diagonal row of four people (as if part of an endless line) opposite a single man with a strongly featured profile. It conveys the artist's sense both of the community and of the individual. The strong profile with the blank facial expression (left), the expressive eyes (right), and the frontal face with the tightly closed mouth (center) are Raphael's way of focusing on the individual responses to the fate of the entire group — the Lithuanian seems to accept his condition, Walter Broe's eyes question it, and there is pent up anger in the face of the man facing the viewer. The three inscriptions on the wall demonstrate the hypocritical piety of the uncaring capitalist society: "God is your friend," "How long since you wrote to mother," and "The wicked are like the troubled sea."

This last inscription is yet another biblical citation — from one of the left's favorite biblical figures, the prophet Isaiah (57:20). Does the artist wish to draw our attention to the way in which Isaiah's sublime sentiments are being misused by a wicked capitalist system that allows men to suffer so?

3. Father and Son

The Jewish context of Raphael Soyer's art is also revealed in his many portrayals of his father. It seems that Raphael was almost obsessed with his father, whom he painted from his earliest days as an artist and continued to paint even after Avrom's death in 1940.

Avrom Sho'er's Yiddish and Hebrew writings in America inevitably take up the subject of immigration and the alienation of the sons from the fathers in the new land. He describes the immigrants as people "uprooted from their motherland" and dispatched "to a strange land, unknown to them and to their forefathers." They are "stricken by that silent sadness of one who is unwillingly displaced and is headed to a place foreign to his mentality, to his habits and customs and to those of his ancestors, a sadness unmitigated by even the faintest hope, an utter despair at being unable to fulfill any of one's wishes and desires."[29] In the new country the immigrant is totally estranged from his environment: "They were all strange [*zarim*] to him... all... She bore him sons, and they were strange to him... all were strange, both she and they." "He worked and labored for strangers and there in the strange shop he slaved for his employer, a stranger to him... among strange workers, whose activities, interests, and everything they did was always strange and incomprehensible to him." "When he became ill his home became too small... in America there is no place to be alone, not even a bed of one's own, not even a table, everything here belongs to strangers. One pays rent to strangers, one rents furniture from strangers..."[30]

However strange Avrom felt in America, however upsetting the transition from Russia to the hurly burly of life in New York, where Hebrew scholars were neither in great demand nor highly respected, his Jewish identity never wavered. For his son, however, the matter of both his father's and his own Jewish identity was a problem. Raphael's ambivalence with

Fig. 18. *Raphael Soyer, A Portrait of the Artist's Father (collection of Jane and David Soyer).*

regard to his father's Jewishness is expressed visually by the two different ways in which he portrays him — as a modern, somewhat "acculturated" man and as a more obviously "Jewish" type. Many years after his father's death he made an idealized, "non-Jewish" portrait of him based on an early photograph (Fig. 18). In another painting the father is shown at his writing desk, in modern dress (Fig. 19). There is a certain ambivalence in the pose; he seems to be writing, but at second look the tool with which he is working resembles a brush more than a pen. There are certainly no Hebrew letters visible on the writing pad. In a later work (Fig. 20) the father is seated, with an open book on his lap and a bookshelf behind him. Here too the book is blank. For someone who knew Hebrew and Yiddish and, as we know, used a Hebrew inscription

[29] Avraham Sho'er, *"Nitpardah ha-havilah," Ha-toren*, vol. 8, 1, Adar 1921, p. 25.

[30] From the story *"Beyn zarim," Ha-toren*, vol. 7, 1921, pp. 9, 10, 11.

Fig. 19.   Raphael Soyer, A Portrait of the Artists's Father, c. 1925 (collection of Raphael Soyer).

Fig. 20.   Raphael Soyer, A Portrait of the Artist's Father (collection of Raphael Soyer).

Fig. 21.   Raphael Soyer, A Portrait of the Artist's Father, 1916/17 (collection of Raphael Soyer).

in at least one of his paintings, this omission appears to be significant. Does it reveal Raphael's discomfort with the fact that his father wrote in Hebrew, and not in a European language?

In the second type of portrayal we observe an exaggerated, almost caricature-like emphasis of the father's Jewishness. This can be seen in a very early watercolor, *Artist's Father* (Fig. 21). One might hypothesize that this work reflects Raphael's lack of ease with his father's very pronounced Jewish identity, an identity from which he, as a young American, wished to distance himself.

Particularly interesting is the occasion when Raphael shows us a double portrait of himself and his father. The *Double Portrait* (Fig. 22) was done in three media — a drawing, an etching, and a painting — indicating Raphael's great interest in this "comparison" between father and son. There is a clear

Fig. 22.   Raphael Soyer, Double Portrait, 1977 (collection of Ezra Mendelsohn).

similarity of features between the two faces, but the father is wearing a hat, a sign of his particularistic, Jewish identity. However, in both the painting and the etching there is a reversal of expectations. The impact of Raphael's physical presence is much less than that of his father's. The artist almost withers away, merging into whiteness, while Avrom's features are sharply sketched in dynamic black suggesting — despite the anxious face — life and vitality. This despite the fact that the father was by this time long since dead. In this struggle between black and white we feel that the dead father draws his energy from his son, while the latter seems to be disappearing altogether.

Works of art in an artist's collection can be a guide to his sources. One of the lithographs in Raphael

Soyer's collection is Lovis Corinth's *Death and the Artist* (Fig. 23) in which we see death represented as a skeleton lurking behind the portrait of the artist. Soyer's *Double Portrait* seems to be inspired by Corinth. The traditional meaning of the *memento mori* in Corinth's picture is applied to Raphael himself. The father's deep roots in Judaism, his black vitality, strengthens him, while Raphael's presence is vitiated by his ambivalence with regard to his own (Jewish) identity. It is interesting in this connection that Raphael chose to copy Filippino Lippi's *Self-Portrait with an Old Man* (Fig. 24). The painter, the son of Fra Filippo Lippi, places himself next to the old man, whose wrinkled and chiseled strong-featured face is contrasted to the smooth and angelic face of the young man. Yet each possesses the same degree of

Fig. 23. Lovis Corinth, Death and the Artist, 1916 (collection of Raphael Soyer).

Fig. 24. Raphael Soyer, A Copy of Filipino Lippi's Self-Portrait with an Old Man, 1961 (collection of Raphael Soyer).

physical reality. The renaissance artist is comparing the different stages of life, while the American is illustrating the apparently unstoppable decline of Judaism in the new generation.

In Raphael's *Self-Portrait with Self-Portraits of Rembrandt, Corot and Degas* the artist once again raises the problem of his identity, this time within the context of art history. But unlike the case with his father, in this work he emerges as an equal. His identity as an artist appears to be secure, while his identity as a Jew, and his standing vis-à-vis his observant and learned father, is very much in doubt. If, as we have seen, immigration to the new world is hard on the older generation, the new generation has also suffered. The artist has rejected what he regards as the narrow, parochial but nonetheless rich and

satisfying world of traditional Judaism — again at a price.

Avrom Sho'er and his son Raphael represent two diametrically opposed positions within the Jewish world — particularistic Judaism, on the one hand, universalism on the other. This contrast is revealed even in their choice of careers: Avrom the writer, a traditional Jewish profession, Raphael the artist, plying a craft that had to contend with the Jewish ban on representational art.[31] It is interesting to note that several other Jewish artists were sons of writers — Nahum Gutman was the son of S. Ben Zion, Yosel Bergner is the son of Melech Ravich. It is probably true to say that of all the major European creative arts in modern times, up until the twentieth century, Jews were far more prominent in music and in literature

[31] In Avrom's autobiographical story *"Kanita haver,"* published in *Sefer ha-yovel hedenu* (New York, 1936), he relates that he too, as a young man, used to draw and that this activity annoyed his father. He quotes his father as saying: "not only [does he read *Haskalah* books] but he also writes poems and draws" (p.

187). It then turns out that even Avrom's father used to draw — he made a *mizrah* as a present for his father-in-law — but later apparently repressed this activity in favor of the traditional role of talmudic scholar.

than in painting. Indeed, Raphael's generation was the first to produce, both in Europe and in America, a large number of gifted Jewish artists who made a lasting contribution to their chosen discipline.

In his role as Hebrew and Yiddish writer Avrom Sho'er held an ideological position strongly opposed to that of his sons. He too refers to blacks (kushiim), but only to show that this nation, along with the Persians, Babylonians, Germans and all the rest belong to one group of mankind, and Israel to another. This is obviously the traditional Jewish way of looking at things, even though Sho'er does take a rather unusual position when he sarcastically urges God to "choose" these nations rather than the Jews, who are not exactly flourishing under His special patronage.[32] The Hebraist also wrote against the temptations of communism, as in his story In the Storm, which describes the unhappy fate of a young woman who abandons Judaism for the revolutionary cause.[33]

Sho'er also has something to say about "faces," which brings us back to the question of his son's portrait painting. Writing in 1921 on the weekly Torah reading in the synagogue, the father of three radical artists returns once again to the vexed problem of "fathers and sons." If the sons are abandoning the ways of their fathers, he writes, it is because the fathers of today, unlike those of the past, have no "face" (panim ayn lanu). According to the Midrash, also related by Rashi, when Joseph was in danger of being lured into bed with Potiphar's wife the face [diokan] of his father Jacob appeared to him, and saved him from temptation. For Sho'er, then, the existence of "face" designates moral authority, without which Judaism must disintegrate and fall.[34] In this context his son's Double Portrait takes on special significance. It is obvious that Raphael agrees that "face" is important, and the picture demonstrates beyond the shadow of a doubt that as far as the artist is concerned his father's face had in fact retained its considerable power. True, on the level of biography the son has not followed in the footsteps of his father — unlike Joseph, who was saved from temptation, he has rejected his father's ways in favor of left-wing universalism. But on a

deeper psychological level, he cannot fight free from his father's dominance, and in his effort to reject his Jewish past he is endangering his very existence — panim ayn lo (he has no face).

Raphael Soyer and his brothers never sought to conceal their Jewishness. Moses actually produced some drawings on specifically Jewish themes. In 1946 he went so far as to illustrate an enthusiastically pro-Zionist book on Jewish folk dances in Palestine; this does not mean that he was a Zionist, but it probably does show that, perhaps as a result of the horrific events of the war, he was prepared, at least temporarily, to lend his support to the Zionist cause.[35] Raphael claimed (see above) that he was not involved with "Jewish content in art," but he did do a large and sympathetic portrait of Golda Meir in 1975 and he also supplied the illustrations for Isaac Bashevis Singer's autobiographical book Lost in America, published in 1981.[36] In a post-war, undated letter to the American artist R.B. Kitaj he wrote that "Concerning the question about your Jewish awareness I agree with your equating the condition of the Jewish people with that of all other oppressed people."[37] We may conclude that this sort of Jewish consciousness, waning and waxing as it did, had always co-existed with a powerful desire to "overcome" Jewish parochialism and separateness. Let Raphael himself have the last word, or almost the last word on this subject. After talking with Golda Meir, the very embodiment of modern Jewish nationalism, he writes in his diary: "From an occasional serious tone in this conversation one realized that the State of Israel is indeed the center of Golda Meir's thought and life."[38] To which we may add — of her life, but certainly not of his.

The Soyers, as we know, did not wish to be considered as "Jewish artists," and who will deny them the right to define themselves and their role as artists as they wished? We hope that we have convinced the reader that their art cannot be understood without reference to a Jewish context, and that it is concerned with and illuminates some of the central dilemmas and conflicts of the Jew in the twentieth century.

[32] "Al ha-nisim ve-al-ha-niflaot," Ramah, vol. 2, 10–11 (21–22), Tevet-Adar, 1939.
[33] "Ba-sufah," Ha-toren, 8 Nov. 1918, pp. 10–11, continued in 15 Nov. 1918, pp. 5–7 and 6 Dec. 1918, pp. 7–9.
[34] Avraham Sho'er, "Parashat ha-shavuah," Ha-doar, 22 Dec. 1921.
[35] Palestine Dances! Folk Dances of Palestine as set down by

Corinne Chochem and Muriel Roth. Drawings by Moses Soyer. Photographs by John Mills, Jr. (New York, 1946).
[36] For the Meir portrait see Soyer, Diary of an Artist, p. 286.
[37] Archives of American Art, roll 1927, frame 849.
[38] Soyer, Diary of an Artist, p. 285.

212

Fig. 1.   J. Lipchitz, Song of the Vowels, 1930–1932. The original plaster model (h 380 cm). Tel Aviv Museum of Art.

THE "DAVID-ORPHEUS" MOTIF IN JACQUES LIPCHITZ*

Avigdor W.G. Posèq

Modern Jewish art pioneers who strove to create an authentic Jewish art, one which would also appeal to the general public, sometimes gave their fantasy free rein in combining direct visual impressions with obscure literary sources. The synthesis resulted in original but seemingly opaque images, which at first sight seem to have little to do with the artists' ideology. Only after a comprehensive enquiry does the singular intercourse of the visual and verbal motifs reveal the Jewish content of these works. We propose to apply this method to one of Jacques Lipchitz's best known compositions, the *Song of the Vowels*.

The problem of whether an artist's imagination is more strongly motivated by words than by images has long been debated, and analysts of the creative unconscious study both the spontaneous verbal associations and impulsive reactions to evocative blots. The stimulating potential of chance shapes and unpremeditated word chains already envisaged by Leonardo,[1] has been widely exploited in modern art. Modern artists sometimes go even further, and in combining the suggestiveness of *objets trouvées*, or in some cases, incidental shapes of their own making, with spontaneous, or even partly subconscious thematic associations, they produce compositions which even they sometimes find difficult to explain. Wishing to decipher the meaning of such works one must reverse the creative process. Starting with the finished product one has to trace

Fig. 1a. J. Lipchitz, Song of the Vowels. Bronze cast. Paris, Rue Saint Martin.

* The present article is a revised version of a lecture on "Jacques Lipchitz's Song of the Vowels," delivered to the Jewish Art Section of the World Congress of Jewish Studies, Jerusalem, June 1993.

[1] The stimulating effect of chance images is recommended by Leonardo, *Treatise on Painting* (Codex Urbinas Lat. 1270), trans. J.P. McMahon (Princeton, 1956), I, 51. See also E.H. Gombrich, "The Image in the Clouds," *Art and Illusion* (London, 1962), 162; H.W. Janson, "The Image Made by Chance in Renaissance Thought," in M. Meiss, ed., *De Artibus Opuscula IX: Essays in Honour of Erwin Panofsky* (New York, 1961), 261. On Leonardo's interest in verbal associations see L.H. Heydenreich, *Leonardo da Vinci* (New York, 1954), 13, 60; also K.R. Eisler, *Leonardo da Vinci: Psychoanalytic Notes to the Enigma* (New York, 1961), 259.

Fig. 1b. J. Lipchitz,
Song of the Vowels
(detail).

the visual and the conceptual ingredients and study their interaction. The recent acquisition by Tel-Aviv Museum of the original plaster model of the *Song of the Vowels* (Fig. 1)[2] was an occasion for the analysis of one of Lipchitz's less understood works, allowing to discern its heretofore unnoticed Jewish significance.

Although the bronze casts of the *Song of the Vowels*, owned by major public collections,[3] have been widely reproduced, and the composition has been recognized as a climax of change in the career of the artist,[4] writers who repeating what Lipchitz himself has said about it have added little to its intelligibility, curiously missing the clues arising out of the artist's own comments. In his biography he says that the

almost four-meter-high monument was preceded by some small sketches which he made in 1928, when experimenting with "transparent" volumes, in which the mass of sculptural forms is only delineated by metal wire. He says that he was delighted with this invention that seemed like drawing freely in space, since in allowing him to render instantaneous impressions, it helped him to break away from the Cubist severity of his earlier works.[5] One of his first assays in the new technique was a representation of a musician, inspired by a vivid experience of the Paris Symphony Orchestra concerts in the Salle Pleyel, where, always sitting in front of the harpists, he became interested in the glittering vibration of their instruments. Fascinated

[2] Cat. *Jacques Lipchitz: From Sketch to Sculpture* (Tel Aviv Museum of Art, December 10, 1991–February 29, 1992), 72–73, no. 27, English trans. 147.

[3] One of them, belonging to the French National Museums, is placed out of doors in the rue Saint Martin in Paris; other casts are in the Zurich Kunsthaus, in the Kroller-Muller at Otterloo, the University of California Franklin D. Murphy Sculpture Garden, in Los Angeles, on the other campus of Cornell University (Ithaca, N.Y.), and in the Nelson A. Rockefeller Collection in New York; cf. N. Barbier, *Cat. Lipchitz: Oeuvres de Jacques Lipchitz (1891–1973)* Collections du musee national

d'art moderne (Paris, 1978), 77–78, no. 33. For Lipchitz's own description of this composition, see J. Lipchitz & H.H. Arnason, *My Life in Sculpture* (New York, 1972), 123–125 (later cited as Lipchitz-Arnason).

[4] A.M. Hammacher, *Jacques Lipchitz: His Sculpture* (New York, 1960), 49, fig. 54. For a full bibliography, see N. Barbier, *Cat. Lipchitz.*

[5] Lipchitz says that he used the "transparents" as "drawing in space," cf. Lipchitz-Arnason, 95f. He discussed the "special quality of 'airness'" of these works in a letter to Roger Vitrae, cf. Hammacher, *Jacques Lipchitz,* 70.

Fig. 2.   J. Lipchitz, Harpist, 1928. Bronze (h 45 cm). New York, Mr. & Mrs. J.B. Brooks Collection.

Fig. 3.   J. Lipchitz, The Harpists, 1930. Bronze (h 45 cm). New York, Reis Family Collection.

by the harmonic reciprocity of the shimmering strings and melody he fashioned a small *Harpist* where the scribble-like linear rhythm expressing the totality of the musician's involvement, also conveys Lipchitz's own more complex audio-visual perception (Fig. 2).[6]

The theme of musical rhythms which, Lipchitz says, had a "hypnotic attraction" for him, was taken up again in another *Song of the Vowels* antecedent, a small composition entitled *The Harpists*, showing two musicians playing highly stylized instruments (Fig. 3).[7] Although originally this work was conceived only as a more solid version of the linear Harpist, Lipchitz freely developed the motif, adding another figure, and combining the two players into a single entity, while their harps assumed the form of outstretched wings. Recalling this involuntary development Lipchitz says that he was always enthralled by incidental forms, and perhaps alluding to Leonardo's recommendation of "images made by chance," he adds that "the work of art must move from the unconscious to the conscious, and then back to the unconscious again."[8] Elsewhere he also mentions the unintentional ambiguity of some of his later works, and records that he occasionally produced such chance effects by pouring hot wax into water. These "semi-automatic" shapes enriched his imagination, and elaborating them he often discovered additional images which he readily incorporated into his works.[9]

Lipchitz does not explain the ambivalence of *The Harpists* but recounts that his Parisian dealer mistakenly labelled it "Harp," and under this name sold it to an American collector. This man found that since the United States' customs then recognized as art only representations of living things, the work would be dutiable as a musical instrument. The difficulty was solved when the buyer, adopting the technique of free verbal association, convinced the officer in charge that 'harp' was a mis-spelling of 'harpy', which the standard dictionary said, was "a kind of bird." However, the sculpture was released only after Lipchitz vouched in the American consulate that this was what his work represented. Though the similarity of 'harp' and 'harpy' no doubt struck him with the same amusement as the chance sculptural forms, he says that he was much gratified not to have to swear that his work represented the legendary bird. Learning later, that the American buyer who presumably knew the funerary connotations of harpies,[10] asked in his will that the sculpture be placed on his grave, Lipchitz designed a suitable base to make it into a proper monument.[11] It seems then, that in the process of progressing from *The Harpists* to the *Song of the Vowels* Lipchitz became aware in this rather odd way, not only that the two musicians could be seen as a bird, but that it could be interpreted as a harpy.

Since as part of his attempt to liberate himself from Cubism he had become interested in Greek mythology, he may have also been attracted to harpies. Larousse defines them as divinities, half women half birds, acting as attendants of Hades. Originally they were known as winds, but as their name was associated with the Greek verb *harpazein*, meaning "to seize" they were regarded as "snatchers" and death spirits. In Homer they are described as winged females who transport people to the other world, and later they were considered as dangerously seductive,[12] and often confused with Sirens, the singing woman-headed creatures, which in Hellenistic literature and art were representatives of music, almost to the same degree as the Muses.[13] The hybrid singers in their turn had an affinity with the human-faced bird *Ba*, the ancient Egyptian spirit of the dead, in whose composite form one also recognizes the prototype of the harpies.[14] The analogy of meaning between the hybrid Egyptian

[6] Lipchitz-Arnason, 103–105, fig. 85.

[7] Lipchitz-Arnason, 115–116, fig. 97.

[8] Lipchitz-Arnason, 195. Lipchitz's interest in involuntary images was shared by Arp, who declared that he interpreted the content of the chance form of his works only after completing them. Cf. R. Motherwell, ed., *Arp: On My Way* (New York, 1948), 70, figs. 18, 123.

[9] Lipchitz discusses chance images in the introduction to a catalogue: *Thirty-Three Semi-Automatics 1955–1956 and Earlier Works 1915–1928* (New York, Fine Arts Associates, March 5–30, 1957), cf. Hammacher, *Jacques Lipchitz*, 73–74; also: Lipchitz-Arnason, 78 and 193f.

[10] On the funerary connotations of harpies, see *Oxford Classical*

Dictionary, s.v. "Harpyiae."

[11] Lipchitz-Arnason, 116.

[12] See *Oxford Classical Dictionary*, ad vocem; *Der Kleine Pauly* (Munich, 1979), 2, 944–945; J. Chevalier & A. Gheerbrant, *Dictionnaire des symbols* (Paris, 1987), 494; also *Webster's New World Dictionary*, s.v. "harpy."

[13] The confusion is reflected among others in the depiction of death spirits identified as "Harpies" in the form of Sirens on the Harpy Tomb of Xantos, cf. s.v. *Oxford Classical Dictionary*. For Sirens see ibid., s.v. "Sirens"; also *Der Kleine Pauly*, s.v. "Seirens."

[14] On the Egyptian origins of the hybrid creatures: Chevalier & Gheerbrant, *Dictionnaire*, 888. On Egyptian representations of

Ba and the Greek harpies as representations of the soul also extends to the harp, which in Antiquity was regarded as a psychogonic instrument whose ravishing, irresistibly alluring melody symbolized the ascension of the soul from earthly to otherworldly reality.[15] Harps were therefore used as symbols of spirituality. In classical art the harp was often confused with a lyre, the attribute of Orpheus, as well known for his journey to the netherworld as for his ability to charm wild beasts with the sound of his music.[16] In his search for universal symbols Lipchitz may have become interested in the conventional connotations of the ancient instruments, and referred to them in the *Song of the Vowels*, transforming the harpy-like configuration of the two harpers into an allegory of music. The putative symbolism of this sculpture was vaguely felt by one of his early biographers, who suggested that the rhythmical forms of the composition evoke the sounds of music played in primitive cultures as a charm against the terrors of the world, and also that its title refers to the melodic ornamentation of the vowels in Gregorian chants.[17] However, there is little to buttress this exegesis. Though Lipchitz says that the work was inspired by a musical experience it is not quite clear why he should associate modern harp melodies with ecclesiastic hymns and how this might be related to primitive rites.

Seeking a better explanation, we may draw some support from Lipchitz's story about the misinterpretation of his preliminary representation of the harpists as a harpy. We do not know how much he learned about the conceptual relation of harps and harpies, but he may have had the mythical birds in mind when in 1930 he created as a monument to his mother,

a zoomorphic figure, half-woman half-bird, carrying an over-grown child on her back (Fig. 4).[18] Shortly afterwards, in the *Song of the Vowels*, he combined the form of a harpy with harp-playing musicians. The occasion was furnished by one of his early admirers, Madame Hélène de Mandrot, who having bought one of Lipchitz's proto-transparent sketches, and later also a version of his *Reclining Woman with a Guitar*,[19] in which the musical instrument is rhythmically integrated into the female form, commissioned him to create a large work for the garden of her villa in the south of France. The lady's appreciation of the hybrid *Woman*, encouraged Lipchitz to propose a similarly ambivalent motif. He traveled to the villa and, enchanted by the location, produced a small preliminary maquette,[20] which, he says, was "a clarification of *The Harpists*." Eventually the sketch was enlarged to the full-size plaster model now in the Tel Aviv Museum (Fig. 1). The first bronze cast was inaugurated in the de Mandrot garden in 1932.[21]

In his commentary on his work's significance no longer refers to the original concert hall experience. He declared instead that the sculpture is associated with the magic of nature and that it evokes an ancient Egyptian prayer.[22] The composition consists of a tall columnar shaft upon which are set the two stylized musicians. The two harps, set at an angle, recall the perspective view of tree-lined avenue that leads to the villa,[23] while the gracefully curved frames of the instruments corresponding to the shapes of the mountains which can be seen in the background suggest that the *Song of the Vowels* may perhaps be understood as an encomium on nature. More significant is the fact that the harps have assumed the

the soul: E.A. Wallis Budge, *Egyptian Magic* (London, 1901, repr. New York, 1971), 113. On the Ba as a soul hovering over the dead, as distinct from the protective genius Ka, see J. Breasted, *Development of Religion and Thought in Ancient Egypt* (New York, 1912, repr. 1959), 56–62.

[15] On the symbolical connotations of harps, see Chevalier & Gheerbrant, *Dictionnaire*, 495, s.v. "Harpe."

[16] On Orpheus's attribute, see *Oxford Classical Dictionary*. Depictions of Orpheus charming beasts are known from Late Antique Roman, Jewish and Christian art. In the catacombs he represents the "messianic prince of peace" while in Byzantine art he is occasionally identified with Christ. For an iconographic survey, see A. Ovadiah & S. Mucznik, "Orpheus Mosaics in Roman and Early Byzantine Mosaics," *Assaph* 1 (1980), 43–56.

[17] Hammacher, *Jacques Lipchitz*, 49.

[18] Lipchitz-Arnason, 109f., fig. 93. On the zoomorphic maternal

image see my "Childhood Fantasy into Archetype Icons in Jacques Lipchitz," *Konsthistorisk tidskrift*, LX (1991), 1, 42–55.

[19] The original version was made in 1928. Lipchitz-Arnason, 103, fig. 83. On the relation of this work to the "transparents," see *Cat. Jacques Lipchitz: From Sketch to Sculpture*, 62.

[20] Lipchitz-Arnason, 122–125, figs. 106, 107. The 36 cm high bronze cast sketch, owned by the Israel Museum in Jerusalem, was exhibited next to the full size plaster model, *Cat. Jacques Lipchitz: From Sketch to Sculpture* 72, f.

[21] Lipchitz-Arnason, 124, fig. 107; Hammacher, *Jacques Lipchitz*, 49.

[22] Lipchitz-Arnason, 125.

[23] Oral communication by Mr. Reuben Lipchitz, the sculptor's brother, to Ms. Dorit Yifat, the Tel Aviv Museum exhibition curator, *Cat. Jacques Lipchitz: From Sketch to Sculpture*, 72.

Fig. 4.   J. Lipchitz, Mother and Child, 1930. Bronze (h 140 cm). Cleveland Museum of Art.

character of powerful wings which seem to lift the entire composition from its socle, and that these wings combine with the two musicians, to form a fantastic bird-like shape, which in evoking a harpy, also recalls in form the Egyptian representations of the soul bird *Ba*. Drawing upon this similarity one might speculate that the twin harpers hovering between heaven and earth embody the Egyptian concept of the duality of soul comprising the *Ba* which inhabits the body and flies over it in death, and the *Ka* which takes over in the hereafter.[24] Considering that Lipchitz's *Song of the Vowels* has to do with music, it could be understood as an allegory of the soul's ravishment of the ancient harp melodies. However, the two harps are neither Egyptian nor classical. Each is composed of a straight vertical column and a curved console from which the strings are stretched to the sounding board, they are easily recognized as modern concert hall instruments. Their pairing might perhaps suggest the so-called "double harp" (which is really a single harp with a double set of strings), but one wonders whether the loosely hanging strings would produce any sort of melody. The kneeling pose of the musicians would also not be practical when playing a concert harp since, unlike Greek harpists, usually shown seated or walking, modern harp players activate pedals. However, ancient Egyptian priest-magicians playing thaumaturgical harp music are often shown kneeling.[25] We cannot say from which painting the pose has been adopted, but the possible reference to Egypt is confirmed by Lipchitz himself. He claims that the title *Song of the Vowels* refers to what he had read somewhere about "a papyrus discovered in Egypt, having to do with a prayer called the *Song of the Vowels* — a prayer that was a song composed only of vowels, and designed to subdue the natural forces." He felt that his sculpture also symbolized the power of man over nature. He goes on to say that in naming it *Song of the Vowels* he created some confusion, since people readily associated it with a poem by

Rimbaud having the same title, which had nothing to do with the ancient papyrus, that had not been discovered at the time when Rimbaud wrote his verse. Lipchitz was unable to explain why the Egyptian prayer and the harps should have come together, except that "both of them were in his mind at the same moment."[26] However, the spontaneous association of the sculptural form with the ancient text, which Lipchitz says, took place only after the work was finished, may not have been arbitrary.

Seeking to unravel the singular word and image association we must start with Rimbaud, one of the most original nineteenth century French poets. His sonnet, "Voyelles," presents in an abbreviated form Rimbaud's concept of the chromatic equivalents of sounds, freely elaborating the visual and tonal correspondences: "A-black, E-white, I-red, U-green, O-blue...."[27] Rimbaud declared that he always endeavored to make his verses visible and palpable,[28] and his theory of mutual audio-visual relations was later interpreted as an *avant la lettre* ideology of a total art experience, propounded by the poet Saint-Pol Roux who, like Rimbaud, was claimed a precursor of Surrealism. Lipchitz may have heard Rimbaud's theory being discussed by his French colleagues, and while exploring the music and form analogies he may have been attracted in the idea of color equivalents of sounds, but it is not immediately clear how his bronze-colored musicians can be related to Rimbaud's theory, and even less so why they should evoke an Egyptian prayer. However, assuming that the creative imagination of an artist is bound by an inner rule of logic, one may perhaps recognize in Lipchitz's linking of his harpists with a "papyrus discovered in Egypt" a spontaneous conflation of the title of Rimbaud's sonnet, with the so-called "Songs of the Harpers," a characteristic genre of Ancient Egyptian lyric, said to have been performed during or after banquets by harp-playing singers.[29] Most of these texts praise the host and the pleasures of his table, but a special

[24] Breasted, *Development of Religion*, 52–57.

[25] On Egyptian harp music, see P. Montet, *Everyday Life in Egypt* (Philadelphia, 1981), 95–96, fig. p. 97.

[26] Lipchitz-Arnason, 123.

[27] A. Adam, ed., *Arthur Rimbaud: Oeuvres completes* (Paris, 1972), 53–53.

[28] F. Musso, *Rimbaud* ([Paris], 1972), 90. Audio-visual correspondences also interested Victor Hugo. It has also been suggested that Rimbaud may have drawn his idea from Cabaner, who used

colored musical notes. His "Le sonnet des sept nombre," written in this manner, is dedicated to Rimbaud, cf. H. Matarasso & P. Petitfils, *Vie d'Arthur Rimbaud* (Paris, 1962), 104–106.

[29] M. Lichtheim, "The Songs of the Harpers," *Journal of Near Eastern Studies* 4 (1945), 178–212; also H. Frankfort, *Ancient Egyptian Religion* (New York, 1961), 83. J. Assman, s.v. "Harfenlieder," *Lexikon der Aegyptologie* (Wiesbaden, 1975), 9 (II.1), 974.

category collectively known as songs of "the time will come" have as their subject the brevity of life, and preach the daily pursuit of happiness, "since nothing is more certain than approaching death, nor more uncertain than the destiny in the aftermath." A famous verse, dedicated to the priest Neferhotep, says "Make a happy day, O priest; [...]may there be singing and music of the harp in your presence. Put misfortune out of your mind, and think only of pleasure. Until that day comes, when you must travel to the 'land of Mertseger', the lover of silence... pass your day in happiness...."[30]

The sentiment conveyed in the Egyptian panegyric would perhaps fit another work on which Lipchitz was working at the same time, namely the enigmatic *Joie de Vivre*. It shows a musician with a stylized string instrument usually identified as a guitar, but possibly a harp (the full-size original model was included in the Tel-Aviv Museum exhibition) (Fig. 5).[31] But the message of the Egyptian harpist is incompatible with the *Song of the Vowels*, which Lipchitz says, symbolizes a wish to control nature. To solve this difficulty we must assume that when he thought of "a papyrus discovered in Egypt having to do with a prayer designed to subdue the forces of Nature" he confused the eulogy of Neferhotep's harpist with another text, also from Egypt, which is not a song but an incantation in one of the so-called "magical papyri." Dating from the time of the Ptolemies to the end of the Roman period (150 B.C. to 200 A.D.), these texts are written in Greek characters and show the combined Greek and Jewish influence of the Hellenistic-Jewish community of Egypt. Some of them even claim the authority of the occult "mysteries which God committed to Moses," and seem to be related to Hebrew prayers. The Jewish influence is particularly evident in the wording of the "Spell of the Seven Vowels," invoking the heavenly "Creator of earth and flesh" who "divided light from darkness" addressing him as "Adonai, Eloai, Sabaot, the God of

gods, IAOOUEI."[32] Adonai, in Hebrew "my lords," is the conventional Jewish form of addressing the Almighty. The plural mode equally characteristic of God's appellation Elohim, is also reflected in Eloai, or Elo'hai, meaning "my Elohim." Sabaot, or S'vaot is the Hebrew word for hosts, often used in conjunction with the word Elohim, i.e., Elohei S'vaot (God of hosts).[33] The word IAOOUEI, after which the Spell is named, brings to mind the hallowed Hebrew name of God, YaHVeH (similar to the ancient Egyptian *y'hw* which translates as "glorious" or "blessed"),[34] written in Hebrew without vowels, and never pronounced. The magic significance of God's name is subject to a long tradition. The seven vowels of the word IAOOUEI also recall the Gnostic "spell of seven vowels," said to contain all the names of God.[35] The word IAOOUEI cannot be a direct transliteration from the Hebrew, which employs only consonants, but in its first part (Iao) one identifies the Hebrew JaH, a common abbreviation of JaHVeH, as in Hallelu-JaH (in Hebrew, "bless Jah," which in European languages is spelled "Alleluja"). IAOOUEI can thus be understood as the plural form of "Iao" (like "Eloai") an arbitrary rendering of JaHVeH, which does not take the plural. Its possible affinity with Hallelu-JaH suggests a form of benediction. All this allows one to recognize in the Hellenistic conjuration a derivation, or even free adaptation, of a Jewish prayer formula, perhaps one of the Psalms where all these names of God as well as the words Hallelu-JaH recur very frequently.[36]

We do not know when or how Lipchitz encountered the magic incantation, but since he himself says that he read about one Egyptian text he might have come across the other as well. He even was correctly informed, when he said that the Spell had not been available to Rimbaud. Though the text was first published in an obscure mid-nineteenth century journal of Antiquarians, it became more widely known only when it was included in a well-known Egyp-

---

[30] Lichtheim, "The Songs of the Harpers," 195; also Montet, *Everyday Life in Egypt*, 96f.

[31] In his biography Lipchitz says that the *Joie de Vivre* was meant to cheer his sick sister. The composition had an inner mechanism which enabled it to turn around. Commissioned in 1927 by the Vicomte Charles de Noailles for the garden of his estate in the south of France, it is now in the Albert Einstein College of Medicine in New York, cf. Lipchitz-Arnason, 96f., fig. 81. The original plaster model of this work included in the Tel Aviv Museum Exhibition was described as "a man and

a woman dancing with a guitar," *Cat. Jacques Lipchitz: From Sketch to Sculpture*, 54, no. 18.

[32] Wallis Budge, *Egyptian Magic*, 176–178, cf. Goodwin, "Fragment of a Graeco Egyptian Work on Magic," *Publications of the Cambridge Antiquarian Society* 7 (1852).

[33] For the Hebrew names of God, see *Encyclopedia Judaica*, 7, 674.

[34] 34. Breasted, *Development of Religion*, 57.

[35] Wallis Budge, *Egyptian Magic*, 57, n. 3.

[36] S.v. "Psalms," *Encyclopedia Judaica*, 13, 1309.

Fig. 5.   J. Lipchitz, Joie de Vivre, 1927. The original plaster model (h 357 cm). Tel Aviv Museum of Art.

tologist's book on Egyptian magic, published eight years after Rimbaud's death.[37] In Lipchitz's Parisian milieu an interest in Ancient Egyptian hymns and in Egyptian things was not unusual.[38] He himself may have been aware of the Egyptian origin of the harpies, and also drew inspiration for his David and Goliath from the Egyptian Narmer Palette,[39] whereas *Joie de Vivre* seems to be inspired by the song of Neferhotep's harper. Whatever the source of Lipchitz's knowledge of the Spell of the Seven Vowels, its free association with the title of Rimbaud's sonnet was presumably reinforced by the phonetic similarity of the word IAOOUEI with the sounds of A,E,I,O,U, discussed by Rimbaud. One can imagine that Lipchitz would be especially intrigued by the relation of the Egyptian text to Hebrew prayers, and as a Jew he would not only recognize the Hebrew names of God, but would also associate these names with the Psalms, which pious Jews recite as a universally effective charm. A particular group of these prayers is typified by the initial words "Song of Degrees" (Ps. 120–133), usually understood as referring to the steps of the Temple where the Psalms were recited, but possibly defining the verses as a Song of Glories. This in turn brings us back to the *Song of the Vowels* which Lipchitz said, symbolizes the "power over Nature."

One must note here, that the conceptual significance of the configuration was not premeditated and Lipchitz seems to have discovered it only in the course of its making, or perhaps when the sculpture was already finished. Considering the process of free word and image associations one would not be surprised if Lipchitz's recollection of the ancient spell was suggested by the form of his work. A person acquainted with the Hebrew alphabet perceives in the loose strings of the sculptural harps the shape of

the Hebrew letter *shin*, a conventional abbreviation of El Shaddai (powerful or omnipotent God) which is often used as an amulet.[40] Twice repeated in the two harps the charm would be especially powerful. The seemingly arbitrary connection of the Hebrew letter with the Egyptian spell, and with the title of Rimbaud's sonnet, no doubt took place on the subconscious level, and Lipchitz himself was apparently not aware of the Jewish connotations of his Song.

In his earlier works he usually preferred mythological themes, but at about that time came to recognize that biblical subjects have an equally universal appeal. He was of course aware that in the Temple liturgy, the recitation of Psalms was accompanied by harp music, and that harp is the attribute of David, not only identifying him as Psalmist but also evoking his attempt to exorcise Saul's mental disorders. The magic spell of David's harp was already postulated in Antiquity, and in Late Antique mosaics he is often shown playing to an assorted assembly of bewitched animals.[41] The iconographic motif, presumably inspired by an apocryphal Psalm,[42] is closely associated with the pagan representations of Orpheus charming the animals, implying a conceptual parallelism of the two poet-musicians. Lipchitz need not have been aware of the far-reaching iconological implications of the David-Orpheus affinity,[43] but he knew of course that both David and Orpheus were depicted as harpists, and in fashioning the twin harpists would be reminded of their equivalence. He may have acknowledged the parallelism in *Joie de Vivre*, where reflecting Lipchitz's interest in polyvalent themes, the musician may be seen either as David or as Orpheus, in addition to representing an Egyptian harper. Assuming that the twin harpists in the *Song of the Vowels* also represent

[37] See above, note 32.

[38] For modern artists' interest in Egyptian hymns, see A. Ozenfant, *Foundations of the Modern Art* (1931), trans. J. Rodker (New York, 1952), 203–24.

[39] The David and Goliath project was not realized; for the maquettes, see *Cat. Jacques Lipchitz: From Sketch to Sculpture*, 84–87, no. 32. On the Egyptian antecedent of the motif see my: "Jacques Lipchitz's David and Goliath," *Source* 8.3 (1989), 22–31.

[40] For the word Shaddai, see *Encyclopedia Judaica*, 7, 67b. On "Shin" see also 14, 1408.

[41] The foremost example of this motif is found in the early sixth century mosaic floor of the synagogue of Gaza, cf. A. Ovadiah, "The Synagogue at Gaza," *Qadmoniot* 1.4 (1968), 124f. H.

Stern, "Un nouvel Orphee-David dans une mosaique du VIe siecle," *Comptes rendus de l'Academie des Inscriptions et Belles Lettres* (1970), 63–79; M. Barasch, "The David Mosaic of Gaza," *Assaph* 1 (1980), 1–42, figs. 1 and 2. See also M. Friedman, *Bilder zur Bibel* (Bayreuth, 1985), 18.

[42] The existence of this supernumerary Psalm referred to as no. 151, and formerly known only from Greek translations, was confirmed by discovery of the Dead Sea Scrolls, cf. J.A. Sanders, *Dead Sea Psalms* (Ithaca, N.Y., 1963), 93–103, and Friedman, *Bilder zur Bibel*, 19. I am grateful to Professor Friedman for this information.

[43] For the David-Orpheus parallelism, see Barasch, "The David Mosaic," passim; also Friedman, *Bilder zur Bibel*, 18ff.

David and Orpheus, their pairing may be understood as alluding to the similar allure of their melodies.[44]

The idealistic message of the composition is given a special resonance by its high socle, not unlike the shaft on which Lipchitz wished to place his David and Goliath.[45] The motif of the columnar base evokes the Parisian Colonne de Vendôme modelled on Imperial Roman prototypes, and commemorating Napoleon's victory at Austerlitz. However, in the *Song of the Vowels* the triumph is not over an enemy. The two musicians who had magic power over nature, celebrate the ecumenical universality of art, reflecting Lipchitz's attempt to create art which being Jewish would also be comprehensible to non-Jewish public.

Summing up this somewhat roundabout iconographical exegesis, we may say that although it may not add much to what Lipchitz himself said about his work, an insight into the free interplay of his visual and verbal mainsprings offers a glimpse of the working of a creative mind, which resulted in an impressive art work with an unexpected Jewish meaning. Implicitly, the analysis also supports the legitimacy, in certain cases necessity, of broadening the scope of critical methodology to include the artist's seemingly non-sequential linking of words and images. In the case of Jacques Lipchitz, who by his own testimony purposefully exploited subconscious associations, such an inquiry is truly indispensable.

---

[44] Lipchitz's juxtaposition of the archetype Greek and biblical artists is paralleled in Amedee Ozenfant's comparison of Achenaton's and St. Francis's hymns to the sun, cf. Ozenfant, *Foundations of the Modern Art*, 203–204. On the symbolisms of pairing, see Chevalier & Gheerbrant, *Dictionnaire*, s.v. "Deux" and "Jumeaux."

[45] See above, n. 39.

224

Fig. 1. Frida Kahlo, My Grandparents, My Parents and I (Family Tree). 1936, Oil and tempera on metal panel, 12 1/8" × 13 5/8". Collection of the Museum of Modern Art, New York. Gift of Allan Roos, M.D., and B. Mathieu Roos.

THE HIDDEN FRIDA: COVERT JEWISH ELEMENTS IN THE ART OF FRIDA KAHLO*

Gannit Ankori

The Mexican artist Frida Kahlo (1907–1954) has recently become one of the best known Latin American artists, something of a "cult" figure.[1] Her posthumous international acclaim, spurred by a rising interest in women artists and in the non-European art of the "other," has produced several important scholarly investigations into the artist's work.[2]

Most texts on Kahlo focus on the artist's unusual life story and treat her art as an "autobiography in paint."[3] Born in Coyoacán, Mexico in 1907, Kahlo was nearly killed in an automobile accident when she was 18 years old. As a result of this accident, throughout her life she suffered from intense physical pain, which found poignant expression in her imagery.[4] Kahlo's emotional life was no less dramatic. In August of 1929, a month after her 22nd birthday, she married world-famous muralist Diego Rivera, who was 24 years her senior. Theirs was a stormy relationship, marked by childlessness, mutual infidelities, divorce and remarriage.[5] The emotional upheavals of Kahlo's life also became prime subjects of her paintings.

In addition to the biographical perspective that dominates the research literature about Kahlo, several scholars have pointed to Christian, pre-Columbian and popular Mexican images that have influenced the artist's work. The object of this paper is to introduce some heretofore unexplored visual and cultural sources — specifically sources that relate to the artist's Jewish ancestry — that informed some of Kahlo's most important paintings.[6]

* Reproduction of all works by Frida Kahlo authorized by El Instituto Nacional de Bellas Artes y Literatura, Mexico.

[1] On Kahlo as a cult figure see Hayden Herrera, "Why Frida Kahlo Speaks to the 90's," *New York Times*, October 28, 1990, Section 2, pp. 1, 41. Herrera writes: "Like a Goddess, she is referred to by her first name only. Madonna, Isabella Rossellini and Cindy Crawford are fans. She has captivated everyone from scholars writing dissertations to Chicano muralists, fashion designers, feminists, artists and homosexuals. According to Sassy, a magazine for teen-age girls, she is one of the 20 women of this century that American girls most admire." Ibid, p. 1.

[2] One of the earliest projects on Kahlo, which pre-dates the surging popular interest in the artist, is Karen and David Crommie's 1966 documentary film entitled *The Life and Death of Frida Kahlo*. The film itself and the taped interviews conducted in preparation for the project are invaluable sources of information. I thank Karen Crommie for making this material available to me. Other significant works on Kahlo began to appear in the late 1970s. In Mexico, Teresa del Conde's *Vida de Frida Kahlo* appeared in 1976 and Raquel Tibol's *Frida Kahlo: crónicas, testimonios y aproximaciones* was published a year later. In the United States, Kahlo's work was included in various anthologies and group shows of women artists, e.g. Karen Petersen and J.J. Wilson, *Women Artists: A Recognition and Reappraisal from the Early Middle Ages to the Twentieth Century* (New York, 1976); and Ann Sutherland Harris and Linda Nochlin, *Women Artists: 1550–1950* (New York, 1976). Other scholars who contributed to our knowledge of Kahlo are Martha Zamora, Laura Mulvey, Peter Wollen, Joyce Kozloff, Nancy Breslau, Edward Sullivan. Undoubtedly the two major books on Kahlo to date are Hayden Herrera's *Frida: A Biography of Frida Kahlo* (New York, 1983) and Helga Prignitz-Poda, Salomon Grimberg, Andrea Kettenmann, eds., *Frida Kahlo: Das Gesamtwerk* (Frankfurt am Main, 1988). Herrera's contribution to the study of Kahlo cannot be over-emphasized. I wish to express my deep gratitude to Herrera for putting her archives at my disposal, providing me with much unpublished source material and for her support. *Das Gesamtwerk* is essentially a catalogue raisonné of the artist's work. It also contains valuable essays and documentary material. Co-author Salomon Grimberg's other writings must be singled out. His research on Kahlo offers illuminating psychoanalytical interpretations of some of the artist's major works. Since 1989, Dr. Grimberg has kindly shared with me publications, photographs and information about Kahlo. I am deeply grateful for his generosity and interest in my work.

[3] Herrera, *Frida*, xii. Unless otherwise noted, the biographical information is based primarily on Herrera's book.

[4] Kahlo's medical history was recounted by the artist in 1946 to Dr. Henriette Begun, a German-born gynecologist who emigrated to Mexico in 1942. A copy of this hand-written medical record is found at the Centro Nacional de Investigación Documentación e Información de Artes Plásticas, Instituto Nacional de Bellas Artes [CeNIDIAP, INBA]. I thank the archivists at CeNIDIAP, particularly Nadia Ugalde, for their kind assistance. See also Hayden Herrera, "The Palette, the Pain, and the Painter," *Artforum* (March 1983), 60–67, for a critical view of Kahlo's manipulative use of her illnesses. On the accident and its aftermath see Herrera, *Frida*, 47–77.

[5] The Kahlo-Rivera relationship is discussed in detail in Herrera's *Frida*. See also Hayden Herrera, "Portraits of a Marriage," *Connoisseur* (March 1982), 124–127. Rivera's own account of this stormy relationship may be found in Diego Rivera with Gladys March, *My Art My Life: An Autobiography* (New York, 1960). See also Bertram D. Wolfe, *The Fabulous Life of Diego Rivera* (New York, 1963).

[6] This study is based on a small section of my doctoral dissertation which deals with Kahlo's self-image.

Jewish Roots

That Kahlo's father, Wilhelm Kahlo, was a Jew of Hungarian-German descent who emigrated to Mexico at the turn of the nineteenth century is a well-known fact never denied by the artist herself.[7] Thus far, Kahlo's relationship to Judaism has been reduced to two amusing anecdotes, which attest both to the artist's casual acknowledgement of her Jewish roots and to her tendency to do so precisely when she felt that Jews were being persecuted or victimized. One incident occurred during a well-attended dinner party at the residence of Henry Ford. As the guests were sitting around the table, Kahlo is reported to have waited for a break in the conversation in order to publicly ask the host, a known anti-Semite, in mock-innocence: "Mr. Ford, are you Jewish?"[8]

The second incident took place at the Wardell Hotel where Kahlo and Rivera were residing during their Detroit sojourn.[9] After discovering that the hotel barred Jews from its premises, both artists declared that they had "Jewish blood" and threatened to leave at once. The hotel management had no choice but to change the discriminatory regulations.[10]

Another demonstration of Kahlo's awareness of the Jewish problem, particularly in the 1930s, was her support for an exhibition of portraits of Jews by Lionel Reiss which took place in New York City in 1933.

The stated purpose of this show was to emphatically refute Nazi racial theories pertaining to the supposed inferiority of Jews. The endorsement of Kahlo and her husband is documented by a photograph of the couple attending the opening of the show.[11]

To be sure, neither Kahlo nor her father ever were practicing Jews. In fact, shortly before her death the artist wrote in her journal that, as a dedicated communist, she "rejects all religions."[12] Yet this ideological statement notwithstanding, a close look at her art reveals that Kahlo's sense of religiosity and spirituality was much more complex.[13]

In the present context, a brief review of several aspects of the artist's relationship to her Jewish heritage will suffice. Like many other twentieth century Mexican artists, Kahlo embraced "Mexicanidad" and, accordingly, integrated non-European, Mexican motifs into her art and life. Her espousal of pre-Columbian "idols" and popular Mexican religious art is usually viewed as a non-religious, political statement of national commitment.[14]

The artist's use of Christian symbols has been variously interpreted by those close to her and by scholars. As Kahlo's youthful letters reveal, her early Catholic upbringing, under the stern tutelage of her devout mother, clearly did not subside even when she was a teenager.[15] Isolde Piñedo Kahlo, the artist's

---

[7]   Wilhelm Kahlo was born in Baden-Baden, Germany in 1872. The original spelling of the name may have been "Kuhlo," writes Martha Zamora, *El pincel de la angustia* (Mexico, 1987), 8. In 1891, following his mother's death and his father's remarriage, Wilhelm emigrated to Mexico. Three years later he married Maria Cardeña who bore him two daughters, Maria Luisa (b. 1894) and Margarita (b.1898). Maria Cardeña died during childbirth, and very shortly afterwards, on 21 February 1898, Kahlo married Matilde Calderón (1876–1932). As soon as they were married, Matilde sent her step-daughters away to a convent school. Wilhelm and Matilde had five daughters of their own, four of whom survived. They are Matilde (1898–1951), Adriana (1902–1968), Frida (1907–1954) and Cristina (1908–1964). "Herr Kahlo," as Frida used to call her father affectionately, died in 1941. See Zamora, 190.

[8]   Herrera, *Frida*, 135.

[9]   Kahlo and Rivera arrived in Detroit on 21 April 1932, as Rivera was commissioned to paint the walls of the courtyard of the Detroit Institute of Art. Rivera completed the murals on 13 March 1933, whereupon Rivera and Kahlo left for New York. For exact chronological data, see *Diego Rivera: A Retrospective* (Detroit, New York and London, 1986), 79–85.

[10]   Herrera, *Frida*, 134. It was Lucienne Bloch who reported these incidents to Herrera. Bloch was Rivera's assistant at the time and became a close friend of Kahlo's. Perhaps her own Jewish consciousness — she is the daughter of the great Jewish composer

Ernest Bloch — made her aware of other people's Jewish identification.

[11]   *Rivera Retrospective*, 86, fig. 181.

[12]   Frida Kahlo's journal is a brownish-red leather bound volume with the initials JK inscribed in gold on the cover. According to Martha Zamora, the book once belonged to John Keats and was picked up in New York by a friend of Kahlo's (Zamora, 227–237, also see Herrera, *Frida*, 263.) Kahlo began to write the journal in the 1940s. Most of the entries are not dated. Some of the original pages have been cut out. In its present form, the diary contains 161 unnumbered pages and is locked in a display case at La Casa Azul — the Blue House that was Kahlo's home and is today the Frida Kahlo Museum. I would like to thank Dolores Olmedo, Director of the Museum, for allowing me to conduct my research and take photographs at La Casa Azul.

[13]   This topic is discussed in detail in my doctoral dissertation.

[14]   See, for example, Janice Helland, "Aztec Imagery in Frida Kahlo's Paintings," *Woman's Art Journal* 11.2 (Fall 1990 Winter 1991), 8–13.

[15]   Matilde Calderón, a devout Catholic, tried to raise her daughters as Catholics and subsequently sent them to a convent school. The influence of Frida's Catholic upbringing is evident in Kahlo's youthful letters to her boyfriend, Alejandro Gómez Arias. On 15 December 1922 she writes: "the only thing that as a friend I advise you is to have enough strength of will to support such

niece, insists that even as an adult Kahlo remained "basically, underneath the Communist rhetoric, always Catholic."[16]

In his study of Kahlo's 1937 painting *Memory*, Salomon Grimberg offers a slightly different view of this issue. A psychiatrist by profession, Grimberg stresses the connection between early childhood beliefs and their imprint on the adult's psyche and argues that Kahlo's use of Christian symbols exposes that, her rational view of herself as an atheist notwithstanding, her deep internal feeling for Catholicism never totally subsided.[17]

Kahlo's Judaism is a different story. In the strict sense of Jewish law Frida Kahlo was not Jewish, as her mother was not a Jew.[18] However, according to the laws that dominated European society during the artist's adult life — the racist laws of Nazism — Kahlo certainly was Jewish. She was well aware of the fact that, had she been living in various parts of Europe during the 1930s and 1940s, she too would have been considered a member of the Jewish faith and as such would have shared the "Jewish fate" as well. Many of Kahlo's Jewish friends report that the artist often spoke of herself as "half-Jewish." After Hitler's rise to power, Kahlo is reported to have been deeply concerned not only about Nazism in general, but specifically about her Jewish relatives who apparently still resided in the vicinity of Baden-Baden.[19]

Indeed, although far removed from practicing Judaism, evidence points to the fact that Kahlo was interested in her Jewish roots and viewed them as part of her "genealogical identity." Traces of this covert identity may be found in at least two major paintings by the artist. As will be shown, it is no coincidence that both were produced in the shadow of Nazism.

Family Tree

In 1936 Frida Kahlo painted a small work entitled *My Grandparents, My Parents and I* (Fig. 1). Now in New York's Museum of Modern Art, it is her only surviving work of 1936, probably one of a total of two paintings she produced that year.[20] Kahlo's scanty output in 1936 was due to several reasons. First, she spent part of the year at the British Hospital in Mexico City, recovering from foot surgery.[21] Secondly, much of the rest of her time was devoted to the affairs of her husband, Diego Rivera. According to Rivera's biographer, Bertram Wolfe, who spent most of 1936 in Mexico and was in daily contact with the couple, Kahlo and Rivera were closer than ever that year, following a period of estrangement during which Rivera had an affair with Kahlo's younger sister Cristina.[22] Wolfe reports that during this period,

pains as God Our Father sends us as a test given the fact that we came into the world to suffer"; quoted in Herrera, *Frida*, 34. But Frida's father insisted that his favorite daughter should receive different instruction: he sent her to the German school, and later to the National Preparatory School, where she acquired a broader, more humanistic education. Consequently, Frida became fluent in English and German and quickly began to abandon Catholicism. In a letter written on 1 January 1924, tell-tale signs of Kahlo's growing religious scepticism can be traced. She writes: "This morning I took communion and prayed to God for all of you... Imagine, yesterday I went to confession in the afternoon, and I forgot three sins and I took communion that way and the sins were big, now let's see, what shall I do, but the thing is that I have begun not to believe in confession and although I might want to, I cannot confess my sins well"; quoted in Herrera, *Frida*, 38–39. I was fortunate to meet Alejandro Gómez Arias, Kahlo's life-long friend, in Mexico before his death. He kindly allowed me to make copies of Kahlo's letters to him and shared his memories of her with me.

16 Isolde Piñedo Kahlo, private interview, Mexico, March, 1989.

17 Salomon Grimberg, "Frida Kahlo's *Memory*: The Piercing of the Heart by the Arrow of Divine Love," *Woman's Art Journal* 11.2 (Fall 1990/Winter 1991), 3–7, esp. 6, n. 1.

18 According to Jewish Halakha, a person is a Jew if born to a Jewish mother or if properly converted.

19 It is interesting to note in this connection, that in the aftermath of the first World War, Kahlo also voiced concern about her German relatives with whom contact had been temporarily lost. In a letter to Alician Gómez Arias, for example, she writes: "Estoy haciendo por averiguar la dirección de una hermana de mí papá que vive en Pforzheim, estado de Baden... Dudo un poco de que pueda conseguirla porque hace ya mucho tiempo que no sabemos de la familia de mi papá, por la guerra." Quoted in Raquel Tibol, *Frida Kahlo: Una Vida Abierta* (Mexico, 1983), 44. As can be imagined, during World War II, the Kahlo family was concerned about their relatives who still resided in Germany.

20 Herrera writes that a now lost Self-Portrait was painted for Dr. Leo Eloesser that year as well, Herrera, *Frida*, 194. Kahlo mentions this portrait in an unpublished letter to Leo Eloesser, her friend and physician, dated "17 de Diciembre de 1936." At the edge of the second page of this two-page, typed letter, Kahlo adds a handwritten message: "Ya terminé la pinturita que Ud me pidio (mi autoretrato)."

21 According to the Begun medical record, Kahlo had her third foot operation that year. Also see Wolfe, *The Fabulous Life*, 306.

22 Wolfe, 356–361. Kahlo's close collaboration with Rivera may also be deduced from her letters of 1936 to Bertram and Ella Wolfe. Many of these letters form part of the Wolfe Collection at the archives of the Hoover Institution on War, Revolution and Peace. I thank Marylin B. Kann of the Hoover archives for her kind assistance. On Rivera's affair with Cristina Kahlo see Herrera, *Frida*, 179–191.

Kahlo was intimately involved with all of Rivera's undertakings. In addition to his paintings, Rivera was working on several literary projects: two joint ventures with Wolfe: a biography of the artist and a book entitled *Portrait of Mexico*,[23] as well as illustrations for a book of Yiddish poems by Isaac Berliner entitled שטאט פון פאלאצן (Shtut fun Palatsn).[24]

Three years after completing *My Grandparents, My Parents and I*, Kahlo met Parker Lesley, a young curator from the United States, who interviewed her at La Casa Azul (the Blue House), her Coyoacàn home. In her characteristically straightforward manner, Kahlo described the painting to the visitor as representing

> me in the middle of this house, when I was about two years old. The whole house is in perspective as I remember it. On top of the house in the clouds are my father and mother when they were married (portraits taken from photographs). The ribbon about me and my mother's waist becomes an umbilical cord and I become a foetus. On the right, the paternal grandparents, on the left the maternal grandparents. A ribbon circles all the group — symbolic of the family relation. The German grandparents are symbolized by the sea, the Mexican by the earth.[25]

The painting was exhibited at Kahlo's first one-woman show at New York's Julien Levy Gallery in November of 1938.[26] Listed in the exhibition catalogue as *My Family*, it was hailed in an article written in conjunction with the show as "an amusing family tree."[27] Some four decades later, this basic interpretation was reiterated by leading Kahlo scholar Hayden Herrera, who characterized the work as a "delightfully whimsical" representation of the artist's family.[28] Its

humor and charm notwithstanding, I propose that this is a serious and key work, that merits further attention.

The Preparatory Sketch

Before examining the final painted version of Kahlo's 1936 "family tree," a look at a pencil drawing of identical size — apparently a preparatory sketch for the painting — may offer a unique view of the artist's creative process (Fig. 2).[29] At the top right corner of the sketch, Kahlo drew and clearly labelled portraits of her paternal grandparents, Henriette Kaufmann and Jakob Kahlo. The two portraits are set against a map of the European continent which includes Germany. A tricolored flag also appears in the background. Since this is a monochrome pencil sketch, one can only assume that the colors of the banner were intended to be the black, red and yellow of the German flag.[30] The names of Kahlo's paternal grandparents are written in bold letters between two lines that form a setting for the portraits. From these, a perpendicular label with the name "Guillermo Kahlo" descends and leads to a portrait of Kahlo's father. Symmetrically, on the left side of the composition, Kahlo sketched portraits of Antonio Calderón and Isabel González, her maternal progenitors, with the map and flag of Mexico behind them. The symbolic lines that mark their union and bear their names lead to a portrait of Kahlo's mother, whose name — Matilde Calderón — is also clearly inscribed.

Below Kahlo's paternal ancestors is an incomplete sketch of a camera. Kahlo's father was a photographer by profession and the camera was his unmistakable attribute.[31] Below the camera, at the bottom right-hand

[23] Bertram D. Wolfe, *Diego Rivera, His Life and Times* (New York and London, 1939); Diego Rivera and Bertram D. Wolfe, *Portrait of Mexico* (New York, 1938).

[24] יצחק בערלינער, "שטאט פון פאלאצן" (מעקסיקע, 1936). Isaac Berliner, *La Ciudad de los Palacios* (Mexico, 1936).

[25] A typed transcript of Parker Lesley's six-page, unpublished interview with Kahlo is among the papers at the Frida Kahlo Museum. A photocopy of the original is in Hayden Herrera's archive. I thank her for making it available to me.

[26] The painting was listed as the seventh entry in the catalogue and titled *My Family*. New York, Julien Levy Gallery, *Frida Kahlo (Frida Rivera)*, 1–13 November [1938]. The "catalogue" is a yellow fold-out sheet with a list of 25 paintings on one side and André Breton's essay on Kahlo, entitled "Préface," printed in French, on the other side.

[27] Bertram D. Wolfe, "Rise of Another Rivera," *Vogue*, 1 Nov. 1938, 131.

[28] Herrera, *Frida*, 8–9.

[29] Kahlo left the drawing unsigned until she gave it to a friend in 1943, whereupon she signed and dated it "Frida Kahlo 1943." The drawing was put up for auction by Christie's on behalf of the original owner in November 1990. See Christie's *Latin American Paintings, Drawings and Sculpture*, New York, November 1990, 134. I thank Vivian Pfeiffer of Christie's for her kind assistance.

[30] Actually, two tricolored flags appear in the drawing. There are two possible explanations for this. The most likely explanation to my mind is, that Kahlo was experimenting with the composition, and since this was merely a preparatory sketch she did not bother to erase the "pentimento." Another reason might be that the second flag was intended to be the Hungarian flag (with its red, white and green stripes and superimposed emblem), since Kahlo's paternal grandparents were Hungarian-German Jews.

[31] The camera reappears as Wilhelm Kahlo's attribute in a 1951 portrait that Frida painted of her father. *Das Gesamtwerk*, fig. 123.

Fig. 2. Frida Kahlo, Preparatory sketch for My Grandparents, My Parents, and I (Family Tree), *1936. Pencil on paper, 12 1/8" ×" 13 3/4", Courtesy of Christie's. New York.*

corner of the composition, the artist drew a school of sperm, symbolizing her father's contribution to her conception and being. At the bottom left side of the composition — the maternal side — a huge egg cell in the process of being penetrated by a large sperm is carefully drawn.

In the preparatory sketch, as in the final painting, Kahlo's parents are placed at the center of the composition. As Kahlo herself said, this double portrait was copied from the couple's 1898 wedding photograph

(Fig. 3). A rough outline of a fetus appears to be attached to Matilde's waist. Below Guillermo's portrait, the patio of La Casa Azul is delineated. A small seated child — presumably Frida as a toddler — sits within.

The preparatory sketch for *My Grandparents, My Parents and I* reveals Kahlo's initial sources of inspiration and some of the ideas that were on her mind in 1936. Most importantly, the lines that label and connect the various family members form a pattern which

Fig. 3. *Guillermo Kahlo, Wedding photograph of Guillermo Kahlo and Matilde Calderón, 1898. Courtesy of CENIDIAP-INBA, Mexico.*

is clearly based on schematic genealogical charts. The planned cartographical background emphasizes the fact that Guillermo and Matilde's union was the result of intermarriage. Hence, Frida Kahlo herself is shown as the product of mixed heritage.

Daughter of Intermarriage

Visual depictions of intermarriage were not unprecedented in Mexican art. In Viceregal New Spain, for example, paintings of *Las Castas* were in great demand (Fig. 4). These works were used as "visual guides" to the various different castes, or offspring of intermarriages, which pervaded the Hispanic New World. This unique genre reappeared in eighteenth century academic art (for example in the paintings of

noted artist Miguel Cabrera), as well as in popular works, often by anonymous limners.[32] In a way, then, by stressing racial diversity, Kahlo's family tree offers a typically Mexican genealogy. The artist emphasized this aspect of her origins time after time, in her diary, in interviews and in all the "biographical sketches" she drafted. In a diary entry, written several months before her death and titled: "Esquema de mí vida," for example, she states:

My Hungarian paternal grandparents — born in Arad, Hungary — already married, went to live in Germany, where some of their children were born, among them my father, in Baden-Baden Germany — Guillermo Kahlo, Maria, Enriquita, Paula and others. He emigrated to Mexico in the 19th century, residing here always, all his life. He married a Mexican girl, mother of my "little" sisters Luisita and Margarita. Upon the very early death of his wife, he married my mother, Matilde Calderón y Gonzáles, daughter among 12 of my grandfather Antonio Calderón of Morelia of the indigenous Mexican Michoacan race and my grandmother, Isabel Gonzáles y Gonzáles, daughter of a Spanish general.[33]

Although Kahlo was well aware of the traditional Mexican mode of representing intermarriage, she chose to turn to a different source of inspiration in 1936, as she was attempting to give visual form to her concept of Self within family. This deliberate choice — to base her painting on contemporary genealogical charts — is highly significant and may be fully understood only within the historical context of the time.

Let us begin with the Nuremberg laws, decrees of racial discrimination issued at the end of 1935 by the Nazi government and geared to promote "racial purity." It goes without saying that, in Nazi terms, intermarriage was considered the most heinous of crimes. One important method of proving or disproving "racial purity" was the delineation of genealogical charts. These became a prominent tool in Nazi Germany.[34]

Repercussions of these racist laws resounded in Mexico. Within the German immigrant community,

[32] *Treasures of Mexico* (Los Angeles, 1978), 37, 121; and The Metropolitan Museum of Art, *Mexico: Splendors of Thirty Centuries* (New York, 1990), 432–433.

[33] This entry follows a three-page text that is dated "Abril 27 — 1954." The artist died on July 13, 1954, one week after her

47th birthday. Unless otherwise noted, I have used my own translations.

[34] Karl A. Scheleunes, *The Twisted Road to Auschwitz: Nazi Policy Toward German Jews 1933*–1939 (Chicago, 1970), 92–132, esp. 130.

Fig. 4. Anonymous, Las Castas, 18th century. Oil on Canvas, 58 1/4" × 40 15/16". Museo Nacional del Virreinato, Tepotzotlán, Mexico.

Nazi and anti-Nazi groups formed. By 1936, Nazi-oriented manuals on how to conduct "genealogical research" were introduced and distributed in the German School of Mexico City. Most of the school's teachers had joined the Nazi party and encouraged their students to sketch their "pure" origins and to chart their "family trees."[35]

Kahlo was profoundly aware of and concerned about these developments. In addition to her general anti-fascist stand — a position she shared with her

---

[35] Marianne O. de Bopp, "The Jewish Exile-Intelligentsia in Latin America as Exemplified by Mexico" in Hans-Bernhard Moeller, ed., *Latin America and the Literature of Exile* (Heidelberg, 1983), 113–136, 374–376, see esp. 119.

communist comrades — she had a special interest in these issues. She herself was of German descent, had attended the German school as a child, spoke and read German and, in her youth, immersed herself in German culture.[36] Furthermore, her German-born father had studied in the town of Nuremberg, as she often stressed, and many of his relatives still resided within the borders of the Third Reich.[37] Finally, according to Nazi laws, Kahlo was a Jew; in Nuremberg terms, "impure."

Thus, Kahlo's adaptation of the genealogical chart as a model for her "family tree" cannot be viewed as merely formal. Her deliberate inversion of the device recommended by her former German school teachers to prove *pureza de sangre*, in order to stress the opposite — her "impure" blood, must be viewed as an expression of her "mixed" origins and a reflection of her implicit identification with her Jewish heritage.

The Other Frida

In a 1943 essay about his wife entitled "Frida Kahlo and Mexican Art," Diego Rivera writes about the predominance of Kahlo's German heritage: "The German... genes of the father — prevailed" he wrote, "wiping out all of the Spanish and allying itself with the Indian genes of the mother."[38] Rivera's comment may seem curious at first, given Kahlo's emphatically expressed Mexicanidad. However, certain psychological factors pertaining to the artist's complex relationship with her parents may explain the profound truth contained in Rivera's statement.

In both the painting and the sketch for *My Grandparents, My Parents and I* Kahlo reveals significant aspects of her relationship with her parents. Kahlo paints her fetus-self on top of her mother's white wedding dress in the general vicinity of Matilde's abdomen. The fetus is based on medical drawings from a book on obstetric medicine by Francis Ramsbotham, which the artist owned (Fig. 5).[39] The fetus is attached by its umbilical cord to a large white bow fastened to the mother's waist. Kahlo's mother is shown here as the provider of the necessary biological "life-line" that enabled Kahlo to enter this world.[40]

But the child-self — that is, Kahlo as a conscious human entity, capable of thinking and making choices — is clearly situated on her father's side. The patio of La Casa Azul — the home the father built for his family — forms a protective womb-like shelter for the little girl, who is literally and figuratively close to her father's bosom.

This visual depiction of Kahlo's relationship to her parents is in accordance with other data about the artist's familial situation. The issue has been dealt with in depth by both Herrera and Grimberg; both offer conclusive evidence that, while her feelings towards her mother were ambivalent if not outright hostile, Frida Kahlo adored her father. She too was his favorite daughter.[41]

---

36 Alejandro Gómez Arias recalled that Guillermo Kahlo sent Frida to the German school of Mexico City despite the objections of Matilde. Later, Kahlo entered the National Preparatory School, apparently because the tuition at the German School was too high. Gómez Arias, private interview and Herrera, *Frida*, 452. Kahlo's affinity with German culture is discussed in detail in my Phd dissertation. One often overlooked example is Kahlo's given name. As her birth certificate indicates, Frida Kahlo was born Magdalena Frida Carmen Kahlo (a copy of the birth certificate is found at the CeNIDIAP archives). Except for a brief period when Rivera tried to convince her to use the name Carmen, Kahlo always used her German name, Frida. Moreover, at various times in her life she further Germanized her name by adding the letter "e" and spelling it "Frieda." Many of her letters to Leo Eloesser, Lucienne Bloch and Ella Wolfe are signed "Frieda." Quite a few of her paintings, drawings, a fresco and an etching are also signed thus. See *Das Gesamtwerk*, figs. 2, 6, 16, 29, 38, 51, 146, 152, 153, 179, 261b. Kahlo also emphasized her knowledge of the German language. Her first self-portrait, for example, includes a German caption on the back of the canvas "HEUTE IST IMMER NOCH" (see *Das Gesamtwerk*, p. 231); her diary includes a German quote from Brecht's *Three Penny Opera*; her library contains many German books.
37 Tibol, *Una Vida Abierta*, 32.
38 "El Alemán analista constructo-destructor y escéptico alucinado — los genes del padre — prevaleció, limpiándolo, contra todo lo español y aliándose a lo indio — genes de la madre." Diego Rivera, "Frida Kahlo y el Arte Mexicano," *Boletín del Seminario de Cultura Mexicana* 1.2 (October, 1943), 99.
39 William V. Keating, ed., Francis H. Ramsbotham, *The Principles and Practice of Obstetric Medicine and Surgery in Reference to the Process of Parturition (with 64 plates and numerous woodcuts)* (Philadelphia, 1865), plate 53, fig. 2.
40 It is interesting to note that Kahlo's other depiction of her mother, a painting entitled *My Birth* (*Das Gesamtwerk*, fig. 37) also emphasizes the biological function of parturition. The face of Kahlo's mother is covered with a sheet, while her body, viewed from an obstetric angle, is reduced to two legs and a vagina. The full significance of Kahlo's use of obstetric models to portray her mother is discussed in detail in my Phd dissertation.
41 See especially Salomon Grimberg's catalogue essay in Dallas, The Meadows Museum, *Frida Kahlo*, February 17–April 16, 1989. Tibol quotes Kahlo as saying that she looked like both her parents: "Yo me parezo físicamente a los dos. Tengo los ojos de mi padre y el cuerpo de mi madre" (I physically resemble both. I have my father's eyes and my mother's body). Tibol, *Una Vida Abierta*, 35. Yet in *My Grandparents, My Parents and I*, Kahlo stresses her resemblance to her paternal grandmother. This is especially true in the drawing.

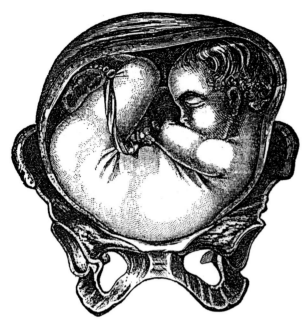

Fig. 5.   Plate 53, fig. 2 from William V. Keating ed., Francis H. Romsbotham, The Principles and Practice of Obstetric Medicine and Surgery in Reference to the Process of Parturition, Philadelphia, 1865.

In a typical passage in her diary Kahlo writes: My childhood was marvelous although my father was a sick man (had vertigoes every month and a half). He was an immense example for me of tenderness, work (photographer as well as painter) and above all of understanding all my problems.

Such is Kahlo's love for her father, that even one of the greatest drawbacks of his life, the illness that dominated and limited his existence, was not considered by the doting daughter a disadvantage that might diminish the "marvelousness" of her childhood. Rather, as other texts reveal, in Kahlo's eyes, it was precisely the illness that supplied proof of her

father's will-power, courage and ability to overcome hardships; it provided an opportunity for the daughter to spend more time with her father; and finally, it became a point of contact and identification between Guillermo and Frida: both individuals were, to a large extent, shaped by their physical disabilities, which became defining factors of their selfhood.[42]

Understanding Kahlo's deep attachment to her father and profound empathy for him, juxtaposed with her negative emotions towards her mother, illuminates the artist's complex and conflicting systems of identification. The deeper we probe this issue the clearer it becomes that beneath the overt layers of Mexicanidad, Kahlo — at some level — always maintained a view of herself as "other." This self-image was, to a large extent, shaped by the artist's strong personal identification with her father, who remained forever an outsider. For although Wilhelm officially became Guillermo, he never really success-fully integrated into Mexican society. All visitors to La Casa Azul in Coyoacàn observed his pronounced "otherness": his unmistakable heavy German accent; the separate "cultural" world he constructed for him-self, filled with European music (the Blue Danube was a favorite), German literature and philosophy.[43]

To be sure, his daughter, Frida, eventually became the epitome of Mexicanidad: she deliberately spoke a "rough" colloquial Mexican vernacular; she drank pulque and demonstratively sang popular Mexican ballads known as "corridos"; she wholeheartedly de-clared her identity with "la raza" and accordingly immersed herself in all things indigenous.[44] But in spite of what, on the face of it, seems to be a great gap between the diametrically opposed cultural worlds of father and daughter, and in spite of Frida's sincere devotion to Mexican culture, never did she sever ties

[42] Kahlo's love for her father is expressed in two of her paintings. One is the 1951 portrait of Wilhelm she painted a decade after her father's death. The other is Kahlo's self-portrait of 1941, which shows her mourning for her father immediately after his death. The latter work is interpreted by Salomon Grimberg in his "Self-Portrait with Bonito," printed by Wolfe's Fine Arts Auctioneers in conjunction with their 19 September 1991 sale. Both works are dealt with in detail in my doctoral dissertation.

[43] Like most immigrants, Wilhelm Kahlo remained within his German milieu. Upon his arrival in Mexico City, he found a job as a cashier in the Cristaleria Loeb, a glassware store founded by Jewish German immigrants . Later he worked at a jewelry store called La Perla, owned by another German friend who had come to Mexico with him in 1891. Throughout his life Wilhelm had few friends. The two that Frida remembered

had strong German accents like Wilhelm himself. See Herrera, *Frida,* 4–8, 18–21.

[44] Kahlo's Mexicanness manifested itself in many other ways. For example, with Rivera she collected pre-Columbian sculpture, popular "retablos" as well as huge "Judas" figures. She decorated her house á-la-Mexicana and wore colorful indigenous costumes and jewelry. She even modified the year of her birth, exchanging 1907 for 1910, thus aligning her personal beginning with the emergence of post-revolution Mexico. This overt Mexicanidad bespeaks a pronounced, conscious effort to stress her love for her country. It could very well be that this extroverted espousal of all things Mexican is a deliberate, demonstrative attempt at belonging, typical of the child of immigrants and quite distinct from the "natural" sense of belonging which characterizes true natives, who often take their identity for granted.

Fig. 6. Henri Rousseau, The Present and the Past, 1899. The Barnes Foundation, Merion, Pennsylvania.

with her paternal European roots. She never could or perhaps never really wanted to reject her father's heritage. Thus, while Frida Kahlo's Mexican identity is exhibited wholeheartedly, with great frequency and with the ideological verve of a manifesto, her "other" identity is expressed implicitly, often through covert symbols. But the Frida who descended from Wilhelm is never far from the surface and she certainly never ceased to exist.

The Influence of Rousseau

Although Kahlo transferred the basic compositional structure of the preparatory drawing to the final painted version of, *My Grandparents, My Parents and I*, the few changes she did make are illuminating. One interesting alteration is the clear demarcation of the sky and the positioning of the grandparents' portraits on clouds. Kahlo probably derived this motif from the wedding photograph of Guillermo Kahlo and Matilde Calderón. Yet unlike their situation in the original wedding photograph, in the painting Kahlo's parents are not positioned "in the clouds." Rather, as Herrera observed, the artist placed her *grandparents'* portraits on "soft cumulus nests."[45] Herrera has suggested that Kahlo used the cloud motif simply because it "amused" her.

A close look at Kahlo's use of this motif points to the artist's indebtedness to an additional visual antecedent, Henri Rousseau's 1899 *The Present and the Past* (Fig. 6). The general stylistic affinity between Le Douanier and Kahlo has often been noted. Mac-Kinley Helm, a North American art historian who in December of 1939, to quote his own words, "had tea with Frida Kahlo de Rivera in the house where she was born," reported that, based on his conversations with the artist, "the modern painter Frida most admires is Henri Rousseau."[46] In conjunction with this comment, Helm cites Rousseau's *The Present and the Past* as an acknowledged visual source for Kahlo's *My Grandparents, My Parents and I*.[47] Yet although Kahlo herself pointed out this link, its full significance has thus far remained unexplored. I suggest that beyond the admitted stylistic influence of Rousseau, Kahlo also derived important conceptual

[45] See Herrera's analysis of the painting in *Frida*, 8–9.
[46] MacKinley Helm, *Modern Mexican Painters* (New York, 1968 [1941]), 167, 170.
[47] Ibid, 169–170.

ideas and themes from the French artist's painting.

Thematically, both *My Grandparents, My Parents and I* and *The Present and the Past* deal with Self, Family and Time.[48] Both works offer images that connect diverse aspects of the artists' past with their present Self. In this respect they are dynamic self-portraits that do not only depict the physical countenance of the artists at a given moment, but also their span of existence within time and space: their past, their familial relations, their place within a geo-social structure.

Both Rousseau and Kahlo utilize artistic conventions such as size, position and portrait-type (face, bust or full-length portraits) in order to visually conceptualize distinct time periods. Rousseau depicts a full-length portrait of himself and his current wife, Josephine, standing behind a flowering tree in a garden. Above the couple, in the sky, the artist's former bearded visage is set alongside the face of his first, deceased wife, Clemence, on fluffy clouds.

Similarly, Kahlo depicts herself as a child in a full-length nude portrait. She too is standing behind a tree in her Coyoacán garden. Above her, the immediate past is represented by her parents' busts, depicted at the time of their marriage. Still higher, in the sky above, and smaller in size, the faces of Kahlo's four grandparents appear on clouds.

Both works emphasize the matrimonial bond as the foundation of the family unit. Another feature common to both paintings is the presence of a blooming tree at a focal point of the composition. In both works the tree connotes the generic, literal idea of a "family tree." In Kahlo's work the tree may have additional meaning. The way she positioned her child-self behind the tree transforms the tree-trunk into a surrogate leg. This pose recalls Kahlo's childhood nickname "Frida pata de palo" (Frida peg-leg). This cruel epithet was given Kahlo as a result of a slight limp caused by the deformation of her right foot.[49]

Between Land and Sea

In addition to the tree and the clouds, Kahlo altered several other elements as she painted the final version of her "family tree." The artist transformed the schematic lines of the genealogical chart, which appeared in the pencil drawing, into red ribbons that connote "blood-lines" or, as Kahlo herself explained, are "symbolic of the family relations." She also replaced the geographical maps and the national flags representing Mexico and Germany with more generalized symbols, the land and the sea. Finally, next to the inseminated egg cell, Kahlo added a womb-like cactus flower in the act of pollination.

These motifs — which were to become recurring symbolic elements in Kahlo's oeuvre — make their initial appearance in this painting. In general terms, they transform the more schematic aspects of the genealogical chart and the blunt national references into more subtle, metaphoric visual language. They also add to the theme of intermarriage the idea of immigration. Indeed, they are influenced by the Yiddish book of poetry by immigrant poet Isaac Berliner, *City of Palaces*, which Rivera was illustrating at the time.

Published in 1936 by Der Weg publishers, three copies of this book are to this day in Kahlo's library. Kahlo was introduced to the poems of Berliner by Diego Rivera who befriended the Yiddish poet and drew a portrait of him as early as 1934.[50] Rivera's collaboration with Berliner involved the translation of the Yiddish texts into Spanish so as to enable the visual artist to draw appropriate illustrations for the poems.

The texts themselves offer a prime example of acculturation. The poems speak emphatically of Mexico — its past and present — but they do so in the language of the "old country." A glossary provided at the end of the volume constitutes a poignant manifestation of the merging of cultures: "Mexican" terms or idioms, which encapsulate untranslatable local ideas, flavors

---

48 A full analysis of these issues is presented in my Phd dissertation. In the present study I shall limit my discussion.

49 Herrera claims that it was caused by a bout with polio when she was six years old; *Frida*, 14. Tibol quotes Kahlo as making this claim: "A los seis años tuve poliomielitis." Tibol, *Una Vida Abierta*, 36. According to Kahlo's medical records which were compiled by Dr. Henriette Begun in 1946, Kahlo bumped her right foot against a tree trunk and subsequently the limb became slightly deformed; Begun medical record and Tibol, *Una Vida Abierta*, 17. In any case, Kahlo's right calf was thinner and weaker than her healthy limb and her foot gave her much trouble

throughout her life. In 1934 the artist had her first foot operation which was followed by numerous other treatments and surgery. In fact, at the time she was painting *My Grandparents, My Parents and I*, she was recuperating from her third operation. Finally, in 1953, the artist's right leg was amputated below the knee. In the 1936 painting — as in subsequent works that allude to Kahlo's ailing limb — the left leg, not the right one, is represented as the troubled one. This, I believe, is because in most of her self-portraits, she painted her mirror-image.

50 The portrait is reproduced in Berliner, 11.

and values, are transliterated into Hebrew characters and defined in Yiddish.[51] The poems themselves incorporate the Yiddish-spelled Mexican terms — fusing the two cultures in verse.

In the introduction to the volume, M. Rosenberg offers a poetics of immigration:

Winds are not always evil. Often they are carriers of fertile seeds across hundreds of miles.

Sometimes you see a flower in the desert and you wonder: who brought it here? how did this beautiful plant come to such a place?

It was the wind that had uprooted it from its home and had brought it hither. And here, in the desert of all places, the seed grew and bloomed, becoming even more beautiful than the flowers back home.[52]

In this metaphoric text Rosenberg makes a general reference to the newly arrived Jewish immigrants in Mexico and to Isaac Berliner in particular. The poet himself dedicates his opening poem to the very same theme: his own immigration and absorption in the new land. The six-page poem, entitled, "On This Side of the Sea", stresses his voyage across the ocean to the land of Mexico, from a European past to a present identification with a new land. Each stanza of the poem begins with the line: "On this side of the sea," stressing the land-sea dichotomy; the final one culminates with a symbol of successful replanting: "On this side of the sea / My tree trunk is already deeply rooted in the land."[53]

With these texts in mind — as they were on Kahlo's mind while she was painting, *My Grandparents, My Parents and I* — let us look once again at the final version of her "family tree." For the first time in her oeuvre, the artist explicitly deals with her father's immigration. Her paternal ancestors clearly originate from the "other side of the sea." Guillermo Kahlo's head is set against a divided background of land and sea: he is visualized as an immigrant, split between

two countries, the old and the new. It is his daughter who completes the process of acculturation. Translating the two metaphors of Berliner's book into visual images, Kahlo presents herself as both flower and tree. The cactus flower, fertilized by the wind-carried pollen from across the sea, is Frida Kahlo herself. Using Rosenberg's metaphor, she represents herself as the newly grown flower of the desert.[54] And finally, the tree that is painted as the artist's surrogate leg could very well be the "tree trunk" that is "rooted deep in the land" on "this side of the sea" — Kahlo's incorporation of Berliner's poetics of immigration into her art.

Thus, Kahlo's seemingly naive and whimsical depiction of her family turns out to be a multi-layered masterpiece with profound personal and cultural meaning. This seminal work provides a glimpse at Kahlo's own view of her complex identity, as she draws on visual, political and literary sources to depict an image of her Self.

The artist appears as a configuration of biological, cultural and environmental components. The "I" of *My Grandparents, My Parents and I* is made up of the egg and the sperm containing racial or genetic factors which produce a "Self" from the fusion of genetic matter from European, Spanish and Indian progenitors. The "I" is also shown as the product of place, a being — flower, tree, child — implanted in the Mexican soil of Coyoacán, after, metaphorically, voyaging from "the other side of the sea." The "I" is a being whose identity is shaped in early childhood within the Oedipal constellation, between father and mother. Kahlo is the girl-child who is protected by her father. With the unabashed nudity of a child, she gazes boldly at the past, the present and the future. Her destiny is determined by various factors, among them her family relations. These include her Jewish roots.

[51] Berliner, 205–207.

[52] ווינטן זענען נישט אלע מאל אן אנשיקעניט. אפט זענען זיי טרעגער פון פרוכטבארע זוימען, וועמען ווינטן פארטראגן אויף הונדערטער מיילן ווייט. זעסט אמאל א בלום אין א וויסטעניש און וואונדערסט זיך: ווער האט זי געבראכט אהער און פון וואנען קומט זי, די שיינע פלאנץ אין אזא ארט? — דער ווינט האט זי אויסגעריסן פון איר היים און זי פארשלייידעט אהער. און דא, דווקא _אין דער וויסטעניש, איז זי זיך צעוואקסן, האט זיך צעבליט שענער און פולער ווי די פלאנצן פון איר היים.

[53] The poem, called "אויף דער זייט ים", appears on pp. 17–22. The final stanza opens thus: אויף דער זייט ים / האב איר טיף שוין פארוואורצלט מיין שטאם.(p. 22).

[54] Herrera interprets the flower as "another scene of fecundation,"

Herrera, *Frida*, 8. My suggestion that the flower is a symbolic portrayal of Kahlo herself is reinforced by the fact that in 1938 and 1939 Kahlo signed several letters with the name Xochitl, which means flower in Nahuatl; Cesar Macazaga Ordoña, *Diccionario de la Lengua Nahuatl* (Mexico, 1979), 115. This was the nickname she used during her affair with Nickolas Muray. Kahlo also painted a symbolic self-portrait of herself as a flower, entitled *Xochitl: Flower of Life*, reproduced in *Das Gesamtwerk*, fig. 57. Copies of Kahlo's letters to Muray are in Herrera's archive. I thank her for making them available to me.

Testimony of a Library

Isaac Berliner's book of Yiddish poems was not the only Jewish book that Kahlo owned. Nor is it the only literary source that influenced the artist's visual imagery. Yet neither Kahlo's interest in her Jewish roots nor the literary and historical dimension of her art have ever been fully investigated. One reason for this oversight may be that while Rivera is always thought of as a painter of history, Kahlo, by contrast, has thus far been considered a "personal" painter, whose profound physical and emotional suffering clouded her interest in the outside world. Rivera is portrayed as a man of the world; Kahlo, as his "self-absorbed," invalid wife.

Yet Kahlo's books tell another story; her library reflects an intense interest in history. Indeed, in her journal she herself writes: "I have read the history of my country and of almost all the peoples."[55] The many volumes that are encased behind the locked glass doors of the wooden bookcases of her Coyoacán home sketch a revealing portrait of the artist's mental world and intellectual pursuits. Even if one takes into account, as one must, the fact that the library does not contain all the books she had read, borrowed or loaned, and, conversely, that perhaps some of the books on the shelves remained unread or were unsolicited gifts — without a doubt the library does have a story to tell.[56]

Many of the titles we encounter on the shelves re-affirm Kahlo's known interests. The numerous books on Mexico — its histories, customs, languages, literature, art, songs and people — testify to the depth of the artist's interest in her country. The literature she amassed spans diverse periods and epochs: pre-Columbian, Colonial, Viceregal, Revolutionary and contemporary. It covers many genres: historical research, fiction, poetry, songs, dictionaries, bi-

ographies, photo-documents, archival material, folklore and other modes of reportage.

Kahlo's interest in the arts is also broader than ever acknowledged. Her feigned anti-intellectualism and "primitif" pose cannot veil the wealth of material she had collected in the form of books and catalogues pertaining to the art of the world. From prehistorical painting to the contemporary art world; from Europe to America, from Oceania to Africa, Kahlo's library contains books and reproductions of all the accepted canonical artworks and numerous other creations of art.

Not surprising in substance, though perhaps in scope and quantity, Kahlo owned dozens of tomes dealing with the Soviet Union and other aspects of communism. The writings of Marx, Lenin and Stalin fill many shelves of her library, and she explicitly states in her diary that she read and re-read all of these books, thus underscoring the seriousness of her commitment to her political convictions.

Kahlo's library also attests to her continuing interest in literature, both popular and "classical," prose as well as poetry. Her somewhat eclectic taste produced a vast collection of world literature by North American, British, Russian, Spanish, Mexican, French and German writers.[57] However, on the wooden shelves of Kahlo's library, a group of "other" books unravel a different tale. It is not the obvious story of the Mexican, communist, artist. It is a narrative told from the margins.

The "Potro"

Among the group of "other" books, the two volumes of Alfonso Toro's *La Familia Carvajal* occupy a special place. Toro's books provide, as the subtitle explicitly states, "an historical study of the Jews and the Inquisition of New Spain in the sixteenth cen-

[55] This entry is dated November 1952. Kahlo writes "He leido la historia de mi país y de casi todos los pueblos."
[56] My detailed study of Kahlo's library is related methodologically to research conducted by proponents of "the social history of ideas," particularly to the work of Robert Darnton; for example, see his "Reading, Writing, and Publishing" in Robert Darnton, *The Literary Underground of the Old Regime* (London, 1982), 167–208, 236–250.
[57] According to the testimony of her friends, Kahlo was an avid reader even in her youth. See, for example, Alejandro Gómez Arias, "Un testimonio sobre Frida Kahlo," in Mexico, Sala Nacional — Palacio de Bellas Artes — Instituto Nacional de

Bellas Artes, *Frida Kahlo: Exposicion Nacional de Homenaje*, Septiembre-Noviembre, 1977, unpaged. "Leía incansablemente. No solamente la biblioteca del padre sino cuanto tenían en sus manos sus compañeros." It should be noted that, unlike Rivera, Kahlo was fluent in both German and English and read in both languages. While some of the books in La Casa Azul belonged to both Rivera and Kahlo, most were Kahlo's. Even when Kahlo was alive, Rivera spent much of his time in his San Angel studio. After her death, Rivera remarried and moved permanently out of the Coyoacán home. All the books discussed in this essay belonged to Kahlo herself.

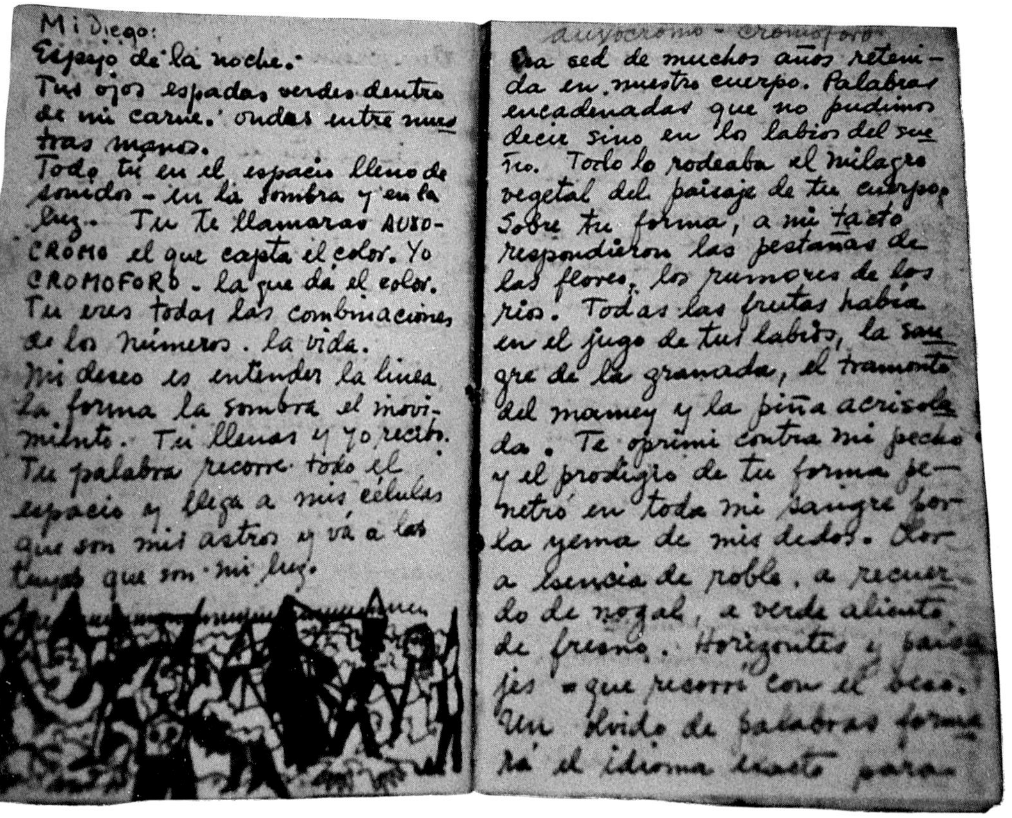

Fig. 7. Frida Kahlo, Diary Entry (Fantasmas), 1944. Frida Kahlo Museum, Coyoacán, Mexico.

tury.''[58] The two volumes, published in 1944 after many years of research, give a detailed account of the history of the persecution of Jews by the Inquisition in Mexico. They include vivid descriptions of interrogation and torture as well as visual illustrations of the inquisitorial procedures.

Is there any significance to the fact that Kahlo owned these two volumes, or was her interest in the Jews of Mexico simply part of her general interest in her country? Furthermore, is there any evidence that the artist actually read the books or that their content affected her in any way? Several sound pieces of evidence — visual and textual — converge in the years 1944–1945 and bear witness to Kahlo's response

to the plight of the Carvajal Jews as recounted by Toro.

In 1944, several pages of Kahlo's diary are filled with words and phrases which are written in what appears to be a ''stream of consciousness'' mode.[59] To be sure, many of the words that appear in this text are common words that may be variously interpreted. But one word stands out, as it is not at all common and is, in fact, obsolete in twentieth century Mexican Spanish. Thus, this ''archaic'' word provides a key to understanding at least a few of Kahlo's thoughts, and consequently, as will be shown, some of her more cryptic visual images. The unusual word is ''potro.''

The ''potro'' is a term taken directly and specifically

---

58 Alfonso Toro, *La Familia Carvajal*, subtitled ''Estudio histórico sobre los judíos y la Inquisición de la Nueva España en el siglo XVI, basado en documentos originales y en su mayor parte inéditos, que se conservan en el Archivo General de la Nación de la ciudad de México'' (Mexico, 1944), 2 volumes.

59 It would be totally irresponsible to attempt to psychoanalyze Kahlo on the basis of this written ''free association session,'' but a textual analysis of these pages reveals certain perceptible connections between the words. Some words are clearly opposites:

''luna, sol''; some are alliterations: ''amor, amarillo''; others provide rhymes: ''año, estaño.'' Certain words seem to point to deeper aspects of Kahlo's psyche, as, for example, she mentions both her parents in different contexts. Teresa del Conde relates this text to the Surrealist movement; see Teresa del Conde, ''La Pintora Frida Kahlo,'' *Surrealisme en Mexico*, Artes Visuales 4, Revista Trimestral, Museo del Arte Moderno, Mexico, Octubre/Diciembre de 1974, 1–5 [English translation 45–46].

Fig. 8.   Auto Inquisitorial, from Anales de la Inquisitión. Madrid, 1841, ill. 13.

from the Inquisition torture chamber.[60] It is a wooden, ladder-like torture device, which is mentioned and illustrated throughout Alfonso Toro's *La Familia Carvajal*.[61] Several pages after Kahlo's "potro" text, a small seemingly undecipherable drawing appears at the bottom of an unrelated text in the artist's diary (Fig. 7). Kahlo labels this tiny sketch "fantasmas," i.e. ghosts. In the drawing, a row of strangely costumed and hooded figures either march or stand in line. These "ghosts," as Kahlo calls them, with their cone-shaped hoods and processional pose can only be understood in comparison with well-known illustrations of the

Inquisition's "auto de fé" (Fig. 8). Kahlo's "ghosts" — spirits from the past — are the "Sambenitos" who were punished and humiliated by the Inquisition.[62]

A separate drawing, done by Kahlo coincidently with the above-mentioned journal entries, provides further evidence that Toro's book and the topic it brought up had an impact on the artist (Fig. 9). Titled "Fantasía" — or should it be "Fantasma"? — the drawing depicts a dismembered foot, which hovers in the sky above. Near it a funnel appears. Below, tears are shed from the large eye turned clock. Orbs, roots, veins and a smaller funnel are also suspended in

---

[60] The entire line appears thus: "Año, estaño, otro potro." The first word, "año" (year), evokes the concept of time. Additional allusions to time recur throughout this word list, specifically words connecting the past with the present, such as "hoy" (today) and "ayer" (yesterday). The second word, "estaño" (tin), is a rhyming association, but also the material upon which Kahlo painted most of her paintings since 1932. "Otro" is the Spanish word for "another." "Otro potro" would then translate into "another torture bed."

[61] Toro describes the "potro" thus: "En la Inquisición de México era éste una especie de camilla inclinada, como de dos metros

de largo por menos de uno de ancho en la parte superior, anchura que iba en diminución hasta no medir sino sesenta centímetros en la parte de abajo. Esta camilla tenía varios travesaños en forma de escalera, de tal suerte dispuestos que entre ellos pudiera meterse el cuerpo del reo, para que todos los travesaños susoidchos, pero especialmente los que quedaban junto a las espinillas, le atormentaran dolorosamente." I, 285. See also 294, note 14, claiming another name for the "potro" was "escalera" (ladder) or "burro" the Mexican term for stepladder.

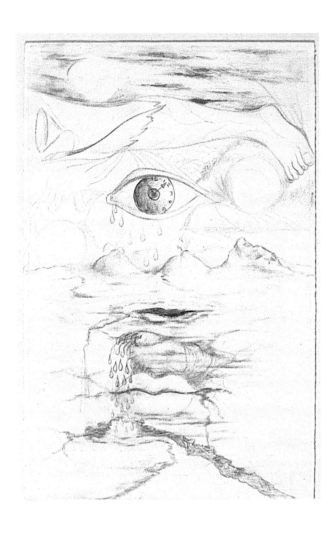

Fig. 9. Frida Kahlo, Fantasía, 1944. Pencil and colored pencil on paper, 9.4" × 6.2". Dolores Olmedo Foundation, Mexico.

Fig. 10. Inquisition torture from Alfonso Toro, La Familia Carvajal. Mexico, 1944, vol. I, p. 280.

the sky. The bottom portion of the drawing is made up of land and sea. The tortured head of a woman and her two breasts seem to float above the water. The rest of the drawing is unclear. Two pairs of lips seem to emerge from a watery foreground.[63]

The face of the tormented woman in Kahlo's 1944 drawing, with her protruding chin and her head violently thrown back, is unlike any of the artist's other figures. This tortured pose seems to be taken directly from the illustrations of Toro's *La Familia Carvajal*. One such illustration depicts a woman being

tortured as boiling oil is applied to her feet (Fig. 10).[64] Another shows Doña Isabel Rodríguez de Carvajal being tortured on the "potro," her head falling back in similar fashion (Fig. 11).[65] The funnel that appears in the 1944 drawing is also an unprecedented motif in Kahlo's art. Significantly, funnels appear in several illustrations in Toro's book. Related to the infamous "water torture," the funnel was used to facilitate the forcing of water down the throats of the tortured, causing their suffocation and subsequent death.[66]

In the Inquisition scenes female victims abound.

---

[62] The "Sambenitos" were "penitents" forced by the Inquisition to wear special costumes as a sign of repentance, see, Seymour B. Liebman, *Los judíos en México y América Central (fe, llamas e Inquisicion)* (Mexico, 1971), 449. The authority on this matter is Henry Charles Lea, whose monumental three-volume work describes the costumes in detail. *A History of the Inquisition of the Middle Ages* (New York, 1955), Volume I, 467–468, and see 389 ff.

[63] At first glance the drawing seems to be related to the surrealistic

works of Salvador Dali, specifically to his use of what he called "critical paranoia." Kahlo's relationship to Surrealism is discussed in detail in my Phd dissertation.

[64] Toro, I, 280.

[65] Toro, illustration opposite p. 288. Also see Toro, II, illustration opposite p. 224.

[66] Funnels appear, for example, in Toro, II, illustrations opposite pp. 240 and 256.

The act of undressing itself was conceived as the initial part of the torture and humiliation.[67] Thus, the nude, tormented body of Kahlo's "Fantasía" (Fantasma?) drawing seems to be directly related to such a "female ghost" of the past.

If indeed Kahlo's diary entries and drawing indicate that she was influenced by Toro's study of the Inquisition, the question remains, why did she feel drawn to these themes in particular? In 1944, Kahlo was in grave physical condition and experiencing acute pain. I suggest that the images from the torture chamber, which she had just encountered in Toro's books, offered vivid accounts of torment with which she could identify. The artist herself points to the connection between her present ordeal and the distant suffering of "kindred spirits" of the past metaphorically, within the drawing itself. The eye-turned-clock motif literally as well as figuratively places "time" inside "vision"; thus Kahlo evokes the relationship between past and

---

[67] One of the most famous visual images pertaining to the Mexican Inquisition is the nude figure of Doña Isabel de Carvajal standing before the inquisitors. See Toro, I, illustration opposite p. 304.

Fig. 11. *Tormento en el potro de doña Isabel Rodríguez de Carvajal, from Alfonso Toro, La Familia Carvajal. Mexico, 1944, vol. I, illustration opposite p. 288.*

Fig. 12. *Frida Kahlo, Without Hope, 1945. Oil on Canvas mounted on Masonite, 11" × 14 1/4". Dolores Olmedo Foundation, Mexico.*

present — the essence of time — through the visual images.[68]

Without Hope

The ideas that began to appear sporadically in drawings and in the artist's private journal in 1944, emerged in 1945 in a powerful oil painting entitled *Without Hope* (Fig. 12). In this disturbing work, Kahlo painted herself as she lay in a four-poster bed, covered with a blanket spotted with cells. Her tear-covered face turns stoically to the viewer, while a strange funnel-like object seems to pour various elements into her mouth. The funnel leans against a wooden contraption which, in turn, seems connected to the bed. The entire scene is placed outdoors within a dramatic setting: a landscape of fissured volcanic rock below, with sun and moon above.

Hayden Herrera's interpretation of this work — to date the most convincing attempt to decode this enigmatic painting — captures the affect that the work engenders, but leaves several crucial links unexplained. Herrera writes:

> In *Without Hope*, 1945, Frida stages her drama in that vast, heaving sea of volcanic rock the Pedregal. The faults and fissures symbolize the violence done to her body. Dramatic action is not clear, but the horror is unequivocal. Frida lies weeping in bed. Between her lips she holds the tip of a huge, membranous funnel — a cornucopia of gore containing a pig, a chicken, brains, a turkey, beef, sausage, and a fish, plus a sugar-candy skull with "Frida" written on its forehead. These she may be vomiting onto the easel that straddles her bed, making the carnage the source of her art. Or the image could refer to those pre-Columbian speech symbols that look like comic strip balloons, with the funnel of butchery symbolizing a scream of rage and horror. Another explanation is that Frida painted *Without Hope* after convalescing from an operation, and that the funnel depicts her disgust when her doctor, full of the best bedside-manner cheer, announced: "Now you can eat anything!"

Since she was so thin, the doctors made her eat pureed food every two hours. On the back of the painting's frame Frida wrote a rhyme: "A mí no me queda ya ni la menor esperanza... Todo se mueve al compás de lo que encierra la panza" (Not the least hope remains to me... Everything moves in time with what the belly contains.) The sheet covering Frida's naked body is dotted with round microscopic organisms that look like cells with nuclei or perhaps eggs waiting to be fertilized. Their form is echoed in the blood-red sun and pale moon that appear together in the sky. Thus Frida once again extends the meaning of her body's misadventures into the opposite worlds of the microscope and the solar system. It could also be that she set the funnel of horror in *Without Hope* between cells and celestial orbs in order not to aggrandize but rather to minimize, by contrast with the great span of things, her own personal miseries. Very likely, too, the simultaneous presence of the sun and the moon refers, as in some of Frida's other paintings, to the Aztec notion of an eternal war between light and dark, or to Christ's crucifixion, where the sun and moon together indicate the sorrow of all creation at the death of the savior. Thus, whether the funnel is a hemorrhage, a miscarried child, a scream, or a force-fed meal, the gore gushing from (or to) Frida's mouth and onto (or from) an easel that evokes a cross can be seen as a ritualistic offering, a personal and imaginary rite that redeems or renews through suffering.[69]

Herrera herself admits that the "dramatic action," as she phrases it, is "not clear," before she ventures to suggest several possible explanations for the various elements of this painting. While there can be no doubt as to the astuteness of her analysis of certain motifs — the fissured landscape, the sun and moon, the cosmic and microscopic setting — other elements remain unexplained. The strange wooden contraption, which Herrera calls an "easel that evokes a cross" is not an easel at all. When Kahlo wanted to paint her own easel — and she did so several times — she

---

[68] Kahlo's frail physical condition is related in the Begun medical records. The motif of the clock within the eye first appears in Kahlo's oeuvre in a 1934 drawing entitled *Ojo Avisor* (*Das Gesamtwerk*, fig. 199). This image may be related to Marc Chagall's 1911 version of *I and the Village* (Museum of Modern Art, New York), where the cow's eye turns into a clock. Chagall,

like Kahlo, connects his present predicament — life as an artist in Paris — with his past, represented by his native Vitebsk. Moreover, he presents himself torn between Judaism and Christianity, as he wears a necklace with a cross around his neck and a ring with a Star of David on his finger.

[69] Herrera, *Frida*, 347–348.

Figs. 13, 13a.   Tormento del agua, from Alfonso Toro, La Familia Carvajal. Mexico, 1944, vol. II, opposite p. 240, and vol. I, p. 289.

produced a faithful copy of the easel she owned at the time.[70] The funnel is another mystery. Herrera speculates with regard to its possible source: a speech sign taken from Aztec codices? a force-fed meal?

The text and illustrations included in Alfonso Toro's *La Familia Carvajal* reveal the hidden source of Kahlo's vision. The funnel — particularly one forced down the throat — and the wooden "ladder-like" contraption are, as previously shown, staple components of the two widespread torments implemented by the Mexican Inquisition: torture on the "potro" and the "water torture." Furthermore, in many of the illustrations in Toro's books it is specifically a

[70]   The identification of the wooden contraption as a "wooden easel suggestive of a crucifix" was first postulated by Joyce Kozloff in her pioneering article "Frida Kahlo," *Women's Studies* 6 (1978), 55. Compare the photograph of her easel (e.g. *Das Gesamtwerk*, 28) with her depiction of it, for example in her 1951 *Self Portrait with Doctor Farill* (*Das Gesamtwerk*, fig. 124).

female victim who is bound to a "bed." The torture victim's position in many of these illustrations, as she helplessly lies on the bed with a sheet or blanket covering hands, is virtually identical with Kahlo's pose in *Without Hope* (Figs. 13, 13a).[71]

Apparently, as we have seen, after having read Alfonso Toro's books and seeing the images reproduced in them, Kahlo was inspired to utilize similar imagery to express her own plight. As Herrera's biographical study of Kahlo lucidly relates, the artist was greatly tormented at the time, both physically and emotionally.[72]

Yet, identifying the source for Kahlo's imagery does not fully solve the mystery of the painting. One pertinent question remains unanswered: what motivated Kahlo, particularly in 1945, to incorporate these unusual images related to the torture of Jews as metaphors for her own pain? In many of her other portraits she used Christian symbols to express her personal "Calvary"; in others, she adopted pre-Columbian motifs to convey her own torment. The images of *Without Hope* are unique in Kahlo's oeuvre.

Close scrutiny of another element of this painting — the cells that dot the blanket that covers Kahlo's body — provides a clue that might help us answer this query. It has been suggested that these may be egg cells awaiting fertilization. However, a close look at these cells indicates that, while several cellular organisms may indeed be eggs in the process of being inseminated, others are markedly different in pattern and color. Kahlo's avid interest and aptitude for biology is well-known. Prior to her accident, she intended to pursue a medical career. Once this plan was thwarted due to her precarious physical condition, she pondered the possibility of executing scientific and microscopic drawings as a way of making a living. It is obvious, that the "circles" in her 1945 painting

were deliberately painted cells of a specific nature.[73]

The cells Kahlo painted in 1945 are clearly related to Diego Rivera's Detroit murals, particularly to the cells Rivera painted on two side panels that flank the north wall of the courtyard of the Detroit Institute of Arts. The general theme of Rivera's 1932-33 panels is the inherent duality of scientific research. In his work, Rivera visually demonstrates how healing and destruction, medicine and war technology, are based on the self-same knowledge. Thus, on the left-hand side, a scene of vaccination appears. Below this panel, a healthy human embryo is depicted surrounded by various diseased cells (Fig. 14). On the right-hand side of the wall, opposite the vaccination scene, a group of men wearing gas-masks is shown in the process of creating poisonous gas. Below this ominous display of war technology, Rivera painted cells that are suffocated by poison gas (Fig. 15).[74]

Kahlo's allusion to Rivera's mural provides a key to a full interpretation of her painting's iconology. The cells that cover Kahlo's body relate to disparate types of organisms. The egg and sperm cells — used here for the first time since Kahlo's 1936 *My Grandparents, My Parents, and I* — refer to the artist's genetic heritage.[75] The cells derived from Rivera's work evoke two of the negative forces that affect human beings — disease and war.

That Kahlo suffered from physical ailments throughout her life and particularly at the time she painted *Without Hope* may explain the fact that diseased cells cover her body both literally and figuratively. Kahlo's depiction of cells adversely affected by poison gas becomes particularly significant when one remembers that it was around this time that the full horrors of the Holocaust were being uncovered. Photographs from the death camps and reports on the plight of the Jews in particular were circulating.

[71] Toro, II, illustration opposite p. 240; also note the funnel that appears in this illustration. See also I, 289.

[72] Herrera, *Frida*, 344-359.

[73] Ibid, 26 and Gómez Arias, private interview. Kahlo's interest in the microscope is reflected in her library as well, where to this day a volume of Dr. J. Pelletan's *Le Microscope* (Paris, 1887) still stands.

[74] My reading of Rivera's iconography is based on Dorothy McMeekin, *Diego Rivera: Science and Creativity in the Detroit Murals* (Michigan State University Press, 1985), 24-32, 43-53.

[75] The egg and sperm cells reappear in 1945 in Kahlo's *Birth*

of Moses, see note 77. Eggs and sperms appear once again in the background of Kahlo's 1951 portrait of her father. Thus it becomes clear that the artist uses this motif when she wishes to allude to her genetic heritage, particularly to her Jewish roots.

[76] *El Libro Negro del Terror Nazi en Europa: Testimonios de escritores y artistas de 16 naciones* (Mexico, 1943). Ziva Amishai-Maisels has brought to my attention the fact that after the Soviet liberation of Maydanek death camp in 1944, the Soviets made a film about the Nazi atrocities there, which they distributed worldwide. Kahlo may have seen this film.

Fig. 14. Diego Rivera, Vaccination Scene and Healthy Human Embryo Surrounded by Diseased Cells, 1933. Fresco, from Detroit Industry murals, North Wall. Copyright The Detroit Institute of Arts. Founders Society Purchase, Edsel B. Ford Fund and Gift of Edsel B. Ford.

Fig. 15. Diego Rivera, The Manufacture of Poison Gas and Cells Suffocated by Poison Gas, 1933. Fresco, from Detroit Industry murals, North Wall. Copyright The Detroit Institute of Arts. Founders Society Purchase, Edsel B. Ford Fund and Gift of Edsel B. Ford.

As early as 1943, a "Black Book of Nazi Terror" was published in Mexico. *El Libro Negro del Terror Nazi*, is to this day in the artist's library, a testimony to her interest and knowledge.[76]

By juxtaposing images of torture devices of the Inquisition with depictions of cells being suffocated by gas, Kahlo points to an obvious parallel. Both the Catholic Inquisitors and the Nazis persecuted Jews. Both oppressors were obsessed with "pureza de sangre," purity of blood. The Inquisition tests for "limpieza" and the Nazi demand for "pureza" seem to have converged in 1944-1945 in Kahlo's painting. Perhaps her genealogical heritage — symbolized by the egg and sperm cells — made it easy for her to empathize with the persecuted Jews of Europe, where she still had Jewish relatives, as well as with the suffering Jewish women of the Inquisition torture chamber.[77]

From the Margins

A study of the "Jewish" books in Kahlo's library has thus far involved three books which pertain to disparate chapters of Jewish history. Alfonso Toro's two-volume *La Familia Carvajal* provides an in-depth account of the persecution of Jews during the Inquisition of New Spain; Isaac Berliner's 1936 book of Yiddish poetry relates to Jewish immigration and acculturation in Mexico; *El Libro Negro del Terror Nazi en Europa* is a 1943 account of contemporary Nazi atrocities as recounted by artists and writers from 16 different European countries.

Additional volumes included in Kahlo's library strengthen the voice of the "books from the margins." Alongside the German "classics" Herr Kahlo left his daughter, other German books — published several years after Wilhelm Kahlo's death — are to be found on Frida Kahlo's bookshelves. Upon closer examination, one observes that many of these were published, like *El Libro Negro*, by a small publishing company that was set up in 1942 by German Jewish immigrants residing in Mexico. Marianne O. de Bopp, who has studied the German Jewish community of Mexico, has written about this publishing endeavor:

> In 1942 the publishing house of "El Libro Libre" was founded in Mexico. The editions of this German press in a Spanish-speaking country, as interesting as they might be for the bibliophile were, with the exception of Anna Segher's *Das siebte Kreuz* (*The Seventh Cross*), perhaps of no particular note. Since they only appeared in an edition of 500-1000 copies, they were soon forgotten.[78]

The fact that Kahlo was among the very select circle that subscribed to this small and specialized publishing effort is not without significance. In light of our previous findings, her interest in the German writings of Jewish authors such as Egon Erwin Kisch, Ernest Sommer and others, and in the Jewish themes they dwelled upon, becomes fully understandable.

Moreover, Kahlo did not limit herself to the German and Spanish literature produced by the small El Libro Libre publishing house. Among her books one may find a rare copy of a Spanish translation of the poetry of Yehudah Halevi, *Poemas sagrados y profanos*. The work of the Hebrew poet of medieval Spain had been translated and prefaced by Maximo José Kahn and Juan Gil-Albert in 1943 and published in a limited edition by another group within the German Jewish community of Mexico.[79] Diametrically opposed in mood and genre, Kahlo also owned Ilya Ehrenburg's picaresque novel on the adventures of the "little Jewish tailor" Lasik Roitschwanz.[80] The presence of these books in Kahlo's library — and more so the influence of some of them on her art — point to the artist's interest in her Jewish roots.

Conclusion

As several scholars have noted, Kahlo's personal suffering is often expressed in her work with the aid of imagery derived from Christian and pre-Columbian

---

[77] In many of the Inquisition documents the persecuted Jews were accused as practitioners of the "ley de Moises" (law of Moses). Perhaps it is no coincidence that in 1945, the same year that she painted *Without Hope*, Kahlo completed *The Birth of Moses*. This painting was instigated by Kahlo's reading of *Moses and Monotheism*, Freud's account of the emergence of the Jewish religion and the origins of the Jewish People. Kahlo's *The Birth of Moses* is a complex painting which cannot be discussed in this context. It is dealt with in detail in my Phd dissertation.

[78] de Bopp, 126–127.

[79] Ibid, 131.

[80] The English translation I used is by Alec Brown: Ilya Ehrenburg, *The Stormy Life of Laz Roitshvantz* (London, 1965). The original Russian version was first published in 1928, the Spanish title in Kahlo's library is *La Vida Agitada de Lasik Roitschwanz*.

art. In the context of modern Mexican painting the use of this imagery is not unusual. In the paintings and drawings examined in this study, Kahlo utilizes other visual antecedents to express her experiences. Her sources — contemporary genealogical charts, poetic metaphors of immigration, Inquisition torture devices and human cells suffocated by poison gas — used particularly during the Nazi era, expose a covert aspect of Kahlo's identity, her "hidden" Jewish roots.

248

A PROPOS DE L'ILLUSTRATION
DU CHANDELIER A SEPT BRANCHES
SUR UN ACTE DE MARIAGE

Victor Klagsbald

Dans un article paru dans le volume dix-huit du *Jewish Art*, Monsieur Sh. Sabar publie la photographie d'une *ketubbah* exécutée pour un mariage célébré à Villefranche-sur-Mer en 1669.[1] La comparaison de l'enluminure avec celle de *ketubbot* nord-africaines plus tardives, conforte Monsieur Sabar dans son opinion quant à l'origine maghrébine du document. Il aurait suffi cependant de lire le texte pour en être certain. Le fiancé Aaron b. Jacob Caniso et la fiancée Simha bat Shelomo Sasportas s'engagent à se soumettre aux "règlements [*takanot*] institués et confirmés par les rabbins exilés du pays de Castille et observés depuis par la Sainte Communauté d'Oran." Le texte du contrat mentionne le nom du fiancé Aaron Caniso, mais celui-ci signe Aaron Cansino.

Lorsqu'en 1509 le Cardinal Ximenes occupe la ville et met à sac le quartier juif, tous les habitants s'enfuient. Revenus, ils reconstituèrent la Communauté autour de quelques familles, notamment les Sasportas et Cansino.[2]

Les deux familles comptent dans leurs rangs rabbins célèbres, poètes, philosophes, mécènes et philanthropes mais également diplomates et agents royaux. Notre fiancé semble être un des fils de Jacob Cansino, agent du roi d'Espagne. A la mort de son frère tué en 1636 par les Bene Raxes, alors qu'il regroupait les troupes espagnoles, Jacob hérita de ses fonctions, qu'il exerça jusqu'à sa mort, le 19 octobre 1666. C'est après la disparition de cet homme d'influence que le Marquis de Los Veles, gouverneur de la région, réussit à déposséder la famille Cansino de ses privilèges, ce qui à terme conduisit à l'expulsion des juifs d'Oran en 1669. Toute la Communauté, 466 âmes, s'embarqua et traversa la Méditerranée. Les réfugiés se rendirent à Nice, Villefranche-sur-Mer et Livourne.

Notre *ketubbah* porte précisément la date fatidique de 1669, et expulsés d'Oran, les familles Cansino et Sasportas ont dû célébrer le mariage à Villefranche-sur-Mer. S'agissant des deux familles dirigeantes de la communauté on peut supposer que le document a été établi et décoré selon la tradition locale. En l'occurence, il s'agit d'une des plus anciennes *ketubbot* séfarades enluminées venues jusqu'à nous. Ce qui caractérise ces *ketubbot* de haute époque est l'espace du texte serré dans un cadre sommé par un arc en fer a cheval dépassé, le tout rehaussé par un décor floral.

La *ketubbah* de Villefranche ajoute à ce schéma la représentation du Chandelier à Sept Branches. Dans une publication précédente, j'ai proposé de voir dans cette évocation de la *menorah* une allusion à l'un des trois devoirs spécifiques de la femme juive: l'allumage des lumières le vendredi soir. Il est vrai que j'ai omis d'expliquer le lien qui existe entre ces deux lumières. Monsieur Sabar exprime ses doutes quant à cette hypothèse en écrivant (p. 174): "Mais si l'artiste avait réellement l'intention d'illustrer les trois devoirs religieux de la femme juive, pourquoi les deux autres, notamment l'immersion rituelle et le prélèvement d'une partie de la pâte ne sont elles pas illustrées...? De plus, les lumières de Shabbat ne sont pas allumées sur un Chandelier à Sept Branches, mais sur un chandelier spécial pour le Shabbat, avec lequel l'artiste devait être familiarisé... Le sens de la *menorah* dans toutes les représentations est apparemment associé avec le Temple et Jérusalem, dont le souvenir doit être rappelé et 'placé au dessus de la joie suprême,' notamment le mariage."

Je rappellerai tout d'abord que je n'ai pas proposé de voir dans l'image de la *menorah* l'évocation des trois, mais d'une seule des obligations religieuses de la

[1] Shalom Sabar, "Sephardi Elements in North African Hebrew Manuscript Decoration," *Jewish Art* 18 (1992), 168–91.
[2] *Encyclopedia Judaica*, vol. 12, p. 1446; Moshe Orfali, "Mazkeret

Yuhasin le-Beit Cansino," in *Asufot: Annual for Hebrew Studies*, ed. Meir Benayahu (Jérusalem, 1988), II, 345ss (hébreu).

Fig. 1   Ketubbah. Villefranche-sur-Mer, 1669. Collection Victor Klagsbald, Paris. (Photo: Studio Lucien Loeb).

femme juive. Si les deux autres sont parfois visualisées sur les pages de titre gravées des rituels de prière, destinés aux femmes, il ne serait peut-être pas du meilleur goût d'en orner un acte de mariage. Mais ceci est secondaire. Monsieur Sabar considère la dessin du point de vue iconographique et y voit le suite des illustrations traditionelles du Tabernacle dans les Bibles hébraïques médiévales de l'Espagne chrétienne; ainsi l'image de la *menorah* sur notre *ketubbah* serait selon lui une évocation du Temple de Jérusalem. Dans un article publié dans la *Revue des Etudes Juives*,[3] j'ai tenté de démontrer que l'hypothèse selon laquelle la représentation de la *menorah* aurait pour dessein de garder vivant le souvenir du Temple, hypothèse formulée par plusieurs historiens de l'art juif, n'est pas acceptable.

L'évocation de la *menorah* est un symbol primordial et autonome et un symbole ne se réfère pas à une réalité tangible mais à une ou plusieurs idées. Si l'artiste avait voulu évoquer le souvenir du Temple il aurait tout simplement décoré la partie supérieure de l'acte par l'image traditionelle du Temple de Jérusalem comme c'est le cas pour un grand nombre de *ketubbot* italiennes et parfois hollandaises. L'auteur pense trouver dans un article de Madame Iris Fishof dans *Journal of Jewish Art* vol. 9 un argument en faveur de sa thèse.[4] Cependant cet article, abondamment illustré, ne montre aucune image de la *menorah*, mais seulement la représentation traditionnelle du Temple de Jérusalem. Il semble donc bien, que le motif sur notre *ketubbah* fasse référence à autre chose. La *menorah* évoque l'espérance messianique, qui sans doute se fait sentir davantage au moment où un jeune couple fonde un nouveau foyer, comme l'écrit à juste titre Monsieur Sabar. Serait-ce une raison suffisante pour l'avoir choisi comme élément de la décoration? Il faut plutôt chercher l'enchaînement associatif ailleurs. Disons d'emblée que la lumière est synonyme de salut (Ps. 27:1), de joie (Esth. 8:16), de vie (Ps. 56:14; Job 33:30), et la *menorah* représente la lumière originelle. Voilà déjà une raison suffisante pour placer son image en tête du document. Mais au delà il y a un rapport mystique qui associe le Chandelier à Sept Branches et les Pains de Proposition à la lumière et aux pains sabbatiques. Les lumières que la femme juive allume à l'entrée du Shabbat sont souvent au nombre minimal de deux en référence aux deux formules bibliques *zakhor* et *shamor* recommandant le respect du Shabbat. Mais ce nombre de deux ne répond pas à une règle absolue. L'auteur de *Magen Avraham* connaît la coutume d'en allumer sept, sans doute en souvenir de la *menorah* du Temple. C'est dans l'oeuvre de R. Yeshayah Horowitz (Shelah) qu'il trouve cette allusion au Chandelier à Sept Branches. L'idée de cette association est si répandue que dans les rituels *Minha ve-Arvit* que l'on trouve sur les bancs de toutes des synagogues, on peut lire parmi les règles d'allumage des lumières du Shabbat: "...et on doit les placer [les sept flammes] en ligne droite, en souvenir du Chandelier du Temple." Tuvia Wexler parle longuement de l'analogie entre les pains (*lehem mishne*) associés à la lumière du Shabbat et les douze Pains de Proposition et la *menorah*.[5] Il semble que c'est un texte du *Zohar* sur *Parashat Eqev* qui est à l'origine de l'association des lumières du Shabbat au Chandelier du Temple.[6] Mais l'évocation la plus claire de la *menorah* par les lumières sabbatiques se lit dans le poème *Azamer Bishevahin* de R. Isaac Luria (Arizal) que l'on chante le vendredi soir juste avant la récitation du *kidush*, la sanctification du Sabbat.[7] A l'époque de la rédaction de notre *ketubbah* la littérature kabbalistique de Safed avait pénétré toutes les communautés du pourtour de la Méditérranée. Si l'artiste s'est inspiré pour l'*iconographie* comme l'écrit Monsieur Sabar, des peintures décorant les manuscrits espagnols médiévaus, la présence du Chandelier à sept branches doit être recherchée, au niveau de l'*iconologie*, dans la littérature mystique citée notamment dans le poème liturgique de R. Issac Luria.

Je voudrais donc confirmer en conclusion que l'image de la *menorah* dans notre cas n'est pas l'évocation du Temple détruit mais bien au contraire l'expression d'espérances, baignées dans la lumière originelle qui a éclairée le Shabbat du premier couple humain.

---

[3]   *Revue des Etudes Juives* 1444 (octobre-décembre 1985), 408–38.

[4]   Iris Fishof, "'Jerusalem above my chief joy': Depictions of Jerusalem in Italian *Ketubot*," *Journal of Jewish Art* 9 (1982), 61–75.

[5]   Tuvia Wexler, *Zefunot bi-Msoret Yisrael* (Jérusalem: Reuven Mass, 1968), p. 67ss.

[6]   Vol. III, fol. 272b. L'auteur remercie Monsieur Joël Touati de lui avoir signalé ce passage.

[7]   Israel Davidson, *Thesaurus...* (New York, 1924), I, no. 2322.

Book Review

Scribes, Script and Books: The Book Arts from Antiquity to the Renaissance, by Leila Avrin. Chicago: American Library Association and London: The British Library, 1991. xxxii + 356 pp., 343 B/W illustrations and figures.

Although this book is not dedicated directly to the field of Jewish art, students of the Hebrew book, its design and manner of production over the ages will find much valuable information. Leila Avrin is best known from her pioneering studies on Hebrew micrography, primarily her dissertation on the earliest dated decorated Hebrew manuscript and the exhibition catalogue *Micrography as Art*.[1] An art historian by training, she has been teaching a course on the arts of the book at the School of Library and Archives Studies of the Hebrew University of Jerusalem.

In this work Avrin sets out "to demonstrate just how the principles of tradition and change have determined the form of the Western book from ancient times to the age of printing" (p. xxxi). However, rather than surveying the material in a chronological order, the author dedicates each of the book's fourteen chapters to a well-defined topic. Thus, there are separate chapters dealing with the book in particular societies (e.g., "The Book in the Ancient World: Mesopotamia," "The Egyptian Book," "The Greek and Hellenistic Book," "The Roman Book," "The Islamic Book"), while others are concerned with the book arts in general (e.g., "Manuscript Illumination," "Papermaking," "Bookbinding"), and three chapters are dedicated to writing systems and the history of the alphabet: "Writing," "The Alphabet," and "Latin Script."

Admittedly, this wide range of topics requires a series of scholars in the respective fields. Avrin, who admirably presents this material in a lucid and attractive narrative, modestly defines her efforts as "chutzpah." But despite the fact that the book lacks scholarly documentation for the many theories (as well as the facts) introduced, it provides the non-expert with an excellent introduction to the history of the book. Instead of footnotes, the author appended for those interested in further reading a basic scholarly

A prophet holding a written scroll, Dura-Europos, 244/5 CE.

bibliography for each topic, arranged by the chapters in her book. In addition, the book is enriched by well-chosen plates (some are, however, too small and too dark), chronological tables, maps, and figures by noted Jerusalem calligraphers Malla Carl and Noah Ophir.

Our readers will naturally find a special interest in the chapter on the Hebrew book (pp. 100–137), which is, as expected, the longest and most thorough. (Additional material on the development of Hebrew script is found in the chapter on the alphabet). This chapter covers the history of the book in Jewish history from

---

[1] See Leila R.K. Avrin, "The Illuminations in the Moshe Ben-Asher Codex of 895 C.E.," Ph.D. dissertation (University of Michigan, 1974). *Micrography as Art* was published by Centre National de la Recherche Scientifique, Paris and the Israel Museum, Jerusalem, 1981 (together with an essay by C. Sirat, "La lettre hébraïque et sa signification").

biblical times till the end of the fifteenth century, but cites examples and practices current in later centuries as well. As with other chapters, there is a brief history and a chronological table at the beginning. However, it is virtually impossible to survey the complicated history of the Jewish people and the many important books which it produced in such a short space. It would have been wiser to expand instead the short chronological table and arrange it in parallel columns, juxtaposing the historical events in Eretz Israel and the various centers of the Diaspora with personalities and major books. The table as it stands now confusingly mixes these categories, and thus oddly lists the works of Maimonides under the heading "Talmudic Period" while important events are missing from the "Rise of European Jewry."

There are many curious facts noted by the author which give the Hebrew book a unique place in the history of Western civilization. For example, "word spacing and justification of margins appear in Hebrew scrolls and codices before these features are found regularly in Greek and Latin books. The fine, almost white leather of some of the Dead Sea Scrolls that resembles parchment dates from a time before the earliest extant parchment codices... In the Islamic era, the earliest dated manuscript with illuminations is a Hebrew codex..." (pp. 102–3); "The relative lack of mistakes in Hebrew Bible codices as compared to Latin and Greek manuscripts has been noted by many..." (p. 124). Furthermore, in modern Israel sheets of parchment for sacred writing are still being produced, and Torah scrolls are written in almost exactly the same manner as in antiquity. In mixing past and present, Avrin discusses the economics of medieval Hebrew manuscripts, side by side with a report on the current costs of making a Torah scroll ($18,000–40,000), an Esther scroll (about $500), and a ketubbah (price depends on material and decoration).

There are many other cases where Avrin goes beyond the time limits defined in the title and the preface. Thus, for example, Sephardi scribe's implements from late nieteenth century Jerusalem (pl. 105) are presented in the vicinity of inkwells from the Roman period (pl. 106). However, it is this curious juxtaposition of the past and present that provides at times unexpected parallels. A case in point is the shape of the ancient receptacle used by the Egyptian scribe (pl. 86), which remarkably resembles the Torah *tik* used by Jewish communities in Islamic lands until the modern era. Despite the fact that the author does not attempt to explain the enormous time gap, this insight opens for the student of ceremonial Judaica a new avenue of research.

The chapter ends with a short survey of the medieval manuscript and its decoration. The author emphasizes the place of micrography from its earliest appearance in Hebrew manuscripts until the contemporary revival. Besides codices, the decoration of other manuscripts (e.g., Esther scrolls, *ketubbot*) is briefly discussed as well. It should be noted that contrary to what the author writes (p. 132), in the Cairo Geniza there are a number of decorated *ketubbot* dated prior to the twelfth century, the earliest being a fragment from Metropolis, Egypt (Cambridge University Library, TS 12.659), dated to 927/8 (or 1027/8).[2]

Finally, there are in this chapter very few minor factual mistakes that should be corrected in future editions: the first revolt against the Romans broke out in 66 not 60 (p. 105); the text of the *mezuzah* is comprised of two passages (not one) in Deut. 6:4–9 and 11:13–21 (p. 110); in the caption to pl. 103 (p. 111) the verses of the *tefillin* are Exod. 13:1–16; according to the *halakha* the minimal number of columns to each of the Torah parchment sheets is three, not two (p. 115); the captions to the "brick" pattern of the Song of Moses and Song of the Sea (p. 116, fig. 15; verse 44 is *not* part of the second Song!) have been confusingly transposed; the Torah *tik* reproduced in pl. 115 (p. 129) is apparently Iraqi, not Persian (though its *rimonim* seem to be Persian indeed).[3]

In sum, Avrin's *Scribes, Script and Books* may be recommended to all those who love and appreciate books. Students of Jewish art will find in it much relevant information and an excellent beginning for research in many aspects that are crucial for understanding the development of the Hebrew book in Western society.

Shalom Sabar

---

[2] See M.A. Friedman, *Jewish Marriage in Palestine: A Cairo Geniza Study* (Tel Aviv and New York, 1980–81), vol. I, p. 97; vol. II, p. 82.

[3] For the design and shape of Iraqi *tikim*, see B. Yaniv, "The Metal Work of Torah Cases From Iraq in the 19th and 20th Centnries," *Pe'amim* 11 (1982), 102–112 (in Hebrew).

DMITRY LION, 1925–1993

Dmitry Lion, who died in Moscow in September 1993 at the age of sixty-eight from a sudden heart attack, was one of the few post-war artists in the U.S.S.R. who identified themselves without fear or confusion as Jewish artists. His entire work from the early 1950s was inspired by the Holocaust. To express his feelings about it he elaborated his highly individual style of drawing, making him one of the most significant figures in the contemporary Moscow art scene. This artistic language influenced a large number of artists, though Lion's own work remained for the most part unexhibited and unpublished until his modest one-man show in 1991. His special way of life in the waning of socialist Russia seemed to be beyond comprehension. The fact that he devoted himself to undesirable, if not prohibited, Jewish themes, lived in poverty, and made no effort to be understood or "acquirable" by the authorities, gave him the reputation of one of the "saints and fools" of Moscow. Nevertheless he was seen as knowledgeable about drawing and as a good teacher. He was an artist, a philosopher of art, and a preacher, who generously shared his views and artistic discoveries with anyone who was interested in understanding them. All the attempts to record his brilliant discourses on art were rejected by him.

Lion participated in many exhibitions of the Russian "underground" abroad, though subversive activities as such did not attract him. Ilya Kabakov, in his recently published memoirs, describes Lion as a "metaphysical" and "spiritual" artist, who tried to express the unbearable realities of his time by a personal, purely spiritual effort, rather than by a strategy

Dmitry Lion

of conceptualism as Kabakov did. Nevertheless it is possible that Lion's use of texts within his drawings influenced the conceptualist movement in its early stages in Moscow.

Large, fresco-like works on paper, devoted to the Holocaust, as well as many drawings and etchings grouped in several main cycles — "Bless those who go," "Three lives of Rembrandt," "Biblical cycle," and others — remained in the little apartment where the artist lived with his family. Many works were purchased for galleries and private collections in Europe, the United States, and Israel, and a good portion belongs to the Tretyakov Gallery and to the Pushkin Museum in Moscow.

Dmitry Lion left a daughter, a talented young graphic artist, and many pupils, who inherited not only the precepts of art but also his pure modernist ideology and high don Quixotism.

Dmitry Lion, Sacrifice of Isaac, c. 1967. Ink on paper.

Lola Kantor-Kazovsky

Self-Portrait, 1974/5. Oil on canvas, 91.5 x 73.5 cm. Private collection. (Photograph courtesy of Michele Vishny.)

MORDECAI ARDON, 1896–1992

Mordecai Ardon, Israel's foremost artist, died in Jerusalem in the summer of 1992, his life having spanned nearly a century. In a retrospective self-portrait, showing himself as a youth, Ardon summarized the facts of his early years. Listing cities where he lived and teachers who inspired him toward a life in art, the dancing letters read "Tuchow" (Poland), where he was born; "Tarnow," a nearby town to which he fled at the age of thirteen to escape his Orthodox family's opposition to becoming a painter; "Berlin," where he was a student at Reinhardt's Schauspielschule des Deutschen Theatres; "Weimar," where he attended Bauhaus classes; "München," where he studied Old Master painting techniques with Max Doerner; and "Jerusalem," which ultimately became his home. The last five lines refer to Ardon's teachers, Itten, Klee, and Kandinsky. Despite paying tribute to his Bauhaus masters, the painting reflects Ardon's lifelong worship of Rembrandt both in its revelation of inner light and in the voluminous sleeve of his garment — a recollection of the so-called *Jewish Bride* — but rendered in twentieth-century cubist planes.

Although depicting himself with a touch of sadness, this was hardly Ardon's characteristic demeanor. All who knew him remember the sparkling smile, sharp mind and ready humor, which occasionally turned to self-mockery. He was a storyteller *par excellence*, who told a tale with great dramatic flair.

Ardon was a man who knew Bible and Midrash and was versed in rabbinic literature and Kabbalah. He spoke six languages fluently, was well read in world literature, and had more than a casual knowledge of music, even avant-garde composers. Ardon deeply admired Eastern and Western art and was knowledgeable about the development of both from the ancient through modern periods. Sumerian sculpture particularly attracted him and he would frequently jest about his own resemblance to some of its bald statuettes. The richness of this background and his extraordinary intelligence contributed to both the content and style of his paintings. It is noteworthy that in this self-portrait he carries not only the tool of his craft — a paintbrush — but also a book. For Ardon, the hand and the mind were inseparable in the creation of art.

While Ardon's subject matter embraced landscape, portraiture, still life, and genre, it was the landscape of Israel that dominated his oeuvre. From his first experience of Jerusalem in 1933, to the very end of his life, Ardon felt a mystical attachment to the earth, which he absorbed and recreated in his art. Although the final decades of his life were spent mostly in his Paris studio, Israel's landscape remained his primary expression. Somehow, in distancing himself physically, he grew closer to it spiritually. Like William Wordsworth's definition of poetry, Ardon's paintings reflect "emotion recollected in tranquility."

Before taking up residence in Paris, he contributed enormously to the development of art in Israel. He taught at the New Bezalel School beginning in 1935 and became director from 1940 to 1952. Among his stellar pupils were Avigdor Arikha, Yaacov Agam and Maryan. From 1952 to 1963 Ardon served as Artistic Advisor to the Ministry of Education and Culture. Despite his heavy schedule, he never abandoned his easel; during these years numerous exhibitions of his paintings were held in museums and galleries throughout the world, culminating in a major retrospective at the Tel Aviv Museum in 1985. At the age of ninety-one he had an impressive exhibition of recent works in London!

Many awards attest to Ardon's achievements: the UNESCO Prize at the Venice Biennale (1954), the Israel Prize (1963), honorary doctoral degrees from the Hebrew University (1974), Tel Aviv University (1981), the Weizmann Institute of Science (1983), and the Mordecai Ish-Shalom Prize (1992). His autobiography, *Unterwegs*, was awarded the Itzik Manger Prize for Yiddish Literature in 1988.

A significant number of Ardon's paintings are in museums and private collections all over the world, and they are greatly cherished. Israel also possesses some of his finest works. In addition to canvases, in Jerusalem one can view the magnificent *Creation* tapestries in Shaare Zedek Hospital and the awesome stained-glass windows, *Isaiah's Vision of Eternal Peace*, in the Jewish National and University Library. Mordecai Ardon's monumental art has enriched the world. He will be sorely missed.

Michele Vishny

KURT WEITZMANN,
1904–1993

When Kurt Weitzmann died at the age of eighty-nine, he had recently signed a contract for the republication of *Die Byzantinische Buchmalerei des 9. und 10. Jahrhunderts* and was proofreading the final draft of his study (written in collaboration with Massimo Bernabo) of the illustrated Octateuch manuscripts. One is an expanded version of his 1934 Habilitationschrift and the other the result of nearly fifty years of research; together these two books attest to Weitzmann's exceptional longevity and scholarly consistency. They embody his greatness as the explorer and systematizer of a shattered artistic heritage, but they barely hint at the remarkable range and extraordinary importance of Weitzmann's contribution to the history of medieval art. In addition to studies of manuscript illumination, Weitzmann's publications include studies of ivory carving, icon painting, frescoes, and mosaics, and comprise not only Byzantine but also Classical, Jewish, Early Christian, Armenian, Western, and Crusader materials, even touching Near Eastern and Islamic art.

Weitzmann was born on 7 March 1904 in Klein-Almerode near Kassel. After attending courses on Ancient and Renaissance art taught by Martin Wackernagel, Arnold von Salis, Adolf von Harnack, Julius von Schlosser, Josef Strzygowski, Karl Maria Swoboda, and Emmanuel Lowy in Munster, Wurzburg, and Vienna, he studied in Berlin with the archaeologist Ferdinand Noack and with the historian of medieval art Adolph Goldschmidt. Weitzmann completed his Ph.D degree under Goldschmidt's direction in 1929, writing a thesis on the Byzantine ivory rosette caskets that was published as the first volume of Goldschmidt and Weitzmann, *Die byzantinischen Elfenbeinskulpturen des X.–XIII. Jahrhunderts*; he then collaborated with Goldschmidt on the second volume of the ivories

corpus and also prepared his Habilitationschrift under Goldschmidt's supervision.

Although Weitzmann was not Jewish, his close affiliation with Goldschmidt tainted him in the eyes of the Nazis, as did his public refusal to embrace National Socialist ideology. He left Germany in 1935 and took up residence in Princeton, where he lived for fifty-eight richly productive years with his wife, the art historian Josepha Weitzmann-Fielder. First as a member of the Institute for Advanced Study and, from 1945, also as a Professor in the Department of Art and Archaeology of Princeton University, Weitzmann continued his studies of Byzantine manuscript illumination, joining a group of scholars headed by Charles Rufus Morey and Albert Mathias Friend, Jr., engaged in a project to prepare a corpus of illustrated manuscripts of the Septuagint. The volume on the Octateuchs is a product of this enterprise as is the 1986 publication of the Cotton Genesis.

In preparing the Septuagint corpus and in teaching the manuscript seminar, Weitzmann came to discern the principles underlying the history of Byzantine manuscript illumination that he set forth in his most influential book, *Illustrations in Roll and Codex: A Study of the Origin and Method of Text Illustration* (Princeton, 1947, revised in 1970). Beginning with the tenet that what survives of ancient and medieval art is but a fragment of a once-vast production, *Roll and Codex* proceeds by reconstructing, through a precise analysis of the archaeological evidence, the general evolution of illustrated manuscripts, and then continues by establishing a method for interpreting extant witnesses.

In contrast to most scholars who saw Christian art emerging step by step from simple symbols and emblematic images to elaborate painted narratives, Weitzmann viewed it as an offshoot of an established tradition; indeed, as he argued most fully in the 1990 Dumbarton Oaks publication of *The Frescoes of the Dura Synagogue and Christian Art*, he believed that it depended largely on a preceding Jewish adaptation of Hellenistic developments. As a result, Weitzmann presented the evolution of Christian art largely as a series of appropriations and adjustments of the ancient heritage.

He outlined his belief in several articles and mainly in "Zur Frage des Einflusses jüdischer Bilderquellen auf die Illustration des Alten Testament" in *Festschrift Theodor Klauser*, in the *Jahrbuch für Antike und*

Christentum, Supplement I (Munster, 1964), pp. 401–15, which was published in English as "The Question of the Influence of Jewish Pictorial Sources on Old Testament Illustrations," in *Studies in Classical and Byzantine Manuscript Illumination*, edited by

H.L. Kessler (Chicago, 1971), pp. 76–95. In this as in his other observations Kurt Weitzmann will continue to teach and guide us even after his death.

Herbert L. Kessler

ERIC ESTORICK,
1913–1993

Eric Estorick was a tower of a man, both in stature and in spirit. He was a man who loved life and knew how to enjoy its delights. He was a man of varied interests, knowledgeable in art and history, politics and science. He was an energetic doer as well as a wonderful conversationalist.

Eric became an art collector and dealer relatively late in life, after the Second World War, when he was still interested in social and political upheaval all over the world.

His interest in the political work of the British socialist Stafford Cripps, who as Chancellor of the Exchequer saved Britain from the high post-war inflation, brought him to write *Stafford Cripps: Master Statesman* (1949). His interest in Cripps stemmed from his days as a student of sociology at New York University. He followed Cripps's career from being a King's Counsellor in 1927, through his expulsion from the Labour Party because of his involvement in the founding of the Anti-Fascist Popular Front in 1938, to his nomination as Ambassador in Moscow. Estorick's previous book, *Stafford Cripps: Prophetic Rebel* (1940), is a masterpiece of a great analytical mind. Eric was still involved with Cripps and his support for the independence of India in 1947. The book *Changing Empire: Churchill to Nehru* (1950) expresses Eric's deep involvement in the decline of the

British Empire and in the fight against colonialism after the Second World War. This, no doubt, was one of the reasons for his deep commitment to the State of Israel.

Eric's work with his devoted late wife Salome benefited the world of art in general and that of Israel in particular. The couple energetically supported many research projects, art collections as well as living artists. Among the artists they supported were Italian Futurists, and mainly the Russian-born Art Deco artist Erté. They created the Seven Arts Ltd. foundation in London and New York, which mainly represented Erté's works and publications.

Eric's love for Jewish art was always "under cover," as he used to say, and mainly his love for folk art. In their travels to find unknown artists Salome and Eric discovered Anatoly Kaplan in Moscow and fell in love with his work. They committed themselves to distribute his books, and helped him and his family survive. It may have been Eric's upbringing in the poor Jewish neighborhood of Brooklyn, and his conversations with his much-loved grandfather, which culminated in his interest in Jewish art, and as a result his interest in the activities of the Center for Jewish Art, which is how I came to know him. The Center's expeditions to the former Soviet Union to discover remnants of Jewish visual culture excited him. He created the Eric Estorick and Salome Dessau-Estorick Fund to support the survey and documentation of Jewish art in the former Soviet Union carried out by researchers from the Center. He was concerned in the organization of the expeditions, fascinated by the minutest details of our finds, and enjoyed hearing the tales of our adventures there. There was always pleasure and keen interest in his company. Eric's memory and that of Salome will not fade — his children Michael and Isobel will continue the work of their parents. We will always remember Eric as a vital and generous man.

Bezalel Narkiss

RECENT PUBLICATIONS

The Alba Bible: Rabbi Moses Arragel's Testament: A Facsimile Edition. London: Facsimile Edition, 1992. 515 folios with 334 miniatures, a limited edition: 500 copies. Includes a companion volume, ed. Jeremy Schonfield, with the following papers on Jewish art: Sonia Fellous-Rozenblat, 'The Biblia de Alba, its Patron, Author and Ideas'; id., 'The Artists of the Biblia de Alba'; id., 'Catalogue Raisonń of the Miniatures'; Adriaan Keller, 'The Making of the Biblia de Alba.'

Alok, Ersin and Mili Mitrani. *Anatolian Synagogues.* Istanbul: Alok Productions, 1992. 414 pp., with numerous figs.

Amishai-Maisels, Ziva. *Depiction and Interpretation: The Influence of the Holocaust on the Visual Arts.* Oxford, New York, Seoul and Tokyo: Pergamon Press, 1993. 570 pp., with numerous figs.

Amit, David. 'The Source of the Architectural Plans of the Synagogues in Southern Judaea.' *Cathedra for the History of Eretz Israel and Its Yishuv* 68 (June 1993), 6–35. In Hebrew, summary in English, p. 199.

Anne Frank in the World: 1929–1945. Amsterdam: Anne Frank Stichting, 1992 [1985] 144 pp., with numerous figs. A catalogue. Text and photo research by Dienke Hondius, Joke Kniesmeijer and Bauco T. van der Wal. In English and Hebrew.

Apor, Éva. Ed. *Catalogue of the Scheiber Library (Oriental Studies 9).* Budapest: Library of the Hungarian Academy of Sciences, 1992. 450 pp., 5293 items, with indices of names, subjects and titles. Compiled by Á. Kárteszi, V. Kordován and I. Ormos.

Art in Tel Aviv, Tel Aviv In Art: The Tel Aviv Collection. Tel Aviv: Gimmel International, 1991. A collection of 10 paintings that recount the history of the first Hebrew city. Limited edition.

At Home Only With God: Believing Jews and Their Children. New York: Aperture, 1992. 64 pp., with numerous figs. Photographs by Arnold Eagle with essay by Arthur Hertzberg.

Auschwitz: A History in Photographs. Bloomington and Indianapolis: Indiana University Press, and Warsaw: Ksiâżka i Wiedza for Auschwitz-Birkenau State Museum, 1993. 295 pp., with numerous photographs. Compiled and ed. by Teresa Świebocka. English edition prepared by Jonathan Webber and Connie Wilsack. First published in Polish in 1990 by the Auschwitz-Birkenau State Museum and Ksiâżka i Wiedza under the title *Auschwitz: Zbrodnia przeciwko ludzkości (Auschwitz: Crime Against Humanity).*

Avishur, Yitzhak. *The Jewish Wedding in Baghdad, vol. I: Customs, Ceremonies and Documents.* Haifa: The University of Haifa, 1990. 225, XVI pp., with figs. In Hebrew, summary in English, pp. I–XVI.

Baruch, Adam. 'Eichmann Recaptured.' *Ariel: A Review of Arts and Letters* 88 (1992), 66–69.

Beit-Arié, Malachi. *The Makings of the Medieval Hebrew Book: Studies in Palaeography and Codicology.* Jerusalem: The Magnes Press, The Hebrew University, 1993. 283 pp., with numerous figs.

Bemporad, Dora Liscia. 'Aspetti dell' arte ebraica in Italia.' In: *La cultura ebraica nell' editoria italiana 1955–1990 (libri e riviste d' Italia 27).* Rome: Centro di Cultura Ebraica della Comunità Ebraica di Roma, 1992, pp. 189–200.

Berenbaum, Michael. *The World Must Know: The History of the Holocaust As Told in the U.S. Holocaust Memorial Museum.* Washington D.C.: Little Brown & Co., 1993. 256 pp., with numerous figs.

Blatas et l'Ecole de Paris. Venice: Tipo-Litografia Armena, 1982. Unpaginated, with numerous figs. In Italian, English and French. A catalogue accompanying an exhibition at the Chiesa San Samuele, 17 July–5 Sept. 1982.

Blatas: Dipinti, disegnie sculture. Venice: Tipo-Litografia Armena, 1987. 61 pp., with numerous figs. In Italian, English and French. A catalogue accompanied an exhibition at the Chiesa di San Stae, 4 July–27 Aug. 1987.

Böhm, Günter. 'The First Sephardic Cemeteries in South America and in the West Indies.' *Studia Rosenthaliana* 25.1 (Spring 1991), 3–14.

Borowsky, Irvin J. Ed. *Artists Confronting the Inconceivable: Award Winning Glass Sculpture.* Philadelphia: American Interfaith Institute, 1992. 136 pp., with numerous figs. Documents an international competition for glass artists to create work that fosters remembrance of Kristallnacht and the Holocaust.

Braeken, Jo. 'Beth Haknesset: Synagogen in België 1865–1914.' *Monumenten en Landschappen* 12.1 (Jan.–Feb. 1993), 13–45.

Branham, Joan R. 'Sacred Space under Erasure in Ancient Synagogues and Early Churches.' *The Art Bulletin* 74.3 (1992), 375–94.

Broshi, Magen. 'How to Recognize a Jew.' *The Israel Museum Journal* 11 (Spring, 1993), 81–84.

Cohen, Jules. 'Chatz en Pach: graveurs en chazzaniem in achttiende-eeuws Amsterdam.' *Studia Rosenthaliana* 26, 1/ 2 (1992), 46–53.

Cortissos, R. S. 'The Amsterdam Sephardi Community.' *Los Muestros: La Boz de los Sefardim* 4 (Sept. 1991), 12–14.

de Silva y Verástegui, Soledad. *La Miniatura Medieval en Navarra.* Pamplona: Grafinasa, 1988. See esp. the chapter on the Hebrew Bible in Pamplona: 'La Biblia Hebred,' pp. 169–88.

Devins, Driscoll P. *Home of the Living: A Venetian Cemetery.* New York: Triton Press, 1992. With numerous photographs.

Dittmar, Peter. *Die Darstellung der Juden in der populären Kunst zur Zeit der Emanzipation.* Munich: K.G. Saur, 1992. 479 pp., with numerous figs.

Doleželová, Jana and Jaroslav Kuntos. *Gems of the Prague Ghetto: From the Workshops of Prague Silversmiths.* Prague: State Jewish Museum, n.d. 15, xxv pp., with numerous figs. Trans. by Joy Turner-Kadeĉková.

Dratwa, Daniel. 'De synagoge in België: Geschiedenis en cultuur.' *Monumenten en Landschappen* 12.1 (Jan.–Feb. 1993), 8–12.

Fiedler, Jiří. *Jewish Sights of Bohemia and Moravia.* Prague: Sefer, 224 pp., with numerous figs. An alphabetic guide book.

Fintz Menascé, Esther. 'Le quartier juif de Rhodes au 19ème siécle.' *Los Muestros: La Boz de los Sefardim* 4 (Sept. 1991), 17–21.

Fishman, Bernard. 'Beth Hamedrosh Hagodol and Other Vanishing Jewish Buildings.' *Generations: The Magazine of the Jewish Historical Society of Maryland* (Summer 1991), 1–3.

Frankel, Ellen and Betsy Platkin Teutsch. *The Encyclopedia of Jewish Symbols.* New York: Jason Aronson, 1992. 256 pp., with numerous drawings.

Frazier, Nancy. *Jewish Museums of North America: A Guide to Collections, Artifacts and Memorabilia.* New York: John Wiley and Sons, 1992. 242 pp., with numerous figs.

Gené, Pierre. 'Anstaltssynagogen in Wien.' *David: Jüdische Kulturzeitschrift* 4.12 (Apr. 1992), 16–17.

——. 'Randbemerkungen zu den Synagogen in Österreich.' *David: Jüdische Kulturzeitschrift* 4.15 (Dec. 1992), 10–26. Synagogues in Vienna, Niederösterreich, Burgenland, Steiermark, Hohenems. With numerous figs.

———. 'Anmerkungen zur Barocksynagoge in Hohenems.' *David: Jüdische Kulturzeitschrift* 5.16 (Apr. 1993), 8–9.

Gens, Leo. 'Salomos 'Hohelied'.' *E & K: Der Estnische Sammler* 2.3 (1992), 53–57.

Glimtar ur judiskt liv i Sverige: Det Judiska Museet i Stockholm. Stockholm: Judiska Museet, 1990. Catalogue of photographs, unpaginated.

Goberman, D. *Masterpieces of Jewish Art, vol. 4: Jewish Tombstones in Ukraine and Moldova.* Moscow: Image, 1993. 52 pp., with numerous figs. Ed. by Alexander Kantsedikas.

Goldberg, Sylvie, Anne. *Dictionnaire Encyclopedique du Judaïsme.* Paris: éditions du Cerf, 1993. 1800 pp., with numerous figs. In collaboration with Véronique Gillet, Arnaud Sérandour and Gabriel Raphaël Veyret.

Grewenig, Meinrad M. *Sabbatgerät: Lamp herunter, Sorg hinauf.* Speyer: Historisches Museum der Pfalz, 1993. 9 pp., with figs.

Gruber, Ruth Ellen. *Jewish Heritage Travel: A Guide to Central and Eastern Europe.* New York: John Wiley and Sons, 1992. 305 pp.

Guide to the Treasures of the Temple Exhibition. Jerusalem: The Temple Institute, n.d., 15 pp., with figs.

Guleryuz, Naim. *The History of the Turkish Jews.* Istanbul: Rekor Ofset A.S, 1992. 2nd edn. 27 pp., with figs.

Gutmann, Joseph. Ed. *The Dura-Europos Synagogue: A Re-Evaluation (1932–1992)* (University of South Florida Studies in the History of Judaism, vol. 25). Atlanta: Scholars Press, 1992. 226 pp., with numerous figs.

Guttmann, Herman Zvi. *Vom Tempel zum Gemeindezentrum: Synagogen im Nachkriegsdeutschland.* Frankfurt am Main: Athenäum Verlag, 1989. Ed. by Sophie Remmlinger and Klaus Hofmann.

Hamáčková, Vlastimila. 'Le cimetiére juif aı Sêvihov.' *Judaica Bohemiae: Státní Zîdovské Muzeum Praha* 28 (1992), 88–92.

Hamáčková, Vlastimila and Jirîna Sédinová. 'The Jewish Cemetery in Trébíč.' *Judaica Bohemiae* 27.1–2 (1991), 82–91.

Heimann-Jelinek Felicitas and Kurt Schubert. Eds. *Spharadim — Spaniolen: Die Juden in Spanien — Die Sephardische Diaspora (Studia Judaica Austriaca vol. XIII).* Eisenstadt: Österreichisches Jüdisches Museum, 1992. 241 pp., with figs. Includes the following essays on Jewish art: Inés Müller, 'Die maurischen Synagogenbauten in Spanien,' pp. 80–87; Kurt Schubert, 'Zusammenleben und Konfrontation,' pp. 87–90; id., 'Die kulturelle Bedeutung des spanischen Judentums,' pp. 90–95; Ursula Schubert and Kurt Schubert, 'Bibeln,' pp. 95–97; id., 'Pesach Haggadot,' pp. 97–106.

Hinker, Annemarie and Heidemarie Uhl. 'Die Grazer Synagoge (1892–1938).' *David: Jüdische Kulturzeitschrift* 4.14 (Sept. 1992), 15–18.

Hyndráková, Anna and Anna Lorencová. 'Systematic Collection of Memories Organized by the Jewish Museum in Prague.' *Judaica Bohemiae: Státní Zîdovské Muzeum Praha* 28 (1992), 53–63.

Israelowitz, Oscar. *Synagogues of the United States: A Photographic and Architectural Survey.* New York: Israelowitz Publishing, 1992. Over 120 photos.

Jacoby, Ruth. 'The Image of the Jew in Antiquity from the Twelfth Century B.C. Until the Third Century A.D.' *Qadmoniot: Quarterly for Antiquities of Eretz Israel and the Bible Lands* 25.3–4, 99–100 (1993), 116–22. In Hebrew.

———. 'The Relationship Between Decoration and Plan in Queen Helena's Tomb in Jerusalem.' *Qadmoniot: Quarterly for the Antiquities of Eretz Israel and the Bible Lands* 26.1–2, 101–102 (1993), 62–63. In Hebrew.

Jets: Jewish Exhibition Travelling Service: Catalog, Fall 1992. New York: National Foundation for Jewish Culture and the Council of American Jewish Museums, 1992. 97 pp., with numerous figs.

Jewish Immigration in Rio Grande do Sul: Life Stories. Rio Grande do Sul: Instituto Cultural Judaico Marc Chagall, 1992. 2 vols. Vol. 1, 104 pp., vol 2, 127 pp., with numerous figs. In Spanish and English.

Judaica Bohemiae 27 (1–2). Prague: Státní Zîdovské Muzeum Praha, 1991. 112 pp., with figs. Includes: Jirîna Sédinová, 'Volksdruck der Megilla Esther,' pp. 45–48; Vladimír Sadek, 'Silber als Symbol der Thora,' pp. 49–53; Jana Šmejkalovaé, 'The Message of the Banner of Marcus Mordecai Mayzl,' pp. 54–63; Jana Purová, 'Restoration of a 19th Century Torah Mantle,' pp. 65–68; Helena Olmerová, 'Ritualbad bei der Pinkas-Synagoge in der Prager Altstadt,' pp. 69–78; Vladimír Sadek, 'David's Star on the Tombstones of the Old Jewish Cemetery in Prague,' pp. 79–81; Vlastimila Hamáčková and Jirîna Sédinová, 'The Jewish Cemetery in Trébíč,' pp. 82–91; Hana Mayerová, 'The Exhibitions of the State Jewish Museum in 1990,' pp. 93–95; Otakar A. Kukla, 'Artistes juifs de l'Ukraine,' pp. 95–97.

Kamenetzki, Samuel. 'Jüdische Friedhöfe in der Reinpfalz.' In: Alfred Hans Kuby. Ed. *Juden in der Provinz: Beiträge zur Geschichte der Juden in der Pfalz zwischen Emanzipation und Vernichtung.* Neustadt a.d. Weinstraße: Verlag Pfälzische Post, 1989. 2nd edn., pp. 227–29. Restoration of cemeteries in the Palatinate.

Kantsedikas, A., Y. Volkovinskaya and T. Romanovskaya. *Masterpieces of Jewish Art, vol. 3: Silver.* Moscow: Image, 1992. 382 pp., with numerous figs. Ed. by Alexander Kantsedikas.

Kasovsky G. *Masterpieces of Jewish Art, vol. 2: Artists from Vitebsk: Yehuda Pen and His Pupils.* Moscow: Image, 1992. 76 pp., with numerous figs. Ed. Alexander Kantsedikas.

Kestenbaum Green, Connie. 'The Elusive Face of King David: Restoring a Mosaic from the Ancient Synagogue at Gaza.' *The Israel Museum Journal* 11 (Spring, 1993), 65–72.

Klagsbald, Victor. 'Sceau de Salomon Bar Ephraim Ben Al Hadad et du symbolisme du croissant de lune et de l'toile.' *Revue des Études Juives* 150.3–4 (July–Dec. 1991), 547–56.

Knoblauch, G. and F. Hollin. *Die Neue Synagoge in Berlin, 1867 (Reprint).* Berlin: Edition Hentrich and Neue Synagoge Berlin — Centrum Judaicum, 1992. Unpaginated, with numerous drawings and plans. Introduction by Heinz Galinski. Includes an article by Hermann Simon, 'Geschichte und Wiederaufbau der Neuen Synagoge.'

Kogman-Appel, Katrin. 'The Iconographical Models of the Illuminated Haggadot from Spain.' *Pe'amim: Studies in Oriental Jewry* 50 (Winter 1992), 29–68. In Hebrew.

Kopel Gurwin: The Artist and his Work: 1923–1990. N.p., 1991. 127 pp., with numerous figs.

Korol, Dieter. 'Il primo ritrovamento di un oggetto sicuramente giudaico a Cimitile: Una lucerna con la rappresentazione della menoräh.' *Boreas: Münstersche Beiträge zur Archäologie* 13 (1990), 94–102, and pls. 18–19.

Künzl, Hannelore. 'Die Frage der jüdischen Identität in den Werken von M. Lilien und anderen jüdischen Künstlern des späten 19. und 20. Jahrhunderts.' *Kairos* 30–31 (1991), 188–216.

———. *Jüdische Kunst von der Biblischen Zeit bis in die Gegenwart.* Munich: C.H. Beck, 1992. 266 pp., with numerous figs.

Kybalová, Ludmila, 'Dated Laces in Synagogal Textiles.' *Judaica Bohemiae: Státní Zîdovsk Muzeum Praha* 28 (1992), 73–79.

Leedy, Walter. 'Eric Mendelsohn's Park Synagogue.' In: Louis T. Milic. Ed. *Cleveland Sacred Landmarks: A Special Issue.* Cleveland: Cleveland State University, 1990, pp. 45–69.

Levine, Lee, I. 'Reconciling Rabbinic Literature and Archeological

Finds.' *Cathedra for the History of Eretz Israel and its Yishuv* 68 (June, 1993), 36–40.

Lewerenz-Weghuber, Christine Ruth. 'Die Juden in Rudolfsheim-Fünfhaus.' *David: Jüdische Kulturzeitschrift* 4.14 (Sept. 1992), 9–12.

Magen, Yitzhak. 'The Samaritan Synagogue at Khirbet Samara.' *The Israel Museum Journal* 11 (Spring 1993), 59–64.

———. 'Samaritan Synagogues.' *Qadmoniot: Quarterly for the Antiquities of Eretz Israel and Bible Lands* 25.3–4, 100–101 (1993), 66–90.

Majzner, Victor and Andrew Majzner. *The Australian Haggadah.* Melbourne: Victor Majzner, 1992. 177 pp., with numerous pls. A copy of an illustrated Haggadah whose original art work was exhibited at the Jewish Museum of Australia in Melbourne and the Great Synagogue in Sydney.

Makover-Assaf, Sharon and Daisy Raccah-Djivre. 'The 'Flowering Vase' Torah Mantle from Morocco.' *The Israel Museum Journal* 11 (Spring, 1993), 73–80.

Mann, Vivian, B. with Emily D. Bilski. *The Jewish Museum — New York.* London: Scala Publications and New York: The Jewish Museum, 1993. 128 pp., with numerous figs. Introduction by Joan Rosenbaum.

Markova, Alla. 'Sephardic Manuscripts in Leningrad.' *Annual: Organization of the Jews in Bulgaria 'Shalom'* 25 (1990), 77–79.

Meah Berachot: An 18th Century Miniature Book of Blessings and Prayers: A Fine Limited Edition Printed on Vellum. London: Facsimile Editions, 1993. Limited edition: 550 copies, with a companion volume written by Iris Fishof and ed. by Jeremy Schonfield.

Mellinkoff, Ruth. *Outcasts: Signs of Otherness in Northern European Art of the Late Middle Ages.* Berkeley, Los Angeles and Oxford: University of California Press, 1993. 2 vols.; vol. 1: text, lviii, 360 pp., vol. 2: pls. See esp. the following chapters: 'Colors,' pp. 33–56; 'Headgear: Holy and Unholy, pp. 57–94; 'Hebrew and Pseudo-Hebrew Lettering,' pp. 95–108; 'Introduction to Unusual Physical Features,' pp. 111–17; 'Physical Distortions and Deformities,' pp. 119–44. 'Skin Blemishes,' pp. 78–116.

Milgrom, Jo. *Handmade Midrash: A Guide for Teachers, Workshops in Visual Theology: Rabbis and Lay Leaders.* Philadelphia, New York and Jerusalem: The Jewish Publication Society, 1992. 177 pp., with numerous figs.

Moore, Clare. Ed. *The Visual Dimension: Aspects of Jewish Art.* Boulder, San Francisco and Oxford: Westview Press, 1993. 184 pp., with numerous figs. Published in Memory of Isaiah Shachar (1935–1977), in cooperation with the Oxford Centre for Postgraduate Hebrew Studies. Includes: Joseph Gutmann, 'Is There a Jewish Art?,' pp. 1–19; Vidosava Nedomački, 'A Contribution to the Discussion 'Is There a Jewish Art',' pp. 21–23; Ursula Schubert, 'The Continuation of Ancient Jewish Art in the Middle Ages,' pp. 25–45; Thérèse Metzger, 'The Iconography of the Hebrew Psalter from the Thirteenth to the Fifteenth Century,' pp. 47–81; Helen Rosenau, 'The Architecture of the Synagogue in Neoclassicism and Historicism,' pp. 83–103; Alfred Moldovan, 'Foolishness, Fakes, and Forgeries in Jewish Art: An Introduction to the Discussion on Judaica Conservation and Collecting Today,' pp. 105–19; Bernhard Blumenkranz, 'The Case for a Central Archives of Jewish Art: An Introduction to the Discussion on the Possibility of Establishing a Central Photographic Archives of Jewish Ceremonial Art,' pp. 121–35; Thérèse Metzger and Mendel Metzger, 'Introduction to the Catalogue of the Bodleian Library Exhibition,' pp. 137–39; id., 'Catalogue of Illuminated Hebrew Manuscripts Exhibited in the Bodleian Library, August-September 1977,' pp. 141–68. Includes also a list of publications by Isaiah Shachar and indices.

Morton Weizman, Sandra. *Artifacts from 'A Coat of Many Colours: Two Centuries of Jewish Life in Canada' (Mercury Series Paper No. 62).* Hull: Canadian Museum of Civilization, 1990. 133 pp., with numerous figs. A catalogue which accompanied an exhibition of the Canadian Museum of Civilization in corporation with the Canadian Friends of Beth Hatefutsoth. In English and French.

Paszkiewiczowie, Hanna i Piotr and Monika Krajewska. *Cmentarze Zydowskie w Warszawie (Jewish Cemeteries in Warsaw).* Warsaw: Wydawnictwo Naukowe PWN, 1992. 69 pp., with numerous figs.

Perry-Lehmann, Meira. 'Prints and Drawings.' *Ariel: A Review of Arts and Letters in Israel* 88 (1992), 36–42.

Piâtkowska, Renata. 'Maurycy Gottlieb (1856–1879).' *Biuletyn: Zydowskiego Instytutu Historycznego* 2 (158), 45–64.

———. Ed. *Maurycy Trêbacz 1861–1941: Wystawa monograficzna: Katalog dziel istniejâcych i zaginionych.* Warsaw: Z.ydowski Instytut Historyczny w Polsce, Muzeum Historii Miasta Lodzi, 1993. 203 pp., with numerous figs. In Polish and English.

Putík, Alexander, Jirîna Sédinová and Jana Dolezélová. *Jewish Customs and Traditions.* Prague: State Jewish Museum, 1992. 84 pp., with numerous figs.

Revel-Neher, Elisabeth. *The Image of the Jew in Byzantine Art (Studies in Antisemitism Series).* Oxford, New York, Seoul, and Tokyo: Pergamon Press, 1992. 133 pp., with numerous figs. Foreword by Marcel Dubois, trans. by David Maizel. Published for the Vidal Sassoon International Center for the Study of Antisemitism (SICSA), The Hebrew University of Jerusalem.

Roditi, Edouard. 'Observations on the Preservation of Jewish Monuments.' *The Jewish Museum of Greece Newsletter* 34 (Winter-Spring 1993), 1–4.

Rosenbaum, Jacob and Belle. *Chronicle of Jewish Traditions: A Sentimental Journey.* New York: Yeshiva University Museum, 1992. 47 pp., with numerous figs. Catalogue of the metalwork of Henryk Winograd depicting scenes of Jewish life from the paintings of Moritz Oppenheim.

Rosenfeld, Moshe. *Hebrew Printing from its Beginning until 1948: A Gazetteer of Printing: The First Books and their Dates with Photographed Title-Pages and Bibliographical Notes.* Jerusalem, 1992. With numerous figs.

Roshkovska, Anna. 'Facts about the Contribution of Jews to the Europeanization of Art and Culture in the Bulgarian Lands: 18th–19th Century.' *Annual: Organization of the Jews in Bulgaria 'Shalom'* 25 (1990), 51–61.

Roth, Michel and Max Warschawski. *Les Synagogues d'Alsace et leur Histoire.* Jerusalem: Chalom Bisamme, 1992. 191 pp., with numerous figs.

Rozen, Minna. 'A Survey of Jewish Cemeteries in Western Turkey.' *The Jewish Quarterly Review* 83.1–2 (July–Oct. 1993), 71–85.

Sabar, Shalom. 'The Sephardi Marriage Contract.' *Ariel: A Review of Arts and Letters in Israel* 88 (1992), 70–83.

Salvaged from the Warsaw Ghetto: the Archives of E. Ringelblum. Warsaw: Museum of the Jewish Historical Institute in Poland, 1993. 51 pp., with numerous figs.

Samely, Alexander. 'The Interpreted Text: Among the Hebrew Manuscripts of the John Rylands University Library.' *Bulletin of the John Rylands University Library of Manchester* 73.2 (1991), 1–20.

Scharf, Rafael F. Ed. *In the Warsaw Ghetto: Summer 1941.* New York: Aperture, 1993. 112 pp., with numerous figs. Photographs by a German soldier, Willy Georg, with passages from Warsaw Ghetto diaries.

Schreckenberg, Heinz and Kurt Schubert. *Jewish Historiography and Iconography in Early and Medieval Christianity, Part I:*

Josephus in Early Christian Literature and Medieval Christian Art; Part II: Jewish Pictorial Traditions in Early Christian Art (Compendia Rerum Iudaicarum ad Novum Testamentum 3.2). Assen: Van Gorcum, 1992. xviii, 310 pp., with numerous figs. Introduction by David Flusser.

Schrijver, Emile G.L. 'On Matatia de Ishack Aboab (1672–1703) and his Calligraphic Art.' *Studia Rosenthaliana* 26.1–2 (1992), 193–201.

Schubert, Ursula. 'Jüdische Buchmalerei im Burgenland.' *David: Jüdische Kulturzeitschrift* 5.16 (Apr. 1993), 3–5.

———. *Jüdische Buchkunst, Part II (Buchkunst im Wandel der Zeiten vol. 3/ II).* Graz: Akademische Druck- u. Verlag, 1992. 225 pp., with numerous figs. An historical introduction by Kurt Schubert and an essay by Otto Mazal.

The Sephardic Journey: 1492–1992. New York: Yeshiva University Museum, 1992. 420 pp., with numerous figs. A catalogue which accompanied the Yeshiva University Museum exhibition, 13 Nov. 1990–31 Dec. 1992. Includes the following papers on Jewish art: Shalom Sabar, 'Manuscript and Book Illustration Among the Sephardim Before and After the Expulsion,' pp. 54–93; Chaya Benjamin, 'The Sephardic Journey — 500 Years of Jewish Ceremonial Objects,' pp. 94–135.

Sheffer, Avigail. 'Ancient Textiles Decorated with Color from the Land of Israel.' In: Chagit Sorek and Etan Ayalon. Eds. *Colors from Nature: Natural Colors in Ancient Times.* Tel Aviv: Eretz Israel Museum, 1993, pp. 66–75. In Hebrew. Summary in English, p. 32*

Simon, Hermann. *The New Synagogue, Berlin: Past — Present — Future.* Berlin: Edition Hentrich, 1992. 48 pp., with figs.

Šmejkalová, Jana. 'The Borderline Between Time and Eternity: A Note on the Symbolism of Synagogal Textiles.' *Judaica Bohemiae: Státní Židovske Muzeum Praha* 28 (1992), 80–87.

Stavroulakis, Nicholas. 'Jewish Amulets Against the Evil Eye.' *Los Muestros: La Boz de los Sefardim* 5 (Dec. 1991), 56–57.

———. *A Salonika Album: Jews and Dervishes.* Athens: Talos Press, 1992. 60 pp., with figs.

Stavroulakis, Nicholas and Timothy DeVinney. *A Jewish Guide to Greece.* Athens: Talos Press, 1992. 280 pp., with numerous figs.

Strom, Yale. *The Expulsion of the Jews: 500 Years of Exodus — A Photo History from the Inquisition to the Present.* New York: S.P.I. Books and Shapolsky Publishers, 1992. 192 pp., with numerous figs.

Le temps des rafles: Le sort des juifs en France pendant la guerre. Paris: Centre de Documentation Juive Contemporaine (C.D.J.C.), 1992. 191 pp., with numerous figs. Catalogue accompanying an exhibition of the C.D.J.C. Curators: Serge Klarsfeld, Hubert Cain and Jean Corcos.

Three Unifold Jubilees: Italian Jewry in Jerusalem. Jerusalem: Museo U. Nahon di Arte Ebraica Italiana, 1992. 18 pp.

van Voolen, Edward. 'Hebraica and Judaica Printed in the Northern Netherlands before 1815 in the Collection of the Jewish Historical Museum of Amsterdam.' *Studia Rosenthaliana* 26.1–2 (1992), 202–23.

Warszawski, Abraham and Abraham Peretz. 'Building the Temple Mount: Organization and Execution.' *Cathedra for the History of Eretz Israel and its Yishuv* 66 (Dec. 1992), 3–46. In Hebrew, summary in English, p. 191.

Wiehn, Erhard Roy. *Jewish Life in Kiev.* Konstanz: Hartung-Gorre, 1992. Unpaginated, with numerous figs. In Russian, German and English.

Wiesemann, Falk. *Genizah — Hidden Legacies of the German Village Jews.* Vienna: The Hidden Legacy Foundation, 1992. 224 pp., with numerous figs. A catalogue for an exhibition by The Hidden Legacy Foundation. Includes the following papers: Falk Wiesemann, ''Hidden Testimonies' of German Rural Jewry: An Introduction to the Exhibition,' pp.15–32; Hans-Peter Baum, 'Jewish Life in Franconia,' pp. 33–50; Leonhard Scherg, 'Urspringen: A Jewish Community, Synagogue and Genizah,' pp. 51–57; Fritz Armbruster, 'Ichenhausen: What Was and What Remains: Stones, Papers — Memories,' pp. 58–65.

Wiśniewski, Tomasz. *Synagogues and Jewish Communities in the Bialystok Region: Jewish Life in Eastern Europe before 1939.* Bialystok: David, 1992. 218 pp., with numerous figs. The second part includes alphabetized information on and drawings of Jewish towns and villages and their synagogues.

Yargina, Z. *Masterpieces of Jewish Art, vol. 5: Wooden Synagogues.* Moscow: Image, 1993. 367 pp., with numerous figs. Ed. by Alexander Kantsedikas.

Young, James. *The Texture of Memory: Holocaust Memorials and Meaning.* New Haven: Yale University Press, 1993. With numerous figs.

Yuniverg, Leonid. *The Jerusalem Museum of the Jewish Book: The Project.* Jerusalem, Tel Aviv: Aticot, 1993. 36 pp.

Zeharia, Shabtai. 'The Synagogue of Senior Geni.' *Etmol: A Magazine for the History of Eretz Israel and the People of Israel* 13.2, 76 (Dec. 1987), 6–7.

Zevi, Fausto. 'Recenti studi e scoperte di archeologia ebraica.' In: La cultura ebraica nell'editoria italiana 1955–1990 (Libri e riviste d'Italia 27). Rome: Centro di Cultura Ebraica della Comunitaı Ebraica di Roma, 1992, pp. 169–84.

Zoltán, Riczu. *Zsidö ´pületek ´s emlkek Nyíregyházán (Jewish Relics and Buildings in Nyíregyháza).* Mátszalka and Nyíregyháza: Armenta Hüsüzem, 1992. 132 pp., with figs. and plans. Summaries in English and German, pp. 125–32.

In the 'List of Publications' in vol. 18 the following articles were wrongly attributed, and we apologize to the author:

Schubert, Ursula. 'Jüdische und Christliche Kunst.' *Jahrbuch des Vorarlberger Landesmuseumsvereins — Freunde der Landeskunde.* Bregenz, 1991, pp. 77–82.

———. 'Das Mittelalterliche Erbe in der Bilderbibel des Moses Dal Castellazzo, Warschau, Jüdisches Historisches Institut, Cod. 1164.' In Alfred Ebenbauer and Klaus Zatloukal. Eds. *Die Juden in ihrer mittelalterlichen Umwelt.* Vienna, Köln and Weimar: Böhlau Verlag, 1991, pp. 205–15.

Compiled by Sarit Shalev-Eyni

CHRONICLE OF EVENTS

Aarau, Aargauer Kunsthaus Aarau. 'Alis Guggenheim (1896–1958).' 18 Oct.–22 Nov. 1992

Amsterdam, Joods Historisch Museum. 'In de voetsporen van Anski: Joods leven in Rusland 1772–1917.' Through 18 Oct. 1992.

———. 'Op zoek in Litouwen.' 11 Sept.–29 Nov. 1992.

———. 'Faces in Focus: Four Centuries of Portraits of Dutch Jews.' 18 Dec. 1992–4 Apr. 1993.

———. 'Andy Warhol: Ten Jewish Portraits.' 18 Dec. 1992–4 Apr. 1993.

Ann Arbor, University of Michigan Hillel. 'Lodz Ghetto: Survival and Destruction of the First Ghetto.' 15–21 Mar. 1993.

Baltimore, Jewish Historical Society of Maryland. 'Fertile Ground: Two Hundred Years of Jewish Life in Baltimore.' Through Feb. 1993. Catalogue, 24 pp.

Baltimore, JCC of Greater Baltimore, Brown Art Gallery. 'Is This Israeli Art?' 2 May–20 June 1993.

Barcelona, Fundación Baruj Spinoza. 'Judíos en Barcelona 1914–1954: Las primeras olas migratorias.' 30 Apr.–29 May 1992.

Basel, Schweizerische Museums für Volkskunde and the Jüdischen Museums der Schweiz. 'Juden im Elsass.' 26 Nov. 1992–15 Aug. 1993.

Be'er Sheva, The Avraham Baron Art Gallery, Ben Gurion University of the Negev and Omanut La'am. "From the Limits of the West' : The Five-Hundredth Anniversary of the Expulsion from Spain: Artists Responding to Judah Halevi's Poem 'Fair-Crested': A Travelling Group Exhibition.' Jan. 1992. Opening: Jerusalem, The Jerusalem Theater, 29 Jan. 1992; Tel Aviv, Artists' House, 9 Feb. 1992 and Be'er Sheva, Ben Gurion University, May 1992. Curator: Haim Finkelstein. Catalogue, unpaginated, with numerous figs.

Berkeley, Judah L. Magnes Museum. 'The Legacy of Boris Deutsch: A Centennial Exhibition.' 24 May–20 Sept. 1992.

———. 'Survivors: Ceramic Sculpture by Andrée Singer Thompson.' 24 May–Sept. 1992.

———. 'Remembrance: Mixed-Media Installation By Lisa Kokin.' 24 May–19 July 1992.

———. 'The 30th Anniversary Exhibition of the Judah L. Magnes Museum.' 11 Oct. 1992–7 Feb. 1993. Catalogue, 39 pp., with figs.

———. 'Kafka, Eve, The Wolf, and My Grandmother's Bread Bowl: Triennial Juried Exhibition.' Through 23 May 1993. Contemporary art by California artists Laurie Polster, Elisse Pogofsky-Harris, William Rosen, and Rachel Schriber.

———. 'The Prophetic Quest: 75th Anniversary of Jacob Landau.' 6 June–19 Sept. 1993. Catalogue.

———. 'Painting with Light: Photographic Aspects in the Work of E.M. Lilien.' Through Sept. 1993.

Berlin, Bauwettbewerb. 'Topographie des Terrors.' 31 Mar.–20 Apr. 1993.

Berlin, Jüdisches Museum, Martin-Gropius-Bau. 'Unser einziger Weg ist Arbeit': Das Getto in Lodz: 1940–1944.' 15 Jan.–22 Mar. 1992. An exhibition from the Jüdisches Museum, Frankfurt am Main.

Berlin, National Foundation for Jewish Culture. 'Council of American Jewish Museums Conference in Berlin.' 14 Jan. 1992.

Boston, Massachusetts College of Art. 'Seeing Through "Paradise": Artists and the Terezín Concentration Camp.' 6 Mar.–4 May 1992. Also in New York, Drawing Center, Jun.–Aug. 1991; Grand Forks, North Dakota Museum of Art, Sept.–Oct. 1991; Houston, Jewish Community Center, Nov.–Dec. 1991; Berkeley,

University Art Museum, Jan.–Mar. 1992; Prague, Kinsky Palacé National Gallery, May–June 1992; and Terezín, Terezín Ghetto Museum, Sept.–Nov. 1992. Curators: Johanna Branson, Michéle Furst and Jeffrey Keough. Catalogue, 88 pp., with numerous figs. See esp. Johanna Branson, 'Seeing Through "Paradise": Art and Propaganda in Terezín,' pp. 37–48; Arno Pařík, 'Art in the Terezín Ghetto,' pp. 49–62; Leo Hass, 'The Affair of the Painters of Terezín,' pp. 63–70; Al Hurwitz, 'Friedl Dicker-Brandeis: the Art Educator as Hero,' pp. 71–81; Arno Pařík, 'Short Biographies of the Terezín artists,' pp. 83–85.

Bratislava, Slovenská Národná Galéria. 'Imro Weiner — Král: 1901 suborneé dielo 1978.' Dec. 1991–Feb. 1992. Catalogue, 85 pp., with numerous figs.

Brookline, Hebrew College. 'The First Seven Days.' 21 Mar.–June 1993.

Brussels, Auschwitz Foundation and the Free University of Brussels. 'Histoire et mémoire des crimes et génocide nazis.' An international congress. Included the following papers on Jewish art: James Young, 'The Rhetoric of Ruins: Jews, Poles and Auschwitz'; S. Samuels, 'Beth Hashoah Museum of Tolerance'; J.R. Boonstra, 'Het Anne Frank Huis: Meer dan allen een historische plek'; D. Dratwa, 'Cheminement de la mémoire de la Shoa en Belgique: Analyse des mémoriaux'; T. Swiebocka, 'Les changements projetés au Musée d' Auschwitz'; I.B.H. Abram, 'Nederlandse musea en de Shoa'; A. Genger, 'Kunst und Ehrunerung: Beispiele aus der gedenkstatten arbeit.'

Brussels, Bibliotheque Royale Albert I. 'Le monde d' Anne Frank, 1929–1945.' 16 Oct.–28 Nov. 1992. Catalogue, 86 pp. Organized by the Anne Frank Foundation of Amsterdam. Also at the Romi Goldmuntz Centrum in Antwerpen, 4–28 Mar. 1993.

———. 'Le livre Yiddish: Fonds Jacques Lew.' 12 Feb.–27 Mar. 1993. Catalogue by Azarius Dobruszkes and Théodore Gutmans, 86 pp.

Brussels, Cercle Ben Gourion. 'Art and Judaica from Israel: Contemporary Designers.' 25–27 Jan. 1992.

Brussels, Goethe Institut. 'Memories of Jewish Poland — 1932: Photographs by Nahum T. Gidal.' 26 Oct.–28 Nov. 1992. Catalogue, 6 pp. An exhibition of Beth Hatefutsot, Tel Aviv.

Brussels, Musée Communal d'Ixelles. 'Le Sphinx de Vienne: Sigmund Freud: L'art et l'archéologie.' 6 May–11 July 1993. Catalogue, 202 pp.

Brussels, Musée Juif de Belgique. 'Belgian Jewish Artists from Israel.' 15 Dec. 1991–21 Mar. 1992. Catalogue by Daniel Dratwa, 20 pp.

———. '1940–1944: Les années ténèbres. Déportation et résistances des Juifs en Belgique.' 13 Sept.–20 Dec. 1992. Curator: Daniel Dratwa. Catalogue by the curator, 46 pp. Includes: 'Jewish Artists in Belgium during the Occupation,' pp. 39–43.

———. 'From Gracia Nasi to Nico Gunzburg: Shadows and Lights of the Antwerp Jewry.' 21 Jan.–23 May 1993. Catalogue by Daniel Dratwa, 40 pp. Also at the Romi Goldmuntz Centrum in Antwerp, 8–17 June 1993.

———. 'Maps and Images from the Holy Land from the 16th century to Nowadays.' Catalogue by Daniel Dratwa, 24 pp.

Brussels, Musée Royaux Art et Histoire. 'Artisanat d'Israel: Kunstambacht uit Israel.' 14 June–28 July 1991. Catalogue, 120 pp. Organized by the Alix de Rothschild Foundation.

Cambridge, MA, Semitic Museum, Harvard University. 'Capturing the Holy Land: M.J. Diness and the Beginnings of Photography in Jerusalem.' Through Dec. 1993. Catalogue.

Cavaillon, Musées et Patrimoine de Cavaillon. 'Esther, Samuel et Rébecca.' 9 Nov. 1992–31 May 1993.

Chicago, Art Institute of Chicago. 'Marc Chagall and the Jewish Theater.' Through 7 May 1993.

Chicago, Spertus Museum. 'Voyages to Freedom: 500 Years of Jewish Life in Latin America.' 3 Nov.–6 Dec. 1992.

———. 'David Bennett: Prophetic Visions.' 21 Sept. 1992–7 Feb. 1993.

———. 'In the Tradition of the Sephardim.' Through Jan. 1993.

———. 'Jews of Turkey: Anyos muchos y buenos.' 27 Sept. 1992–2 Jan. 1993.

———. 'The Holy Land: Then and Now.' Through 23 May 1993.

Cincinnati, Hebrew Union College — Jewish Institute of Religion, Skirball Museum. 'An Eternal People: The Jewish Experience.' 11 May–July 1993.

———. 'New Forms for Traditional Art: Works by Susi Guggenheim-Weil.' 11 May–July.

Collegeville, Berman Museum of Art at Ursinus College. 'Voyages to Freedom: 500 years of Jewish Life in Latin America.' 15 Nov.–20 Dec. 1992.

Columbus, The Liturgical Art Guild of Ohio. The Thirteenth Biennial Exhibition: 'Contemporary Works of Faith '93.' 7 Mar.–4 Apr. 1993.

Cracow, Ariel Gallery. 'Paweł Vogler: Memories, Paintings, Drawings.' Opening: 6 June 1992.

Cracow, Gologórski and Rostworowski Gallery. 'Osias Hofstatter.' Opening: 7 June 1992. On loan from the Herzliyah Museum.

Cracow, Judaic Museum in the Old Synagogue. 'Anna Małecka-Beiersdorf: Paper Cut-Out — Inspirations with Jewish Art.' Opening: 6 June 1992.

Denver, Mizel Museum of Judaica. 'The City of David: Discoveries from the Excavations.' 12 Sept.–15 Nov. 1992.

———. 'Hanukkah: Festival of Lights.' 30 Nov.–31 Dec. 1992.

———. 'Discovering Denver Jewish Artists.' 20 Dec. 1992–28 Feb. 1993. Curator: Jack Henry Kunin. Catalogue by the curator, unpaginated.

———. 'In Fitting Memory: The Art and Politics of Holocaust Memorials.' 15 Mar.–31 May 1993. By Ira Nowinski and Sybil Milton.

———. 'Israel: The Western Wall: Photographs by Andy Katz.' 14 June–22 Aug. 1993.

———. 'Aliya 33: Housing the German Immigrant in Tel Aviv.' 14 June–22 Aug. 1993. By Jack Henry Kunin.

Detroit, Janice Charach-Epstein Museum Gallery and Jewish Community Center of Metropolitan Detroit. 'Feast of Lights: Art and Tradition of Hanukkah Lamps.' 1992. Curator: Anita Plous. Catalogue ed. by the curator, 32 pp., with figs. Includes an essay by Joseph Gutmann, pp. 5–14.

Ein Harod, Mishkan Le'Omanut: Museum of Art. 'Judith Weinshall Liberman: The Holocaust Wall Hanging.' 25 Apr.–25 June 1992.

Eisenstadt, Österreichisches Jüdisches Museum. 'Die Juden in Spanien bis 1492.' Opening: 18 May.–26 Oct. 1992.

———. 'Spanisches und Spaniolisches Judentum.' A conference. 17–21 June 1992. Included the following paper on Jewish art: Emile G.J. Schrijver, 'Hebräische Kalligraphie bei den holländischen Sepharden im 17. und 18. Jh.'

Elkins Park, The Temple Judea Museum of Keneseth Israel. 'The Work of Our Hands: A Five Year Retrospective.' 25 Sept. 1989–19 Jan. 1990. Curator: Judith B. Maslin. Catalogue, unpaginated.

Ellis Island, Ellis Island Immigration Museum. 'Jews in America.' Through June 1993.

Emeden, Ostfriesische Landesmuseums Emden. 'Zeugnisse einer zerstöhrten Vergangenheit: Jüdisches Kultgerät aus Emden 1639–1806.' 1 July–30 Aug. 1992. Catalogue by William B. Gross, Rafi Grafmann and Annette Weber, 31 pp., with figs.

Essen, Alte Synagoge Essen. 'Synagoga — Ecclesia in der christlichen Kunst.' 12 Mar.–9 May 1993. Photographs by Herbert Jochum.

Frankfurt am Main, Jüdisches Museum. 'Sehnsucht Jerusalem.' Opening: 25 June 1992.

———. 'Mikwe: Geschichte und Architektur jüdischer Ritualbäder in Deutschland.' 10 Sept.–15 Nov. 1992.

———. 'Zedaka: Jüdische Sozialarbeit im Wandel der Zeit: 75 Jahre Zentralwohlfahrtsstelle der Juden in Deutschland 1917–1992.' 3 Dec. 1992–28 Feb. 1993. Catalogue ed. by Frank Kind and Esther Alexander-Ihme, 447 pp., with numerous figs. See esp. the following paper: Anne Alter, 'Armut und Wohltätigkeit in der Kunst der Aschkenasim,' pp. 44–57.

Haifa, Museum of Music and Ethnology. 'Azerbaijan: Mountain Jews and Urban Muslims.' Opening: 28 July 1992. Curator: Nina Benzoor. Catalogue ed. by the curator, 159 pp., Includes: Shalom Sabar, 'The Kettubbah among Mountain Jews.' pp. 137–31. In Hebrew and English.

Hohenems, Jüdisches Museum Hohenems. 'Beit haChaim: Haus des Lebens: Der jüdische Friedhof in Hohenems.' 24 Apr.–12 July 1992. With Photographs of Arno Gisinger

———. 'Abraham und Abraham: Zwei Religionen — Ein Kalender: Kinderzeichnungen zu Bibellesungen im jüdischen und christlichen Jahreskreis.' 25 Sept.–18 Oct. 1992.

———. 'Georg Chaimowicz: 'Lieber Papa!': Kinderzeichnungen 1936 bis 1946, 'Lebensspur': Werke 1957 bis 1990.' 25 Apr.–16 May 1993.

———. 'Genisa: Das verborgene Erbe der deutschen Landjuden.' 15 Sept.–7 Nov. 1993.

Houston, JCC of Houston. 'Endurance Through Faith: Sephardic Watercolors by Joan Elion and Tina Goldstein.' Through 20 Mar. 1993.

Istanbul and Izmir, 'Jewish Art in Turkey.' A symposium organized by the Center for Jewish Art of the Hebrew University of Jerusalem. 23 Aug.–2 Sept. 1993. Included tours of Jewish monuments, historical, social and cultural background lectures as well as the following lectures on Jewish art: Ruth Jacoby, 'Architecture of the Synagogues in Turkey'; id., 'Ancient Synagogues in Asia Minor'; Bezalel Narkiss, 'Sacred Objects of Synagogues in Turkey'; id., 'Home Ritual Objects in Turkey'; id., 'Jewish Graveyards in Turkey'; Nikos Stavroulakis, 'Ritual Textiles'; id., 'The Image of the Jew in 19th Century Ottoman Art'; Shalom Sabar, 'Ketubbah Ornamentation in the Western Ottoman Empire'; id., 'Hebrew Book Printing and Decoration in the Ottoman Empire'; Stella Kent, 'In Search of Our Roots: Presentation of Documentation by the Kadikoy Group, Istanbul'; Nurhan Atasoy, 'Jewish Decorative Arts in the Ottoman World.'

Jackson, Museum of the Southern Jewish Experience. 'A Heritage Revealed: The Jewish Presence in Arkansas.' Through Dec. 1993.

Jerusalem, Bezalel Academy of Art and Design and the Torah Culture Department of the Ministry of Education and Culture. 'The Synagogue's Structure in Israel: 1948-1992.' 1992. Curator: Siona Shimshi. Catalogue, 82 pp., with numerous figs. and plans. Includes a symposium with A. Elhanani, Nurit Ashkenazi, Samuel Ben Sasson, Rabbi Zeev Gotthold, Brachiah Lipschitz, David Cassutto, Elhanan Reiner, Ran Shehori, Ephraim Shilo and Siona Shimshi, pp. 14-24, 72-81.

Jerusalem, Misgav Yerushalayim. The Fourth International Congress of Misgav Yerushalayim: 'Hispano-Jewish Civilization after 1492.' Included the following papers on Jewish art: David Cassuto, 'The Synagogues of the Sephardic Diaspora after the

Expulsion'; Gloria Mound, 'The 18th Century Synagogue in Minorca'; Zusia Efron, 'Decoration and Forms of the Jewish-Sephardic Gravestones in the Balkans'; Santiago Palomero Plaza, 'The Sephardic Museum in Toledo.'

Jerusalem, The Israel Museum. 'Daniel Libeskind: The New Extension of the Berlin Museum with the Jewish Department.' Opening: 8 Sept. 1992. In cooperation with the Berlin Senate Department for Building and Housing, the Berlin Senate Department for Cultural Affairs, and the Berlin Museum.

———. 'In a Single Statement: Works by Zelig Segal.' Opening: 15 Dec. 1993.

———. 'Painting the Bible in Rembrandt's Holland.' 7 May–25 Aug. 1993.

———. 'Marc Chagall: Dreams and Drama.' Through 31 Jan. 1994.

Jerusalem, Judaica Jerusalem. 'Judaica: Rare Books, Manuscripts, Documents and Jewish Arts.' Exhibition and auction, 10–11 June 1992. 479 lots.

———. Exhibition and auction, 5 Nov. 1992. 515 lots.

———. Exhibition and auction, 3 Mar. 1993. 522 lots.

———. Exhibition and auction, 7 June 1993. 466 lots.

Jerusalem, Mayanot Gallery — Yael Gahnassia. 'Jerusalem — 25th Anniversary of Reunification.' Opening: 28 May 1992.

Jerusalem, Mishkenot Sha'ananim. 'Lehie Talmor: Horowitz the Storyteller: Cahier de Voyage.' Opening: 8 Nov. 1992.

Jerusalem, Society for Jewish Art. The Twenty-Fifth Annual Conference of the Society for Jewish Art: 'Treasures of Judaica: Recent Discoveries and New Studies in Jewish and Israeli Art.' 7–8 Apr. 1992. Included: Gideon Ofrat, Iris Fishof, Aviezer Ravitzki, Ran Shehori, Siona Shimshi and Gershon Shaked, 'Jewish and Israeli Identity in Art: A Symposium.' Ruth Jacoby, 'The Mystery of the Burial Site of Helena, Queen of Adiabene'; Yitzhak Magen, 'Discoveries in the Field of Ancient Samaritan Synagogues'; Sarit Shalev-Eyni, 'Italian Sources of the Kaufmann Haggadah'; David Cassuto, 'Unusual Italian Torah Ark Curtains in the Collection of Museo Nahon, Jerusalem'; Yitzhak Einhorn, 'From the Mysteries of Jewish Symbolism: The Meaning of the Rooster on Jewish Objects'; Naomi Feuchtwanger-Sarig, 'The Custom of Binding the Torah: A Reevaluation'; Naomi Cassuto, 'The First Torah Ark in Livorno'; Orpa Slapak, 'From Cochin to Jerusalem: An Old Synagogue from South India Restored in the Israel Museum'; Haya Friedberg, 'Contemporary Jewish Ceremonial Art: Between Commodities and Objects d'Art'; Alexander Mishori, 'The Motif of Purity in the Ceramic Works of Moshe Gershuni'; Avigdor Posèq, 'The Jewish "Pieta Rondanini"'; Shlomit Steinberg,' "Palm Tree Circle" and "Cypress Circle": Motifs in the Work of the Israeli Artist Israel Rabinowitz.'

Jerusalem, World Union of Jewish Studies. The Eleventh World Congress of Jewish Studies. 22–29 June 1993. Included the following papers on Jewish art: Israel Roll, 'Figurative Arts among Jews of Late Antiquity'; Dalia Levit-Tawil, 'Eschatology and the Temple Motif at the Dura Europos Synagogue'; Bracha Yaniv, 'The Torah Case in the Mishnaic and Talmudic Period'; Sarit Shalev-Eyni, 'The Nudity of Pharaoh's Daughter in Christian and Jewish Iconography'; Hava Baer, 'Architectural Motifs in Bibles and Qur'ans of the Middle East'; Vivian Mann, 'Decorated Hebrew and Arabic Books: Mutual Influences in Spain and the Sephardi Diaspora'; Gabrielle Sed-Rajna, 'Some Further Data on the Diagrams in the Manuscripts of Rashi's Commentary of the Torah'; Elisabeth Revel-Neher, 'The Double-Page of the Tabernacle Objects in Sephardic Bibles and its Relationship to Byzantine Iconography'; Michel Garel, 'Illustrations Concealed within Reputedly Pure Decoration in Hebrew Medieval Manuscripts'; Evelyn M. Cohen, 'The Sister Haggadah and its 'Poor Relation''; Katrin Kogman-Appel, 'The Second

Nuremberg Haggadah and the Yehudah Haggadah: Were They Made by the Same Artists?'; Yael Zirlin, 'The Problems of Identifying the Origin of a Manuscript: Hamburg, Cod. Hbr. 155'; Naomi Feuchtwanger-Sarig, 'Yiddish 'Minhagim' Books in Netherlands, for Ashkenazim, Sefaradim and for Gentiles'; Iris Fishof, 'Joseph Son of David of Leipnik: An 18th–Century Scribe and Illuminator'; Ziva Amishai-Maisels, 'Chagall's 'Golgotha': Sources and Meanings'; Mirjam Rajner, 'Chagall and Russian Futurism: 'The One-and-a-Half Eyed Archer''; Ruth Apter-Gabriel, 'In the Spirit Of An-sky: Jewish folk Art Motives in Russian-Jewish Art'; Dora Kogan, 'Symbolism in the Art of Naum Gabo and Anton Pevsner'; Hillel Kazovsky, 'Sarrah Shor in the Period of the 'Kultur-Lige,' 1919–1924'; Vera Reider, 'Biblical Themes in Russian Avant-Garde Graphics in the 1970s–1980s'; Helen Kantor-Kazovsky, 'Dmitry Lion: Jewish Experience in Soviet Non-Official Art'; Elena Lebedeva, 'A. Tishler as a Jewish Artist'; Jana Doleželová, 'Torah Binders in East Europe'; Jerzy Malinowski, 'Jewish Avant Garde Art in Poland, 1910–1939'; Stephen Feinstein, 'Three European Artistic Responses to the Holocaust: Kleinman, Otreba and Sozansky'; Grigory Ostrovsky, 'The Circle of Jewish Artists in Galicia in the 1930s'; Milly Heyd and Ezra Mendelsohn, 'The Burden of the Past and the Vision of the Future: American Artists of Jewish Origin'; Haya Friedberg, ''The Burial': Turning Point in Larry Rivers's Art'; Evelyn L. Greenberg, 'Toward the 21st Century: New Directions in American Synagogue Architecture'; Marcia Reines Josephy, ''Wise-Hearted Men, Wise-Hearted Women': Jewish Arts and Crafts in Contemporary America', Avigdor W.G. Posq, 'Jacques Lipchitz's 'Song of Vowels''; Gannit Ankori, 'Covert Jewish Elements in the Art of Frida Kahlo'; Norman L. Kleeblatt, 'Merging Homosexual and Jewish Identities in Late 20th–Century American Art'; Norma Grinberg and Sergio Samis, 'Creating Modern Jewish Art Objects in Brazil'; David M. Cassuto, 'First Holy Arks in Spanish-Portuguese Synagogues in Italy'; Ralf Busch, 'Johann Lund and his Vision of the 'Tempel Salomonis,' the Models of Hamburg and Halle'; Hannelore Künzl, 'Mikva'ot in Germany: 18th–19th Centuries'; Thomas C. Hubka, 'Wooden Synagogues in Poland: The Architecture of a Pre-Hassidic Popular Culture'; Kazimierz and Maria Piechotka, 'The Synagogues of Lvov'; Shlomit Steinberg, ''The Birth of Light, The Creation by Fire': The Creation of Adam and Eve in Abel Pann's Paintings, 1920–1925'; Igor Aronov, 'The Influence of Russian Art on Joseph Zaritsky'; Ilya Rodov, 'Origin and Developments in the Work of Shalom Moskovitz from Safed'; Bezalel Narkiss, 'Reports on Documentation in Israel, Poland, the Former Soviet Union, Morocco, United States and England'; Eli Davis, 'The Menorah in Hebrew Amulets'; Kazimierz and Maria Piechotka, 'On the Unpromised Land: The Architecture of Polish Synagogues during the 16th–19th Centuries'; Eric Meyers, 'What Can the Archaeology of the Ancient Synagogue Tell Us about Rabbinic Judaism?'; Gideon Foerster, 'Planning and Designing of Synagogues in the Roman and Byzantine Periods'; Rachel Hachlili, 'Synagogue Decoration according to Community Decisions and Recommendations'; David Amit, 'Iconoclasm in Ancient Synagogues in Eretz Israel.'

Jerusalem, Yad Vashem: The Holocaust Martyrs' and Heroes' Remembrance Authority. 'Memories of the Holocaust: Avraham Sapir: An Exhibition of Paintings.' Opening: 9 Dec. 1992.

———. 'Ernst Degasperi: Yügerstütter Zyklus — Light in the Darkness.' Opening: 10 Feb. 1993.

———. '''Shtetel'': The Jewish Town Through the Eyes of its Artists.' Opening: 15 June 1993. Curator: Bela Shomer-Seizik. Collection of Mishkan Le-Omanut Museum of Art, Ein Harod.

London, Bloomsbury Book Auctions. 'Valuable Hebrew Printed

Books and Manuscripts.' 17 Sept. 1992. 348 lots.

London, British Library. 'Hebrew Illuminated Manuscripts from Iberia.' Nov. 1992–March 1993.

———. 18 Mar. 1993. 348 lots.

London, Sotheby's. 'Western Manuscripts and Miniatures.' 22 June 1993. 102 lots. Included some Hebrew manuscripts (lots 76–79).

Los Angeles, Hebrew Union College Skirball Museum. 'Purim Masks and Passover Haggadot.' Through 25 Apr. 1993.

———. 'Italian Ketubbot.' 27 Apr.–27 June 1993.

Los Angeles, Martyrs Memorial and Museum of the Holocaust. 'In Fitting Memory: Perspectives on an Evolving Tradition of Holocaust Memorials.' 23 June–20 Aug. 1992. Photographs by Ira Nowinsski and text by Sybil Milton. A traveling exhibition organized by the Judah L. Magnes Museum, Berkeley, and the Living Memorial to the Holocaust-Museum of Jewish Heritage, New York.

———. 'Yizkor Books: Memorial to Destroyed Communities.' Opening: 1 Sept. 1993.

———. 'Yochka Lipshitz: Photography as Personal Memory.' Opening: 1 Sept. 1993.

Los Angeles, University of Judaism, Platt Art Gallery. 'Traditions: Jewish Arts and Crafts by Wendy Rabinowitz, Mordechai Rosenstein and Maria Gotsban.' 14 Mar.–25 Apr. 1993.

———. 'Images: Art as Tikkun: Healing and Transformation.' 14 July–29 Aug. 1993.

Madrid, Comisión Nacional Judía Sefarad 92, Quinto Centenario. 'Sefarad: The Jews of Spain from the Golden Age to Expulsion.' Opening: 5 June 1992.

Mexico City, Mexico City's Bilingual University. 'Fragmentos de la Memoria: Bela Gold.' Opening: 14 July 1992.

Miami Beach, Community Center. 'Mosaic: Jewish Life in Florida.' Through Apr. 1993.

Munich, Historischer Arbeitskreis Sendling und Israelitische Kultusgemeinde München. '"Der Gute Ort": Ausstellung zum Alten Israelitischen Friedhof an der Thalkirchner Straße.' Nov. 1991. An essay by Karl W. Schubsky, 15pp., with figs.

New Rochelle, Gladys and Murray Goldstein Cultural Center, Temple Israel. 'Lvov: Heartland of the Jewish Past.' Opening: 20 Sept. 1992. Curator: Liora Finkenberg. Catalogue, unpaginated.

New York, Adine Fine Art Gallery. 'Ethics of the Fathers: A Message for the Ages by Yonah Weinrib.' 17 May–26 Apr. 1993.

New York, American Guild of Judaic Art. 'National Jewish Art Week.' 14–20 Mar. 1993.

New York, Christie's. 'Important Silver, Objects of Vertu, Russian Works of Art and Judaica.' Auction, 22 Apr. 1993. 566 lots.

New York, The Dime Savings Bank. 'Bracha Turner: Views of the City of Safed in Pen and Ink.' 11 Jan.–20 Sept. 1993.

New York, Emunah of America and Joy Schonberg Galleries: Fine Judaica Auctioneers and Appraisers. 'Emunah of America Charity Auction: Important Judaica and Works of Art.' Auction, 6 Nov. 1993. 154 lots.

New York, Guggenheim Museum Soho. 'Marc Chagall and the Moscow Jewish Chamber Theater Murals.' Through Jan. 1993.

New York, Hebrew Union College, Joseph Gallery. 'Midrash with Spoiled Milk: Photomontage by Barbara Rose Haum.' Through 17 Apr. 1993.

———. 'The Collector's Room: Selections from the Judy and Michael Steinhardt Judaica Collection.' Opening: 24 May 1993. Curator: Cissy Grossman. Catalogue, unpaginated.

New York, Holocaust Resource Center. 'The Overlooked Holocaust: The Devastation of the Sephardic Communities.' Through 24 June 1993.

New York, International Center of Photography. 'The Photographs of Roman Vishniac: Man, Nature and Science 1930–1985.' 29 Jan.–18 Apr. 1993.

New York, The Jewish Museum.'Bridges and Boundaries: African Americans and American Jews.' 22 Mar.–19 July 1992. In collaboration with the National Association for the Advancement of Colored People (NAACP).

———. 'Convivencia: Jews, Muslims, and Christians in Medieval Spain.' 20 Sept.–20 Dec. 1992.

———. 'From the Inside Out: Eight Contemporary Artists.' 13 June–14 Nov. 1993. Curator: Susan Tumarkin Goodman. Catalogue, 59 pp., with numerous figs.

———. 'The Best Day of the Week: An Exhibition for Families.' Through June 1994.

New York, The Library of the Jewish Theological Seminary of America. 'Text and Context; The Development and Dissemination of Medieval Sephardic Culture.' Through 5 Feb. 1992.

New York, The New York Public Library. 'Assault on the Arts: Culture and Politics in Nazi Germany.' Through 28 May.

New York, Rockland Center for Holocaust Studies. 'Because It Can Happen Again: Works by Tibor Spitz.' Through 29 Apr. 1993.

New York, Swann Galleries. 'Hebraica and Judaica: Books and Manuscripts, Broadsides, Illustrated Books, Graphics, Ephemera, Maps, Megillot, Posters, Postcards, Prints, Watercolors, Objects and Ceremonial Art.' Auction, 25 June 1992.

New York, UJA — Federation of New York. 'Chuppah: Jewish Bridal Canopies by Shula Mustacchi.' Through 22 July 1993.

New York, Yeshiva University Museum. 'Sefer Shel Or: Book of Light by Douglas Florian.' Through Dec. 1992.

———. 'An Enduring Tradition: Wood Inlay in Jewish Ceremonial Art by Yehudah Jacobs.' 6 Dec. 1992–June 1993.

———. Dreams of the Bible: Paintings by Uri Shaked.' Through 15 Feb. 1993.

———. 'The World of Itshak Holtz: A 20th-Century Genre Painter.' Oct. 1992–July 1993. Curator: Susan B. Parkoff. Catalogue, 22 pp., with figs.

———. 'Creations for the Life of a Jewish Family by Susi Guggenheim-Weil.' 24 Jan.–18 Apr. 1993.

———. 'Jewish Ceremonial Objects by Lorelei and Alex Gruss.' Apr.–Sept. 1993.

———. 'Aishet Hayil: Woman of Valor.' Through June 1994. Catalogue ed. by Sylvia A. Herskowitz and Sarah L. Schmerler, 70 pp., with numerous figs.

New York, YIVO Institute for Jewish Research. 'Monuments of Memory: Photographs by Ira Nowinski.' Through 4 Sept. 1993.

Paris, Fondation Kikoïne, Couvent des Cordeliers. 'Kikoïne et ses amis de l'Ecole de Paris.' 11 May–20 June 1993. Catalogue by Leila Voight, unpaginated, with numerous figs.

Philadelphia, JCC of Greater Philadelphia, Klein Branch, Fred Wolf Jr. Gallery. 'Contemoporary Ketuboth.' Through 26 Apr. 1993.

Philadelphia, Philadelphia Museum of American Jewish History. 'Contemporary Artifacts 1992.' 17 Nov. 1992–3 Jan. 1993. Catalogue, 20 pp., with figs.

———. 'The Chapter Paintings by Archie Rand.' Through 17 Apr. 1993.

Philadelphia, Temple Judea Museum of Keneseth Israel. 'The Work of Our Hands: A Five Year Retrospective.' 25 Sept. 1989–19 Jan. 1990

———. 'The Past Continues: Work of Samuel Bak.' 6 Oct.–20 Dec. 1991. Curator: Judith B. Maslin. Catalogue by the curator, 15 pp., with figs.

———. 'Women's Voices, Prayers and Amulets by Carol Hamoy.' 22 Mar.–16 June 1993.

Phoenix, Plotkin Judaica Museum. 'The Shtetl: A Faint Memory:

Lithographs by William Gropper.' 28 Mar.–30 June 1993

——. 'The Warsaw Ghetto: Woodcuts By Stefan Mrozewski.' 28 Mar.–30 Jun. 1993.

Portland, Mittleman JCC. 'Yetzirah: Jewish Ceremonial Pottery by Lia Lynn Rosen.' Through 31 Mar. 1993.

——. 'Sephardi Women of Turkey: Photographs by Audrey Daniel.' 3–28 May 1993.

Princeton, Institute of Semitic Studies, The Princeton University Committee for Jewish Studies, The Association for Society and Culture. 'The Second International Congress of Yemenite Jewish Studies.' 28–30 June 1992. Included the following lectures on Jewish art: Tsipporah S. Greenfield, 'The Jewelry of the Jewish Bridegroom of Maswar as Judaica'; Carmela Abdar, 'Women's Costumes and Appearance in a Jewish-Yemenite Village as a Reflection of Social-Religious Status'; Ester Muchawsky-Schnapper, 'Ceremonial Objects in Yemenite Synagogues.'

Riverdale, The Judaica Museum, Hebrew Home for the Aged at Riverdale. 'Artists of Vitebsk Academy: Work by Students of Yehuda Penn.' 15 Aug.–30 Oct. 1993.

——. 'Tsirl Waletzsky: Jewish Papercuts.' Through 15 Apr. 1993.

——. '"If I Forget Thee, O Jerusalem": From the Collection of Abraham and Deborah Karp.' 5 Apr.–29 Oct. 1992.

——. 'Integral and Integrated? : Four Hundred Years of Jewish Life in Ichenhausen, Bavaria.' 20 Dec. 1992–23 May 1993. Catalogue, 19 pp. The exhibition was prepared by the Haus der Bayerischen Geschichte and the Stiftung Ehemalige Synagoge Ichenhausen — Haus der Begegnung as 'Juden auf dem Lande: Beispiel Ichenhausen.'

Rockville, JCC of Greater Washington, Goldman Art Gallery. 'Heaven on Earth: Divine Crafts for Jewish Homes and Traditions.' Through 1 Apr. 1993.

San Francisco, Craft and Folk Art Museum. 'Jewish Papercuts.' 7 Nov. 1992–2 Jan. 1993.

——. 'Hand Bookbinders of California.' 7 Nov. 1992–2 Jan. 1993.

San Francisco, Elizabeth S. Fine Museum, Congregation Emanu-El. 'The Liturgical Papercuts of Archie Granot.' 25 Aug.–6 Dec. 1992.

——. 'Antiques from the Archives.' 30 Aug.–Sept. 1993.

San Francisco, The Jewish Museum San Francisco. 'Resistance and Rescue.' Through 15 Aug. 1993.

San Francisco, One Bush Street. 'Identities Lost and Found: Russian Jewish Artists from 1920s–1990s.' 19 Aug.–30 Nov. 1992. Curator: Sonia Melnikova-Lavigne. Included the following artists: Marc Chagall, Meer Akselrod, Efim Royak, Natan Altman, Komar and Melamid, Vladimir Yankilevsky, Grisha Bruskin, Alek Rapoport, Simon Okstein, Alexander Gurevich, Alexander Khomsky and others.

Sofia, Ministry of Culture and the Organization of the Jews in Bulgaria 'Shalom'. 'Jewish Artists in Bulgaria.' Oct. 1991. Catalogue by Tatyana Dimitrova and Andrei Daniel, 23 pp., with figs.

South Yarra, The Jewish Museum of Australia. 'Courage to Care: Rescuers of Jews During the Holocaust.' Opening: 29 June 1992.

——. 'The Golem.' Opening: 28 Feb. 1993. Curator: Barrie Kosky.

——. 'Sephardim — Jews of Spain' 15 Aug.–Dec. 1993.

Tallin, The Estonian National Museum. 'The Jewish Cultural Heritage in Tartu.' 18 Dec. 1992–31 Jan. 1993.

Teaneck, Temple Emeth Experiential Museum. 'Life Cycle of the Syria-Sephardic Jewish Community.' Through Apr. 1993.

Tel Aviv, Beit Hatefutsoth: The Nahum Goldmann Museum of the Jewish Diaspora. 'Aliya '90: The Exodus of the Jews from the Soviet Union to Israel.' Winter, 1990–1991. Catalogue of numerous photographs, unpaginated.

——. 'In the Footsteps of Marrano Families.' Opening: 21 Dec. 1992. Includes a book ed. by Ruth Porter and Sarah Harel-Hoshen, *Odyssey of the Exiles: The Sephardi Jews 1492–1992.* 207 pp., with numerous figs.

——. 'Sephardi Itinerary, 1992: Photographs by Frederic Brenner.' Opening: 21 Dec. 1992.

——. 'Jews in Bulgaria, Spring 1991: Photographs by Doron Bacher.' Opening: 15 Apr. 1993.

Tel Aviv, Eretz Israel Museum. 'A Touch of the Past: Hands on Archaeology: Special exhibition for the blind and visually impaired.' Summer, 1992. Curator: Irit Ziffer. Catalogue ed. by the curator, 167, * pp. In Hebrew, preface in English, pp. 3*–17*.

Tel Aviv, Sotheby's. '19th-and 20th-Century Paintings, Drawings and Sculpture.' Auction, 20 Oct. 1992. 124 lots.

——. 'Important Judaica: Books, Manuscripts and Works of Art.' Auction, 14 Apr. 1993.

——. '19th and 20th Century Paintings, Drawings and Sculpture.' Auction, 4 Oct. 1993. 150 lots.

——. 'Important Judaica: Books, Manuscripts, Works of Art and Paintings.' Auction, 5 Oct. 1993. 307 lots.

Tel Hai, The Museum of Photography at Tel Hai Industrial Park. 'Vintage Prints from Antique Photographs of the Holy Land.' Opening: 23 Nov. 1992.

Toronto, Beth Tzedec Reuben and Helene Dennis Museum. 'From Our Permanent Collection: Passover — Holy Day of Spring; Ghetto Currency; Nererin Collection of Ritual Objects; Israeli Independence — 45 Years.' 28 Mar.–Oct. 1993.

Trenton New Jersey State Museum. 'A Day in the Warsaw Ghetto: A Birthday Trip in Hell.' 15 May–27 Jun. 1993.

Warsaw, National Museum in Warsaw. 'Polish Painting in the Ewa and Wojtek Fibak Collection.' 23 May–9 Aug. 1992. Also at the National Museum in Poznań, 22 Aug.–25 Oct. 1992. Catalogue by Barbara Brus-Walinowska, Władysława Jaworska, Agnieszka Morawińska and Agnieszka Lawniczakowa, 271 pp., with numerous figs. See esp. Agnieszka Morawińska, 'Paintings without Adjectives,' pp. x–xviii, and the painters Piotr Michałowski, pp.6–15; Zygmunt Menkes, pp. 196–211 and Alicja Halicka, pp. 218–24.

Washington D.C., B'nai B'rith Klutznick Museum. 'Bezalel: The Evolution of a Heritage.' 30 June–Sept. 1993.

Washington, D.C., National Museum of American History, Smithsonian Institution. 'The Past as Memory and Model.' 20 Apr.–30 June 1993.

West Bloomfield, Charach-Epstein Museum Gallery, JCC of Metropolitan Detroit. 'Jews of Greece.' Through 29 July 1993.

——. 'Faith and Survival: Documentation of the Life of Ethiopian Jews by Peggy Myers.' Through 29 July 1993.

——. 'The Collectors III.' 5 Aug.–9 Sept. 1993.

Compiled by Sarit Shalev-Eyni

Contributors to this issue

Gannit Ankori is working towards her Ph.D in the Department of Art History at the Hebrew University, where she teaches modern art and aesthetics.

Harold Brodsky is an Associate Professor at the Department of Geography at the University of Maryland.

Ralf Busch is the Director of the Hamburger Museum für Archäologie und die Geschichte Hamburgs. He has published extensively on Jewish history in northern Germany, and lectures on Jewish art at the Technische Universität Braunschweig.

Laura Rachel Felleman Fattal, Ph.D., is the Curator of Education at the Zimmerli Art Museum at Rutgers, the State University of New Jersey.

Naomi Feuchtwanger-Sarig is a Ph.D Candidate in the Department of Art History, and a Lecturer at Bar-Ilan University.

Mira Freidman is a Professor of Art History at Tel Aviv University.

Evelyn L. Greenberg is a historian of Jewish art, formerly from Washington, D.C., and now residing in Jerusalem.

Milly Heyd is a Senior Lecturer at the Department of Art History at the Hebrew University, specializing in modern and modern Jewish art.

Elliott Horowitz is a Senior Lecturer in Jewish history at Bar-Ilan University. His article received the Richard and Joan Scheuer Award from the Hebrew Union College Jewish Institute of Religion for the best article on Jewish art and architecture in 1992-93.

Lola Kantor-Kazovsky is a Graduate Student of the Department of Art History at the Hebrew University and a Researcher at the Center for Jewish Art.

Victor Klagsbald is an art historian and a collector of Judaica.

Bianca Kühnel is a Senior Lecturer at the Department of Art History at the Hebrew University, and specializes in medieval art history.

Yaffa Levy is a Researcher in the manuscript division of the Center for Jewish Art.

Ezra Mendelsohn is a Professor at the Institute of Contemporary Jewry and in the Department of Russian Studies at the Hebrew University.

Luisa Mortara Ottolenghi is a former Professor of Codicology and History of Illumination at the University of Milano and Cagliari. She is President of the Jewish Documentation Center, Milano.

Ilona Pataki-Brestyánski is a Professor Emerita of Art History at the Academy of Applied Arts, Budapest, and was the Chief Curator of the Hungarian National Gallery.

Joseph Patrich is a Senior Lecturer at the Department of Archaeology at the University of Haifa.

Avigdor W.G. Posèq is a Senior Lecturer of Art History at the Hebrew University and at Tel Aviv University, and specializes in Renaissance art and modern sculpture.

Y.L. Rahmani is Chief Curator, retired, of the Israel Antiquities Authority.

Shalom Sabar is a Lecturer in the Departments of Art History and Folklore at the Hebrew University.

Sarit Shalev-Eyni is a Researcher at the Center for Jewish Art.

Michele Vishny is an art historian and author and serves as Special Consultant on twentieth-century art to the Spertus Museum, Chicago.

Annette Weber is a Curator of Judaica at the Jewish Museum in Frankfurt am Main.

FRIENDS OF THE CENTER FOR JEWISH ART

The CJA is grateful to all the contributors whose generosity over the years has enabled us to continue our research projects, scholarships, publications, teaching and educational programs.

Founders
Philip and Muriel Berman, Allentown, PA
Dorot Foundation, New York
Eric Estorick and Salome Dessau-Estorick Fund, London
Getty Grant Program, Santa Monica, CA
Richard and Bea Levy, Boca Raton, FL
Dr. Ruth Mellinkoff, Los Angeles
S.H. and Helen R. Scheuer Family Foundation, New York
The late Maurice Spertus, Tel Aviv–Chicago

Patrons
Morris E. Curiel, Madrid–Curaçau
Jacobo and the late Asea Furman, Santiago, Chile
William and Lisa Gross, Ramat Aviv, Israel
Erica and the late Ludwig Jesselson, New York
Masto Foundation, Switzerland
Rich Foundation, Paris
Washington, D.C. Chapter of the AFHU
Benjamin and Barbara Zucker, New York

Sponsors
Stanley and the late Selma Batkin, New Rochelle, NY
Nancy Berman and Alan Bloch, Los Angeles
Walter and Jeanny Bick, Richmond Hill, Ontario
Abraham and Rachel Bornstein, Brookline, MA
Dr. Yonat and the late Michael Floersheim, Zurich
Victor Klagsbald, Paris, France
Fanny and Leo Koerner Charitable Trust, Cambridge, MA
Prof. James H. and Emily Marrow, Princeton, NJ
Dr. Franklin Murphy, Los Angeles
P.E.F. Israel Endowments Funds, New York
Isaac and Bonnie Pollack, New York
Leona Z. Rosenberg, Chicago
Harold and Kitty Ruttenberg, Pittsburgh
Richard and Joan Scheuer, New Rochelle, NY
Jerome and Ellen Stern, New York
Joseph Steiglitz and Family, Tel Aviv
Henry and Beate Voremberg, Fort Lee, NJ

Donors
Mr. and Mrs. Sam Angel, Vancouver
Dr. Alfred Bader, Milwaukee
Morris and Beverly Baker, Bloomfield, MI
British Council, Tel Aviv
Maurice and Marilyn Cohen, Newton, MA–Palm Beach, FL
Lloyd Cotsen, Los Angeles
Harry and Lillian Freedman, Newton, MA
Daniel Friedenberg, New York
Ruth and the late Leon Gildesgame, Mt. Kisco, NY
Martin Goldberg, Toronto
Regina Heim, Zurich
George Jaffin, New York
Dr. Manfred and Anne Lehmann, New York
Isi Leibler, Victoria, Australia
Lucius N. Littauer Foundation, New York
Pauline and the late Michael Lockman, Jerusalem
Friends of Mordechai Narkiss in his memory

The State of Lower Saxony, Germany
Dr. Leonard Polonsky, Barnet, England
Project Judaica, Washington, D.C.
Martha Samson, Jerusalem
Jules Samson, Downsview, Ontario
William Silberkleit, Marina del Rey, CA
Isaac Sinaiko, Cerritos, CA
Mr. and Mrs. Robert and David Smith, Arlington, VA
Gerard and Brigette Stern (Henriette Noetzlin Fund), Geneva
Jane Stern, Washington, D.C.
Leonard J. Winchester, Terrace Park, OH

Contributors
Joshua and Ita Aber, Yonkers, NY
Friends of Ita Aber in her honor
Morris Altman, Toronto
American Academy for Jewish Research, New York
Harry and Lore Bauer, Lawrence, NY
David Berg, New York
Mr. and Mrs. William Berman, Walnut Creek, CA
Norman and Diana Bernstein, Washington, D.C.
Dr. Eli and Batia Borowski, Jerusalem
Hubert and Larissa Cain, Paris
Endowment Fund of Houston
Albert and Dorothy Gellman, Toronto
Yehuda Golan, Jerusalem
Dr. Jack and Esther Goldman, New Rochelle, NY
Judith Goldman, Houston
Jewish Agency, Aviezar Fund, Jerusalem
Jerome Kaplan, Rockville, MD
Larry and Linda Levenstein, Toronto
Richard and Frances Luban, Encino, CA
Ester Mazor, Washington, D.C.
Ministry of Education, Center for Oriental Jewish Heritage, Israel
Dr. Alfred and Jean Moldovan, New York
Henry and Bella Muller, Niagara Falls, Ontario
National Council on Art in Jewish Life, New York
Ben and Cynthia Pollard, Gerrard's Cross, England
Dan and Joanna Rose, New York
Jacob and Belle Rosenbaum, Monsey, NY
Joseph and Sheila Rosenblatt, New York
Herman Russ, New York
Sam and Esther Sarick, Willowdale, Ontario
Sion Segre-Amar, Torino, Italy
Romie and Blanche Shapiro, New York
Julius and Lillian Silberg, Sarasota, FL
Ivan and Marilyn Soclof, Beachwood, OH
Eugene Spertus, Carson, CA
Joan Strausberg, New York
Jean Sulzberger, New York
Judith Sulzberger Foundation, New York
Dr. Marvin and Gerry Teitelbaum, Los Angeles
Florence Urbach, Don Mills, Ontario
Carl and Genia Urbont, Larchmont, NY
Yehezkel and Zahava Vered, Ramat Gan, Israel

Leon and Sandra Weiner, Houston
Rubin Zimmerman, Tel Aviv
Leonard and Selma Zoref, Roslyn, NY

Annual Members
Rebecca Ackerson, Coral Gables, FL
Sylvia Altholz, Brooklyn
Tamar Baumgold, New York
Harold and Vivian Beck, Coral Gables, FL
Hyman and Freida Bernstein, Laurel, MD
Leon and Mala Betensky, Washington, D.C.
Raymond Blank, Bridgeport CT
Maxine Blendis, Toronto
Jack and Irma Bochner, Yonkers, NY
Alberto Boralevi, Torino, Italy
Dr. Weert Börner, Bonn, Germany
Sy and Joan Bram, Los Angeles
Dr. B. Bromberger-Barnea, Jupiter, FL
Linda Bronfman, Toronto
Cabrera Casting
Mildred Cafritz, Rockville, MD
William B. and Hilda Clayman, Youngstown, OH
Annette Cohen, Philadelphia
Edward S. Cohen, Jerusalem
Elaine Lustig Cohen, New York
Joseph and Rebecca Cohen, Bronx
Morris Cooper, Farmington Hill, MI
Nita Corinblit, Van Nuys, CA
Mel and Judy Croner, San Rafael, CA
Norbert and Paulette Cymbalista, Geneva
Elcan Diesendruck, San Paulo, Brazil
Frank Dobia, Victoria, Australia
Ruth Eis, Oakland, CA
Vera Eisenberger, Vienna
Frank and Elaine Farbenblum, Rockville, MD
Eugene and Edith Feiger, Toronto
Mr. and Mrs. Arthur Fentin, Boyton Beach, FL
Mr. and Mrs. Martin Fine, Miami
Dorothy Freedman, Elkins Park, PA
Moses Freedman, Washington, D.C.
Rabbi Elliot Gertel, Chicago
Mr. and Mrs. Gabriel Gilead, Chicago
Bela Gold, Mexico City
Milton Gottesman, Washington, D.C.
Archie and Susan Granot, Jerusalem
Dr. Charles and Julie Greenbaum, Rydal, PA
Judah Gribets, New York
Gene and Cissy Grossman, Irvington-on-Hudson, NY
Helena and Irving Grossman, Toronto
Dr. Katia Guth-Dreyfus, Basel
Perry Haber, Tel Aviv
Fred and Cheryl Halpern, Livingston, NJ
Prof. Milton and Miriam Handler, New York
Alexander Hassan, Washington, D.C.
Ortrun Hirche, Rotterbergstasse, Germany
Helene Hixon, Chevy Chase, MD
Roberta Holland, Providence, RI
Prof. Hans Otto Horch, Neuwied, Germany
Prof. Thomas Hubka, Milwaukee, WI
Gurion and Ruth Hyman, Toronto
Devra Jacobson, Wilmette, IL
Dr. Jack and Minda Jaffe, Shaker Heights, OH
Jewish Community Center, Louisville, KY
Norman and Sybil Kahn, Shawnee Mission, KS

Michael and Marsha Kaniel, Jerusalem
Dr. Abram Kanof, Raleigh, NC
Irene Kaplan, Silver Spring, MD
Rochelle Rubinstein and Alan S. Kaplan, Toronto
Michael Kaufman, Sunrise, FL
Patrick A. Kenny, Silver Spring, MD
Sherwin and Louise Kershman, Houston
Shirley H. Kerze, Altamonte Springs, FL
Prof. Herbert Kessler, Baltimore
Alan and Reva Kirschberg, New York
Bill and Gertrude Kissiloff, New York
Harold Klug, Don Mills, Ontario
Charles and Robyn Krauthammer, Chevy Chase, MD
Abe Kremer, Fair Lawn, NJ
Alan and Arlene Kurtis, Palm Beach, FL
Rabbi Sol and Gabriela Landau, Coral Gables, FL
Alexander and Ann Lauterbach, Van Nuys, CA
Joseph and Sandra Lepelstat, North Bellmore, NY
Joseph and Sheila Levy, London
Eva Leiblich-Fernandes, Mainz, Germany
Willy Lindwer, Amstelveen, Holland
Dr. Thomas and Hinda Litman, Hopkins, MN
Stanley and Judy Lucas, Cincinnati
Richard Lurie, Martshalltown, South Africa
Bernard Lustig, Stamford, CT
Edith Lustig, Brooklyn
William Margulies, London
Arthur and Gitel Marx, Brooklyn
Dr. William and Rosalind Merkow, Hartland, WI
Miriam Milman, Tannay, Switzerland
Albert and Judith Milstein, Chicago
Lena Minkoff Memorial Foundation
Margaret Morse, Miami Beach
Dr. Abraham and Avis Lee Neiman, Chicago
Moses and Esther Nussbaum, New York
Henry and Sophie Olshin, East Meadow, NY
Luisella Montara Ottolenghi, Milano, Italy
Arthur and Gladys Pancoe, Glencoe, IL
Rabbi Norman Patz, Cedar Grove, NJ
Felix D. Posen, London
Steve and Jeremy Potash, Oakland, CA
Helen S. Potaznik, New York
Ralph and Marcia Preiss, Poughkeepsie, NY
Haim and Ruth Rabinowitz, Jerusalem
Michael and Nancy Reich, Mamaroneck, NY
Jacques and Esther Reutlinger, Berkeley, CA
Ira and Brigitte Rezak, Stonybrook, NY
Harold and Barbara Richman, Hartford, CT
Rubenovitz Museum, Chestnut Hill, MA
I. Rubinstein, Los Angeles
Harold and Joyce Saffir, Glencoe, IL
David and Ellen Saltman, Holyoke, MA
Bertil and Esther Schonkopf, Stockholm
Arnold and Mary Schwarzbart, Knoxville, TN
Costanza Segre Montel, Torino, Italy
Edyth Siegel, Stamford, CT
Silver & Ziskind, New York
Gene and Ruth Slater, Pasadena, CA
Dorothy Soclof Katz, Memphis, TN
Philip and Sylvia Spertus, Taylor, TX
Dr. Moses A. and Dr. Susanne Spira, Beverly Hills
Estate of Leon Sturman, Rochester
Temple Sinai, Pittsburgh
Barbara Trellis, Pittsburgh

269

SUPPORT THE CENTER FOR JEWISH ART
by becoming a member of THE INTERNATIONAL SOCIETY FOR JEWISH ART, *KLIL*

As a member of the International Society for Jewish Art you will receive the annual journal *Jewish Art*, as well as newsletters informing you of the latest research projects, study tours and publications of the CJA. In addition, members are entitled to a 30% reduction on all CJA publications.

Annual membership dues of US$ 150 per household assist the CJA to continue its innovative research in all fields of Jewish art, from antiquity to the present.

An annual contribution of $1,000, as part of the Director's Circle, entitles a member to a free copy of all CJA publications.

☐ Yes, I would like to become a member of the International Society for *Jewish Art*. Enclosed is my check, payable to the International Society for *Jewish Art, KLIL*, POB 4262, Jerusalem 91042, Israel. If you require an American tax deduction receipt, please write out and send your check to the American Friends of the Hebrew University, 11 East 69th Street, New York, N.Y. 10028, earmarked for student scholarships of the Center for Jewish Art.

Name _____

Address _____

Telephone _____ (home) _____ (work) _____

Date _____

Signature _____

For more information about the Center, please contact:

The Center for Jewish Art
POB 4262, Jerusalem 91042
Israel
Tel.: 972-2-586605
Fax: 972-2-586672

In the U.S.A.:
Nancy Wellins
1691 Lawrence Road
Mohegan Lake, NY 10547
Tel/Fax (914) 528-7324

JEWISH ART: ANNUAL OF THE CENTER FOR JEWISH ART OF THE HEBREW UNIVERSITY OF JERUSALEM

Notes to Authors

Manuscripts, editorial communications, and books for review should be addressed to the Editor, *Jewish Art*, P.O.Box 4262, Jerusalem 91042, Israel.

Articles
Only original, previously unpublished articles can be considered.

Manuscripts should be submitted on a floppy diskette, in ASCII format for IBM compatible computers, together with a *double-spaced* printout of article, notes, and a list of illustrations. References should appear in *endnotes* (see below) in a separate file on the diskette and *double-spaced* at the end of the manuscript; captions to photos (see below) should appear in a List of Figures.

Notes
References in endnotes (not footnotes) should include all the following information, in this order:
— Author's full name (forename, initial, surname), followed by a comma.
— Title of the work referred to (articles in double quotation marks followed by a comma, then the title of the work or periodical in which it appears. Periodicals and works published separately *underlined*).
— Volume, number, and year (for periodicals).
— Place and year of publication in parenthesis (for books).
— Page, folio, and plate numbers where relevant.
Titles of works of art should be underlined.

Photographs
All the photographic reproductions that are to accompany the article should arrive with the manuscript, and with the copyright holder's permission. Black and white photographs should be glossy prints, preferably 12 x 9 cm. Color transparencies should be positive Ektachrome at least 6 x 6 cm. All photographs should be copied (xeroxed) and the copy sent with the manuscript. The *copy* should be clearly marked with figure number and top-bottom orientation.

Photographs, manuscripts, and diskettes will be returned upon request. Please enclose a stamped, self-addressed envelope.

DATE DUE